한국어 학습 총서 03

Korean Vocabulary Practice for Foreigners

English Version

Advanced Level

고급

외국인을 위한

한국어 어휘 연습

연세대학교 한국어학당 편

연세대학교 출판문화원

Preface

The Korean Language Institute of Yonsei University celebrated its 53rd anniversary this year. Throughout the years, the Korean Language Institute has published teaching materials for conversational Korean, practice workbooks, and much more. However, as the number of students that are learning Korean increases, their demands became more diverse. As a result of a rise in demands to practice Korean vocabulary, it became necessary to increase teaching materials for practicing vocabulary words.

'Korean Vocabulary Pratice for Foreigners' is divided into three books: Beginner, Intermediate, and Advanced. This book was published in order to build the vocabulary of Korean language students while increasing their proficiency in the language. Also, this book was written to prepare students for the various kinds of Korean Proficiency Examinations that currently exist. Vocabulary words that form part of the text book and that may appear on the Korean Proficiency Examinations have been carefully chosen and along with each word an explication of its meaning and example sentence have been provided. Also, a section of various practice problems is included so that students can make good use of the words they have learned.

'Korean Vocabulary Pratice for Foreigners' can be used as a complimentary textbook at the Korean Language Institute for learning vocabulary or can be used by students who are studying Korean on their own. We hope that 'Korean Vocabulary Pratice for Foreigners' can be used to efficiently teach vocabulary to students of the Korean language while improving their proficiency.

Yonsei University Language Research and Education Center
Korean Language Institute Compilation Committee

머리말

연세대학교 한국어학당은 올해로 창립 53주년을 맞이했습니다. 연세대학교 한국어학당은 그동안 회화 교재, 언어기능별 교재, 활용연습용 교재 등 많은 교재를 집필, 출간하였습니다. 그러나 한국어를 배우는 학습자들이 늘면서 그들의 요구도 다양해졌습니다. 특히 한국어 어휘 학습에 대한 학습자들의 요구가 높아져 어휘 학습용 교재가 필요하게 되었습니다.

'외국인을 위한 한국어 어휘 연습'은 초급, 중급, 고급의 3권으로 구성되었습니다. 이 책은 한국어를 공부하는 학습자들의 어휘력을 향상시켜 한국어 숙달도를 높이기 위해서 출간하게 되었습니다. 특히 '외국인을 위한 한국어 어휘 연습'은 현재 시행되고 있는 다양한 한국어능력 평가 시험에 대비하도록 구성되었습니다. 한국어 교재와 한국어능력 평가 시험에서 다루어지고 있는 어휘를 등급에 맞게 선정하여 각 어휘의 의미를 설명하고 예문을 제시하였습니다. 또한 다양한 문제를 통해 학습한 어휘를 활용할 수 있도록 구성하였습니다.

'외국인을 위한 한국어 어휘 연습'은 한국어교육기관에서 어휘 학습을 위한 부교재로 활용할 수 있으며 혼자서 공부하는 학습자는 자습용으로 활용할 수 있습니다. '외국인을 위한 한국어 어휘 연습'이 한국어 학습자들이 효율적으로 어휘를 학습하여 한국어능력을 향상할 수 있도록 하는 데 기여할 수 있기를 바랍니다.

연세대학교 언어연구교육원 한국어학당 교재편찬위원회

Introductory Remarks

01 'Korean Vocabulary Practice for Foreigners (Advanced)' is a compilation of vocabulary words deemed essential for foreign students learning Korean at the advanced level.

02 This book has been divided into 17 different lessons depending on the class of words and form of expressions by verbs, nouns, adjectives, adverbs, onomatopoeias and mimetic words, prefixes and suffixes, proverbs, idioms, and Chinese character phrases.

03 Each lesson within this book has around 30~50 vocabulary word entries included and explained. The total amount of vocabulary words including the headwords, synonyms, antonyms, related words, etc. comes to about 1000 words. These vocabulary words have been decided from existing teaching materials from the Institution of Korean Language Education, statistics about basic vocabulary from the National Korean Language Research Organization, and on basis of the frequency and level of difficulty of the sample words that are used in the Korean Language Test(TOPIK).

04 Each lesson is divided mainly into vocabulary explanations and practice questions. First, the vocabulary explanations have definitions and examples to sufficiently help the student understand, and the Vocabulary Practice Questions have questions in order to accurately check if the student has correctly learned the vocabulary words.

05 The part of speech will be written next to each word. If the word is a Noun(명사), it will expressed as N(Noun), a Verb(동사) as AV(Action Verb), and an Adjective(형용사) as DV(Descriptive Verb).

06 The vocabulary words are put into the alphabetical order of 가나다.

07 Each vocabulary word includes pronunciation, English translation, definition, usage, expressions, synonyms, antonyms, related words, examples, etc.

08 The example sentences are written using appropriate grammar that students at the advanced level should be able to understand.

09 The vocabulary practice questions are presented in various forms. Especially, taking into consideration students who are preparing for the Korean Language Test (TOPIK), the questions have been formatted to fit the style of this test.

10 For students who are learning at the advanced level, Yonsei University's Korean Language Institute would like to inform you that topics that will help with fluency and natural speaking such as proverbs and idioms, Chinese character phrases, etc. have also been split into definitions and practice questions in the 「Application Practice」 book by KLI.

11 In this vocabulary index, each lesson has been ordered by 가나다 order including the headwords, synonyms, antonyms, and related words. Also in the vocabulary index, the pages in which the words appear are annotated as well.(Proverbs, sayings, Chinese character phrases, and idioms are all orderded seperately in 가나다 order.)

12 The clauses for each vocabulary word which include definitions and examples were referenced from Doosan Dong-a's 「Yonsei's Korean Dictionary」 and the National Korean Language Institute's 「Standard Korean Dictionary」.

일러두기

01 '외국인을 위한 한국어 어휘 연습 (고급)'은 한국어를 배우는 외국인을 위한 어휘집으로 고급 단계에서 필수적으로 알아야 할 어휘를 소개하였다.

02 이 책은 품사와 표현의 성격에 따라 동사, 명사, 형용사, 부사, 의성어 · 의태어, 접두사 · 접미사, 속담, 관용어, 한자성어의 총 17개의 과로 되어 있다.

03 이 책은 각 과마다 약 30~50개 정도의 어휘를 표제어로 제시하여 설명하였다. 총 어휘 개수는 표제어, 유의어, 반의어, 관련어 등을 포함하여 약 1000여개에 이른다. 이 어휘들은 기존 한국어교육기관의 교재와 국립국어연구원 통계의 기초 학습 어휘와 한국어능력시험(TOPIK)의 기출 어휘를 토대로 사용 빈도와 난이도에 따라 선정되었다.

04 각 과는 크게 어휘설명과 연습문제 두 부분으로 구성되어 있다. 먼저 어휘 설명 부분에서는 의미 설명과 예문을 통해 학습자들이 어휘에 대해 충분히 이해할 수 있도록 했고, 어휘 연습 문제 부분에서는 앞서 배운 어휘를 정확하게 이해했는지 확인할 수 있도록 했다.

05 어휘 제시 순서는 각 과 별로 가나다순에 따른다.

06 각 어휘 항목에는 발음, 번역, 의미 설명, 활용 구문, 활용 표현, 유의어, 반의어, 관련어, 예문 등이 포함되어 있다.

07 활용 구문에서는 Noun(명사)는 'N(Noun)'으로, Verb(동사)는 'AV(Action Verb)'로, Adjective(형용사)는 'DV(Descriptive Verb)'로 표시했다.

08 예문은 고급 단계의 학습자의 수준에 적절한 어휘와 문법 표현을 사용하여 제시하였다.

09 어휘 연습 문제는 다양한 유형으로 구성하였다. 특히, 한국어능력시험(TOPIK)을 준비하는 학습자들을 고려하여 한국어능력시험과 문제유형이 같거나 유사한 문제들을 수록하였다.

10 고급 수준의 학습자의 경우 한국 문화에 대한 이해를 도움과 동시에 보다 유창하고 자연스러운 한국어를 구사할 수 있도록 하기 위해 속담과 관용어, 한자성어 등도 의미 설명과 연습문제 두 부분으로 나누어 수록했으며 이 부분은 연세대학교 언어연구교육원 한국어학당의 교재 「활용연습」을 차용하였음을 밝혀둔다.

11 단어 색인에는 각 과에서 주요하게 다룬 표제어는 물론 표제어의 유의어, 반의어, 관련어도 모두 포함하여 가나다순으로 제시하였다. 단어 색인에는 단어가 제시된 페이지를 제시하였으며 속담, 격언, 한자성어, 관용어도 따로 가나다순으로 제시하였다.

12 어휘 항목의 의미 설명과 예문 등은 두산동아의 『연세한국어사전』, 국립국어원의 『표준국어대사전』을 참조하여 제시하였다.

Subject Map

Chapter	Subject	Number of Vocabulary Words
1	Verbs I	33
2	Verbs II	39
3	Verbs III	38
4	Nouns I	45
5	Nouns II	45
6	Nouns III	47
7	Adjectives I	44
8	Adjectives II	44
9	Adjectives III	43
10	Adverbs I	31
11	Adverbs II	38
12	Adverbs III	23
13	Onomatopoeias, Mimetic words	40
14	Prefixes, Suffixes	20
15	Proverbs	40
16	Idioms	60
17	Chinese character phrases	40

내용구성

과	주제	어휘개수
1	동사 I	33
2	동사 II	39
3	동사 III	38
4	명사 I	45
5	명사 II	45
6	명사 III	47
7	형용사 I	44
8	형용사 II	44
9	형용사 III	43
10	부사 I	31
11	부사 II	38
12	부사 III	23
13	의성어 · 의태어	40
14	접두사 · 접미사	20
15	속담	40
16	관용어	60
17	한자성어	40

차례 Contents

동사 I

01

Verbs I

01 동사 I

001
가라앉다

[가라안따] to sink

when an object that was floating on top of water sinks to the bottom or when the wind or current of water becomes calmer

[Usage] N에 가라앉다
N으로/로 가라앉다

[Expression] 배가 가라앉다 a ship sinks
열이 가라앉다 fever goes down
흥분이 가라앉다 excitement dies down

[Example] 배는 큰 바위에 부딪힌 후 물 밑으로 가라앉았다.
After the ship ran into a large boulder, it sank to the bottom of the water.

경기 내내 계속되는 응원 열기 속에서 관중들의 흥분은 가라앉을 줄 몰랐다.
Even while cheering with fervor throughout the entire game, there was no sign of calming the audience's excitement.

002
가르다

[가르다] 1. to divide 2. to cut with a blade 3. to split

1. to separate into different parts

[Usage] N을/를 N으로/로 가르다

[Example] 아이들이 편을 셋으로 갈라서 놀이를 했다.
The children decided to divide into three different teams and played.

2. to cut something by using a blade

[Usage] N을/를 N으로/로 가르다

[Example] 생선의 배를 가르고 내장을 뺐다.
The fish's stomach was cut in order to take out the innards.

3. to divide/cut something by forcing it apart

[Usage] N을/를 가르다

[Example] 화살이 과녁을 향하여 바람을 가르고 날아갔다.
The arrow split the air as it flew towards the target.

003
가리다[1]

[가리다] to cover

to obscure something so that it is not visible or not penetrable

[Usage] N을/를 가리다

[Expression] 나는 너무 무서워서 손으로 두 눈을 가려 버렸다.
I was so scared that I covered my eyes with my hands.

그는 모자로 얼굴을 가리고 나무 그늘에서 낮잠을 자고 있었다.
That person covered their face with their hat and slept underneath the shade of a tree.

004
가리다[2]

[가리다] 1. to differentiate 2. to be picky 3. to be shy 4. to be potty-trained

1. to choose one option out of many different choices

[Usage] N을/를 가리다

[Example] 수많은 출품작 중에서 입상작을 10점만 가리는 것은 여간 어려운 일이 아니었다.
It was an extremely hard task to choose only 10 works out of all works entered.

2. to like only what you want to like and ignoring what you do not like

[Usage] N을/를 가리다

[Example] 음식을 가리지 말고 골고루 먹어라.
Do not be a picky eater and try to eat various types of food.

3. to choose to disassociate from strangers due to shyness

[Usage] N을/를 가리다

[Example] 아이가 낯을 가려 엄마한테만 안긴다.
The child is shy and will only stay in its mother's arms.

4. when a child is potty-trained and knows how to go to the bathroom by his/herself

[Usage] N을/를 가리다

[Example] 우리 조카는 두 살밖에 안 됐는데 대소변을 다 가린다.
My niece is only two years old but has already been potty-trained.

005
감다

[감따] 1. to wind 2. to wrap 3. to wind

1. to wind a string or rope around something

[Usage] N을/를 N에 감다
N을/를 N으로/로 감다

[Antonym] 풀다 to unwind

[Example] 그는 다친 발목에 붕대를 칭칭 감고 있었다.
He was wrapping his injured ankle in bandages.

2. to wrap one's arms or legs around someone else's body

[Usage] N을/를 N에 감다
N을/를 N으로/로 감다

[Synonym] 두르다 to wrap

[Antonym] 풀다 to unravel

[Example] 두 사람은 서로의 허리에 팔을 감고 걸었다.
The two people wrapped their arms around each other's waists as they walked.

3. to rewind something like a spring or tape

[Usage] N을/를 감다

[Antonym] 풀다 to unwind

[Example] 비디오는 다 보시면 처음으로 감아서 반납해 주세요.
If you are finished watching the video, please rewind and then return it.

006
감수하다

[감수하다] to endure

to suffer reproach and anguish without any protest

[Usage] N을/를 감수하다

[Expression] 고통을 감수하다 to endure anguish
책임을 감수하다 to bear the responsibility
비난을 감수하다 to endure the criticism
불이익을 감수하다 to endure the disadvantages

[Example] 많은 고통을 감수한 결과 오늘의 성공을 이루었다.
I achieved success today after enduring much pain.

내가 잘못을 저지른 이상 어떠한 비난이라도 감수하겠다.
As I have done wrong, I will endure all criticism and more.

007
강구하다

[강구하다] to seek out

to actively try to find a suitable solution to a problem

[Usage] N을/를 강구하다

[Expression] 방법을 강구하다 to seek out a method
대책을 강구하다 to seek out a countermeasure

[Example] 문제의 심각성을 인식하고 해결 방법을 강구하고 있다.
I've taken into account the severity of the issue and am trying to find a suitable solution.

당국은 다시는 이 같은 대형 화재가 일어나지 않도록 대책을 강구해야 할 것이다.
The authorities have to seek out actively a countermeasure so that a large fire like this will never happen again.

008
갚다

[갑따] 1. to repay 2. pay back

1. to repay or return something that you have borrowed

[Usage] N에/에게 N을/를 갚다

[Synonym] 돌려주다 to return

[Antonym] 빌리다 to borrow

[Example] 그는 기일 내에 은행 빚을 갚을 수가 없었다.
He couldn't repay his debt to the bank by the deadline.

2. to pay back someone after being indebted to them or pay back someone due to a grudge

[Usage] N에/에게 N을/를 갚다

[Synonym] 보답하다 to repay

[Example] 고마운 선생님의 은혜를 어떻게 갚을 수 있을까?
How am I supposed to repay the kindness of a teacher I am thankful to?

009
개다[1]

[개다] to fold

to fold clothes or bedding into a neat fashion

[Usage] N을/를 개다

[Antonym] 펴다 to unfold

[Example] 아침마다 이부자리를 개어 이불장에 넣는 것은 귀찮은 일이다.
It is troublesome to fold my bedding and place it back into the bedding cabinet every morning.

여기저기 던져져 있던 옷들을 개어 정리하니 방이 훨씬 넓어 보였다.
After folding all of the clothes that were thrown haphazardly around the room, the room looked much more spacious.

010
개다[2]

[개다] to mix

to mix a powdery substance into water, oil, etc. in order to blend the two together

[Usage] N을/를 개다

[Example] 이 가루약은 반드시 물에 개어 잡수세요.
The only way to consume this powdered medicine is to mix it in water.

밀가루를 물에 갠 후 거기에 야채를 넣으세요.
After mixing the flour into the water, add the vegetables to the mixture.

011
개의하다

[개이하다] to be bothered

(mostly used as negative expressions) to constantly have something on your mind and be worried about it

[Usage] N을/를 개의하다
N에 개의하다

[Example] 별 일 아니니까 개의할 것 없습니다.
It's not a big deal so there is no need to be bothered by it.

남의 말에 개의하지 않고 내 신념대로 밀고 나가겠다.
I refuse to be bothered by other opinions and will only act on my own beliefs.

012
거두다

[거두다] 1. to harvest 2. to gather 3. to gain 4. to handle 5. to raise 6. to obtain

1. to harvest grains, fruits, etc.

[Usage] N을/를 거두다

[Example] 가을에는 논에서 곡식을 거두느라 손길이 바쁘다.
My hands are busy trying to harvest grains from the rice fields during the fall.

2. to gather objects that have been dispersed

[Usage] N을/를 거두다

[Example] 주인은 종업원에게 손님들의 식사가 끝나면 바로 그릇을 거둬 오라고 지시했다.
The owner told the employee to gather plates as soon as customers were done eating.

3. to gain good results

[Usage] N을/를 거두다

[Example] 처음으로 출전한 팀이 전년도 우승팀을 꺾고 승리를 거두었다.
Even though it was their first time competing, they won over last year's winning team.

4. to handle a corpse

[Usage] N을/를 거두다

[Example] 선장은 침몰한 선박에서 시신을 거두어 장례를 치루었다.
The captain recovered the corpse from the sunken ship and proceeded with a funeral.

5. to take care of or raise one's child, an orphan, etc.

[Usage] N을/를 거두다

[Example] 김 목사님은 부모 없는 아이들을 거두어 돌보신다.
Pastor Kim raises orphans.

6. to obtain money or objects from people

[Usage] N 을/를 거두다

[Example] 후원자들에게서 기부금을 거두어 선거운동을 준비했다.
They collected donations from sponsors and prepared the election campaign.

013
거들다

[거들다] 1. to assist 2. to interfere

1. to assist and help someone with their task

[Usage] N을/를 거들다

[Synonym] 돕다 to help

[Example] 영수는 학교를 그만두고 아버지께서 하시는 장사를 거들었다.
Youngsoo quit school and assisted his father with his business.

2. to interfere on someone else's words or actions

[Usage] N 을/를 거들다

[Example] 친구를 위해서 한마디 거들다가 나까지 호된 꾸지람을 들었다.
I interfered on my friend's behalf and got included in the severe scolding as well.

014
거르다[1]

[거르다] to skip

to skip something in a continuous sequence

[Usage] N을/를 거르다

[Expression] 식사를 거르다 to skip meal
끼니를 거르다 to skip meal

[Example] 혼자 사니까 바쁠 때는 끼니를 거를 때가 많아요.
Because I live by myself, there are many times when I skip meals because I am busy.

영수는 하루도 거르지 않고 새벽마다 우유 배달을 했다.
Youngsoo never skipped a day delivering milk at the break of dawn.

015
거르다[2]

[거르다] to filter/sift

to filter solids or sediments out of liquid by using a strainer or filter paper in order to collect just the liquid

[Usage] N을/를 N에 거르다
N 을/를 N으로/로 거르다

[Example] 밀가루를 곱게 체에 걸러 그릇에 담아 두었다.
I sifted the flour through a strainer and placed the finer powder into a bowl.

된장을 물에 푼 후 체로 걸러 내어 맑은 된장국을 끓였다.
After dissolving the bean paste into the water, I sifted the mixture through a strainer to make a clearer bean paste soup.

016
거스르다[1]

[거스르다] 1. to go against 2. to defy 3. to offend

1. to go against the natural flow of things and instead go in the opposite direction

[Usage] N을/를 거스르다

[Example] 국민들은 시대를 거스르는 구시대의 법을 폐지할 것을 요구했다.
The citizens demanded the abolition of old era laws that went against the current era.

2. to defy someone's wishes, words, rules

[Usage] N을/를 거스르다

[Expression] 지시를 거스르다 to defy the orders

[Antonym] 따르다 to obey

[Antonym] 그는 부모의 뜻을 한 번도 거스른 적이 없는 모범생이었다.
That model student has never defied his parents' wishes.

3. to offend someone

[Usage] N을/를 거스르다

[Expression] 기분을 거스르다 to offend someone

신경을 거스르다 to get on someone's nerves

비위를 거스르다 to bother someone

[Example] 나는 선배의 비위를 거스르지 않으려고 선배가 시키는 대로 다 했다.
I did as my senior asked because I did not want to offend him.

017
거스르다[2]

[거스르다] to give change

to receive more money than the listed price and give the change back

[Usage] N을/를 거스르다

[Related Word] 거스름돈 change

change 택시 기사는 잔돈을 정확히 거슬러 주었다.
The taxi driver gave me exact change.

천 원을 내고 백 원짜리 동전을 하나 거슬러 받았다.
I gave 1,000 won and received a 100 won coin in change.

018
거치다

[거치다] 1. to pass 2. to go through

1. while traveling, you stop by or pass through the area

[Usage] N을/를 거치다

[Example] 대구를 거쳐 부산으로 갔다. I passed through Daegu to go to Busan.

2. to go through a process or steps

[Usage] N을/를 거치다

[Example] 학생들은 초등학교부터 중학교, 고등학교를 거쳐 대학에 입학하게 된다.
Students start from elementary school and go through junior high school and high school in order to be admitted into a university.

019
걷다

[걷따] 1. to roll 2. to gather 3. to collect 4. to cease

1. to roll up something that has sagged down or clear something that has been covered.

[Usage] N을/를 걷다

[Expression] 소매를 걷다 to roll up one's sleeves

커튼을 걷다 to roll/gather the curtains

[Example] 소녀가 소매를 걷자 하얀 피부가 드러났다.
As soon as the girl rolled up her sleeves, her white skin was exposed.

2. to gather and clean things that have been dispersed

[Usage] N을/를 걷다

[Example] 비가 올 것 같으니까 빨래부터 걷어라.
Since it looks like it's going to rain, gather up the laundry outside.

3. to gather money or objects from people

[Usage] N을/를 걷다

[Example] 동료들에게 축의금을 걷어 결혼하는 직원에게 전달했다.
We collected congratulatory money from our colleagues and gave it to the co-worker getting married.

4. to cease something that you started

[Usage] N을/를 걷다

[Example] 자금 사정이 나빠져서 벌여 놓은 사업들을 다 걷어 버렸다.
Because my financial condition isn't good, I ended up ceasing all of the businesses I had started.

020
걸리다

[걸리다] 1. to activate 2. to receive a call 3. to hang 4. to hang in the air
5. to rely on 6. to be included 7. to violate/breach 8. to be trapped
9. to be dissatisfied 10. to become ill

1. to be activated, to start

[Expression] 시동이 걸리다 the engine starts

[Example] 엔진에 이상이 생겼는지 열쇠를 돌려도 자동차의 시동이 걸리지 않았다.
There must be something wrong with the engine since even when I turned the key, the engine would not start.

2. to receive a call

[Expression] 전화가 걸려 오다 receive a call

[Example] 광고 방송이 나가자 문의 전화가 계속해서 걸려 왔다.
After the commercial aired, we received a lot of calls from people making inquiries.

3. to hang off of something

[Usage] N에 걸리다

[Example] 경찰은 창문 옆에 걸린 사진을 보면서 질문을 시작했다.
The police started the questioning after seeing the picture hung on the wall next to the window.

4. the sun or moon is floating in the sky

[Usage] N에 걸리다

[Example] 해는 서산머리에 걸려 있었다.
The sun was floating over the top of the western mountain.

5. when future perspectives rely on something

[Usage] N에 걸리다

[Synonym] 달리다 to hang

[Example] 이건 제 장래가 걸린 문제예요. My future relies on this problem.

6. a reward is included

[Usage] N에 걸리다

[Example] 육상은 가장 많은 금메달이 걸려 있는 종목이다.
Track and field is the sports category with the most gold medals rewarded.

7. to violate or breach a rule/law

[Usage] N에 걸리다

[Example] 그는 규정에 걸리는 일은 하지 않았다.
That person never did anything to violate the rules.

8. to become entrapped

[Usage] N에 걸리다

[Example] 나는 마치 최면에 걸린 사람처럼 그 사람의 지시를 따랐다.
I followed that person's commands as if I was hypnotized.

9. to be dissatisfied with what you see or feel

[Usage] N에 걸리다

[Expression] 마음에 걸리다 something bothers you and stays on your mind

[Example] 식사 때 찾아 온 손님을 차 한 잔만 대접해 보낸 게 마음에 걸린다.
I felt dissatisfied with sending off a dinner guest after serving them just a cup of tea.

10. to become ill; to become infected

[Usage] N에 걸리다

[Expression] 병에 걸리다 to become ill

[Example] 목이 아픈 것을 보니 목감기에 걸린 것 같다.
Seeing that I have a sore throat, I think I may have caught a cold.

021
겪다 [격따] 1. to suffer 2. to meet with

1. to suffer through events that are hard or will be a valuable experience

[Usage] N을/를 겪다

[Example] 인간은 고통을 겪고 이겨 나가는 가운데 성장하는 법이다.
Humans develop into better people by suffering hardships.

2. to meet with people and maintain relationships with them

[Usage] N을/를 겪다

[Example] 사람은 겪어 봐야 알고 물은 건너봐야 안다.
You must first cross the water to know it, and you must interact with people to fully know them as well.

022
기울이다

[기우리다] 1. to lean 2. to devote to

1. to lean towards something

[Usage] N을/를 N에/에게 기울이다

N을/를 N으로/로 기울이다

[Example] 어머니는 몸을 기울여 내 이마를 들여다보았다.

My mother leaned towards me to look at my forehead.

2. to devote all of one's efforts to one thing

[Usage] N 을/를 N에/에게 기울이다

[Expression] 주의를 기울이다 to give attention to

정성을 기울이다 to devote oneself earnestly

노력을 기울이다 to devote all effort to

심혈을 기울이다 to devote one's heart and soul

[Example] 화가 김민수 씨는 10년 동안 심혈을 기울여 만든 작품들을 모아서 전시회를 열기로 했다.

Painter Kim Minsoo has decided to have an exhibition of the paintings he has poured his heart and soul into for the last ten years.

023
기인하다

[기인하다] to result from

something results from a cause

[Usage] N에/에서 기인하다

[Example] 무역 적자는 주로 수출 부진에 기인한 것이다.

Deficit in the trade commerce usually results from a slump in exports.

서울의 땅값 상승은 인구 증가에서 기인하였다.

The rise in Seoul's land value resulted from a rise in population.

024
기피하다

[기피하다] 1. to avoid 2. to shirk one's responsibilities

1. to avoid something because you dislike it

[Usage] N을/를 기피하다

[Example] 요즘 세대는 한자어의 사용을 기피하는 경향이 있다.

In modern society, there is a tendency to avoid Sino-Korean words.

2. to shirk one's public duties and responsibilities

[Usage] N을/를 기피하다

[Example] 종교적인 이유로 병역 의무를 기피하는 사람들이 있다.

There are people who use religious reasons to shirk their military service.

025
기하다

[기하다] 1. to aim for 2. to arrange a date

1. in order to achieve something, you work to meet the requirements and carefully proceed to reach your goal

[Usage] N에 N을/를 기하다

[Expression] 신중을 기하다 to aim to be careful
안전을 기하다 to aim to be safe
완벽을 기하다 to aim to be perfect
만전을 기하다 to aim for perfection

[Example] 봄철 화재 예방에 만전을 기해 주시기 바랍니다.
Please aim for perfect prevention of fires in the spring.

2. (use the structure of '**기하여**') to arrange a date and act according to that date

[Usage] N을/를 기하다

[Example] 오늘 새벽 4시를 기해 폭풍 주의보가 발효되었다.
A storm warning was issued at four in the morning today.

026
꺼리다

[꺼리다] 1. to avoid 2. to be reluctant

1. to avoid or dislike something because it may bring harm to you

[Usage] N을/를 꺼리다

[Example] 그 사람은 남 앞에 나서서 말하기를 꺼리는 성격이다.
That person is the type to avoid speaking up in front of people because of his personality.

2. to be reluctant because there is something that you are dissatisfied with

[Usage] N에 꺼리다

[Expression] 마음에 꺼리다 to be reluctant because of your gut instinct
양심에 꺼리다 to bother your conscience and cause you to be reluctant.

[Example] 나는 양심에 꺼릴 만한 일은 하지 않았다.
I didn't to do things that would remain on my conscience.

027
꼬이다[1]

[꼬이다] 1. to be twisted 2. to get complicated 3. to be irritated

1. to become twisted or entangled

[Usage] N이/가 꼬이다

[Example] 실들이 꼬여서 그걸 푸느라고 반나절을 보냈다.
I spent a quarter of a day detangling the entangled threads.

2. when something you were doing gets complicated and doesn't go your way

[Usage] N이/가 꼬이다

[Expression] 일이 꼬이다 the situation is complicated

[Example] 하는 일마다 잘 풀리지 않고 꼬이기만 한다.
Everything I do doesn't flow well and gets complicated.

3. to be irritated with something

[Usage] N이/가 꼬이다

[Expression] 성격이 꼬이다 to become irritated with something

[Example] 그는 매사를 비판적인 시각으로 보는 탓에 성격이 꼬인 사람으로 오해 받을 때가 많다.
Because that person views everything critically, people always misunderstand him as an irritable person.

028
꼬이다²

[꼬이다] to manipulate

to use sweet words or actions to fool people and manipulate them into doing deeds

[Usage] N을/를 꼬이다

[Example] 게임기로 아이를 꼬여서 금품을 요구한 유괴범이 한 달 만에 잡혔다.
The kidnapper who used game consoles to kidnap kids and then demand ransom was caught within a month.

그 사람은 비싼 이자를 쳐 주겠다고 주부들을 꼬여 거액의 돈을 끌어 모았다.
That person manipulated housewives into giving a large sum of money by promising them high interest rates.

029
꼬이다³

[꼬이다] to infest

when insects or people are gathered into one area and are disorganized

[Usage] N이/가 N에 꼬이다

[Example] 더러우면 파리가 꼬이는 법이다. If it is dirty, flies will come and infest it.

사고 현장에는 구경꾼들이 꼬이기 시작했다.
The scene of the accident became infested with bystanders.

030
꾸다

[꾸다] to borrow

to borrow something/money after promising to repay someone

[Usage] N에서/에게서 N을/를 꾸다

[Example] 후배한테 돈을 꾸느니 차라리 한 끼 굶는 게 낫겠다.
I would rather starve a meal than borrow money from a junior.

새로 이사 갈 집은 워낙 비싸서 많은 돈을 꾸어다 보태야 했다.
Because the house we wanted to move into was so expensive, we had to borrow a large sum of money in order to pay for it.

031
꾸리다

[꾸리다] 1. to pack 2. to manage

1. to pack items

[Usage] N을/를 꾸리다

[Example] 동생은 여행을 많이 다녀서 그런지 배낭을 꾸리는 솜씨가 아주 능숙하다.
The way my younger sibling packs his backpack efficiently must be because he travels frequently.

2. to manage your work in a way to propel ahead; live your life efficiently

[Usage] N을/를 꾸리다

[Expression] 가게를 꾸리다 to manage a shop
가정을 꾸리다 to manage a household
살림을 꾸리다 to manage the housekeeping
생계를 꾸리다 to manage the means of living

[Example] 아내는 어려운 형편 속에서도 살림을 잘 꾸려 나가고 있다.
My wife's housekeeping is not affected by the family's poor circumstances.

032
꿰다

[꿰다] 1. to string through 2. to skewer 3. to be well-informed

1. to string a thread or a rope through a hole so that it goes through to the other side

[Usage] N을/를 N에 꿰다

[Example] 여기저기 떨어져 있는 동백꽃들을 주워 실에 꿰어 꽃목걸이를 엮었다.
I picked up fallen camellia flowers and strung them into a flower necklace.

2. to pierce an object onto a stick or skewer

[Usage] N을/를 N에 꿰다

[Example] 우리는 잡은 물고기를 꼬챙이에 꿰어 불에 구워 먹었다.
We skewered the fish we caught and cooked them over the fire so that we could eat them.

3. to be well-informed about a situation or work

[Usage] N을/를 꿰다

[Example] 그는 그 지역에 관한 것이라면 손바닥 들여다보듯이 훤히 꿰고 있다.
That person is so well-informed that he knows that area like the back of his hand.

033
끊기다

[끈키다] 1.to be cut off 2. to be disconnected 3. conversation is cut off
4. call is disconnected 5. traffic is stopped 6. flow of people has stopped

1. something that has been connected has been cut into two pieces

[Example] 전쟁 후 철로가 끊겨 통행할 수 없게 되었다.
After the war, the railroad tracks were cut off and no one could pass through.

2. something that has been done continuously gets disconnected so that it can't be finished

[Example] 손자가 죽음으로써 윤 씨 집의 대가 끊겨 버렸다.
After their grandson died, the Yoon line was cut off.

3. the conversation is temporarily cut off

[Example] 우리의 대화는 곧 끊겼고 한동안 침묵이 계속되었다.
Our conversation cut off right away and a silence fell over us.

4. call is disconnected

[Example] 통화 도중에 전화가 끊기지 않았더라면 범인의 위치를 찾아낼 수 있었을 텐데…….
If the call didn't get disconnected, we could have discovered the criminal's whereabouts......

5. traffic is stopped

[Example] 우리 고향은 깊은 산중에 있어서 눈만 오면 교통이 끊긴다.
Because my hometown is located deep within the mountains, all traffic is cut off when it snows.

6. flow of people, etc. is stopped

[Example] 이십여 년 전에는 관광객으로 붐볐는데 지금은 휴일에도 인적이 거의 끊기다시피 한산하다.
Twenty years ago, the area was crowded with tourists but nowadays the flow of people has stopped even on holidays and the area is quiet.

01 연습문제

[1-10] 다음 밑줄 친 부분과 의미가 비슷한 것을 고르십시오.

Choose the word that is similar to the underlined word.

1. 우리는 세 명씩 편을 나누어서 놀이를 했다.

❶ 가르다　❷ 감다　❸ 거르다　❹ 끊다

2. 어린 시절에는 들녘에 나가 참새 쫓는 일을 돕곤 했다.

❶ 거들다　❷ 취하다　❸ 챙기다　❹ 부담하다

3. 제가 저지른 실수인 만큼 저에 대한 비난은 달게 받겠습니다.

❶ 갚다　❷ 갈다　❸ 기피하다　❹ 감수하다

4. 갑자기 현금이 필요한 일이 생겨서 친구에게 급하게 돈을 빌렸다.

❶ 꾸다　❷ 걷다　❸ 얻다　❹ 받다

5. 두 남녀는 서로의 허리에 팔을 두르고 사이좋게 걸어가고 있었다.

❶ 풀다　❷ 감다　❸ 매다　❹ 묶다

6. 음식을 가려 먹는 습관은 어린이의 정상적인 성장을 저해할 수 있다.

❶ 소식하다　❷ 과식하다　❸ 편식하다　❹ 단식하다

7. 엄청난 시련들을 겪고 나서야 인생에서 가장 중요한 것이 무엇인지 깨달았다.

❶ 맞서다　❷ 지내다　❸ 경험하다　❹ 회복하다

8. 자신의 신념에 따라 결정한 일이라면 세상의 이목 같은 건 신경 쓰지 말고 밀고 나가는 것이 옳다고 본다.

❶ 꺼리다　❷ 가리다　❸ 거스르다　❹ 개의하다

9. 보건복지부는 전염성이 강한 유행성 결막염이 확산되기 전에 조기 차단하는 방안을 찾고 있다.

❶ 풀다 ❷ 강구하다 ❸ 해결하다 ❹ 기울이다

10. 청년실업률이 치솟고 있는데도 청년들은 급여나 근무 조건 등의 측면에서 대기업과 현격한 차이가 나는 중소기업 취업을 꺼리는 상황이다.

❶ 선호하다 ❷ 좌우하다 ❸ 기피하다 ❹ 개의하다

[11-13] 다음 밑줄 친 부분과 의미가 반대인 것을 고르십시오.

Choose the word that is the opposite of the underlined word.

11. 다 마른 빨래들을 잘 개어 옷장 안에 정리해 놓았다.

❶ 펴다 ❷ 짜다 ❸ 접다 ❹ 손질하다

12. 그 선수는 지난 번 경기 때 부상한 무릎에 붕대를 감고 출전했다.

❶ 열다 ❷ 풀다 ❸ 뜨다 ❹ 벗다

13. 남에게 돈을 꾸어 부모님 선물을 사느니 그냥 정성이 담긴 꽃 한 송이를 드리겠어.

❶ 갚다 ❷ 아끼다 ❸ 벌다 ❹ 꿰다

[14-17] 다음 ( )에 알맞은 것을 고르십시오.

Choose the word that fits best in the parenthesis.

14. 수년 전에는 관광객으로 붐비던 곳이었는데 그 사건 후로 인적이 거의 ( ).

❶ 그쳤다 ❷ 막혔다 ❸ 끊겼다 ❹ 떨어졌다

15. 직장 생활에 쫓기다보니 규칙적인 생활을 하기는커녕 끼니를 ( ) 일도 자주 있다.

❶ 꺼리는 ❷ 거르는 ❸ 미루는 ❹ 마다하는

16. 최근에는 조각품에 대한 기호가 크게 떨어져 상업 화랑에서도 전시회를 (   ) 것으로 나타났다.

❶ 벌이는 ❷ 광고하는 ❸ 병행하는 ❹ 기피하는

17. 주변에서 흔히 볼 수 있는 천연재료인 모래가 최첨단 정보 기술의 주원료가 된다는 사실을 아는 사람은 많지 않다. 모래 그 자체는 값어치가 낮지만 화학 처리나 가공 과정을 (   ) 새로운 물질을 만들면 반도체의 핵심 소재가 되기도 한다.

❶ 견뎌 ❷ 겪어 ❸ 거쳐 ❹ 걸러

[18-19] 다음 밑줄 친 부분의 의미가 <u>다른</u> 것을 하나 고르십시오.

Choose the underlined word that has a different meaning from the other underlined words.

18.

❶ 음식을 <u>가리지</u> 말고 골고루 먹어야 한다.
❷ 아이가 심하게 낯을 <u>가려</u> 아무에게나 맡길 수가 없다.
❸ 사고의 원인을 <u>가리기</u> 위해서 온갖 노력을 기울이고 있다.
❹ 범인은 얼굴을 <u>가릴</u> 목적으로 모자와 마스크를 쓰고 있었다.

19.

❶ 아침식사를 <u>거르는</u> 주된 이유는 '시간부족' 인 것으로 나타났다.
❷ 할아버지께서는 하루도 <u>거르지</u> 않고 우리 형제의 도시락을 싸 주셨다.
❸ 하루라도 운동을 <u>거르면</u> 불안해지는 사람은 운동중독을 의심해 보아야 한다.
❹ 녹차 잎을 곱게 <u>거른</u> 맑은 차를 마시면 내 영혼까지 맑아지는 느낌이 든다.

[20-21] 다음 중 동사의 쓰임이 잘못된 것을 고르십시오.

Choose the sentence in which the verb is used incorrectly.

20.

❶ 게으름을 부리는 사이에 숙제가 일주일 치나 걸려 있다.

❷ 올림픽에서 금메달이 가장 많이 걸려 있는 종목은 육상이다.

❸ 차에 시동이 걸리지 않는데 엔진 부분을 점검해 보아야겠다.

❹ 나라를 짊어지고 나갈 청소년들에게 우리의 미래가 걸려 있다.

21.

❶ 부모님은 온갖 정성을 기울여서 자식들을 키운다.

❷ 높은 목표를 세운 만큼 남다른 연습을 기울이지 않으면 안 된다.

❸ 심혈을 기울여 완성한 작품을 그렇게 쉽게 남의 손에 넘겨줄 순 없다.

❹ 매사에 주의를 기울이지 않으면 방심하는 순간에 큰 사고가 날 수 있다.

[22-30] 다음 (　　)에 공통적으로 들어갈 단어의 기본형을 쓰십시오.

Find the one word that fits in the parentheses and write the most basic form.

22.

❶ 그는 어떤 수단과 방법을 써서라도 빚부터 (　　　)겠다고 마음먹었다.

❷ 사장님께서 저에게 베풀어 주신 은혜는 평생이 걸리더라도 꼭 (　　　)도록 하겠습니다.

23.

❶ 해가 중천에 떴으니 얼른 일어나서 이불도 (　　　)고 방청소도 좀 해라.

❷ 오전 내내 가을비가 주룩주룩 내리더니 오후가 되어서야 날이 (　　　)었다/았다/였다.

❸ 아이가 가루약을 잘 먹지 못할 때는 약을 물에(　　　)어/아/여 주는 것도 한 방법이다.

❹거짓말처럼 맑게 (　　　)은/ㄴ 푸른 하늘을 바라보니 마음속의 우울함이 다 사라진 느낌이었다.

24.

❶ 진통제를 먹자 곧 통증이 (　　　)었다/았다/였다.

❷ 배는 바위에 부딪힌 충격으로 물속으로 (　　　)고 말았다.

❸ 그의 자세한 설명을 듣고 나서야 겨우 마음이 (　　　)었다/았다/였다.

❹ 유족들의 흥분이 (　　　)기를 기다려 장관은 이번 사건에 대한 입장을 표명했다.

25.

❶ 지금처럼 경기흐름을 쉽게 예측할 수 없는 시기에는 투자에 신중을 (　　　)는 것이 현명하다.

❷ 국방부 장관은 회의에서 군 본연의 임무 수행에 만전을 (　　　)을/ㄹ 것을 당부했다.

❸ 앞으로는 보안 문제를 해결할 수 있는 기술적인 부분에 보다 완벽을 (　　　)도록 해야 한다.

❹ 방송통신위원회는 지난 5월 17일 12시를 (　　　)어/아/여, 2개월 째 유지되어 온 사이버 경보단계를 해제한다고 밝혔다.

26.

❶ 그는 부모의 뜻을 한번도 (　　　)은/ㄴ 적이 없는 효자였다.

❷ 만원으로 아이스크림 6개를 사고 1,000원을 (　　　)어/아/여 받았다.

❸ 생태계의 파괴는 인간이 자연의 법칙을 (　　　)은/ㄴ 대가라고 할 수 있다.

❹ 우리 과 직원들은 까다로운 과장의 비위를 (　　　)지 않으려고 늘 신경을 곤두세우고 있다.

27.

❶ 그는 소나기가 그치고 해가 나기가 무섭게 천막을 (　　　)었다/았다/였다.

❷ 큰 스님은 오갈 데 없는 어린 아이들을 10여 명이나 (　　　)었다/았다/였다.

❸ 이번 선거전에서는 야당이 여당에게 큰 득표 차이로 대승을 (　　　)었다/았다/였다.

❹ 모교에 대형 도서관을 건립하기 위해 동창회에서 기금을 (　　　)고 있다.

28.

❶ 베인 손에 붕대를 (　　　)고 글씨를 쓰려고 하니 불편하기 짝이 없다.

❷ 그 친구는 나를 보자마자 팔을 내 목에 (　　　)고 반가움의 표시를 했다.

❸ 여자아이는 머리를 (　　　)고 빗으로 곱게 빗으니 어엿한 아가씨 같았다.

❹ 타고 있던 놀이기구가 아래로 떨어지듯 갑자기 내려갈 때는 나도 모르게 눈을 (　　　)고 말았다.

29.

❶ 성격이 (　　　　)은/ㄴ 사람은 대개 언행이 부정적이다.

❷ 나는 회사일로 눈코 뜰 새 없다는 동생을 (　　　　)어/아/여 여행을 가기로 했다.

❸ 하는 일마다 술술 잘 풀릴 때가 있는가 하면 이상하게 (　　　　)기만 할 때도 있는 법이다.

❹ 결혼반지의 디자인은 가는 선이 (　　　　)어/아/여 단단한 노끈이 만들어지듯 부부를 단단하게 이어준다는 의미를 갖고 있다.

30.

❶ 구슬을 실에 정성스럽게 (　　　　)어/아/여 목걸이를 완성했다.

❷ 그는 외국인이면서도 한국 역사의 주요 인물을 줄줄 (　　　　)고 있다.

❸ 그는 닭고기를 꼬챙이에 (　　　　)어/아/여 불에 구우면서 손님 맞을 준비를 하고 있었다.

❹ 그는 이 지역에서 평생 살아서 이곳에 관한 것은 모르는 것 없이 훤히 (　　　　)고 있다.

동사 Ⅱ

02

Verbs Ⅱ

02 동사 II

001
날리다[1]

[날리다] to have fly/float

to have an object ride the wind and move around

[Usage] N이/가 날리다

[Expression] 먼지가 날리다 to have dust fly

낙엽이 날리다 to have fallen leaves fly

깃발이 날리다 to fly a flag

눈보라가 날리다 to have snow fly

[Example] 거리는 흙먼지만 날리고 무척 황량하였다.
There was a lot of dust in the air which made everything dreary.

봄에는 꽃가루가 날려 눈병에 걸리는 사람이 많다.
Because a lot of pollen floats in the air during the spring, many people have eye infections.

002
날리다[2]

[날리다] 1. to make fly 2. to disperse into the air 3. to make yourself known 4. to flit around 5. to lose money

1. to make fly

[Usage] N을/를 날리다

[Example] 개막식에는 비둘기를 하늘로 날리는 순서가 있었다.
At the commencement ceremony there was a part where they made doves fly.

2. to throw or disperse into the air

[Usage] N을/를 날리다

[Example] 아이들은 깃발을 날리며 환호성을 질렀다.
The children flew the flag and cheered.

3. to make yourself known

[Usage] N을/를 날리다

[Expression] 이름을 날리다 to make a name for yourself

명성을 날리다 to create a reputation for yourself

[Example] 민수의 어머니는 1960년대에 명성을 날리던 영화배우였다고 한다.
It is said that Minsoo's mother was a famous actress in 1960 with quite a wonderful reputation.

4. to move around your body quickly

[Usage] N을/를 날리다

[Expression] 몸을 날리다 to have your body fly around

주먹을 날리다 to throw a punch

[Example] 상대는 공중으로 몸을 훽 날리더니 내 머리에 일격을 가했다.
My opponent flew up into the air and attacked my head.

5. to lose money due to incorrect handling

[Usage] N을/를 날리다

[Expression] 돈을 날리다 to lose all of your money
재산을 날리다 to lose all of your savings

[Example] 주식 투자를 잘못 해서 전 재산을 날리는 사람도 있다.
There are many people who lose all of their savings due to bad investments.

003
넘나들다

[넘나들다] to cross freely

to cross borders or lines back and forth, freely

[Usage] N을/를 넘나들다

[Example] 여러 나라의 국경을 넘나들며 장사를 하는 사람들이 있다.
There are many people who do business in different countries and cross international borders freely.

김 교수는 정치학, 역사학, 언어학 등 학문의 여러 분야를 넘나들며 논문을 쓴다.
Professor Kim writes theses across many different subjects such as politics, history, and language.

004
넘보다

[넘보다] 1. to peek 2. to covet 3. to underestimate

1. to peek in order to see something fully

[Usage] N을/를 넘보다

[Example] 동생은 남의 대문 안을 넘보고 있다가 들킨 사람처럼 화들짝 놀랐다.
My younger sibling was so startled that he looked like someone who had just been caught peeking into someone's front gate.

2. to covet something that belongs to someone else

[Usage] N을/를 넘보다

[Example] 상대 선수는 경험이 부족해 우승을 넘볼 만한 실력이 못되니까 자신감을 가지고 해 보세요.
Your opponent lacks the experience to even covet first place, so become more confident.

3. to think lightly of someone/something

[Usage] N을/를 넘보다

[Example] 미국과 러시아는 우주 과학에 있어서는 어느 나라도 넘보지 못할 기술을 지니고 있다.
America and Russia are both countries that should not be taken lightly when it comes to space technology.

005
누리다

[누리다] to enjoy/be blessed with

to enjoy something over a long period of time

[Usage] N을/를 누리다

[Expression] 행복을 누리다 to enjoy bliss
자유를 누리다 to enjoy freedom
인기를 누리다 to enjoy popularity
권세를 누리다 to enjoy authority

[Example] 요즘은 댄스 그룹들이 솔로 가수들보다 인기를 누리고 있는 듯하다.
Lately, it seems that dance groups are enjoying more popularity than solo singers.

귀족은 봉건 사회에서 이익과 특권을 많이 누렸던 특권 계급이었다.
In the feudalism era, the aristocrats were a level of people who enjoyed profits and many privileges.

006
누비다

[누비다] 1. to quilt 2. to cross back and forth

1. to place cotton in between two pieces of fabric and sew lines

[Usage] N을/를 누비다

[Expression] 이불을 누비다 to quilt a blanket
바지를 누비다 to sew pants

[Example] 어머니는 겨울이면 솜을 넣어 누빈 옷을 우리 형제에게 입혔다.
My mother used to dress my brothers and me in quilted clothes when it became winter.

2. to cross back and forth without and reluctance

[Usage] N을/를 누비다

[Example] 영국 공연단은 전국을 누비며 공연을 하러 다녔다.
The performance group from England crossed back and forth across the nation while performing

007
다듬다

[다듬따] 1. to trim 2. to trim off 3. to smooth out 4. to warm up

1. to trim something so that a form appears

[Usage] N을/를 다듬다

[Expression] 머리를 다듬다 to trim your hair
손톱을 다듬다 to trim your nails

[Example] 머리가 길어서 좀 다듬으러 미용실에 가는 길이에요.
My hair has gotten long so I'm going to the hair salon in order to get it trimmed.

2. to rid of parts that you don't need and make it something that is useful

[Usage] N을/를 다듬다

[Example] 요리하는 일도 쉽지 않지만 재료를 깨끗이 다듬는 일도 손이 많이 가는 일이다.
Cooking is not an easy feat but neither is preparing ingredients so that they are clean and ready for use.

3. to smooth out things like text to make it flow better

[Usage] N을/를 다듬다

[Example] 출판사에 넘길 원고를 다듬기 위해 책상에 앉았다.
I prepared to smooth out some parts in my manuscript before turning it over to the publisher by sitting at my desk.

4. to clear your voice so that you can speak or sing better

[Usage] N을/를 다듬다

[Example] 심호흡을 하고 목소리를 다듬고 전화 수화기를 들었다.
I breathed deeply and cleared up my voice before picking up the telephone receiver.

008
다지다

[다지다] 1. to make firm 2. to strengthen yourself 3. to solidify 4. to finely chop

1. to press on or step on something constantly in order to make it firm

[Usage] N을/를 다지다

[Expression] 흙을 다지다 to pack the dirt
땅을 다지다 to pack the earth

[Example] 역 주변에 아파트를 짓기 위해 땅을 단단히 다지는 중이다.
They are in the process of packing the dirt in order to make it more firm so that apartments can be built there.

2. to strengthen yourself; to prepare yourself

[Usage] N을/를 다지다

[Expression] 마음을 다지다 to strengthen one's mind
각오를 다지다 to prepare one's resolution

[Example] 이번 계획을 성공적으로 이끌기 위해서는 새로운 각오를 다져야 합니다.
In order to make our new plans a success, we must become much more resolute.

3. to solidify the basics or base

[Usage] N을/를 다지다

[Expression] 기반을 다지다 to solidify the base
기초를 다지다 to solidify the basics

[Example] 이번 정상 회담의 목적은 양국 경제 협력의 기반을 다지는 데에 있다.
The purpose of this summit is to solidify the groundwork of cooperation between the two countries concerning the economy.

4. to chop meat, vegetables, or something finely with a knife

[Usage] N을/를 다지다

[Expression] 고기를 다지다 to mince the meat

마늘을 다지다 to dice the garlic

[Example] 간장에 파와 마늘을 곱게 다져 넣어 양념장을 만들었다.

I chopped onion and garlic finely and combined it with soy sauce in order to make a marinade.

009
다짐하다

[다짐하다] 1. to commit oneself to something 2. to make sure

1. to commit oneself into doing something so that you succeed

[Usage] N을/를 다짐하다

AV겠다고 다짐하다

[Example] 이번 시험에서 꼭 합격하겠다고 굳게 다짐했다.

I wholly committed myself to getting an acceptable test score for this exam.

2. to assure that something you did or do will be successful

[Usage] N에/에게 N을/를 다짐하다

N에/에게 AV겠다고 다짐하다

[Example] 나는 아내에게 다시는 담배를 피우지 않겠다고 다짐했지만 일주일이 못 가서 다시 피우게 되었다.

I assured my wife that I would be successful in quitting smoking but I didn't even last a week.

010
달다[1]

[달다] 1. to hang 2. to install 3. to add to 4. to record

1. to hang an object in one specific area

[Usage] (N에) N을/를 달다

[Expression] 깃발을 달다 to hang the flag

단추를 달다 to sew on a button

[Example] 우리 집은 국경일에 반드시 대문에 태극기를 단다.

On a national holiday, our household always hangs the Korean flag on our front door.

2. to install an object or equipment

[Usage] (N에) N을/를 달다

[Expression] 전화를 달다 to install a phone

에어컨을 달다 to install air conditioning

[Example] 공부방이 너무 더워서 에어컨을 달았더니 정말 쾌적해요.

Since my study room was so hot, we installed air conditioning and it's very comfortable now.

3. to add on a definition, explanation, particle or postposition, or a condition to a piece of text or words

[Usage] (N에) N을/를 달다

[Expression] 각주를 달다 to add a footnote

조건을 달다 to add a condition

[Example] 한문 원문에 토를 다니까 읽기가 훨씬 쉽다.
The original Chinese text is much easier to read after adding in particles.

4. to keep track of bills in an account book

[Usage] (N에) N을/를 달다

[Expression] 술값을 달다 to keep a bar tab

외상값을 달다 to keep an account book of bills

[Example] 오늘 술값은 장부에 달아 주세요.
Please add today's bar bill to my tab.

011
달다²

[달다] to weigh

to weigh something on a scale

[Usage] (N에) N을/를 달다

[Expression] 고기를 저울에 달다 to weigh meat on a scale

몸무게를 달아 보다 to measure one's weight

[Example] 주인은 금의 무게를 저울에 달아 보고 가격을 제시했다.
The owner weighed the gold on a scale and asked for a price relative to the weight.

무게를 달아야 하니까 저울 위에 소포를 올려놓으세요.
Please place the package on the scale because we need to weigh it.

012
달다³

[달다] 1. to become red-hot 2. to become flushed 3. to become fretful

1. to have a metal or rock become red-hot

[Usage] N이/가 달다

[Example] 난로가 빨갛게 달아 방안이 후끈거린다.
The heater became red-hot and heated the room.

2. to feel flushed because you are feeling feverish or excited

[Usage] N이/가 달다

[Example] 내 약점을 지적당하자 나도 모르게 얼굴이 뜨겁게 달아 올랐다.
I unconsciously became flushed after being criticized on my weakest point.

3. to become fretful and impatient because you feel disappointed or distressed

[Usage] N이/가 달다

[Expression] 애가 달다 to become anxious

속이 달다 to be anxious

몸이 달다 to be anxious and fidget

[Example] 내가 고백했는데도 그녀가 아무런 반응을 안 보이니 애가 달아서 어찌해야 할지 모르겠다.
Even when I confessed my love, the girl had no response and I felt so fretful that I don't know what to do with myself.

013
대다

[대다] 1. to apply 2. to supply 3. to park or anchor 4. to compare 5. to indicate 6. to be on time for

1. to place against something

[Usage] N을/를 N에 대다

[Expression] 손을 대다 to place one's hand against something
입에 대다 to place to one's lips

[Example] 그는 술잔을 입에 댔다가 마시지 않고 내려놓았다.
He placed the wine glass to his lips but didn't drink from it and just placed it back down.

2. to supply or provide for something

[Usage] N을/를 N에 대다

[Example] 어머니는 수술비를 댈 돈이 없어서 퇴원하기로 마음먹었다.
My mother didn't have any money to put towards the surgery bill so she decided to discharge from the hospital.

3. to park a car or anchor a boat in one, fixed area

[Usage] N을/를 N에 대다

[Example] 주차장이 따로 없는 사람들은 집 앞에 차를 대기도 한다.
Those who do not have a driveway or parking lot just park their cars in front of their homes.

4. to make a comparison with

[Usage] N을/를 N에 대다

[Example] 길고 짧은 건 대 봐야 안다.
You must compare lengths in order to see if it is longer or shorter.

5. to indicate someone's response

[Usage] N을/를 대다

[Expression] 증거를 대다 to show evidence
핑계를 대다 to say an excuse

[Example] 내가 모임에 참석하지 못한 이유를 대려면 너무 많다.
There are too many reasons for me to explain why I couldn't participate in the meeting.

6. to be aware of an appointment and be early to it

[Usage] N에 대다

[Example] 약속시간에 대어 오느라고 얼마나 일찍부터 서둘렀는지 모른다.
You don't know how quickly I rushed in order to make it to this appointment.

014
더듬다

[더듬따] 1. to fumble around for 2. to search for 3. to recollect 4. to stutter

1. to feel around for something that you can't see

[Usage] N을/를 더듬다

[Example] 문을 열고 어두운 벽을 더듬어 전등을 켰다.
After I opened the door, I felt around on the wall in the dark to turn on the light.

2. to search for something by going over many different points

[Usage] N을/를 더듬다

[Expression] 흔적을 더듬다 to retrace the traces left behind
길을 더듬어 찾아가다 to retrace a path

[Example] 국토 순례의 길을 걸으며 선인들의 발자취를 더듬어 볼 생각입니다.
I have decided to retrace the footsteps of virtuous men in a cross-country pilgrimage.

3. to retrace a thought or something from your memory in order to remember it

[Usage] N을/를 더듬다

[Expression] 기억을 더듬다 to retrace a memory
추억을 더듬다 to retrace a recollection

[Example] 술을 한 잔 하면 지난 고통의 세월을 더듬어 보곤 한다.
When I drink, I often retrace my memories of pain from months past.

4. to stutter or stumble over words

[Usage] N을/를 더듬다

[Expression] 말을 더듬다 to stutter

[Example] 내 동생은 많은 사람 앞에 서면 긴장을 하여 말을 심하게 더듬는다.
When my younger sibling is in front of a large group of people, he becomes very anxious and stutters severely.

015
돌리다

[돌리다] 1. to turn 2. to operate 3. to alter 4. to pass around 5. to be indirect 6. to divert 7. to shift blame

1. to turn in one direction using one point or line as the starting point

[Usage] N을/를 돌리다

[Expression] 바퀴를 돌리다 to spin
다이얼을 돌리다 to turn the dial

[Example] 소년은 지구본을 돌리면서 여러 나라의 수도를 하나하나 찾아보았다.
The boy turned the globe to find the capitals to many nations.

2. to operate so that the functions are put into action

[Usage] N을/를 돌리다

[Expression] 세탁기를 돌리다 to operate the washing machine
공장을 돌리다 to have the factory operate

[Example] 바느질로 먹고 사는 아주머니는 끊임없이 재봉틀을 돌리고 계셨다.
The old woman who makes a living out of sewing was constantly operating her sewing machine.

3. to alter the position of something

[Usage] N을/를 N으로/로 돌리다

[Expression] 몸을 돌리다 to turn the direction of the body
시선을 돌리다 to shift the line of vision

[Example] 교수는 창밖으로 시선을 돌리고 있더니 조용히 입을 열었다.
The professor had shifted his line of vision out to the window when he quietly began to talk.

4. to pass or deliver around an item

[Usage] N을/를 N으로/로 돌리다

[Expression] 떡을 돌리다 to pass around rice cakes
신문을 돌리다 to deliver the newspaper

[Example] 개업 기념으로 상가 전체에 떡을 돌렸다.
To celebrate the grand opening of the business, I passed around rice cakes to the whole shopping district.

5. to be indirect with your words

[Usage] N을/를 돌리다

[Example] 제발 말을 빙빙 돌리지 말고 요건만 간단하게 말해라.
Please stop beating around the bush and say only the main points.

6. to divert from the topic

[Usage] N을/를 돌리다

[Example] 그는 자기에게 불리한 얘기가 나오자 화제를 돌리려고 애를 썼다.
He tried extremely hard to change the subject once words that worked against him were spoken.

7. to shift the blame or praise to someone else

[Usage] N을/를 N의 탓으로 돌리다
N을/를 N의 공으로 돌리다

[Example] 사업 부진을 남의 탓으로 돌리지 말고 자신의 잘못을 인정해야 한다.
Do not try to shift the responsibility of your business depression on someone else and just acknowledge it yourself.

016
뒤지다[1] [뒤지다] 1.to rummage 2. to search through

1. to rummage through something thoroughly in search of something

[Usage] N을/를 뒤지다

[Expression] 가방을 뒤지다 to rummage through a bag
집 안을 뒤지다 to rummage throughout the house

[Example] 지갑 안을 뒤지니 천 원짜리 하나가 나왔다.
I found a 1,000 won bill after rummaging through my wallet.

2. to search thoroughly through a book or documents etc.

[Usage] N을/를 뒤지다

[Expression] 사진첩을 뒤지다 to search through a photo album
학적부를 뒤지다 to search through the school register

[Example] 그들은 차근차근히 책을 뒤지며 자료를 찾았다.
They methodically searched through the book in order to find data.

017
뒤지다[2]

[뒤지다] 1. to fall behind 2. to lag 3. to be behind

1. to fall behind someone else's pace

[Usage] N보다 뒤지다

[Example] 산길에 익숙하지 않은 나는 열심히 걸어도 계속 다른 사람보다 뒤졌다.
Because I wasn't used to mountainous roads, no matter how fervently I walked I always fell behind other people.

2. to lag or fall behind in skills or level compared to other people

[Usage] N에/에게 뒤지다

[Example] 그의 업무 처리 능력은 결코 다른 사람에게 뒤지지 않는다.
His skill in completing tasks doesn't not in any way fall behind other people.

3. to be behind on a standard

[Usage] N에 뒤지다

[Expression] 시대에 뒤지다 to be behind on a generation
유행에 뒤지다 to be behind on the fads

[Example] 요즘 사람들은 유행에 뒤질세라 패션에 관심을 갖고 따라가려고 애쓰는 것 같다.
People nowadays dress to and have a lot of interest in fashion because they are afraid they will be behind on the newest fads.

018
드러나다

[드러나다] 1. to emerge 2. to be revealed

1. to emerge 2. to be revealed

[Usage] N이/가 드러나다

[Example] 구름이 걷히자 산봉우리가 드러났다.
The mountain peak emerged after the clouds cleared.

2. to have a truth that was hidden, become revealed

[Usage] N이/가 드러나다

[Expression] 비밀이 드러나다 to reveal secrets
사실이 드러나다 to reveal the truth

[Example] 피의자들은 범죄 사실이 백일하에 드러나자 잘못을 시인했다.
After the crime of the suspect was revealed like broad daylight, he admitted his wrongdoing.

019
때우다

[때우다] 1. to patch up 2. to make shift 3. to pass time 4. to make due

1. to patch up something that has become perforated or broken with a different piece

[Usage] N을/를 때우다

[Expression] 이를 때우다 to patch up teeth
구멍을 때우다 to patch up a hole

[Example] 썩은 이를 백금으로 때웠다.
They patched up the rotten tooth with white gold.

2. to have a makeshift meal with simple food

[Usage] N을/를 (N으로/로) 때우다

[Expression] 끼니를 때우다 to have makeshift meal
점심을 때우다 to have a makeshift lunch

[Example] 너무 바빠서 점심을 빵하고 우유로 때웠어요.
I was so busy that I had to have a makeshift meal of only bread and milk.

3. to pass time when you don't have much to do

[Usage] N을/를 때우다

[Expression] 시간을 때우다 to pass the time

[Example] 친구가 올 때까지 비디오를 보면서 시간을 때웠다.
I watched videos to pass the time until my friend came.

4. to make due with other options

[Usage] N을/를 N으로/로 때우다

[Example] 생일인 걸 깜빡해 선물을 준비 못해서 축하한다는 말로 때웠다.
I had forgotten that it was his birthday and didn't prepare a gift, so made due with just wishing him a happy birthday.

020
뚫다

[뚤타] 1. to pierce 2. to overcome

1. to pierce 2. to overcome

[Usage] N을/를 뚫다

[Expression] 구멍을 뚫다 to pierce a hole
터널을 뚫다 to drill a tunnel
길을 뚫다 to make a way
세계시장을 뚫다 to break through the global market

[Example] 터널을 뚫으면 두 지역 간의 교류가 한층 활발해질 것으로 전망된다.
If we drill a tunnel, it is predicted that the exchange between these two areas will be more active.

2. to break through and overcome an ordeal, obstacle, or other hardships

[Usage] N을/를 뚫다

[Expression] 고난을 뚫다 to overcome hardship
장애를 뚫다 to overcome a hindrance
경쟁을 뚫다 to break through the competition

[Example] 그는 많은 고난과 역경을 뚫고 지금의 위치에 이르게 되었다.
He overcame many hardships and adversity to get to where he is today.

021
뜨다[1]

[뜨다] 1. to float 2. to get loose 3. to be excited

1. to float on the surface of the water or rise in the air off of a surface because it doesn't sink

[Usage] N이/가 N에 뜨다

[Expression] 물에 뜨다 to float in water
해가 뜨다 the sun rises

[Example] 우리는 수평선 위로 조금씩 뜨고 있는 붉은 해를 바라보며 가슴속으로 저마다의 소원을 빌었다.
As we watched the the sun rise little by little over the horizon, each of us made a wish in our hearts.

2. to become loose after not sticking so that a space in between is formed.

[Usage] N이/가 뜨다

[Expression] 벽지가 뜨다 to have the wallpaper become loose
장판이 뜨다 to have the papered floor become loose

[Example] 풀칠이 잘못되어 벽지와 장판이 떠서 다시 도배해야 했다.
Because we glued down the wallpaper and papered floor wrong, it became loose and we have to redo the walls and the floor.

3. (used as a figure of speech) to become excited and restless

[Usage] N이/가 N에 뜨다

[Expression] 마음이 뜨다 to become excited
허영에 뜨다 to be caught up in vanity

[Example] 소풍 생각에 마음이 떠 있어 공부가 되지 않는다.
When I think of the excursion, I get so excited that I am unable to study.

022
뜨다[2]

[뜨다] 1. to scoop up 2. to spoon 3. to slice 4. to cut

1. to scoop up or take out an item that was immersed

[Usage] N을/를 N에 뜨다

[Example] 어머니는 큰 대접에 국을 뜨고 거기에 밥을 말아 주셨다.
My mother scooped up some soup into a large soup bowl and mixed together with rice for me.

2. to spoon up food and eat it

[Usage] N을/를 뜨다

[Example] 먼 길 가는데 아무리 바빠도 한술 뜨고 가거라.
No matter how busy you are, since you're traveling a long way please eat something.

3. to slice something like fish into thin slices

[Usage] N을/를 뜨다

[Example] 생선의 살로는 회를 뜨고 남은 뼈로는 생선 매운탕을 끓였다.
After slicing the fish into sashimi, I took the leftover bones and made a spicy fish soup.

4. to only cut and buy the fabric that you need

[Usage] N을/를 뜨다

[Example] 할머니는 시장에서 옷감을 떠서 손수 한복을 지으셨다.
My grandmother went to the marketplace and bought some fabric and made her own traditional Korean clothes.

023
뜨다3

[뜨다] 1. to leave 2. to die/depart

1. to leave the place that you were at

[Usage] N을/를 뜨다

[Expression] 고향을 뜨다 to leave your hometown

[Example] 큰오빠는 도시로 가서 꼭 출세하겠다며 고향을 떴다.
My older brother left our hometown to the city, saying that he would become successful.

2. to die/depart

[Usage] N을/를 뜨다

[Expression] 세상을 뜨다 to depart from the world

[Example] 아버지는 어머니가 돌아가시자 외로움을 못 이기시고 얼마 후 세상을 뜨셨다.
My father couldn't overcome the sadness he felt after my mother died and departed the world soon after.

024
마다하다

[마다하다] to refuse

to decline or refuse

[Usage] N을/를 마다하다

[Example] 김 대리는 집에 좋은 일이 있는지 술자리도 마다하고 일찍 귀가했다.
Mr. Kim must have a happy event at home because he declined to participate in the drinking party and left to return home early.

오랜만에 한국에 왔더니 어릴 적 친구가 먼 길을 마다하지 않고 나를 만나러 와 주었다.
Even when I was located far away, my friend didn't refuse to visit me because it had been a long time since I visited Korea.

025
말리다[1]

[말리다] to dissuade

to dissuade someone from doing an act

[Usage] N을/를 말리다

[Expression] 싸움을 말리다 to dissuade someone from fighting

[Example] 싸움을 말린다는 것이 오히려 부채질하는 결과가 되었다.
Trying to dissuade the fight actually was an act of fanning the fire.

친구가 홧김에 과음하는 것 같아 술을 그만 마시라고 말렸다.
I dissuaded my friend from drinking any more because it seemed like he was overdrinking in a fit of anger.

026
말리다[2]

[말리다] 1. to be rolled 2. to become involved

1. to be rolled or wrapped on something

[Usage] N에 말리다

[Example] 아버지께서 사 오신 신문지에 말린 것이 무엇인지 아이들이 모두 궁금해했다.
The children were curious of what was wrapped in newspaper that their father had bought..

2. to become involved or participate suddenly in an occurrence

[Usage] N에 말리다

[Example] 그는 정치적 사건에 말려 도중에 학교를 그만둔 사람이었다.
He became involved in a political event and had to quit school.

027
반기다

[반기다] to greet

to greet warmly

[Usage] N을/를 반기다

[Example] 어머니는 휴가 나온 아들을 얼싸안으시면서 반기셨다.
The mother hugged and greeted her son warmly who had taken leave from the army.

친구 가족 분들은 집 앞까지 나와서 우리를 반겨 주셨다.
My friend's family came out to the front of the house to greet us.

028
반하다

[반하다] 1. to go against 2. to rebel against

1. (usually used in the form '반하여') to go against or be contradictory

[Usage] N에 반하다

[Example] 농림어업의 인구는 감소하고 그에 반해 3차 산업 부문의 취업 인구가 증가할 것으로 예측된다.
The population in the agricutural, the forestry, and the fishery business is declining whereas the tertiary industries' field employment is expected to increase.

2. to rebel against someone's opinion or rules by opposing them or violating them

[Usage] N에 반하다

[Example] 규칙에 반하는 행동을 하면 규정에 따라 처벌을 받게 된다.
If you violate the rules then you must receive punishment according to the regulations.

029
배다[1]

[배다] 1. to permeate 2. to become a habit 3. to become accustomed to

1. to have liquid or a smell soak or permeate through

[Usage] N에 배다

[Expression] 땀이 옷에 배다 to have sweat soak through clothes
기름이 종이에 배다 to have oil soak through the paper
냄새가 몸에 배다 to have a smell permeate throughout the body

[Example] 뛰어 왔더니 옷에 땀이 다 배었다.
Sweat has soaked into my clothes because I ran here.

2. to become habituated and familiar

[Usage] N에 배다

[Expression] 일이 손에 배다 to have work habituated and familiar to my hands
욕이 입에 배다 to have cursing become habituated

[Example] 그 식당 직원들은 친절이 몸에 배어 있다.
The employees of that restaurant have kindness habituated in their bodies.

3. to become accustomed to a feeling or thought so that you feel it deeply or it lingers for a long time

[Usage] N에 배다

[Example] 농악에는 우리 민족의 정서가 배어 있다.
The instrumental music of peasants is something that the Korean people have become accustomed to.

030
배다[2]

[배다] 1. to conceive 2. to become pregnant 3. to become compact

1. to conceive 2. to become pregnant 3. to become compact

[Usage] N을/를 배다

[Expression] 아이를 배다 to conceive a child
새끼를 배다 to conceive offspring

[Example] 우리 집 개가 새끼를 배서 몸이 무거운지 힘들어한다.
Our pet dog seems tired because of her heavy body due to conceiving offspring.

2. to become pregnant (for fish who have eggs)

[Usage] N에 배다

[Example] 잡은 고기에 알이 배어 통통했다.
The fish that we caught was pregnant and full of eggs so the stomach was fat.

3. to have the arms, legs, etc. become compact with muscle

[Usage] N에 배다

[Example] 계단을 오르락내리락했더니 다리에 알이 뱄다.
My legs have formed muscles after going up and down the stairs.

031
버티다

[버티다] 1. to endure 2. to stand up to 3. to remain firm

1. to bear for a long time and endure

[Usage] N에 버티다

[Example] 그는 갖은 악조건에도 불구하고 오지에서 한 달 동안 버텨 냈다.
He endured a whole month in the uncharted land even with a slew of unfavorable conditions.

2. to not give in and stand up to or resist

[Usage] N에/에게 버티다

[Example] 말단 사원이 상급자의 부당한 압력에도 잘 버티고 있다.
The lower-level employee is standing up well to the unreasonable pressure that his superior is exerting on him.

3. to remain firm on a subject and not swaying

[Usage] N이/가 버티다

[Example] 대문 안에 들어서자 무시무시하게 큰 개가 버티고 있었다.
As soon as I walked into the main gate, there was a large and fearsome dog present and remaining in it's place.

032
부딪치다

[부딛치다] 1. to collide 2. to be confronted 3. to face 4. to take on

1. to collide with something hard

[Usage] N과/와 부딪치다
N에/에게 부딪치다

[Synonym] 부딪히다 to collide

[Example] 빙판길에서 미끄러져 서로 정면으로 부딪친 차들이 크게 부서졌다.
The cars that slid on the icy road and collided with each other head on were destroyed.

2. to be confronted suddenly and unexpectedly

[Usage] N에 부딪치다

[Synonym] 부딪히다 to be confronted

[Example] 경제적 난관에 부딪친 회사는 결국 문을 닫고 말았다.
The business was confronted with some economic hardship and eventually had to close its doors.

3. to face someone when you didn't purposely try to

[Usage] N과/와 부딪치다

[Synonym] 부딪히다 to face

[Example] 그들은 헤어진 지 10년 만에 서울에서 우연히 부딪쳤다.
They met each other randomly in Seoul after being separated ten years ago.

4. to take on without avoiding it. to take on directly. to take on in a confrontation

[Usage] N에 부딪치다
N과/와 부딪치다

[Example] 피해자와 직접 부딪치면 감정이 상하기 쉬우니 보호자와 만나서 차분하게 이야기해 봐라.
If you face the victim directly, feelings can be hurt easily, so meet with a guardian and speak while calm and collected.

033
부리다[1]

[부리다] 1. to use 2. to show

1. to use your talent or wit

[Usage] N을/를 부리다

[Expression] 꾀를 부리다 to use your wit
요술을 부리다 to use a trick

[Example] 아이들이 틈만 나면 놀러 가려고 꾀를 부렸다.
Children used every opportunity to use their wit in order to go play.

2. to show bad personality traits or bad disposition

[Usage] N을/를 부리다

[Expression] 늑장을 부리다 to dawdle
욕심을 부리다 to show greed
기승을 부리다 to show reluctance to yield
어리광을 부리다 to be childish

[Example] 아이가 갑자기 학교에 가지 않겠다고 고집을 부려 나를 난처하게 했다.
My child suddenly stated that he refused to go to school and showed stubbornness, making me embarrassed.

034
부리다[2]

[부리다] to control

to control or manipulate animals or lower people and make them do whatever you want

[Usage] N을/를 부리다

[Expression] 마소를 부리다 to control horses or cattle
일꾼을 부리다 to control workers

[Example] 우리 아버지는 평생 소를 부리며 농사를 짓고 살았다.
My father has lived his life controlling cows to help harvest and farm.

그 집은 대단한 부자여서 많은 노비를 부리고 있었다.
Their household is so rich that they control many servants.

035
부추기다

[부추기다] 1. to put a person up to 2. to instigate

1. to put a person up to doing something

[Usage] N을/를 부추기다

[Example] 노조 위원장은 노동자들을 부추겨 임금 협상을 위한 파업에 동참하게 했다.
The president of the union put the laborers up to a strike in order to achieve a negotiation in wages.

2. to instigate by irritating someone or instigating a situation so that it becomes serious

[Usage] N을/를 부추기다

[Expression] 싸움을 부추기다 to instigate a fight
경쟁심을 부추기다 to instigate competition
과소비를 부추기다 to instigate over-consumption
물가 상승을 부추기다 to instigate the rise in prices

[Example] 근거 없는 유언비어는 사회적 혼란을 부추길 뿐이다.
Rumors that are groundless only help to instigate societal disorder.

036
부치다[1]

[부치다] to fry

to fry/cook/griddle pancakes or foods with a batter on a frying pan greased with oil

[Usage] N을/를 부치다

[Expression] 계란을 부치다 to fry eggs
전을 부치다 to fry panfried food

[Example] 계란 지단을 부쳐 채를 썰어 떡국 위에 올려놓는다.
I fried some eggs, cut it into thin slices, and then place them on top of the rice cake soup.

비가 오는 날 빈대떡을 부쳐서 온 가족이 나눠 먹었다.
Our whole family ate pancakes on a rainy day after cooking them.

037
부치다[2]

[부치다] to lack

to be beyond one's capacity or too much for a person

[Usage] N에 부치다

[Expression] 힘에 부치다 to lack in strength
실력이 부치다 to lack in skills

[Example] 주말에는 긴 여행에 체력이 부쳐서 집에서 꼼짝하지 않고 쉬고 있었다.
I lacked the strength to go on a lengthy vacation this weekend so I stayed at home and rested instead.

자식들 공부시키는 것이 힘에 부쳐서 고등학교를 졸업한 큰아들을 대학에 보낼 수 없었다.
I no longer had the strength to earn money to further my children's education that I failed to send my eldest son to college.

038
부치다[3]

[부치다] to fan

to use a fan, etc. to create wind

[Usage] N을/를 부치다

[Expression] 부채를 부치다 to fan using a fan

[Example] 그는 신문지를 부채 삼아 얼굴에 부쳤다.
He used the newspaper as a fan to fan his face.

그 사람은 더위를 참을 수 없다는 듯이 부채를 힘껏 부치고 있었다.
He fanned himself as if he could not endure the intense heat.

039
비추다

[비추다] 1. to illuminate 2. to shine on 3. to compare to

1. to illuminate something by using something else with light

[Usage] N을/를 비추다

[Example] 따뜻한 봄 햇살이 정원의 잔디밭을 비추고 있었다.
The warm spring sun illuminated the grass in the garden.

2. to shine on or shine through

[Usage] N을/를 N에/에게 비추다

[Example] 필름을 햇빛에 비추어 사진을 확인해 보았다.
I held up the film to have the light shine through and checked the photos.

3. (usually used in the '...에 비추어' form) to compare an object to something related to it

[Usage] N을/를 N에 비추다

[Expression] 경험에 비추다 to compare from experience
상식에 비추다 to compare from common sense
형편에 비추다 to compare from circumstances

[Example] 내 경험에 비추어 생각해 보면 네 행동은 지나친 감이 있다.
When I compare from my past experiences, I feel that your actions were excessive.

02 연습문제

[1-10] 다음 밑줄 친 부분과 의미가 비슷한 것을 고르십시오.

Choose the word that is similar to the underlined word.

1. 다시 돌아오기 어려운 기회니만큼 학생시절의 자유를 마음껏 누리고 싶다.

❶ 지내다 ❷ 즐기다 ❸ 누비다 ❹ 살리다

2. 2년여에 걸쳐 시나리오를 다듬은 끝에 마침내 영화 제작에 들어가게 되었다.

❶ 손을 보다 ❷ 손을 대다 ❸ 손을 쓰다 ❹ 손이 가다

3. 나는 두 번 다시 그곳에 가지 않겠다고 스스로 다짐했다.

❶ 결정하다 ❷ 결심하다 ❸ 선택하다 ❹ 지원하다

4. 체육관에 에어컨을 설치해서 학생들이 쾌적한 환경에서 운동할 수 있게 되었다.

❶ 빼다 ❷ 얻다 ❸ 달다 ❹ 배다

5. 이 방은 손바닥만 한 내 하숙방에 비하면 무척 큰 편이다.

❶ 대다 ❷ 달다 ❸ 향하다 ❹ 못하다

6. 그 유명인들이 곧 결혼할 거라는 소문이 이번 기자회견을 통해 사실로 밝혀졌다.

❶ 발견되다 ❷ 드러나다 ❸ 기인하다 ❹ 지정되다

7. 그는 더 많은 보수를 주겠다는 경쟁 회사의 제의를 마다하고 지금까지 자신을 키워 준 현재의 회사에서 계속 근무하기로 했다.

❶ 꺼리다 ❷ 거스르다 ❸ 경험하다 ❹ 거절하다

8. 심의 규정에 어긋난 광고를 할 경우에는 상당한 액수의 벌금이 부과된다.

❶ 따르다 ❷ 반하다 ❸ 부딪치다 ❹ 비뚤어지다

9. 두 사람은 학교를 졸업한 지 20년 만에 우연히 길에서 만났다.

❶ 싸우다 ❷ 부딪치다 ❸ 지나치다 ❹ 어울리다

10. 운동 연습 중에 체력이 부쳐서 도저히 더 이상 할 수가 없었다.

❶ 힘들다 ❷ 충분하다 ❸ 필요하다 ❹ 모자라다

[11-12] 다음 밑줄 친 부분과 의미가 반대인 것을 고르십시오.

Choose the word that is the opposite of the underlined word.

11. 요즘은 여행 생각으로 마음이 떠 있어 좀처럼 일에 집중할 수가 없다.

❶ 날다 ❷ 반기다 ❸ 반기다 ❹ 가라앉다

12. 지배국의 압박에 끝까지 버텨서 마침내 자유를 되찾았다.

❶ 견디다 ❷ 비기다 ❸ 항복하다 ❹ 넘어지다

[13-18] 다음 (　　)에 알맞은 것을 고르십시오.

Choose the word that fits best in the parenthesis.

13. 옆집 아이는 얼마 전에 구입한 자전거로 온 동네를 (　　) 다닌다.

❶ 거치며 ❷ 겪으며 ❸ 누리며 ❹ 누비며

14. 갑자기 전기가 나가는 바람에 어둠 속을 (　　) 불을 켤 만한 것을 찾았다.

❶ 갈라 ❷ 뚫어 ❸ 더듬어 ❹ 추측하여

15. 최근에는 상업성보다 음악성으로 승부를 거는 신인 가수들이 가요계의 정상을 (　　) 있다고 한다.

❶ 넘보고 ❷ 기울이고 ❸ 쳐다보고 ❹ 마음먹고

16. 그는 10대 1의 경쟁을 (　　) 원하던 기업에 입사했다.

❶ 뚫고　❷ 거치고　❸ 이기고　❹ 채우고

17. 그 사람은 친지들이 모두 (　　) 불구하고 무리하게 사업을 확장하더니 결국 큰 손해를 입었다고 한다.

❶ 말리는데도　❷ 개의하는데도　❸ 마다하는데도　❹ 동의하는데도

18. 대지를 적시는 봄비가 내리자 꽃들은 마치 그 봄비를 (　　) 활짝 피었다.

❶ 마시듯　❷ 겨루듯　❸ 반기듯　❹ 당기듯

[19-20] 다음 밑줄 친 부분의 의미가 다른 것을 하나 고르십시오.

Choose the underlined word that has a different meaning from the other underlined words.

19.

❶ 경찰이 용의자의 방을 뒤지니 사건의 단서가 하나하나 발견되었다.
❷ 그는 신입사원임에도 불구하고 업무 능력이 선배 사원에게 뒤지지 않는다.
❸ 영수는 다른 아이들보다 몇 걸음 뒤지는 듯하더니 갑자기 속도를 내기 시작했다.
❹ 그 후보는 여론조사에서는 1위보다 10% 정도 뒤졌지만 실제 선거에서는 1위로 당선되었다.

20.

❶ 그 사장은 아랫사람을 함부로 부리는 걸로 악명이 높다.
❷ 우리 아이는 요술을 부리는 요술쟁이 이야기를 제일 좋아한다.
❸ 우리 아이가 한번 고집을 부리기 시작하면 아무도 감당할 수가 없다.
❹ 다음 주부터는 본격적인 한여름 더위가 기승을 부릴 거라는 예보가 있었다.

[21-23] 다음 중 동사의 쓰임이 잘못된 것을 고르십시오.

Choose the sentence in which the verb is used incorrectly.

21.

❶ 너무 바쁘면 김밥 한 줄로 점심을 때울 때도 있어요.

❷ 어머니 생신 선물을 미역국 끓여 드리는 걸로 때웠어요.

❸ 강의 시간이 비어 있을 때는 그림을 그리면서 시간을 때워요.

❹ 부모님 회갑인데 국내 여행 대신에 친척들을 모시고 큰 잔치를 해서 때울까 해요.

22.

❶ 왜곡된 정보로 사회 혼란을 부추기는 일은 없어야 한다.

❷ 그는 친구들이 부추기는 바람에 학교 대표 선거에 출마하게 됐다.

❸ 새로 발표된 교육 정책이 오히려 사교육을 부추긴다는 주장이 있다.

❹ 지난주에 있었던 추돌 사고를 부추긴 것은 운전자의 졸음운전이었던 것으로 판명되었다.

23.

❶ 신문지를 부채 삼아 부치며 더위를 식혔다.

❷ 일 년간의 계획을 꼼꼼히 세워서 책상 앞에 부쳐 두었다.

❸ 힘에 부치는 여행이었는지 아이는 돌아와서 몸살을 심하게 앓았다.

❹ 할아버지 회갑 잔치를 하루 앞두고 어머니는 전을 부치느라 애쓰신다.

[24-30] 다음 (　　)에 공통적으로 들어갈 단어의 기본형을 쓰십시오.

Find the one word that fits in the parentheses and write the most basic form.

24.

❶ 가을바람에 낙엽이 (　　)는 길을 걸으면서 지난 추억을 떠올렸다.

❷ 그 날 체육 대회에서는 색색가지 풍선을 (　　)는 행사도 진행됐다.

❸ 그는 전 재산을 주식에 투자했다가 1년 만에 전부 (　　)었다고/았다고/였다고 한다.

❹ 그는 80년대 최고의 권투선수로 이름을 (　　)다가 돌연 은퇴해서 아쉬움을 남긴 바 있다.

25.

❶ 비행기 출발 시간에 (　　　)으려면/려면 서둘러야겠어요.

❷ 우리 부모님은 자식들 학비를 (　　　)느라고 노점상까지 하셨다.

❸ 작은 골목에 차를 (　　　)어/아/여 놓으면 통행에 불편을 줍니다.

❹ 전시회장에 전시되어 있는 작품에 손을 (　　　)으면/면 안 됩니다.

26.

❶ 사람들이 땅을 밟아 단단하게 (　　　)는/ㄴ다.

❷ (　　　)은/ㄴ 고기에 소금과 후추를 뿌려 놓았어요.

❸ 성공하려면 자신의 의지를 더 굳게 (　　　)으세요/세요.

❹ 기초를 잘 (　　　)어야/아야/여야 건물이 튼튼하고 오래 간다.

27.

❶ 앞머리는 조금만 (　　　)고 옆머리는 짧게 잘라 주세요.

❷ 영민은 노래 부르기 전에 한껏 목청을 (　　　)었다/았다/였다.

❸ 갖은 야채를 깨끗이 (　　　)어서/아서/여서 소금을 살짝 뿌려 놓았다.

❹ 성격이 꼼꼼한 그는 문장을 (　　　)고 또 (　　　)었다/았다/였다.

28.

❶ 그 고학생은 새벽에 신문을 (　　　)는 아르바이트를 한다.

❷ 그 사람은 상황이 불리해지자 얼른 말을 (　　　)었다/았다/였다.

❸ 실패의 원인을 남의 탓으로 (　　　)지 말고 자신의 잘못을 반성해야 한다.

❹ 나는 방 안에 있는 물건들을 정리할 테니 동생에게는 청소기를 (　　　)으라/라고 했다.

29.

❶ 일이 아직 손에 (　　　)지 않아서 실수할 때가 많다.

❷ 고기 냄새가 옷에 (　　　)어/아/여 좀처럼 없어지지 않는다.

❸ 가게의 구석구석에 아버지의 노력과 땀이 (　　　)어/아/여 있다.

❹ 굴비를 먹어보려고 손에 들었더니 노랗게 꽉 찬 알이 (　　　)어/아/여 있었다.

30.

❶ 그는 체중계에 몸무게를 (　　)아/어/여 보았다.

❷ 뜨거운 용광로 속의 쇠가 벌겋게 (　　)어/아/여 있었다.

❸ 아이들이 나무에 색종이로 만든 별을 (　　)었다/았다/였다.

❹ 발표 결과를 기다리는 지원자들은 애가 (　　)아/어/여 가만히 앉아 있을 수가 없었다.

동사 Ⅲ

03

Verbs Ⅲ

03 동사 III

001
살피다

[살피다] 1. to look carefully 2. to analyze

1. to look around carefully and thoroughly

[Usage] N을/를 살피다

[Expression] 사방을 살피다 to look around on all sides

주변을 살피다 to look around your surroundings

[Example] 횡단보도를 건널 때는 주위를 잘 살피고 나서 건너야 한다.
When you cross the street, you must look at your surroundings carefully before crossing.

2. to analyze or calculate the circumstances or situation

[Usage] N을/를 살피다

[Expression] 문제점을 살피다 to analyze the problem

민심을 살피다 to analyze the popular sentiment

[Example] 이 글에서는 사회의 고령화로 인해 대두되고 있는 노인 복지 문제에 대해 살펴보고자 한다.
This text is analyzing the rise in problems of welfare for the aging due to an aging society.

002
삼가다

[삼가다] 1. to be careful 2. to refrain from

1. to be careful of one's behavior or words

[Usage] N을/를 삼가다

[Expression] 말을 삼가다 to watch your words

행동을 삼가다 to watch your behavior

[Example] 사고 원인에 대한 근거 없는 예단은 사회 불안을 조장할 수 있으므로 삼가야 한다.
Prejudgment without any evidence of the real cause of the accident can aggravate societal instability, so you must be careful.

2. to refrain from doing something that you are reluctant to do

[Usage] N을/를 삼가다

[Expression] 술을 삼가다 to abstain from alcohol

문밖출입을 삼가다 to refrain from leaving the house

[Example] 봄철 황사가 심한 시기에는 야외활동을 삼가는 것이 바람직하다.
Please abstain from leaving the house when the yellow dust period is extreme during the spring.

003
새기다

[새기다] 1. to carve 2. to keep in mind

1. to carve words or pictures into trees, rocks, or iron so that they appear

[Usage] (N에) N을/를 새기다

[Expression] 도장을 새기다 to carve a seal
팔에 문신을 새기다 to tattoo on your arm
목판에 그림을 새기다 to carve a picture on a woodblock
도자기에 문양을 새기다 to carve a pattern on ceramics

[Example] 고려 시대에는 여러 차례 대장경을 새기는 등 목판 인쇄술이 발달했다.
During the Koryeo dynasty, the printing techniques of carving the sacred writings of Buddha on wood blocks were very advanced.

2. to keep in mind so that you do not forget

[Usage] N을/를 N에 새기다

[Expression] 마음에 좌우명을 새기다 to keep a motto in mind
가르침을 머리에 새기다 to keep the teachings in mind

[Example] 정직은 그가 마음에 새겨 두고 있는 좌우명이다.
Honesty is the motto that he keeps in mind.

004
섭렵하다

[섬녀파다] 1. to be well-versed 2. to be well-read

1. to be well-versed in a variety of things

[Usage] N을/를 섭렵하다

[Example] 방대한 문화 유산을 모두 섭렵하기에는 시간이 너무 부족하다.
There is not enough time to be well-versed in the vast amounts of cultural heritage.

2. to be well-read in a variety of books or documents

[Usage] N을/를 섭렵하다

[Expression] 책을 섭렵하다 to be well-read in books
자료를 섭렵하다 to be well-read in documents

[Example] 졸업 논문을 쓰기 위해서 섭렵해야 할 자료들이 산더미처럼 쌓여 있다.
There is a pile of documents I must be well-read on in order to write my graduate thesis.

005
소요되다

[소요되다] to require

to require or need

[Expression] 시간이 소요되다 to require time
경비가 소요되다 to require expense

[Example] 마라톤 완주에 소요되는 시간은 2시간 반 정도로 예상되고 있다.
It is predicted that in order to finish the marathon, the required time will be around two and a half hours.

당국은 소실된 문화재를 복구하는 데 약 40억 원의 공사비가 소요될 것이라고 밝혔다.
It was revealed by the authorities that it would take four billion won to restore the cultural assets that had been destroyed by fire.

006
속단하다

[속딴하다] to judge hastily

to make hasty conclusions without paying close attention

[Usage] N을/를 속단하다
N을/를 N으로/로 속단하다
N을/를 N이라고/라고 속단하다

[Example] 조사가 끝나기도 전에 상황을 속단하지 마라.
Do not make hasty conclusions about the situation before the investigation is over.

철수 씨를 처음 봤을 때는 옷차림만 보고 노숙자라고 속단했었다.
When I first saw Chulsoo, I made the hasty conclusion that he was homeless based on his clothes.

007
솟다

[솓따] 1. to soar 2. to rise 3. to gush 4. to surge out 5. to rise

1. to rise from bottom to top

[Example] 타자가 친 공이 공중으로 높이 솟았다.
The ball that the batter hit soared high into the air.

2. to have the sun or moon rise

[Related Words] 솟아오르다 to fly up

[Example] 해가 중천에 솟아서 방 안이 환했다.
The room was bright because the sun was high in the sky.

3. to have liquid gush out from the inside to the outside

[Expression] 땀이 솟다 to sweat profusely
샘물이 솟다 to gush spring water

[Example] 가만히 있어도 땀이 송송 솟을 만큼 무덥다.
It is so hot that even if you stay still, you will sweat profusely.

4. to have feelings or strength surge out

[Expression] 기운이 솟다 to have feelings surge
용기가 솟다 to have courage surge

[Related Words] 치솟다 to surge

[Example] 체구도 작은 사람이 어디서 그런 기운이 솟는지 모르겠다.
I don't know where all this energy surges out from such a small person.

5. to have a tall building or mountain rise high from the ground

[Example] 서울 한복판에는 남산이 우뚝 솟아 있다.
In the center of Seoul, Nam mountain rises high.

008
수습하다

[수스파다] to patch up

to take care of a disordered and anxious mental state or patch up and organize a situation

[Usage] N을/를 수습하다

[Expression] 문제를 수습하다 to patch up a problem
사태를 수습하다 to patch up a situation

[Example] 흩어진 민심을 수습하는 것이 급선무입니다.
Taking care of a scattered popular sentiment is urgent business.
장례식이 끝나고 사건도 어느 정도 수습되자 검찰의 심문 수사가 본격적으로 시작되었다.
After the funeral was finished and the situation was somewhat patched up, the prosecution started their interrogation.

009
시달리다

[시달리다] to suffer

to suffer agony or vexation

[Usage] N에/에게 시달리다

[Expression] 빚에 시달리다 to suffer from debt
가뭄에 시달리다 to suffer from drought
격무에 시달리다 to suffer from a heavy workload

[Example] 명절 때면 하루 종일 조카들에게 시달리곤 했다.
During the holidays, I was often bothered by my nieces and nephews all day long.
여름 더위에 시달려 쇠약해진데다가 식욕까지 떨어져 기운을 차릴 수 없었다.
I couldn't muster any energy after suffering from weakness and loss of appetite due to the intense summer heat.

010
쏠리다

[쏠리다] 1. to lean 2. to focus

1. to have an object lean to one side

[Usage] N으로/로 쏠리다

[Example] 버스가 급정거하자 사람들이 와락 앞으로 쏠려 넘어졌다.
All of the people leaned and fell towards the front of the bus when it braked suddenly.

2. to focus your vision or mind on a subject

[Usage] N에/에게 쏠리다
N으로/로 쏠리다

[Example] 올해의 우승 향방에 팬들의 비상한 관심이 쏠리고 있다.
The fans' focuses are soaring on which team will win this year.

011
씨름하다

[씨름하다] 1. to wrestle (Korean folk wrestling) 2. to wrestle with

1. to have two people grab the thigh band (satba) and use strength or skill to trip their opponent in order to win

[Usage] N과/와 씨름하다

[Example] 우리 동네에서는 김 할아버지 댁 손자와 씨름해서 이긴 사람이 없다.
There is no one who has won in our neighborhood against grandfather Kim's grandson in Korean wrestling.

2. to use all of your strength or determination in order to wrestle or tackle a subject so that you can conquer or achieve it

[Usage] N과/와 씨름하다

[Expression] 책과 씨름하다 to tackle the books
문제와 씨름하다 to wrestle with a problem

[Example] 저도 대학교 때 학교 공부하랴 공무원 시험 준비하랴 시간에 쫓기면서 밤늦게까지 책하고 씨름했었어요.
During my college years, there was not enough time to both study and prepare for my civil servant exam so I was forced to tackle the books until late at night.

012
애쓰다

[애쓰다] to make an effort

to make a great effort using all of your mind and strength in order to achieve something

[Usage] N에 애쓰다

[Example] 김 과장은 요즘 새로 맡은 일의 준비 작업에 무척 애쓰고 있다.
Mr. Kim, our section chief, is making an intense effort to prepare for the new work assigned to him.

이번 행사의 성공적인 개최를 위해 제일 애쓰신 분은 정 교수님입니다.
The one who made the most effort to make this event a success is Professor Chung.

013
얽매이다

[엉매이다] 1. to be tied down 2. to be shackled

1. to be tied down by a rope or string

[Usage] N으로/로 얽매이다

[Example] 그는 정체를 알 수 없는 이들에 의해 이미 손발이 밧줄로 얽매여 있었다.
His hands and feet were already tied down by ropes by people he did not know the identities of.

2. to be shackled down or restrained and unable to move freely

[Usage] N에/에게 얽매이다

[Example] 나는 규율에 얽매이는 것이 싫어 기숙사 생활을 원하지 않았다.
I didn't want to live in the dormitories because I didn't like being shackled down by regulations.

014
엇갈리다

[얻깔리다] 1.to miss 2. to crisscross 3. to have a disagreement

1. (used primarily with '길') to miss each other in meeting

[Usage] N과/와 엇갈리다

[Example] 어머니를 마중 나갔다가 어머니와 길이 엇갈리는 바람에 헛수고를 했다.
My attempt to greet my mother was in vain because we missed each other in meeting after going separate ways.

2. to crisscross each other every which way

[Usage] N과/와 엇갈리다

[Example] 너덧 개의 불빛이 엇갈리며 움직이고 있었다.
Four or five lights crisscrossed as they moved.

3. to jumbled or have a disagreement in opinion or thought

[Usage] N과/와 엇갈리다

[Example] 두 사람은 주장이 서로 엇갈려 좀처럼 타협을 보지 못하고 있었다.
The two people disagreed in their opinions so it was hard to come to a compromise.

015
엿보다

[엳뽀다] 1. to peek 2. to get a sense of 3. to wait for

1. to peek through secretly

[Usage] N을/를 엿보다

[Example] 도둑은 숨어서 가게 주인이 하는 행동을 엿보고 있었다.
The robber hid and peeked in to watch the actions of the store owner.

2. to get a sense of a truth

[Usage] N을/를 엿보다

[Example] 우리는 속담이나 격언에서 선인들의 지혜를 엿볼 수 있다.
We can get a sense of virtuous men and their wisdom through proverbs and sayings.

3. to wait for a specific moment

[Usage] N을/를 엿보다

[Expression] 때를 엿보다 to wait for a time
기회를 엿보다 to wait for a chance

[Example] 이제나 저제나 기회를 엿보고 있던 그녀는 비로소 자리에서 일어나 방을 빠져나갔다.
She got up and escaped the room after waiting for the opportunity to run.

016
왜곡하다

[왜고카다] to distort

to distort the facts by interpreting it differently

[Usage] N을/를 왜곡하다

[Expression] 진실을 왜곡하다 to distort the truth
역사를 왜곡하다 to distort history

[Example] 검찰이 진실을 왜곡하고 은폐했다고 비난의 소리가 높다.
The criticism directed toward the prosecution for distorting and concealing the truth is high.

전 세계 인터넷 사용자들이 참여해 만드는 인터넷 백과사전에서 역사를 왜곡하는 내용이 다수 발견되어 논란이 되고 있다.
Distorted history discovered in an online encyclopedia edited by internet users from all around the world is becoming a big controversy.

017
유치하다

[유치하다] to lure

to lure events or businesses

[Usage] N을/를 유치하다

[Expression] 외자를 유치하다 to lure foreign capital
시설을 유치하다 to lure facilities

[Example] 정부는 앞으로 공익사업에도 민간 자본을 적극 유치하기로 결정했다.
The government has decided to actively lure private capital for public services as well.

각국의 대사들은 올림픽 대회를 자국에 유치하기 위해 치열한 로비 활동을 벌였다.
There is intense lobbying from each country's ambassador in order to have the Olympics in their home land.

018
잠기다[1]

[잠기다] 1. to be locked 2. to be closed 3. to fasten

1. to be locked with a padlock or a bolt

[Example] 잠겨 있는 줄 알았던 문은 손을 대니 뜻밖에도 활짝 열렸다.
Even though I thought the door was locked, as soon as I touched it, it opened wide.

2. to be closed so that nothing can go through

[Example] 수도꼭지가 잠긴 줄 알고 다른 일 하다가 와서 보니 물이 넘치고 있었다.
I thought I had turned the faucet handle off and did something else before coming back to discover that water was overflowing.

3. to fasten clothes with buttons

[Example] 여고생인 동생은 교복 단추가 모두 잠겼는지 확인하고 집을 나섰다.
My younger sibling who is a high school student checked to see if all of the buttons on her clothes were fastened and then left the house.

019
잠기다[2]

[잠기다] 1. to be flooded 2. to be submerged in 3. to be lost in 4. to be hoarse

1. to be flooded in water; to be immersed under water

[Usage] N에 잠기다

[Expression] 물에 잠기다 to be immersed under water

[Example] 지난 번 홍수로 고향 땅이 물에 잠겼다.
My hometown was immersed under water after the flood last time.

2. to be submerged in fog or smoke

[Usage] N에 잠기다

[Expression] 안개에 잠기다 to be submerged in fog

[Example] 오랜만에 나와 본 서울의 거리는 아침 안개 속에 온통 회색으로 잠겨 있었다.
The Seoul streets that I haven't seen in a long time were submerged in gray fog.

3. to be flooded with thoughts or feelings

[Usage] N에 잠기다

[Expression] 생각에 잠기다 to be flooded with thoughts
기쁨에 잠기다 to be overcome with happiness
슬픔에 잠기다 to be overcome with sadness

[Example] 갑자기 아버지가 돌아가셨을 때 우리 가족은 슬픔에 잠겨 있을 틈도 없이 살아갈 일을 걱정해야 했다.
There was no chance for my family to be overcome with sadness after my father passed away because we had to worry about our future.

4. to be hoarse to the point where you can not make a sound

[Expression] 목이 잠기다 to have your throat hoarse

[Example] 노래 연습을 많이 했더니 목이 꽉 잠겼다.
My throat was hoarse after practicing singing too much.

020
저미다

[저미다] 1. to slice 2. to make ache

1. to cut with a knife into thin slices

[Usage] N을/를 저미다

[Expression] 고기를 저미다 to slice meat
생선을 저미다 to slice fish

[Example] 생선전은 생선들을 얇게 저며서 밀가루와 달걀을 씌우고 기름에 부쳐서 만드는 전통 음식이다.
Fish pancakes are a traditional dish made by slicing the fish into thin slices, covering it in flour and egg, and then frying it in oil.

2. to make the heartache

[Usage] N을/를 저미다

[Expression] 슬픔이 마음을 저미다 to have sadness make your heartache
그리움이 가슴을 저미다 to have longing make your heartache

[Example] 돌아가신 어머니와 비슷한 연세의 할머니들을 뵐 때면 어머니에 대한 그리움이 가슴을 저몄다.
Every time I met someone who was of similar age to my mother who had passed, my heart ached with longing.

021
주저앉다

[주저안따] 1. to drop down 2. to settle down 3. to collapse 4. to quit

1. to drop down weakly in place

[Usage] N에 주저앉다

[Example] 그는 갑작스러운 소식을 듣고 충격을 받아서 그 자리에 주저앉아 버렸다.
He dropped to his knees from shock after hearing the sudden news.

2. to settle down in a specific place or state

[Usage] N에 주저앉다

[Example] 그는 한국에 잠깐 다니러 왔다가 그대로 주저앉게 되었다.
He ended up settling for good in Korea after initially only coming to visit shortly.

3. to have something stacked or standing collapse

[Expression] 건물이 주저앉다 to have a building collapse

[Example] 운동장 가에 세워진 건물은 폭격으로 반이 주저앉아서 지금 쓸 수 있는 것은 교실 두 개뿐이었다.
There are only two classrooms that are usable in the building next to the sports field after half of it collapsed from the bombing.

4. to quit while in the process of doing something

[Example] 나는 절망적인 순간에도 아내의 내조 덕분에 주저앉지 않고 힘을 낼 수 있었다.
I was able to work through even my most hopeless moment and not quit thanks to my wife's assistance.

022
주저하다

[주저하다] to hesitate

to hesitate and not act due to indecision

[Usage] N을/를 주저하다

AV기를 주저하다

[Synonym] 망설이다 to hesitate

[Example] 노래를 부를까 말까 주저하다가 기회를 놓치고 말았다.

I lost my chance to sing after hesitating and wavering between singing or not singing.

집주인은 오랜 세월 살아온 집을 남의 손에 넘기기가 아쉬워서 팔기를 주저하고 있다.

The home owner is hesitating to sell and turn over the home to someone else after living there for many years.

023
주춤하다

[주춤하다] to falter

to falter in the process of doing something due to surprise or hesitation

[Example] 그는 나를 보자 놀랐는지 주춤하고 걸음을 멈추었다.

He must have been surprised to see me because his walking faltered.

자금 사정이 악화되면서 기술 개발이 주춤한 상태이다.

As the financial condition deteriorates, the development of new skills falters.

024
지나치다

[지나치다] 1. to pass 2. to overlook

1. to pass by a place without staying or stopping by

[Usage] N을/를 지나치다

[Example] 매일 가던 단골 술집을 오늘은 그냥 지나쳐 왔다.

Although I had become a regular at the bar, today I just passed it.

2. to overlook a situation or phenomenon without questioning it or taking interest in it

[Usage] N을/를 지나치다

[Example] 우리는 장애우들의 불편과 고통을 남의 일처럼 무심코 지나쳐 버리고 있지는 않은지 되돌아 볼 필요가 있다.

We need to review again if we are overlooking the discomfort and pain of the disabled like it is not our business.

025
지다[1]

[지다] 1. to set 2. to wither 3. to be washed out

1. to have the sun or moon set in the West

[Expression] 해가 지다 to have the sun set

달이 지다 to have the moon set

날이 지다 to have night time fall

[Antonym] 뜨다 to rise

[Example] 이미 달은 서산에 졌는데 동녘 하늘에서 해가 솟지 않는다.
Even though the moon has already set in the western mountains, the sun is not shining from the east.

2. to have flowers or leaves wither and fall

[Expression] 꽃이 지다 to have a flower wither
낙엽이 지다 to have leaves wither

[Antonym] 피다 to bloom

[Example] 세차게 몰아친 비바람 탓에 꽃들이 만개하기도 전에 다 져 버렸다.
Before the flowers were in full bloom, they all withered from the violent storm.

3. to have a stain or something that was stuck on something be washed out

[Expression] 때가 지다 to have a dirt washed out
얼룩이 지다 to have a stain washed out/be stained

[Example] 옷에 묻은 커피 얼룩이 세제를 사용해도 안 진다.
The coffee stain on my clothes does not wash out even with detergent.

026
지다[2]

[지다] 1. to carry 2. to owe 3. to bear responsibility 4. to be in debt to

1. to carry something on your back in order to move it

[Usage] N을/를 N에 지다

[Expression] 짐을 등에 지다 to carry a load on your back
배낭을 등에 지다 to carry a backpack on your back

[Example] 나와 동생은 이불과 옷 보따리를 등에 지고 걷기 시작했다.
My sibling and I carried the bundles of clothes and blankets on our back and began to walk.

2. to owe a favor or to be indebted to

[Usage] N에/에게 신세를 지다

[Expression] 신세를 지다 to be indebted to

[Example] 유학하는 동안 그 사람에게 신세를 많이 졌는데 어떻게 다 갚아야 할지 모르겠다.
I don't know how to repay him after being indebted to him throughout my time studying abroad.

3. to bear responsibility or bear the work of something

[Usage] N을/를 지다

[Expression] 책임을 지다 to bear responsibility
부담을 지다 to bear the burden

[Example] 이번 사태가 저로 말미암아 발생한 만큼 제가 모든 책임을 지고 사퇴하겠습니다.
Because this situation was caused by my actions, I will bear all of the responsibility and resign.

4. to be in debt to with money

[Usage] N을/를 지다

[Expression] 빚을 지다 to be in debt

[Example] 사업을 확장하느라고 김 사장에게 진 빚을 다 갚고 나니 속이 시원하다.
After paying the debt I was in from Mr. Kim, I feel relieved.

027
짚다

[집따] 1. to place hand on 2. to examine 3. to point out 4. to guess

1. to place hand on the ground, wall, or cane in order to rest on it

[Usage] N을/를 짚다

[Expression] 땅을 짚다 to place hand on the ground
지팡이를 짚다 to walk with a cane

[Example] 아버지는 현기증이 나시는지 두 손으로 땅을 짚고 자리에서 일어나셨다.
My father must have felt vertigo because he stood up from the ground after placing both hands on the ground.

2. to examine one's health by using hands

[Usage] N을/를 짚다

[Expression] 맥을 짚다 to examine a pulse
머리를 짚다 to examine a head

[Example] 아이가 자꾸 보채서 이마를 짚어 보니 열이 있었다.
After examining my child's forehead due to his whining, I discovered that he had a fever.

3. to point out one specific thing out of many options

[Usage] N을/를 짚다

[Example] 아이는 손가락으로 글자를 하나하나 짚어 가며 동화책을 읽어 나갔다.
The child pointed to each letter while reading the children's story.

4. to guess in order to understand a situation

[Usage] N을/를 짚다

[Expression] 잘못 짚다 to guess wrong
마음을 짚다 to guess someone's feelings
허점을 짚다 to guess someone's weak point

[Example] 그 선수의 장점은 상대팀의 허점을 짚어서 공격할 줄 안다는 것이다.
This athlete's strong point is his ability to guess his opponent's weak point and attack it.

028
차지하다

[차지하다] 1. to be in possession of 2. to occupy 3. to take up

1. to be in possession of something

[Usage] N을/를 차지하다

[Expression] 농토를 차지하다 to be in possession of farmland

재산을 차지하다 to be in possession of assets

[Example] 형제간에 서로 유산을 차지하려고 다툼이 일어나는 경우가 비일비재하다.
It is a frequent occurrence to have siblings fight to be in possession of the inheritance.

2. to occupy a place

[Usage] N을/를 차지하다

[Example] 어른들이 외출하자 아이들이 안방을 차지하고 숨바꼭질을 시작했다.
As soon as the adults left the home, the children occupied the master bedroom and started to play hide and seek.

3. to take up occupation in a space or in a proportion

[Usage] N을/를 차지하다

[Example] 이번 선거에서 여당은 다수 의석을 차지하는 데 실패했다.
The ruling party failed to take up the majority number in parliamentary seats.

029
참견하다

[참견하다] to interfere

to interfere in affairs that are not yours or unnecessarily act like you know or meddle

[Usage] N에 참견하다

[Expression] 일에 참견하다 to interfere in business

말에 참견하다 to interfere in a conversation

[Example] 남의 일에 공연히 참견하는 것은 주제 넘는 일이다.
To interfere unnecessarily in someone else's business is presumptuous.

아버지는 요즘 심심하신지 방마다 다니며 아이들에게 잔소리를 하시고 부엌일에까지 참견하신다.
It seems that my father is bored because he goes from room to room nagging the children and even interfering in the kitchen.

030
챙기다

[챙기다] 1. to pack 2. to do 3. to take 4. to take care of

1. to pack or take items that you need

[Usage] N을/를 챙기다

[Expression] 짐을 챙기다 to pack your luggage

서류를 챙기다 to pack the documents

[Example] 나는 세면도구를 챙겨 들고 바깥으로 나왔다.
I took my face wash and came outside.

2. to do/take without forgetting

[Usage] N을/를 챙기다

[Expression] 밥을 챙겨 먹다 to eat regularly
옷을 챙겨 입다 to wear clothes that are needed

[Example] 나는 무슨 일이 있더라도 하루 세 끼는 꼬박꼬박 챙겨 먹는다.
No matter what happens, I make sure to eat all three meals.

3. to take something as your own

[Usage] N을/를 챙기다

[Expression] 몫을 챙기다 to take your share
거스름돈을 챙기다 to take your change

[Example] 사장은 회사에서 부당 이익을 챙긴 혐의로 검찰에 기소되었다.
The owner was prosecuted on the suspicion of taking illegal profits from the business.

4. to take care of someone

[Usage] N을/를 챙기다

[Example] 난리 중이라 제 한 몸 챙기기도 힘든 상황에 그녀는 어른들까지 모시고 사느라 고생이 막심했다.
She also took care of the elderly in a period of war where it was hard to even take care of herself.

031
처하다

[처하다] 1. to face 2. to punish

1. to face certain circumstances or positions

[Expression] 위기에 처하다 to face danger
역경에 처하다 to face adversity

[Example] 우리는 살아가는 동안에 수없이 많은 난관과 역경에 처하게 된다.
Throughout our lives, we must face countless difficulties and adversities

2. to punish through policy or penalty

[Usage] N을/를 N에 처하다

[Example] 이번 사건의 책임자를 엄벌에 처하기로 했다.
It has been decided that they will punish the person responsible for this situation with a severe punishment.

032
추구하다

[추구하다] to seek

to seek something by constantly following it in order to achieve something

[Usage] N을/를 추구하다

[Expression] 이윤을 추구하다 to seek profit
행복을 추구하다 to seek happiness

[Example] 기업은 영리 추구를 목적으로 한다.
The main goal of a business is to make profit.

사람은 저마다 자신의 행복을 추구하기 마련이다.
It is destined for each person to seek their own happiness.

033
치르다[1]

[치르다] 1. to go through 2. to suffer 3. to host

1.to go through and achieve a big or important ordeal

[Usage] N을/를 치르다

[Expression] 시험을 치르다 to go through a test
잔치를 치르다 to hold a big celebration
장례식을 치르다 to hold a funeral

[Example] 아들 결혼에 시어른 초상까지 큰일들을 연달아 치렀으니 이모님이 병나실 만도 해요.
It is expected that my aunt fall ill after having to go through both her son's wedding as well as the mourning of her parents-in-law consecutively.

2. to suffer through hardship

[Usage] N을/를 치르다

[Expression] 곤욕을 치르다 to suffer difficulty
옥고를 치르다 to suffer the hardship of prison life

[Example] 그는 대학 시절 반정부 시위에 참가하여 옥고를 치른 경험이 있다.
He suffered the hardship of prison life after participating in an antigovernment protest during college.

3. to host guests

[Usage] N을/를 치르다

[Example] 정초에 며칠 동안 손님을 치르느라고 눈코 뜰 새 없었어요.
I was extremely busy at the beginning of January being a host to guests.

034
치르다[2]

[치르다] 1. to pay for 2. to repay

1. to pay for something that must be paid with money or the equivalent

[Usage] N을/를 치르다

[Expression] 돈을 치르다 to pay with money
값을 치르다 to pay the cost

[Example] 주인 여자에게 돈을 치르고 그는 가게를 나왔다.
He paid the owner with money and left the shop.

2. to repay the cost; to pay back

[Usage] N을/를 치르다

[Expression] 대가를 치르다 to repay the cost
죄 값을 치르다 to pay the price of a misdeed

[Example] 죄 없는 사람들에게 큰 피해를 입혔으니 당신도 그만한 대가는 치러야 한다.
Since you have given much harm to innocent people, you must repay the cost of your actions.

035
타고나다

[타고나다] to be born with

to be born with

[Usage] N을/를 타고나다

[Expression] 복을 타고나다 to be born with fortune
성격을 타고나다 to be born with a certain personality
운명을 타고나다 to be destined
재능을 타고나다 to be gifted

[Example] 그는 주위 사람을 배려할 줄 아는 성품을 타고났다.
He was born with a personality to be considerate.

동생은 타고난 가창력 덕분에 출전하는 노래 대회마다 높은 평가를 받더니 결국 톱 가수가 되었다.
Because my younger sibling is gifted with a good voice, he received high marks in every singing competition he participated in and eventually became a top singer.

036
펼치다

[펼치다] 1. to spread 2. to show 3. to realize

1. to spread by unfolding

[Usage] N을/를 펼치다

[Expression] 책을 펼치다 to spread the book open
부채를 펼치다 to spread open a fan
날개를 펼치다 to spread wings

[Example] 나는 사진첩을 펼쳐 어린 시절의 그리운 얼굴들을 되새겨 보았다.
I spread open the photo album and meditated over the faces I longed to see.

2. to show in a way that people can see or hear and catches their attention

[Usage] N을/를 펼치다

[Expression] 춤을 펼치다 to show off a dance
경기를 펼치다 to show a game
수사를 펼치다 to show an investigation

[Example] 아이스 발레단은 빙판 위에서 환상적인 무대를 펼쳤다.
The ice ballet company showed a fantastic performance on top of the ice rink.

3. to realize your thoughts, dreams, plans and put them into action

[Usage] N을/를 펼치다

[Expression] 꿈을 펼치다 to realize your dreams
이상을 펼치다 to realize your ideal

[Example] 어려운 사람을 돕고 싶다는 꿈을 펼치기 위해 의사가 되었습니다.
I became a doctor in order to realize my dream of wanting to help people in need.

037
품다

[품따] 1. to carry 2. to conceal 3. to harbor

1.to go through and achieve a big or important ordeal

[Usage] N을/를 (N에) 품다

[Expression] 암탉이 알을 품다 to incubate (a hen)

보따리를 가슴에 품다 to carry the bundle against one's chest

[Example] 젊은 엄마가 갓난아기를 가슴에 품고 어딘가로 가고 있었다.
The young mother carried her infant against her chest and made her way somewhere.

2. to conceal so that something is not visible to others

[Usage] N을/를 (N에) 품다

[Example] 가슴에 품고 있던 편지를 은밀히 꺼내어 그에게 전해 주었다.
I secretly gave him the letter I had concealed in my arms.

3. to harbor thoughts or feelings in your mind

[Usage] N을/를 (N에) 품다

[Expression] 연정을 품다 to harbor a crush

희망을 품다 to harbor hope

의문을 품다 to harbor questions

[Example] 시골내기인 나는 도시로 가면 성공할 수 있을 거라는 순진한 희망을 품고 상경했다.
I came to Seoul from the countryside harboring a naive hope that I would succeed in the city.

038
헤아리다

[헤아리다] 1. to count 2. to count 3. to consider

1. to count a number

[Usage] N을/를 헤아리다

[Expression] 동전을 헤아리다 to count coins

나이를 헤아리다 to count age

[Example] 주머니 속의 동전을 헤아려 보니 겨우 버스 탈 차비만 있었다.
After counting the coins in my pocket, I found that I barely had enough money to ride the bus.

2. to count a large number or come to a certain number

[Usage] N을/를 헤아리다

[Example] 그날 대회에는 십만을 헤아리는 군중이 모였다.
That competition amounted to a hundred thousand people in the crowd.

3. to consider

[Usage] N을/를 헤아리다

[Expression] 고통을 헤아리다 to consider difficulty

심정을 헤아리다 to consider feelings

사정을 헤아리다 to consider circumstances

[Example] 하루 종일 수많은 손님을 응대해야 하는 저희 일의 고충을 헤아려 주십시오.

Please consider the difficulty of our work of responding to customers all day.

03 연습문제

[1-10] 다음 밑줄 친 부분과 의미가 비슷한 것을 고르십시오.

Choose the word that is similar to the underlined word.

1. 이 연구에서는 고령화 사회의 문제점과 그 대책에 대해 살펴보고자 합니다.

❶ 물어보다 ❷ 알아보다 ❸ 반론하다 ❹ 검색하다

2. 정확한 사고 원인이 밝혀지기 전에 성급하게 판단하는 것은 금물이다.

❶ 속단하다 ❷ 결정하다 ❸ 엇갈리다 ❹ 주저하다

3. 화재로 훼손된 절을 복구하는 데 6 개월가량 걸릴 것으로 보인다.

❶ 지나다 ❷ 치르다 ❸ 소요되다 ❹ 헤아리다

4. 선거를 앞두고 개최되는 합동 토론회에 유권자들의 관심이 집중되고 있다.

❶ 쏠리다 ❷ 처하다 ❸ 쌓이다 ❹ 밀리다

5. 문화 관광부는 우리의 대표적인 음식인 김치를 세계적으로 보급하기 위해 노력하고 있다.

❶ 애쓰다 ❷ 다루다 ❸ 근무하다 ❹ 매달리다

6. 지나치게 전통에 얽매이기보다는 시대의 요구에 부응할 수 있는 유연성이 필요하다.

❶ 걸리다 ❷ 반하다 ❸ 해방되다 ❹ 구속되다

7. 이것은 그분의 성의의 표시니까 주저하지 말고 받으세요.

❶ 망설이다 ❷ 속단하다 ❸ 지나치다 ❹ 왜곡하다

8. 그는 상대방이 반론을 제기하자 잠시 주춤하더니 그것에 대한 자신의 주장을 계속했다.

❶ 더듬다 ❷ 당황하다 ❸ 방황하다 ❹ 머뭇거리다

9. 그 여자는 남의 일에 자꾸 끼어들어서 다른 사람의 미움을 산다.

❶ 엿보다 ❷ 챙기다 ❸ 참견하다 ❹ 어울리다

10. 시장 후보는 국가의 미래가 청년들에게 달려 있으니만큼 청년들이 꿈을 실현할 수 있는 시를 만들겠다고 공약했다.

❶ 꾸다 ❷ 품다 ❸ 펼치다 ❹ 피우다

[11-12] 다음 밑줄 친 부분과 의미가 반대인 것을 고르십시오.

Choose the word that is the opposite of the underlined word.

11. 사방에 봄꽃들이 형형색색 피어서 참으로 아름답다.

❶ 지다 ❷ 뜨다 ❸ 떨어지다 ❹ 가라앉다

12. 주부들이 모두 할인 행사 매장으로 쏠렸는지 다른 층은 생각보다 한산했다.

❶ 모이다 ❷ 옮기다 ❸ 흩어지다 ❹ 갈라지다

[13-20] 다음 (　　)에 알맞은 것을 고르십시오.

Choose the word that best fits in the parenthesis.

13. 건강을 위해서 지나친 흡연을 (　　).

❶ 합시다 ❷ 삼갑시다 ❸ 피웁시다 ❹ 끊읍시다

14. 그는 온갖 중국역사책을 다 (　　) 꽤 유식하다.

❶ 뚫어서 ❷ 누벼서 ❸ 다듬어서 ❹ 섭렵해서

15. 두 사람은 계속 길이 (　　) 끝까지 못 만나고 말았다.

❶ 갈라져서 ❷ 왜곡돼서 ❸ 지나가서 ❹ 엇갈려서

16. 그 단체 회원들은 언론사들이 진실을 (　　　) 국민을 오도하고 있다고 주장했다.

❶ 거슬러　❷ 인정해　❸ 납득해　❹ 왜곡해

17. 그녀는 악기에 관한 재능을 (　　　) 무슨 악기든지 몇 번만 해 보면 금방 능숙해진다.

❶ 펼쳐서　❷ 누려서　❸ 타고나서　❹ 헤아려서

18. 그 자동차 회사는 결함이 잇달아 발견되자 사태를 (　　　) 위해 총력을 기울이겠다고 다짐했다.

❶ 가리기　❷ 때우기　❸ 수습하기　❹ 왜곡하기

19. 기업의 제일의 목적은 영리를 (　　　) 것이지만 최근에는 이윤의 사회 환원에도 많이 참여하고 있다.

❶ 추적하는　❷ 추구하는　❸ 추월하는　❹ 추출하는

20. 재정위기에 시달리는 유럽의 한 국가는 중국을 비롯한 외국의 투자를 (　　　) 위해 노력하고 있다는 보도가 있었다.

❶ 유치하기　❷ 진행하기　❸ 주최하기　❹ 거절하기

[21-22] 다음 밑줄 친 부분의 의미가 다른 것을 하나 고르십시오.

Choose the underlined word that has a different meaning from the other underlined words.

21.

❶ 물건을 샀으면 당연히 값을 치러야지요.
❷ 우리 아버지께서 장손이어서 명절 때마다 어머니는 친척과 손님을 치르느라고 고생하신다.
❸ 그 전자 제품 회사는 고객 불만에 대한 초기 대응의 실패로 지금 엄청난 대가를 치르고 있다.
❹ 검찰청장은 이번 사건을 재수사해서 죄를 지은 자는 반드시 죄값을 치르도록 하겠다고 목소리를 높였다.

22.

❶ 그런 상황에 처하면 누구든지 그렇게 행동했을 것이다.

❷ 법원은 부산 살인 사건의 범인을 무기 징역형에 처하기로 했다.

❸ 나는 어떤 위험에 처해도 남의 도움은 받지 않으리라 결심했다.

❹ 그 분은 내가 역경에 처했을 때마다 손을 내밀어 도와주신 분이다.

[23-24] 다음 중 동사의 쓰임이 잘못된 것을 고르십시오.

Choose the sentence in which the verb is used incorrectly.

23.

❶ 해외 출장을 위해 필요한 짐을 미리 챙겨 놓았다.

❷ 하숙집 아주머니는 마치 친부모님처럼 나를 잘 챙겨 주신다.

❸ 사장님의 기대에 어긋나지 않도록 회사 일을 잘 챙기고 있다.

❹ 부모님은 내가 혼자 살면서 밥을 잘 못 챙겨 먹을까 봐 늘 걱정하신다.

24.

❶ 암탉이 알을 품고 있으니 가까이 가지 마세요.

❷ 그는 밀서를 가슴에 품고 멀리 중국 만주까지 갔다.

❸ 그는 그녀에게 오래 전부터 품어 온 사랑의 마음을 고백해야겠다고 마음먹었다.

❹ 그는 평소에 머릿속에 품고 있던 몇 가지 아이디어를 거침없이 이야기했다.

[25-30] 다음 (　　)에 공통적으로 들어갈 단어의 기본형을 쓰십시오.

Find the one word that fits in the parentheses and write the most basic form.

25.

❶ 이번 전시 작품에서는 젊은 작가들의 이상을 (　　　　)을/ㄹ 수 있다.

❷ 그는 기회를 (　　　　)다가 주인이 방 안으로 들어간 틈에 창고로 뛰어 들어갔다.

❸ 이번 전시회에는 어린이들의 풍부한 상상력과 창의성을 (　　　　)을/ㄹ 수 있는 작품들이 대거 출품되었다.

❹ 범인은 가게 밖에서 몰래 (　　　　)다가 주인이 없는 틈을 타서 범행을 저지른 것으로 드러났다.

26.

❶ 아버지는 내 나무 필통에 이름을 ( )어/아/여 주셨다.

❷ 할아버지께서 가르쳐 주신 가훈을 늘 마음속에 ( )고 있다.

❸ 그 기둥에는 신화 속에 나오는 신들의 얼굴이 ( )어져/아져/여져 있다.

❹ 그는 '준비된 자를 이길 자는 없다'는 좌우명을 가슴에 ( )고 오로지 공부에만 열중했다.

27.

❶ 수년간 자금 압박에 ( )던 대기업이 결국 문을 닫았다.

❷ 그는 자금난에 ( )다 못해 그만 사채에 손을 대고 말았다.

❸ 그 사장은 격무에 ( )며 밤낮 없이 일하다가 쓰러지고 말았다.

❹ 휴일이면 놀아 달라는 아이들에게 ( )느라고 편히 낮잠도 못 잔다.

28.

❶ 밤하늘의 별을 ( )다가 어느 새 잠들어 버렸다.

❷ 국가대표 선수들이 대거 참가한 그 경기에는 십만 명을 ( )는 관중들이 모였다.

❸ 사고로 가족을 잃은 유가족들의 슬픔을 우리가 어떻게 다 ( )을/ㄹ 수 있을까?

❹ 병원 측에서는 할머니의 어려운 사정을 ( )어서/아서/여서 병원비의 일부를 감해 주었다.

29.

❶ 그 분에게는 어려울 때마다 신세를 ( )게 된다.

❷ 잘못을 한 사람이 책임을 ( )는 것이 당연하다.

❸ 소가 무거운 짐들을 등에 ( )고 터벅터벅 걸어간다.

❹ 급하게 집을 마련하느라고 어쩔 수 없이 빚을 좀 ( )었다/았다/였다.

30.

❶ 문이 ( )어/아/여 있어서 열쇠로 열고 들어갔다.

❷ 영수는 뭔가 깊은 생각에 ( )은/ㄴ 듯 아무 말도 하지 않았다.

❸ 응원 연습을 한 탓인지 목이 ( )어/아/여 목소리가 나오지 않는다.

❹ 어제 하루 동안 내린 비로 한강 공원이 물에 ( )어/아/여 버렸다.

명사 I

04

Nouns I

04 명사 I

001
가상

[가상] imagination

something that is not real or not known if it is real or not, is assumed to be true

[Usage] N을/를 N이라고/라고 가상하다

[Expression] 가상공간 imaginary space

가상의 적 imaginary enemy

[Example] 인터넷 게임의 공간은 현실이 아닌 가상의 공간이다.
Internet games are imaginary spaces and not real.

환경 오염으로 인한 재난 상황을 가상한 영화들이 속속 개봉되고 있다.
Movies that imagine the world after a disaster due to environmental pollution have been releasing one after another.

002
가입

[가입] registration

register or become a member of an organization or group

[Usage] N에 가입하다

[Expression] 가입자 member

가입비 registration fee

가입 신청서registration form

[Antonym] 탈퇴 withdraw

[Example] 만 원이면 신입 회원 가입비로 충분하다.
10,000 won is enough for the new membership fee.

한국 전통 음악에 관심이 있어서 국악 동아리에 가입하기로 했다.
I decided to join the Korean classical music club because I am interested in Korean traditional music.

003
가치

[가치] 1. value 2. value

1. an object that has significance or importance

[Usage] AV을/ㄹ 가치가 있다

[Expression] 희소가치 scarce value

경제적 가치 economic value

가치가 있다 to have worth

가치가 높다 to have high value

가치가 떨어지다 to fall in value

[Expression] 그런 가치 없는 일에 너무 시간을 낭비하지 마라.
Do not waste your time on worthless things.

2. universal validity which is the goal of human spirit

[Expression] 가치관 values

가치 기준 standard of value

낡은 가치관 old values

보수적 가치관 conservative values

가치를 추구하다 to pursue values

[Example] 교사는 학생들이 올바른 가치관을 형성할 수 있도록 도와주어야 한다.
School teachers must help students so that they develop proper values.

004
각오

[가고] resolution

resolution of the mind to take on future tasks or tasks you must endure

[Usage] AV을/ㄹ 각오를 하다

[Expression] 각오가 서다 to decide your resolution

각오를 다지다 to strengthen your resolution

[Example] 군인들은 전쟁터에서 죽을 각오로 싸웠다.
The soldiers fought on the battle fields with the resolution to die.

결심과 각오만 단단하다면 무슨 일이든지 해 낼 수 있다.
With determination and resolution, you can achieve anything.

005
간섭

[간섭] interference

meddling in a stranger's business wrongfully

[Usage] N에/에게 간섭하다

[Expression] 간섭을 받다 to receive interference

간섭에서 벗어나다 to escape from interference

[Example] 부모의 지나친 간섭으로 아이는 삐뚤어져만 갔다.
The parents' extreme interference made the child into a rebel.

당신이 뭔데 남의 일에 이래라저래라 간섭하는 거요?
Who do you think you are to interfere in someone else's business?

006
갈등

[갈뜽] conflict

like how arrowroot and wisteria tangle, when the goals or interests of an individual or group are opposed or cause conflict

[Expression] 노사 간의 갈등 conflict between labor and management

갈등이 생기다 conflict arises

갈등이 심하다 conflict is hostile

갈등을 겪다 to endure conflict

갈등을 해소하다 to resolve conflict

[Example] 사측과 노조의 갈등도 깊어져 그 회사의 회생 가능성은 점점 낮아지고 있다.
The conflict between the business and labor union has gotten so big that the probability of the resurrection of the business is becoming lower.

저는 제 결혼을 반대하는 부모님과의 갈등이 점점 심해지고 있어서 고민입니다.
The conflict between my parents and I over my marriage is becoming so serious that it is troubling me.

007
감소

[감소] decline

decline in quantity or number. reducing in quantity or number

[Usage] N이/가 감소하다
N을/를 감소시키다

[Expression] 인구 감소 decline in population
감소 추세 decline trend

[Antonym] 증가 rise

[Example] 이 장치는 매연 감소에 효과가 있다.
This equipment causes a decline in smoke.

수출이 감소하고 수입이 증가해서 나라 살림이 어려워지고 있다.
The country's economy is not fairing well because exportation declined while importation rose.

008
개방

[개방] 1. opening 2. opening

1. opening up a door or space so that you can go freely in and out

[Usage] N에/에게 N이/가 개방되다
N에/에게 N을/를 개방하다

[Expression] 개방 시간 open time
등산로 개방 open trail

[Antonym] 폐쇄 closing

[Example] 이 박물관은 평일에만 일반 시민에게 개방된다.
This museum opens its doors to regular citizens only on weekdays.

2. undoing things you prohibited or guarded and making it so that there is a free exchange

[Usage] N에/에게 N이/가 개방되다
N에/에게 N을/를 개방하다

[Expression] 개방 정책 open-door policy
수입 개방 opening of imports
시장 개방 opening of market

[Antonym] 폐쇄 closing

[Example] 한국의 교육이 발전하기 위해서는 교육 시장의 개방이 이루어져야 한다고 봅니까?
Do you think that for the advancement of Korean education there must be an opening of the education market?

009
격려

[경녀] encouragement

encouraging so that courage or will is stimulated

[Usage] N을/를 격려하다

[Expression] 격려금 incentive
격려의 말 words of encouragement
격려가 되다 to be words of encouragement
격려를 받다 to receive encouragement

[Example] 나는 시험을 앞두고 초조해하는 친구를 격려해 주었다.
I encouraged my friend who was worried before the test.

부모님의 격려가 없었다면 그 일을 끝까지 할 수 없었을 것이다.
If I didn't have encouragement from my parents, I would've not been able to finish that task.

010
경고

[경고] warning

giving warning so that one is careful or they restrain themselves. also the actual warning

[Usage] N에게 경고를 하다
N에게 경고를 주다
N에게서 경고를 받다

[Expression] 경고문 warning
경고를 무시하다 to ignore the warning

[Example] 접근하지 말라는 경고를 무시하고 가까이 다가갔다.
I ignored the warnings to stay away and went closer.

의사들은 지나친 다이어트가 건강에 치명적인 악영향을 줄 수 있다고 경고한다.
Doctors warn that excessive dieting can have fatal consequences on your health.

011
경향

[경향] tendency

when a phenomenon, phase or behavior leans towards one tendency

[Expression] 새로운 경향 new tendency
현실 도피적 경향 tendency to avoid reality

경향을 띠다 to be tinged with tendency
경향을 보이다 to show tendency

[Example] 평균 혼인 연령이 과거에 비해 높아지는 경향을 보인다.
The average age at which people are getting married are showing an upward trend.

이 책은 대학 입학 시험의 출제경향을 분석하고 그것에 맞는 공부법을 제시하고 있다.
This book analyzes the tendency of questions that were on the college entrance exam and also provides studying suggestions according to the questions presented.

012
고정관념

[고정관념] stereotype

one's consciousness or concept that doesn't easily change and will decide one's behavior

[Expression] 고정관념을 갖다 to have a stereotype
고정관념을 지니다 to carry a stereotype
고정관념을 깨다 to break the stereotype
고정관념에서 벗어나다 to break free from a stereotype

[Example] 사람은 저마다 자기중심적인 고정관념을 지니고 살게 마련이다.
All people have self-centered stereotypes that they live with.

남녀의 역할에 대한 뿌리 깊은 고정관념으로 인해 여전히 남녀 역할 분배에 불평등이 존재하고 있다.
Because of the deeply rooted stereotypes regarding gender roles, there is still unequal division present.

013
골치

[골치] brain

means 'the head' or 'the brain'

[Expression] 골칫거리 trouble
골치(가) 아프다 brain hurts
골치가 쑤시다 brain hurts
골치(를) 앓다 to be worried
골치를 썩이다 to have a headache

[Example] 쓰레기 문제로 온 동네가 골치를 앓고 있다.
The whole neighborhood's heads hurt because of the trash problem.

이 일은 골치를 썩인다고 해결될 일이 아니다.
This is not something that will be solved just from worrying your head over.

014
교양

[교양] refinement

nobility achieved by education, knowledge, or common sense; also vast knowledge about culture

[Expression] 교양과목 cultural studies
교양서적 cultural publications
교양이 있다 to be cultured
교양이 풍부하다 to be abundant in culture
교양을 쌓다 to build refinement

[Example] 옷은 비록 남루하게 입었으나 그 남자는 대화 속에 분명히 교양과 지성미를 풍기고 있다.
Although his clothes are shabby, you can tell by the way he speaks that he is cultured and intelligent.

교양교육은 지식의 단순한 전수가 아니라 사물에 관한 종합적인 이해, 비판적인 인식에 중점을 두고 있다.
Cultural studies are not placing emphasis on merely receiving the information but the combination of a balance between understanding and being critical of an object.

015
구조[1]

[구조] rescue

helping and saving someone who is in dangerous circumstances

[Usage] N을/를 구조하다

[Expression] 구조대 rescue team
구조 신호 rescue signal
구조 활동 rescue operations
인명 구조 lifesaving

[Example] 바다에서 표류하던 난민들이 지나가는 배에 구조를 요청했다.
The refugees who were drifting on the sea requested help from a passing ship.

소방관들은 화재가 발생하면 불을 끄랴 사람들을 구조하랴 위험을 무릅쓰고 정신없이 뛰어 다닌다.
Firefighters run around in chaos when a fire breaks out while trying to extinguish the fire, save people, and also face danger.

016
구조[2]

[구조] structure

part or elements of a whole; also what makes up the framework

[Expression] 구조물 construction
구조도 construction plan
구조주의 structuralism

[Example] 이 제품은 구조가 간단하여 가격이 싸고 고장이 적다.
Because the construction of this product is simple, the price is cheap and it hardly ever breaks.

우리는 유리창이 많고 지붕의 경사가 급한 일본식 구조의 기와집에서 살게 되었다.
We lived in a Japanese-structured home with many windows and a steep, tiled roof.

017
권력

[궐력] authority

official authority or strength that allows you to make people obedient or control people

[Expression] 권력자 authoritative person
권력층 power structure
권력 투쟁 struggle for authority
권력이 있다 to have authority
권력을 잡다 to seize authority

[Example] 이제 인간의 역사에서 권력과 부를 몇 사람이 독점할 수 있는 시대는 지나갔다.
The era in our history when only a few people can dictate and have authority has now passed.

옳지 못한 방법으로 권력을 쟁취한 집단은 권력을 유지하기 위해 범죄 집단을 비호하는 경우가 많다.
Groups that have seized authority through illegal ways usually use illegal groups to try and maintain their authority.

018
권리

[궐리] a right

a right or lawful strength you are entitled to in a particular situation or to a person

[Usage] AV을/ㄹ 권리가 있다

[Expression] 권리를 가지다 to have a right
권리를 행사하다 to exercise your right
권리를 주장하다 to assert your right
권리를 침해하다 to violate your right

[Example] 민주주의 국가에서는 국민의 자유와 권리가 보장된다.
In a democratic nation, the freedom and authority of the people are protected.

국민들이 투표에 참여해 소중한 국민의 권리를 행사했다.
The citizens that participated in the voting, exercised their precious rights.

019
규제

[규제] restriction

using a rule or regulation to create a limit or control so that no one can go over the limit

[Usage] N이/가 규제되다
N을/를 규제하다

[Expression] 규제책 plans of restriction
규제가 풀어지다 restriction is lifted
규제를 강화하다 to strengthen the restriction

[Example] 방송에서는 무분별한 외래어 사용을 규제하고 있다.
There is a restriction on broadcasting programs from thoughtless using words of foreign origin.

정치 규제를 받아 온 인사들이 이제 자유로운 정치 활동을 할 수 있게 되었다.
The people who were subjected to a restricted political activity are now allowed to engage freely in politics.

020
극복

[극뽁] recovery

recovery from harsh circumstances or distress

[Usage] N이/가 극복되다
N을/를 극복하다

[Expression] 위기 극복 recovery from danger
불황 극복 recovery from a slump
가난 극복 recovery from poverty

[Example] 그들은 불굴의 정신으로 국난을 극복하여 민족과 국가를 지켰다.
With an iron will, they recovered from the national crisis and protected the nation's people as well as the nation.

김 사장은 피나는 노력 끝에 가난을 극복하고 오늘날의 기업을 일으켜 세웠다.
Mr. Kim recovered from poverty through painstaking work and raised his business to the business that it is today.

021
근거

[근거] 1. basis 2. base

1. a basis for the formation of a phenomena or the reason for the formation of a thought

[Usage] N에 근거하다
AV는 근거가 되다

[Expression] 근거가 있다 basis is present
근거를 대다 basis is shown
근거를 제시하다 basis is exhibited

[Example] 그 정치인이 뇌물을 받았다는 소문은 근거 없는 헛소문이었다.
The rumor that the government official received bribes was baseless.

2. a central place where you prepare and rest in order to do an action, a base where you do an action

[Expression] 근거지 base
생활의 근거 basis of living

[Example] 사업이 망해서 집을 파는 바람에 하루아침에 생활의 근거를 잃었다.
After selling my home due to going bankrupt, my life has lost its basis overnight.

022
기념

[기념] commemoration

commemoration of a meaningful event or honorable person so that people will not forget them and will constantly think of them

[Usage] N을/를 기념하다

[Expression] 기념식 memorial ceremony
기념관 memorial
기념품 souvenir
결혼기념일 wedding anniversary

[Example] 우리의 만남을 기념하기 위해 축배를 들기로 했다.
To commemorate our meeting, we had a celebratory drink.

중장년층 남성 가운데 결혼기념일이나 아내의 생일을 한 번도 챙겨 본 적이 없다고 대답한 사람이 꽤 많았다.
Amongst men in the late 40's, there are many that answered saying that they had never celebrated their wedding anniversary or wife's birthday.

023
기부

[기부] donation

giving money, assets, etc. so that you can help many people

[Usage] N을/를 기부하다

[Expression] 기부금 donation
기부문화 donation culture

[Example] 결식아동을 후원하는 재단에 매달 5만원씩 기부하고 있어요.
I am donating 50,000 won every month to a foundation that sponsors starving children.

아무리 부자라도 1억 원이라는 큰돈을 기부하기란 쉬운 일이 아니에요.
No matter how rich you are, donating one hundred million won is no easy feat.

024
기증

[기증] donation

giving goods to someone as a gift or a commemoration free of charge

[Usage] N을/를 기증하다
N을/를 기증받다

[Expression] 기증자 donor
기증품 a gift
장기 기증 organ donation
시신 기증 body donation

[Example] 이 서류는 신체 장기 기증 재단에서 발급한 일종의 서약서였다.
These documents were a sort of written oath from the bodily organs donation foundation.

복지 시설이 들어설 부지는 어느 독지가로부터 기증을 받은 것이다.
The land that the welfare facilities will be built on was a donation from a philanthropist.

025
난리

[날리] 1. war 2. uproar 3. fuss

1. war or a disturbance

[Expression] 난리가 나다 war happens
난리가 터지다 war breaks out
난리를 치르다 war is carried out

[Example] 임진왜란 때 경상도 전역이 난리를 치렀다.
During the Japanese Invasion of Korea in 1592, the whole area of Kyungsang-do was in war.

2. due to disaster or conflict, the whole world is in an uproar or world order is chaotic

[Expression] 난리가 나다 to have an uproar
난리를 겪다 to experience an uproar
난리를 치르다 to have an uproar

[Example] 홍수로 집과 가축들이 모두 떠내려가서 난리가 났다.
There is an uproar because both the home and all of the livestock were carried away by the flood.

3. words used to describe a small disturbance

[Expression] 난리가 나다 there is a fuss
난리를 부리다 to be fussy
난리를 피우다 to throw a fit

[Example] 아이는 엄마가 장난감을 사 주지 않는다고 울고불고 난리를 피웠다.
The child threw a fit while crying because his mother didn't buy him the toy that he wanted.

026
납득

[납뜩] acceptance

acknowledge and understanding someone else's words, behavior, or circumstances

[Usage] N이/가 N에/에게 납득되다
N을/를 납득하다
N을/를 납득시키다

[Expression] 납득이 가다 to be convinced

[Example] 나는 그의 돌출 행동을 납득하기 어려웠다.
It was hard for me to accept his sudden actions.

그런 사소한 문제로 자살했다는 사실이 납득이 가지 않았다.
I couldn't accept that he committed suicide due to such a trivial problem.

027
노릇[1]

[노른] 1.role 2. duty

1. (used behind a noun which shows an occupation or one's duty) a word making little of one's job or position

[Usage] N노릇을 하다

[Expression] 선생 노릇 acting like a teacher
관리 노릇 acting like administration

[Example] 나는 한때 영화감독 밑에서 조수 노릇을 했다.
At one period in time, I worked as an assistant under a movie director.

2. (used behind a partial noun) the task undertaken

[Usage] N노릇을 하다

[Expression] 사람 노릇 role as a human
아버지 노릇 role as a father

[synonym] 구실 function

[Example] 돈도 벌어야 하고 가정도 잘 이끌어야 하니 한 집안의 가장 노릇을 하기가 그리 쉬운 게 아니다.
The role as head of the house is no easy feat because not only do you need to earn money but you also have to lead the household well.

028
노릇[2]

[노른] circumstances

(used dependently) (according to a situation)pitiful circumstances or situation

[Usage] DV은/ㄴ 노릇이다
AV을/ㄹ 노릇이다

[Example] 지금 기분이 나쁘다고 해서 아까운 직장을 그만두는 것은 어리석은 노릇이다.
Quitting your good job just because you're in a bad mood is immature.

아무도 찾을 수 없게 꽁꽁 숨겨 놓았던 패물이 없어지다니 정말 귀신이 곡할 노릇이다.
It's mysterious that the jewelry I hid so that no one could find, has disappeared.

029
님비현상

[님비현상] NIMBY (not in my backyard) syndrome

an evasion phenomena where although they accept that garbage incineration plants or nuclear dump sites are necessary, residents feel that they are unpleasant facilities and do not want them to be located in their area; also called regional scale selfishness

[Example] 님비현상은 자기 지역을 지키기 위한 것이라고도 볼 수 있으므로 이를 단순히 비판만 하기는 어렵다.
It is hard to simply criticize the NIMBY syndrome because it is all to protect one's own area.

정부는 자기 지역에 화장장 건립하는 것을 반대하는 님비현상을 극복하기 위해 여러 가지 대책을 마련 중이다.
The local government is preparing many measures to counter the NIMBY syndrome that might arise from the building of a crematorium.

030
단골

[단골] 1. regular hangout 2. a regular

1. a regular hangout that is already determined and where you do business; the abbreviation of 단골집

[Expression] 단골집 regular hangout
단골 가게 store where you are a regular

[Example] 그는 매일 가던 단골집을 오늘은 그냥 지나쳤다.
He just passed his regular hangout today, instead of going in.

2. (between a store or business) a pre-determined place to do business or which you always seek out; also just a regular

[Expression] 단골손님 a regular
단골로 가다 to go as a regular

[Example] 그 식당 아저씨의 친절은 처음 온 손님도 단골로 만들었다.
Because of the restaurant owner's kindness, he made even first-time customers into regulars.

031
대비

[대비] preparation

preparing in advance to endure a future ordeal

[Usage] N을/를 대비하다
N에 대비하다

[Expression] 대비책 ways to prepare

[Example] 갑자기 어려운 일을 당했을 때를 대비하여 저축이 필요하다.
You need to have savings in preparation for any sudden, difficult matters you may be faced with.

행사 책임자는 만일의 사태에 대비하여 행사장 곳곳에 경비원을 배치했다.
The person in charge of the event placed guards all around the event hall to prepare should anything happen.

032
대중화

[대중화] popularization

becoming popular and familiar amongst the public

[Usage] N이/가 대중화되다
N을/를 대중화시키다

[Example] 그는 대중 가수로서는 드물게 국악의 대중화에 노력을 기울였다.
He chose to turn his efforts to popularizing Korean traditional music, which is rare for a popular singer.

요즘 여러 지방자치단체에서 자기 지방의 토속주를 대중화시키려는 노력들을 하고 있다.
Nowadays, many local governments are working to popularize their folk liquors.

033
대책

[대책] countermeasure

plans or means to handle a certain situation

[Expression] 대책 회의 council
대책이 있다 to have countermeasures
대책을 세우다 to raise countermeasures
대책을 마련하다 to prepare countermeasures
대책을 강구하다 to consider countermeasures

[Example] 연료난을 해소하기 위한 대책을 강구했다.
We considered many different countermeasures to solve the shortage in fuel.

이번 지진으로 인한 피해를 최소화하기 위해 해당 관계자들이 모여 대책 회의를 가졌다.
There was a council with relevant parties to discuss countermeasures that would minimize the damage caused by the recent earthquake.

034
덜미

[덜미] 1. scruff 2. back of body

1. the back of your neck and towards the bottom of it

[Expression] 목덜미 scruff of neck
뒷덜미nape of neck

[Example] 뒷머리를 짧게 잘랐더니 목덜미가 시리다.
Ever since I cut the back of my hair, the back of my neck is cold.

2. a part close to the back of your body

[Expression] 덜미를 잡다 to grasp by nape
덜미를 낚아채다 to snatch nape
덜미를 잡히다 to be caught red-handed

[Example] 김 과장은 회사의 기밀 서류를 경쟁 회사에 넘겨주려다가 상사에게 덜미를 잡혔다.
Mr. Kim was caught red-handed by his superior trying to hand over classified documents to a rival business.

035
등장

[등장] appearance

appearing on a stage or platform, appearing in a novel as a character

[Usage] N이/가 N에 등장하다

[Expression] 등장인물 character

[Antonym] 퇴장 exit

[Example] 요즘 광고에는 동물들도 많이 등장한다.
Nowadays, animals also make appearances in commercials.

그 배우는 관객들의 환호와 박수 속에 무대 위로 등장했다.
That actor appeared on the stage amid the audiences' cheers and applause.

036
마련

[마련] arrangement

arranging from consideration

[Usage] N이/가 N에/에게 마련되다
N을/를 마련하다

[Example] 나는 그에게 일자리를 마련해 주었다.
I arranged a job for him.

아파트 단지 곳곳에 놀이터 시설이 마련되어 있다.
There are playgrounds arranged all over the apartment complex.

037
마찰

[마찰] 1. rub 2. friction

1. pressing one thing against another and moving one or both backward or forward

[Usage] N이/가 마찰되다
N을/를 마찰하다

[Example] 조난자들은 두 손을 마찰하여 체온을 유지하려고 했다.
The survivors rubbed their hands together to try and maintain body heat.

2. conflict or trouble between two people caused by disagreement in opinions

[Expression] 마찰을 빚다 to cause conflict
마찰을 피하다 to avoid conflict
마찰을 일으키다 to raise conflict

[Example] 임금 협상에서 노사 간에 마찰이 빚어졌다.
The negotiation about wages caused conflict between labor and management.

038
매너

[매너] manners

the way you behave or your attitude; manners or how you proceed in your daily life

[Expression] 매너가 있다 to have manners
매너가 없다 to have no manners
매너가 좋다 to have good manners
매너가 나쁘다 to have bad manners

[Example] 저 선수는 경기하는 매너가 참 좋다.
That athlete's attitude towards how he plays the game is good.

마구잡이로 옆 차선에 끼어드는 매너 없는 운전자가 많다.
There are many mannerless drivers who do the reckless act of cutting into the car lane next to them.

039
매장[1]

[매장] store

a place that sells items

[Expression] 가구 매장 furniture store
주류 매장 liquor store
전문 매장 specialty store
매장이 들어서다 to enter a store
매장을 열다 to open a store

[Example] 백화점의 1층에는 주로 잡화 매장이 들어서 있다.
There are usually miscellaneous shops on the first floor of department stores.

요즘 와인이나 속옷 등 한 가지 품목만 파는 전문매장들이 많아졌다.
Nowadays, Specialty stores that only sell one item such as only wine or undergarments increased.

040
매장[2]

[매장] 1. burial 2. social ostracism 3. underground

1. corpse or remains are buried in the ground

[Usage] N이/가 N에 매장되다
N을/를 N에 매장하다

[Example] 옛날에는 자신이 죽은 후 화장하는 것을 꺼리고 매장을 원하는 사람이 절대적으로 많았으나 요즘에는 화장을 하겠다는 사람이 점점 늘고 있다.
Long ago, there were many people who were reluctant to be cremated after death and the majority wanted to be buried, but nowadays the number of people who want to be cremated is growing.

2. making it so that a certain person cannot be active in society or a word that can be compared to disproval

[Usage] N이/가 (N에서) 매장되다
N을/를 (N에서) 매장시키다

[Example] 그렇게 비열한 인간은 사회에서 매장을 시켜야 한다.
Underhanded people like that should be ostracized from society.

3. resources or minerals being buried underground

[Usage] N 에 매장되다

[Example] 지구에 매장되어 있는 지하자원은 결코 무궁무진하지가 않다.
Underground resources that are underground in the earth are not necessarily inexhaustible.

041
모집

[모집] recruitment

gathering people or objects who meet certain requirements; also collecting things like donations across a large area

[Usage] N이/가 모집되다
N을/를 모집하다

[Expression] 모집 인원 volume of recruitment
모집 광고 advertisement of recruitment

[Example] 우리 회사에서는 중국어에 능통한 신입사원을 모집하고 있다.
Our business is recruiting new employees who are fluent in Chinese.

저출산 현상으로 초등학생의 수가 감소함에 따라 초등 교원을 양성하는 교육 대학에서도 신입생 모집 정원을 축소하고 있다.
Because the low birth rate phenomena is causing a decline in elementary school children, the recruitment quota in new students for elementary school training in education colleges is also declining.

042
무작정

[무작쩡] being thoughtless

thoughtlessly doing something without planning ahead for it. not keeping in mind future events

[Example] 그는 아무런 계획 없이 무작정으로 집을 나왔다.
He left his house thoughtlessly without any plans.

우리 오빠는뚜렷한 목적도 없이 무작정의 기대로 서울로 갔다.
My elder brother went to Seoul thoughtlessly with no definite goal.

043
바이러스

[바이러쓰] 1.virus 2. computer virus

1. a small pathogenic, microorganism that sticks to live cells as in influenza or polio and can only be seen with a microscope

[Example] 면역력이 약한 아이들은 바이러스에 감염되기 쉽다.
Children who have weak immune systems are easily infected with viruses.

2. a computer virus has the function where it can copy itself and can not only change the way computer programs can run, but can also copy the virus or another version of itself into the program and give commands

[Example] 컴퓨터 바이러스를 막기 위해 백신 프로그램을 설치했다.
In order to prevent computer viruses, I installed a vaccine program.

044
바자회

[바자회] bazaar

a market that opens in order to gather funds for the public or social services

[Expression] 바자회가 열리다 to open a bazaar
바자회를 열다 to hold a bazaar
바자회를 개최하다 to host a bazaar

[Example] 바자회를 열거나 바자회에 참여해 본 적이 있습니까?
Have you ever held or participated in a fundraiser?

백화점 지하 매장에서 불우 이웃 돕기 바자회를 개최합니다.
We are hosting a fundraiser to help underprivileged neighbors in the underground market of the department store.

045
반응

[바능] response

a reaction to a stimulus or an action, also as a phenomena

[Usage] N이/가 N에 반응하다

[Expression] 반응이 있다 there is a response
반응이 빠르다 response is fast
반응을 보이다 response is shown

[Example] 선생님의 농담이 재미가 없었는지 학생들이 아무런 반응을 보이지 않았다.
The teacher's joke must have not been funny because there was no response from the students.

눈동자에 불빛을 비추어 보아도 아무 반응이 없는 걸 보니 이 고양이는 이미 죽은 것 같다.
Because there is no response even after shining a light into its pupils, I think the cat is already dead.

04 연습문제

[1-12] 다음 밑줄 친 부분과 의미가 비슷한 것을 고르십시오.

Choose the word that is similar to the underlined word.

1. 다른 사람의 사생활에 지나치게 (　　　)을/를 하면 불쾌감을 줄 수 있다.

❶ 가상　❷ 경고　❸ 경쟁　❹ 간섭

2. 다양한 산업용 로봇이 (　　　)하면서 많은 노동자가 일자리를 잃게 되었다.

❶ 경쟁　❷ 등장　❸ 가입　❹ 변화

3. 자본 시장이 외국에 대폭 (　　　)됨에 따라 국내 시장의 잠식이 우려되고 있다.

❶ 개최　❷ 개방　❸ 규제　❹ 보존

4. 공무원은 정당, 기타 정치 단체의 결성에 관여하거나 이에 (　　　)할 수 없다.

❶ 대비　❷ 등장　❸ 가입　❹ 중재

5. 새 국제법이 발효됨으로써 국제적 (　　　)을/를 해소하고 협력을 촉진할 수 있게 되었다.

❶ 모순　❷ 고정관념　❸ 이해관계　❹ 갈등

6. 사기도박을 벌인 일당이 검찰에 (　　　)을/를 잡혔다.

❶ 덜미　❷ 머리　❸ 약점　❹ 주도권

7. 김 부장은 사표 쓸 (　　　)을/를 하고 사장님께 반대 의견을 냈다.

❶ 결정　❷ 각오　❸ 고민　❹ 가정

8. 오늘날 범죄는 점점 지능화되는 (　　　)이/가 있다.

❶ 분위기　❷ 경향　❸ 상황　❹ 전략

9. 아이들이 잘 못하더라도 부모님들이 (　　　)을/를 해준다면 아이들은 더욱 힘을 내고 자신감을 가지게 될 것이다.

❶ 격려　❷ 치료　❸ 해결　❹ 보상

10. 환경 보호를 위하여 일회용품의 사용을 (　　　)하고 있다.

❶ 기증　❷ 장려　❸ 확대　❹ 규제

11. 나는 그 공장의 사원 (　　　)에 응시하기로 마음먹었다.

❶ 모집　❷ 경쟁　❸ 수집　❹ 수용

12. 알레르기란 특별한 질병이 없으면서도 외부 자극에 민감하게 (　　　)해서 체질적 장애를 일으키는 것을 말한다.

❶ 치료　❷ 반응　❸ 대비　❹ 규제

[13-16] 다음 (　　　)에 들어갈 말로 알맞지 않은 것을 고르십시오.

Choose the word that does not fit in the parenthesis.

13. 이 운동화는 바닥의 충격을 (　　　) 장치가 설계되어 있다.

❶ 완화시키는　❷ 단축시키는　❸ 흡수하는　❹ 감소시키는

14. 인터넷이 (　　　)되면서 정보의 양은 급격하게 많아지기 시작하였다.

❶ 일반화　❷ 보편화　❸ 산업화　❹ 대중화

15. 여성학 강의를 들으면서 여자에 대한 나의 (　　　)이/가 완전히 깨졌다.

❶ 편견　❷ 개념　❸ 선입견　❹ 고정관념

16. 결혼 날짜를 잡으면 여자 쪽 집에서는 혼수를 (   )하느라 바쁘기 마련이다.

❶ 대비 ❷ 준비 ❸ 장만 ❹ 마련

[17-20] 다음 밑줄 친 부분과 의미가 비슷한 것을 고르십시오.

Choose the word that is similar to the underlined word.

17. 최근 수출이 늘어나서 경기가 회복됨에 따라 실업률이 감소하고 있다.

❶ 축소되다 ❷ 증가하다 ❸ 낮아지다 ❹ 짧아지다

18. 이 소설은 청소년들이 친구들과의 갈등을 극복하는 과정을 감동적으로 보여 주고 있다.

❶ 이겨내다 ❷ 처리하다 ❸ 제거하다 ❹ 감수하다

19. 아무리 변호사라지만 큰 범죄를 저지른 죄인을 감싸고도는 그의 행동은 정말 납득할 수가 없다.

❶ 이해 ❷ 설명 ❸ 찬성 ❹ 인정

20. 그는 차남이지만 형이 외국에 나가 있어서 형 대신 맏아들 노릇을 하고 있다.

❶ 준비를 하다 ❷ 책임을 지다 ❸ 역할을 하다 ❹ 흉내를 내다

[21-22] 다음 밑줄 친 부분이 잘못된 것을 고르십시오.

Choose the underlined word that was used incorrectly.

21.

❶ 오늘 학교에서 화재에 대비한 가상 훈련을 했다.
❷ 생일은 한 생명이 태어난 것을 기념하고 축하하는 날이다.
❸ 불법 어로 행위를 하는 자는 법에 따라 처벌한다는 충고가 적혀 있었다.
❹ 달리 해결 방법이 없는 문제를 가지고 온종일 생각에 잠긴 김 대리는 점점 골치가 아파 왔다.

22.

❶ 노사 간의 갈등이 파업으로 발전되었다.

❷ 그는 선배의 권유로 학교 운동부에 가입하였다.

❸ 평균 결혼 연령이 과거에 비해 높아지는 경향을 보인다.

❹ 채소 장수 할머니는 평생 모은 돈을 모두 고아원에 기증했다.

[23-24] 다음 중 제시된 술어를 공통적으로 사용할 수 있는 것을 고르십시오.

Choose one word that can be used for all of the given verbs.

23.

강구하다	마련하다	세우다	협의하다

❶ 규제 ❷ 대책 ❸ 근거 ❹ 권리

24.

있다	없다	높다	떨어지다

❶ 근거 ❷ 마찰 ❸ 가치 ❹ 권력

[25-27] 다음에 제시된 단어의 관계가 다른 것을 하나 고르십시오.

In the given words, choose the one where the relationship is different.

25. ❶ 노릇-구실 ❷ 갈등-극복 ❸ 매너-예의 ❹ 매장-파는 곳

26. ❶ 개방-폐쇄 ❷ 등장-퇴장 ❸ 감소-증가 ❹ 의무-책임

27. ❶ 마련-준비 ❷ 교양-과목 ❸ 낭비-현상 ❹ 단골-손님

[28-29] 밑줄 친 부분의 의미가 다른 것을 하나 고르십시오.

Choose the word that has the different meaning from the underlined word.

28.

❶ 바다에서 표류하던 난민들이 지나가는 배에 구조를 요청했다.
❷ 화재 현장에 출동한 119 구조 요원들이 신속한 구조 활동을 벌였다.
❸ 물에 빠져 허우적대던 아이가 신고를 받고 출동한 경찰에 구조되었다.
❹ 내가 어렸을 때 살던 집은 방 둘에 조그마한 욕실이 달린 간단한 구조의 빨간 기와집이었다.

29.

❶ 그 녀석은 꼬마들을 동네에 다 모아들여 골목대장 노릇을 하곤 했다.
❷ 왕이 어린 나이로 즉위하자 왕실의 웃어른이 왕의 후견인 노릇을 했다.
❸ 내가 아무리 설명해도 아이가 자기 고집을 꺾지 않으니 답답한 노릇이다.
❹ 그는 차남이지만 형이 외국에 나가 있어서 대신 맏아들 노릇을 하고 있다.

[30-34] 다음 (　　)에 공통적으로 들어갈 단어를 쓰십시오.

Find the one word that fits in the parentheses.

30.

❶ 컴퓨터에 (　　　)이/가 침투해 전산 업무가 마비되었다.
❷ 강력한 항생제가 나온 뒤로 사람들의 관심은 훨씬 고치기 어려운 (　　　)에 의한 질병이나 암에 쏠렸다.

31.

❶ 이 기계는 (　　)이/가 간단하여 가격이 싸고 고장이 적다.
❷ 우리 회사는 유통 (　　)을/를 개선하여 생산성을 향상시키고자 애를 쓰고 있다.

32.

❶ 그렇게 비열한 인간은 사회에서 (　　)을/를 시켜야 한다.
❷ 이곳에는 많은 양의 원유와 천연가스가 (　　)되어 있다.
❸ 장례식이 끝난 후 할아버지의 시신은 선산에 (　　)되었다.

33.

❶ 홍수가 크게 나서 온 동네에 (   )이/가 났다.

❷ 같은 부서의 동료들이 나더러 승진을 했으니 한턱내라고 (   )이다.

❸ 할아버지께서는 (   )이/가 나는 바람에 가족들과 생이별하게 된 이야기를 내게 자주 들려주셨다.

34.

❶ 양국 간에 무역 (   )이/가 점점 커지고 있다.

❷ 딱딱한 두 물체가 (   )하면 불꽃이 일기도 한다.

❸ 여당과 야당이 사소한 일로 의견이 (   )하는 바람에 정국이 경색되었다.

[35-36] **다음 글을 읽고 질문에 답하십시오.**

Read the following passage and answer the questions.

> 요즘 텔레비전을 켜면 출연자들이 영어를 우리말처럼 자주 쓰는 모습을 심심찮게 볼 수 있다. 이에 따라 문화체육관광부에서는 방송에서의 무분별한 영어 사용을 (㉠)하기 위한 (㉡)을/를 (㉢)하기로 했다.

35. ㉠에 알맞은 것을 고르십시오.

❶ 촉진　　❷ 격려　　❸ 비난　　❹ 규제

36. ㉡과 ㉢에 알맞은 것을 고르십시오.

❶ 대책-마련　　❷ 방안-개최　　❸ 실험-시행　　❹ 훈련-실시

명사 Ⅱ

05

Nouns Ⅱ

05 명사 Ⅱ

001
배려

[배려] consideration

taking interest and care for some with your heart

[Usage] N을/를 배려하다

[Expression] 배려를 아끼지 않다 to not be stingy with consideration

[Example] 친구가 세심한 배려를 아끼지 않아 이 곳 생활은 아무런 불편이 없다.
Because of my friend's never-ending careful consideration, living here has not been inconvenient at all.

그 당시 등록금이 없었던 그는 스승의 배려로 공부를 계속할 수 있었다.
He was able to continue studying through his teacher's consideration even when he had no money for tuition.

002
배출[1]

[배출] discharge

emitting a substance

[Usage] N이/가 N으로/로 배출되다
N을/를 N으로/로 배출하다
N을/를 N으로/로 배출시키다

[Expression] 배출구 vent
노폐물 배출 discharging of waste

[Example] 폐수를 함부로 하천에 배출한 업체가 적발되었다.
The company that was illegally discharging waste water into the river was exposed.

쓰레기 종량제가 실시되자 쓰레기의 배출이 크게 줄었다.
After the volume-rate garbage disposable system was implemented, the volume of waste has vastly reduced.

003
배출[2]

[배출] production

training talented people and sending them into society

[Usage] N이/가 N으로/로 배출되다
N을/를 N으로/로 배출하다
N을/를 N으로/로 배출시키다.

[Example] 훌륭한 인재를 배출하는 것이 우리 학교의 목표이다.
Our school's goal is to produce excellent and talented people.

육군 사관 학교는 초급 장교를 배출하는 군사 교육 기관이다.
The Korean Military Academy is a military training institution that produces beginning level officers.

004
보급

[보급] dissemination

evenly distributing something across many different areas so that it reaches and spreads

[Usage] N이/가 보급되다
N을/를 보급하다
N을/를 보급시키다

[Expression] 보급률 distribution rate

[Example] 텔레비전이 보급되기 전에는 라디오 연속극이 대단한 인기를 끌었다.
Before the spread of televisions, soap operas on the radio gained an immense amount of popularity.

전문가들은 주택난 해소를 위해서는 저렴한 임대 주택 보급이 시급하다고 보고 있다.
Experts are saying that the spread of affordable rental houses is urgent if we want to solve the housing shortage.

005
보람

[보람] reward

the good results or satisfaction you receive after doing a deed; also the worth of a deed that causes you to have pride or self-esteem

[Usage] N이/가 보람되다
AV은/ㄴ 보람이 있다
AV은/ㄴ 보람을 느끼다

[Expression] 보람차다 to be rewarding

[Example] 그 동안 노력한 보람도 없이 계획은 실패했다.
Even with all of the effort, the plans failed without any reward.

부모님들은 자식들이 잘 사는 모습을 보면서 고생한 보람을 느낍니다.
Parents feel rewarded even through the hardship if they see their children living well.

006
보상

[보상] 1. compensation 2. compensation

1. (as fixed by law) an amount of money or other things used to compensate for damage or loss and is of equal value

[Usage] N을/를 보상하다
N을/를 보상받다

[Expression] 보상금 compensation money
피해 보상 compensation for damage

[Related Words] 배상 recompense

[Example] 승용차를 도난당했을 때는 그 사실을 경찰서에 신고해야만 보상을 받을 수 있다.
If your car has been stolen, the only way to receive compensation is to report it to the police.

2. achieving good results as compensation in a different area than the one you feel inferior to whether it be physically or mentally

[Usage] N을/를 보상받다

[Expression] 보상 심리 compensation mentality

[Example] 지나친 교육열의 바탕에는 부모들이 자신이 이루지 못한 것들을 아이를 통해 보상받고자 하는 심리가 있다.
Parents who have an extreme passion for education have a mentality of trying to receive compensation through their children for the things that they did not achieve.

007
복제

[복쩨] reproduction

making a reproduction of the original; also making a copy

[Usage] N이/가 복제되다
N을/를 복제하다

[Expression] 복제품 reproduction
복제인간 human clone
불법복제 illegal reproduction

[Related Words] 복사 copy

[Example] 불법 소프트웨어들이 대량으로 복제되어 유통되고 있다.
Illegal softwares are being mass-reproduced and distributed.

우리나라의 연구팀에서 세계 최초로 애완견을 복제하였다.
A research team from our nation cloned a pet dog for the first time in the world.

008
분리

[불리] separation

dividing and separating things

[Usage] N이/가 분리되다
N을/를 분리하다
N을/를 분리시키다

[Example] 기업의 소유와 경영은 분리되는 것이 바람직하다.
The separation of a business' ownership and administration is desirable.

환경보호를 위해 재활용할 수 있는 쓰레기를 분리해서 버려야 한다.
In order to preserve the environment, we must throw away regular trash and trash that can be recycled separately.

009
분석

[분석] analysis

taking apart things that are tangled or complicated and dividing them by their individual element or properties

[Usage] N이/가 (N으로) 분석되다
N을/를 분석하다

[Expression] 분석력 analytical skills
심리 분석 analysis of psychology
원인 분석 analysis of cause

[Example] 공업용 폐수가 하천 오염의 주된 원인으로 분석되었다.
The main cause of the pollution of the river has been analyzed to be because of industrial waste water.

같은 작품에 대한 분석이 비평가에 따라 달라질 수 있다.
The analysis of the same piece can change depending on the critic.

010
비난

[비난] criticism

finding fault with someone's mistake or flaw and talking about it negatively

[Usage] N을/를 비난하다

[Expression] 비난이 일다 criticism rises
비난이 거세다 criticism is harsh
비난이 쏟아지다 criticism pours out
비난을 받다 to receive criticism

[Antonym] 칭찬 praise

[Example] 부실공사를 한 건설 회사에 비난이 쏟아졌다.
There was a pouring out of criticism towards the construction company that did poor construction.

남을 비난하기는 쉬워도 자신을 반성하기는 어렵다.
Although it is easy to criticize others, it is hard to reflect on yourself.

011
빈곤

[빈곤] 1. poverty 2. lack

1. the state of being poor makes life hard to live

[Expression] 빈곤하다 to be poor
빈곤한 살림 lifestyle of poverty
빈곤한 생활 living in poverty
빈곤에 시달리다 to suffer through poverty

[Synonym] 가난 poverty
궁핍 destitution

[Example] 많은 나라가 경제적 빈곤에서 벗어나려고 노력하고 있다.
Many nations are trying to break free from economic poverty.

2. content, etc. is empty because it is not true or lacking

[Expression] 빈곤하다 to be lacking
빈곤한 지식 lacking knowledge
빈곤한 상상력 lacking imagination

[Synonym] 부족 deficiency
빈약 meager

[Example] 그 회사는 기술력이 빈곤하여 제품개발에 실패했다.
That company failed in product development because they lacked in technical skills.

012
사교육

[사교육] private education

education which an individual or private organization privately gives

[Expression] 사교육비 private education fee
사교육 시장 private education market
사교육을 받다 to receive private education
사교육을 시키다 to make someone do private education

[Antonym] 공교육 public education

[Example] 사교육비의 증가로 자녀수가 곧 재력의 상징으로 통하는 시대가 왔다.
With the rise in private education fees, the era where the number of children led to a symbol of wealth came.

공교육에 만족하지 못하는 부모들 때문에 사교육 시장이 점점 커지고 있다.
The market for private education is becoming bigger and bigger because of parents who are not satisfied with public education.

013
사례[1]

[사례] precedent

an example that happened before a certain event

[Expression] 사례가 있다 example is present
사례가 많다 to have many cases
사례를 들다 to give an example

[Example] 전에 이런 사례는 없었기 때문에 어떻게 처리해야 할지 모르겠어요.
Because there was not precedent from before, I don't know how to handle this.

일부 업체들이 경비 절감을 이유로 폐수와 매연을 불법 배출하는 사례가 적지 않다.
There are many cases of businesses illegally dumping waste water and exhaust in order to cut down in expenses.

014
사례[2] [사례] reward

showing gratitude to someone through words, actions, or wealth

[Usage] N에게 사례하다

N에게서 사례를 받다

[Expression] 사례금 compensation

[Example] 혼사가 이루어지면 중매쟁이는 상당한 사례를 받기도 한다.
If marriage is achieved, the matchmaker may receive a significant compensation.

사례하는 뜻으로 점심이라도 사고 싶은데, 시간 좀 내 주십시오.
Please spare me some time because I want to buy you lunch as a token of my gratitude.

015
사이트 [사이트] site

a place where information is gathered, an aggregate on a web server where information is saved

[Expression] 웹 사이트 website

게임 사이트 game site

인터넷 사이트 internet site

사이트에 접속하다 to access a site

[Example] 자주 접속하는 인터넷 사이트가 있나요?
Is there an internet site that you frequently access?

관심 있는 사이트들은 즐겨찾기에 저장해놓으면 편리해요.
If there are sites that you are interested in, it is convenient to save them into your bookmarks.

016
상황 [상황] situation

the shape or circumstances that certain things happen

[Usage] AV /DV는/은/ㄴ 상황에 처하다

[Expression] 상황실 situation room

한계상황 critical situation

상황이 어렵다 to be in difficult situation

상황이 불리하다 situation is unfavorable

[Example] 겨울철에 등산할 때는 눈사태와 같은 돌발적인 상황에 대비해야 한다.
If you hike in the winter, you must prepare for unexpected situations such as avalanches.

학생들의 교육 환경과 그들이 처한 상황을 점차적으로 개선시켜야 한다.
We must progressively improve the educational environment and situations of our students.

017
생계

[생계] living

the means in which you live your life; also the circumstances of your current life

[Expression] 생계비 living expenses
생계가 어렵다 living is hard
생계를 잇다 to continue living
생계를 꾸리다 to make a living
생계를 유지하다 to maintain a living

[Example] 밀가루 값과 쌀값이 오르자 서민층은 생계에 큰 타격을 입었다.
Ordinary people suffered a huge blow in their living when prices for flour and rice rose.

군고구마를 팔아 어렵게 생계를 잇던 모자가 교통사고를 당해 생계가 막막하다고 한다.
The future of the mother and son who sold roasted sweet potatoes as a living, is grim after they were involved in a car accident.

018
생명력

[생명녁] 1. life force 2. vital force

1. the force needed to maintain life for an organism

[Expression] 강인한 생명력 strong life force
끈질긴 생명력 persistent life force
왕성한 생명력 full vitality
생명력이 강하다 to have powerful life force

[Example] 이 식물은 생명력이 강해서 아무 데나 뿌리를 내리고 자란다.
This plant has such a strong life force that it will settle its roots anywhere and grow.

2. the force that allows for essential functions in objects or phenomena

[Example] 그 가수는 타고난 가창력에다가 성실함까지 지니고 있어서 생명력이 긴 듯싶다.
That singer's vitality will be long-lived because of his inborn singing ability and sincerity.

019
선입견

[선입껸] prejudice

a fixed point of view or idea towards a target that is already in your mind

[Expression] 선입견을 품다 to bear prejudice
선입견을 가지다 to have prejudice
선입견을 버리다 to throw away prejudice

[Example] 관찰자는 미리 어떤 선입견을 가지고 관찰에 임해서는 안 된다.
Observers must not have previous prejudices while undertaking observations.

다른 나라의 문화를 연구할 때는 선입견이나 편견 없이 해야 한다.
When studying the culture of other countries, you must not have any prejudices or biases.

020
선정

[선정] selection

choosing a person or item from a variety that will fit best with a certain goal

[Usage] N이/가 N으로/로 선정되다
N을/를 N으로/로 선정하다

[Expression] 작품 선정 selection of piece
사업자 선정 selection of business

[Example] 회장은 정리 해고 문제를 우선 처리 사안으로 선정하였다.
The president selected to first deal with the layoff.

각 군마다 한 마을씩 시범 마을로 선정하면 정부가 이를 적극 지원한다고 했다.
The government stated that it would actively support if every county selected one village as a model village.

021
설립

[설립] establishment

creating a new association or organization

[Usage] N이/가 설립되다
N을/를 설립하다

[Expression] 설립자 founder
설립연도 year of establishment

[Example] 유니세프는 전 세계 어린이들을 돕기 위해 설립되었다.
UNICEF was established to help children all around the world.

부자들 중에는 자선단체를 설립해서 운영하는 사람이 많다.
Amongst wealthy people, there are many that have established and are operating charities.

022
성향

[성향] tendency

when the property or mind is inclined to lean towards one direction

[Usage] N적인 성향이 있다
N적인 성향이 강하다
AV는 성향이 있다
AV는 성향이 강하다

[Example] 그는 보수적인 성향을 지닌 정치가였다.
He was a statesman who retained conservative tendencies.

그녀는 외동딸로 귀엽게 자라 애정을 독차지하려는 성향이 강하다.
Because she grew up as the only daughter who received a lot of affection, she has the strong tendency to try and monopolize affection.

023
소신

[소신] principle

something that you believe and insist on

[Expression] 소신껏 to the best of one's principles
소신대로 by your principle
소신을 가지다 to have principles
소신을 밝히다 to reveal one's principles
소신을 굽히다 to compromise one's principles

[Example] 그 사람은 소신도 없는 단순한 기회주의적 출세주의자이다.
He is simply an opportunistic social climber with no principles.

내 동생은 다른 사람의 눈치를 보지 않고 자신의 소신대로 일하는 사람이다.
My sibling is someone who works according to his principles and does not regard other people's eyes.

024
수명

[수명] 1. life expectancy 2. lifespan

1. the period in which an organism is alive.

[Expression] 평균 수명 average life expectancy
수명이 길다 life expectancy is long
수명이 짧다 life expectancy is short
수명이/을 다하다 life expectancy has expired
수명을 연장하다 to lengthen life expectancy

[Example] 의료 기술의 발달은 인구 증가의 결정적 요인이 되었고, 또 평균 수명의 연장에 크게 이바지하였다.
The development of medical skills was a big contributor to the rise in population and the lengthening of life expectancy.

2. (of items and facilities, etc.) the period of use

[Expression] 수명이 길다 lifespan is long
수명이 짧다 lifespan is short
수명이/을 다하다 lifespan has expired

[Example] 신제품은 기존 제품보다 수명이 5년은 더 길다.
The new product has a lifespan that is five years longer than the existing product.

025
시도

[시도] attempt

trying something as an experiment

[Usage] N이/가 시도되다
N을/를 시도하다

[Expression] 시도를 꾀하다 to plan an attempt

[Example] 1958년에 국내에서 최초로 로켓 발사시험이 시도되었다.
In 1958, there was the first domestic attempt to launch a rocket.

우리는 문제를 해결하기 위해 여러 가지 방법을 시도해 보았으나 모두 헛수고였다.
In order to solve the problem, we attempted many different methods but it was all in vain.

026
시련

[시련] ordeal

extreme hardship

[Expression] 시련이 닥치다 ordeal approaches
시련을 겪다 to endure an ordeal
시련을 당하다 to undergo an ordeal
시련을 극복하다 to overcome an ordeal
시련에 부딪치다 to be faced with an ordeal

[Synonym] 고난 hardship
역경 adversity

[Example] 우리의 앞길에 어떠한 시련이 닥쳐도 이겨낼 수 있을 것이다.
No matter what ordeal approaches us in the future, I know that we can overcome it.

할머니의 얼굴은 많은 시련을 겪으며 살아온 듯 잔주름이 가득했다.
It seemed as though my grandmother suffered many ordeals because her face was full of fine wrinkles.

027
시설

[시설] facilities

large equipment or tools that were made so that many people could comfortably use it communally or made for people's convenience, also the work involved in creating the facilities

[Expression] 시설물 facilities
편의시설 amenities
오락시설 recreational facilities
교육시설 educational facilities
시설을 갖추다 to make preparations for facilities

[Example] 우리 병원은 최첨단의 시설과 기술을 자랑한다.
Our hospital has cutting edge facilities and skills that we are proud of.

그 건물은 주차시설뿐만 아니라 각종 편의시설을 갖추고 있어서 편리하다.
That building not only has a parking lot, but also has many other amenities that make it convenient.

028
안목

[안목] discerning eye

skill or knowledge that allows one to judge the worth of an object or distinguish it

[Expression] 안목이 있다 to have a discerning eye
안목이 높다 to have an experienced eye
안목이 뛰어나다 to have an excellent discerning eye
안목을 기르다 to develop a discerning eye
안목을 가지다 to have a discerning eye

[Example] 그림을 보는 그의 안목은 듣던 대로 탁월했다.
His eye for paintings was as excellent as I had heard.

뭔가 큰 결정을 내릴 때는 눈앞의 이익만 보지 말고 장기적인 안목으로 신중히 판단해야 한다.
When making a big decision, do not only look at the benefits that are right in front of you but decide from a long-term perspective.

029
안정[1]

[안정] stability

not changing and maintaining a constant state

[Usage] N이/가 안정되다
N을/를 안정시키다

[Expression] 안정세 remaining stable
물가 안정 stability of price
안정을 이루다 to achieve stability

[Antonym] 혼란 chaos

[Example] 거품이 빠진 부동산 경기가 안정을 되찾고 있다.
The bubble state of the real estate business is beginning to regain its stability.

정부에서는 가을에 쌀을 사들여 봄에 내놓음으로써 쌀값을 안정시키는 데 힘쓰고 있다.
The government is concentrating its efforts into buying rice in the fall and putting it out for sale in the spring in order to stabilize the price of rice.

030
안정²

[안정] tranquility

the ease and calm of the physical and mental aspect

[Usage] N을/를 안정시키다

[Expression] (신경)안정제 tranquilizer
안정하다 to become at ease
안정을 취하다 to have tranquility
마음의 안정을 잃다 to lose tranquility in one's mind

[Example] 응급실에 있는 저 환자는 절대적인 안정이 필요합니다.
That patient in the emergency room needs absolute tranquility.

시험 생각만 하면 마음이 안정되지 않아 잠을 이룰 수 없었다.
Because my heart was uneasy every time I thought about my exam, I was unable to sleep.

031
앨범

[앨범] 1. photo album 2. CD album

1. a book in which photos are posted in in order to order and preserve them; photo album

[Expression] 졸업 앨범 graduation album
결혼 앨범 wedding album
앨범을 펴다 to open the album

[Example] 그녀는 죽은 남편이 그리울 때면 앨범을 뒤적이곤 한다.
When she misses her dead husband, she browses through the photo album.

2. a place where one person's or a group's songs are gathered; CD album

[Expression] 가요 앨범 pop album
앨범을 내다 to make an album
앨범을 제작하다 to produce an album

[Example] 그들은 당분간 방송 활동을 중단하고 재충전의 시간을 가진 후 앨범 제작에 나설 계획이라고 한다.
They have stated that their plans include stopping their television appearances for now so that they can recharge and then work on producing an album.

032
엉망

[엉망] wreck

a state of unsettled disorder and resolution where a situation or object has become disheveled and mishmashed in a way that one cannot grasp the meaning

[Expression] 엉망진창 wreck
엉망으로 wrecked
엉망이다 to be a mess
엉망이 되다 to become a wreck

[Example] 일찍 내린 서리로 농사가 하루아침에 엉망이 되고 말았다.
Due to an early frost, the farming has become a wreck overnight.

건설 회사가 아파트 공사를 엉망으로 하는 바람에 이곳저곳에서 하자가 발생하자 주민들이 이 회사를 상대로 손해배상 청구소송을 제기했다.
The residents filed for an action for damages against the construction company that had built the apartment haphazardly once flaws began appearing here and there.

033
여건

[여껀] conditions

conditions that have been given from the beginning of a task

[Expression] 생활 여건 living conditions
경제적인 여건 economic conditions
여건이 허락하다 conditions permit
여건을 갖추다 to possess conditions
여건을 마련하다 to arrange conditions

[Example] 경제적 여건만 허락되면 공부를 계속 할 생각입니다.
If economic conditions permit, I am thinking about continuing my studies.

그는 어려운 여건 속에서도 좌절하지 않고 열심히 살았다.
Even in hard conditions, he was not breaking down and living diligently.

034
열의

[여리] enthusiasm

all the devotion you can muster into achieving something

[Usage] N에 대한 열의가 있다
N에 대한 열의가 높다
N에 대한 열의가 대단하다
N에 대한 열의를 보이다

[Example] 그는 학문에 대한 열의가 대단히 높은 사람이다.
He is someone who has an extremely high enthusiasm for learning.

똑똑한 사람이지만 일에 대한 열의가 없다는 게 큰 단점이다.
He is smart but his greatest flaw is that he has no enthusiasm for work.

035
예외

[예외] exception

something that is apart from the average; something that breaks free from common or customary rules

[Expression] 예외 규정 exception rules
예외적 현상 exceptional phenomena
예외적 상황 exceptional conditions
예외없이 without exception
예외로 처리하다 handle as an exception

[Example] 환경 문제는 선진국이나 후진국이나 예외가 있을 수 없다.
There should be no exception concerning environmental problems for either developed countries or underdeveloped countries.

농촌의 황폐화 바람은 이 지역도 예외로 남겨두지 않았다.
This area is not an exception to the trend of rural areas becoming desolated.

036
오염

[오염] pollution

the act of polluting or the state of being plluted

[Usage] N이/가 오염되다
N을/를 오염시키다

[Expression] 환경오염 environmental pollution
대기오염 air pollution
수질오염 water pollution
토양오염 ground pollution
오염물질 pollutant

[Example] 수질오염으로 인한 산소 부족으로 물고기가 떼죽음을 당했다.
Because of water pollution, fish suffered death en masse due to lack of oxygen.

오염물질을 대기 중으로 배출하는 업체는 의무적으로 공해 방지 시설을 갖춰야 한다.
Businesses that emit pollutants into the air are required to prepare pollution control facilities.

037
온라인

[온라인] online

the computer's terminal is connected with the central processing unit and a communication link and can send information, the state where the central processing unit is under direct control

[Expression] 온라인 행정 online administration
온라인 시스템 online system
온라인으로 송금하다 to wire money online

[Example] 요즈음에는 거의 모든 은행에 온라인 시설이 갖추어져 있어서 돈을 받을 사람의 통장 번호만 알면 쉽게 보낼 수 있다.
Nowadays, most banks have online facilities ready so that even if you only know the recipient's bank account number, you can easily send money.

저희가 추천하는 시스템을 구축하면 시간과 공간의 제약을 받지 않고 온라인으로 정보를 제공받을 수 있습니다.
If you establish the system that we recommend, you will not be restricted by space and time and can receive information online.

038
요구 [요구] 1. request 2. demand

1. requesting something because it is something that you need

[Usage] N이/가 요구되다
N을/를 요구하다

[Expression] 요구액 amount demanded
요구 사항 claims requested
요구 조건 terms requested

[Related Words] 청구 claim

[Example] 노동자들은 다음과 같은 요구 조건을 걸고 농성을 시작하였다.
The laborers had a sit-in concerning the following terms requested.

2. demanding for a certain behavior; also expectation of that behavior

[Usage] N이/가 요구되다
AV으라고 /라고 요구하다
N을/를 요구하다

[Expression] 요구서 written request
요구에 응하다to yield to demand

[Related Words] 요청 request

[Example] 경찰이 증인에게 목격한 것을 진술하라고 요구하였다.
The policeman demanded that the witness be truthful in what he saw.

039
운명1 [운명] destiny

including humans, a power that is inescapable and not only transcends all but controls all; also pre-determined life or circumstances

[Usage] AV을/ㄹ 운명이다
AV을/ㄹ 운명을 타고 나다

[Expression] 운명론 fatalism
운명의 장난 irony of fate
타고난 운명 inborn destiny

[Example] 사람이 늙어서 죽는 것은 피할 수 없는 운명이다.
It is inescapable destiny for a human to grow old and die.

둘은 곧 헤어져야만 할 운명이라는 사실을 잘 알고 있었다.
Both knew the truth that it was their destiny to part.

040
운명2 [운명] death

the end of a person's life

[Usage] N이/가 운명하다

[Example] 아버님께서는 운명하시기 전에 공평하게 유산을 배분해 주셨다.
Before my father met his fate, he divided his inheritance fairly.

그는 병원에서 임종하는 가족도 없이 간암으로 쓸쓸히 운명을 했다.
He met his lonely fate from liver cancer without even family visiting him on his deathbed.

041
위기

[위기] crisis

dangerous moment, risky moment

[Usage] N이/가 위기에 빠지다
N이/가 위기에 처하다

[Expression] 위기감 sense of crisis
위기를 넘기다 to pass a crisis
위기를 극복하다 to recover from a crisis

[Example] 그는 뛰어난 말재주로 위기를 모면할 수 있었다.
He was able to avoid crisis due to his gift with speaking.

금융 위기가 닥치자 우리 회사는 존폐의 위기에 처하게 되었다.
When we ran into financial crisis, our business was faced with the crisis of bankruptcy.

042
위협

[위협] threat

a warning that punishment or harm will follow if a certain thing is done or not done

[Usage] N을/를 위협하다
N에게 위협을 주다
N에게서 위협을 받다
N에게서 위협을 당하다

[Example] 대기 오염의 심화로 인간의 생존이 위협을 받고 있다.
Due to the intensification of air pollution, there is a threat to human survival.

미세 먼지는 눈에 보이지 않지만 우리의 건강을 위협하는 것이므로 집안 곳곳을 걸레로 자주 닦는 것이 좋다.
Fine dust is not visible to the naked eye but because it is a threat to our health, it is good to clean with a rag in all areas of the home.

043
유전

[유전] heredity

phenomena where physical and psychological characteristics are passed onto the next generation

[Usage] N이/가 N에게 유전되다
N이/가 N에게 유전하다

[Expression] 유전자 gene
유전병 hereditary disease
유전 공학 genetic engineering

[Example] 현장에 남겨진 혈흔의 유전자를 감식하여 범인을 찾았다.
The culprit was caught by identifying the genes in the bloodstain left at the scene.

생물의 변이가 자손에게 유전한다고 가정해야 진화를 설명할 수 있다.
One must assume that changes in organisms are hereditary in order to explain evolution.

044
장르

[장르] 1. genre 2. genre

1. foreign word meaning area or division; variety or category

[Example] 이번 음악제는 오페라, 교향곡 등 다양한 장르의 작품이 연주될 예정이다.
At this music festival, various genres of works are going to be played such as opera, symphonies, etc.

2. traits in literary works that divide them into varieties like poems, novels, essays, plays, critiques, children's poems, and children's stories

[Example] 이 작가는 시, 소설, 희곡 등 장르를 불문하고 다양한 작품들을 내놓고 있다.
This author is putting out many different works regardless of genres like poems, novels, and plays.

045
재충전

[재충전] recharge

when an electric condenser accumulates electrical energy again or also metaphorically means the power or skills accumulated or renewed from a break

[Expression] 재충전을 하다 to recharge
재충전의 시간을 갖다 to have time to recharge

[Example] 재충전할 수 있는 배터리들은 보통 전자 제품에 사용되는데 특히 휴대용 기기에 흔히 사용된다.
Rechargeable batteries are commonly used in consumer electronics, especially portable devices.

새해 첫 평가전을 치룬 축구 대표팀은 며칠 동안 쉬면서 재충전에 들어갔습니다.
The Korean national soccer team is resting for a few days in order to recharge after playing their first warm-up match of the year.

05 연습문제

[1-10] 다음 (　　　)에 알맞은 것을 고르십시오.

Choose the word that fits best in the parenthesis.

1. 눈앞의 이익만 보지 말고 장기적인 (　　　)으로/로 신중히 판단해야 한다.

❶ 분석　　❷ 안목　　❸ 의도　　❹ 시야

2. 남북분단은 한국 사람들에게 엄청난 (　　　)을/를 가져다주었다.

❶ 시련　　❷ 소신　　❸ 상황　　❹ 비난

3. 우리나라 소비자가 인터넷을 통한 상품 구매 (　　　)이/가 세계적으로 매우 높다는 설문 조사 결과가 나왔다.

❶ 형편　　❷ 성향　　❸ 안목　　❹ 가치관

4. 태권도 관계자들은 태권도를 전 세계에 (　　　)하기 위해 애쓰고 있다.

❶ 시도　　❷ 설립　　❸ 가입　　❹ 보급

5. 정부는 이번 홍수로 농부들이 입은 피해에 대하여 가구당 천만 원 씩 (　　　)해 주기로 결정했다.

❶ 비난　　❷ 선정　　❸ 보상　　❹ 요구

6. 나는 논문을 쓰기 위해 그 작가의 작품을 세밀하게 연구하고 (　　　)하였다.

❶ 해결　　❷ 판결　　❸ 분석　　❹ 시도

7. 아버지가 돌아가신 후 어머니의 적은 수입으로 어렵게 (　　　)을/를 이어가고 있다.

❶ 생계　　❷ 생활　　❸ 생명　　❹ 현실

8. 한국 음식은 무조건 다 매울 거라는 (　　　)을/를 가진 외국인들이 적지 않다.

❶ 관념　　❷ 선입견　　❸ 철학　　❹ 이론

9. 이제 우리는 고령화 사회에 걸맞게 노인들을 (　　　)하는 사회 환경을 만들어 나가야 한다.

❶ 격려　❷ 배려　❸ 배출　❹ 요구

10. 나는 어떤 고난이 닥쳐도 내 (　　　)을/를 굽히지 않겠다.

❶ 자부심　❷ 결정　❸ 마음　❹ 소신

[11-13] 다음 (　　　)에 들어갈 말로 알맞지 않은 것을 고르십시오.

Choose the word that does not fit in the parenthesis.

11. 헬렌 켈러는 불굴의 정신으로 (　　　)을/를 극복하여 전 세계 장애인들에게 희망을 주었고, 다양한 활동으로 '빛의 천사'로도 불렸다.

❶ 장애　❷ 시련　❸ 한계　❹ 여건

12. 그 회사는 기술력이 (　　　)하여 제품개발에 실패했다.

❶ 가난　❷ 부족　❸ 빈곤　❹ 빈약

13. 수원 화성은 1997년에 세계문화유산으로 (　　　)되었다.

❶ 등록　❷ 지정　❸ 선정　❹ 지시

[14-17] 다음 밑줄 친 부분과 의미가 비슷한 것을 고르십시오.

Choose the word that is similar to the underlined word.

14. 살인 누명을 쓰고 10년 동안이나 억울하게 감옥살이를 했던 사람이 국가에 손해배상을 요구했다.

❶ 문의　❷ 갈구　❸ 청구　❹ 신청

15. 이 장학재단은 돌아가신 회장님의 유언에 따라 1995년에 설립됐다.

❶ 세워지다　❷ 생산되다　❸ 제시되다　❹ 건설되다

16. 엄청난 양의 공장 폐수가 정화되지 않은 채 강으로 배출되고 있다.

❶ 흘러가다 ❷ 버려지다 ❸ 유출되다 ❹ 내보내지다

17. 아직 시골에서는 오염되지 않은 신선한 공기를 마실 수 있다.

❶ 정화되다 ❷ 더러워지다 ❸ 물들다 ❹ 규제되다

[18-19] 다음 밑줄 친 부분이 잘못된 것을 고르십시오.

Choose the underlined word that is used incorrectly.

18.

❶ 사람이 늙어서 죽는 것은 피할 수 없는 운명이다.
❷ 핵무기는 인류의 안전에 큰 위협이 아닐 수 없다.
❸ 십중팔구라는 말은 열에 여덟이나 아홉 정도로 거의 예외가 없음을 뜻한다.
❹ 영국의 한 연구소에서 동물의 복사 실험에 성공해 인간의 질병을 치료할 수 있는 가능성을 열었다.

19.

❶ 그는 바쁘다는 핑계로 방을 엉망으로 해 놓고 다녔다.
❷ 우리 팀은 연패를 기록하여 예선 탈락의 위기에 놓이게 되었다.
❸ 둥지를 벗어난 아기 새는 몇 번의 시도 끝에 하늘로 날아올랐다.
❹ 민수는 그녀에게 강한 열의를 느꼈지만 차마 표현은 못하고 있다.

[20-21] 다음 중 제시된 술어를 공통으로 사용할 수 있는 것을 고르십시오.

Choose one word that can be used for all of the given verbs.

20.

하다	당하다	받다

❶ 비난 ❷ 시련 ❸ 오염 ❹ 시도

21.

있다	높다	뛰어나다	기르다

❶ 체력 ❷ 재력 ❸ 안목 ❹ 생명력

[22-23] 다음 중 제시된 술어를 사용할 수 없는 것을 고르십시오.

Choose one word that cannot be used with the given verb.

22.

갖추다

❶ 여건 ❷ 자격 ❸ 생계 ❹ 시설

23.

시키다

❶ 오염 ❷ 배출 ❸ 요구 ❹ 보급

[24-26] 다음 밑줄 친 부분과 의미가 반대인 것을 고르십시오

Choose the word that has the opposite meaning from the underlined word.

24. 유럽 국가들은 각국의 경제권을 <u>통합</u>하여 강대국의 경제적 위협을 견제하고자 했다.

❶ 흡수 ❷ 분리 ❸ 정리 ❹ 분석

25. 모든 사람이 그를 이구동성으로 <u>칭찬</u>한다.

❶ 배려 ❷ 보상 ❸ 위협 ❹ 비난

26. 요즘 학원에 보내거나 과외를 시키는 부모들이 늘어감에 따라 사교육에 드는 비용도 점점 증가하고 있다.

❶ 공교육 ❷ 수업 ❸ 상담 ❹ 학원

[27-32] 다음 ( )에 공통적으로 들어갈 단어를 쓰십시오.

Find the one word that fits in the parentheses.

27.

❶ 뜻밖의 일이 한 사람의 ( )을/를 뒤바꿀 수도 있다.
❷ 삼촌은 모든 것이 사람의 노력과 관계없이 ( )에/에게 달려 있다고 생각하는 사람이다.

28.

❶ 아직도 세계 곳곳에는 평화와 ( )을/를 위협하는 요인들이 도사리고 있다.
❷ 이번 국무회의에서는 치솟는 물가를 잡기 위해 물가 ( )을/를 당면 과제로 다루었다.

29.

❶ 신생 독립 국가들은 경제가 발전하지 못해서 ( )에 허덕이고 있다.
❷ 모임이 있을 때마다 화제의 ( )으로/로 대화가 잘 이루어지지 않는다.
❸ 현대인은 옛날 사람들에 비해 물질적으로는 풍요하지만 정신적으로는 무척 ( )하다.

30.

❶ 봉사 활동은 힘이 드는 반면에 ( )을/를 느낄 수 있다.
❷ 누구든지 자기의 삶에서 뜻과 ( )을/를 찾을 수 있어야 한다.
❸ 두 시간이나 기다린 ( )도 없이 사장과는 면접도 못하고 사무실에서 쫓겨나고 말았다.

31.

❶ 요즘 운동선수들의 약물 복용 (　　)이/가 늘고 있다.
❷ 이런 (　　)은/는 없었기 때문에 어떻게 처리해야 할지 모르겠다.
❸ 여행객들이 귀금속을 몰래 국내에 반입하는 (　　)이/가 해마다 늘고 있다.
❹ 업체들이 경비 절감을 이유로 폐수와 매연을 불법 배출하는 (　　)이/가 적지 않다.

32.

❶ 플라스틱 제품은 (　　)이/가 반영구적이다.
❷ 의학 기술의 발달로 인간의 평균 (　　)이/가 늘어났다.
❸ 모든 기계는 험하게 사용할수록 (　　)이/가 짧아지는 법이다.
❹ 이 세탁기 개발자의 말에 따르면 새로 나온 이 세탁기는 기존의 제품보다 (　　)이/가 5년 쯤 더 길 거라고 한다.

명사 Ⅲ

06

Nouns Ⅲ

06 명사 Ⅲ

001
재테크 [재테크] financial technology

a shortened phrase of 'financial affairs technology,' it is when a business or a person embarks on certain financial activities so that they can receive financial profit

[Expression] 재테크를 하다 to do financial technology
재테크에 능하다 to be skillful in financial technology

[Example] 재테크의 3대 원칙은 안정성, 수익성, 유동성이다.
The three fundamental rules of financial technology are stability, gains, and circulation.

이번 세미나는 부동산 등 재테크시장의 전망을 알아보고 올바른 투자전략을 어떻게 세울지 모색해 보는 기회가 될 것이다.
This seminar will be a chance to get a feel for the correct strategies for investing and also to gain an outlook on the real estate and financial technology markets.

002
재활용 [재화룡] recycle

taking wastes and changing the use or recycling and reusing them

[Usage] N을/를 N으로/로 재활용하다
N이/가 N으로/로 재활용되다

[Expression] 재활용품 recyclables

[Example] 폐휴지를 재활용해서 공책과 신문 등을 만들기도 한다.
They recycle used papers to make notebooks, newspapers, etc.

플라스틱 통과 우유 곽을 재활용해서 장난감을 만들었다.
We took plastic containers and milk cartons and recycled them to make toys.

003
쟁점 [쟁쩜] issue

matters or field that is at the center of a dispute

[Expression] 주요쟁점 major issue
최대의 쟁점 largest issue
정치적 쟁점 political issue
쟁점으로 떠오르다 to come up as an issue
쟁점으로 부각되다 to become a negative issue

[Example] 이 문제는 사회과학 전반에서 하나의 쟁점으로서 계속 논쟁의 대상이 되어 왔다.
This problem has constantly been an object of dispute in the top half of issues in social science.

노사 양측은 지금까지 쟁점이 되었던 문제들을 건설적으로 해결해 나가기로 했다.
Labor and management have decided to go about solving the issues that been a problem up until now, in a constructive way.

004
적성

[적썽] aptitude

temperament or adaptive skills suitable for a certain task; also the same character or personality

[Expression] 적성검사 aptitude test
적성에 맞다 to match with one's temperament
적성을 살리다 to utilize one's aptitude

[Example] 자동차 운전이 그의 적성에 딱 맞는 일이었다.
Driving cars is a perfect fit for his temperament.

대학에 진학할 때는 자신의 적성에 맞는 전공과를 선택해야 한다.
When entering college, you must choose a major that fits with your temperament.

005
전략

[절략] 1. strategy 2. tactic

1. a means or a plan for achieving a goal in war

[Expression] 전략적 후퇴 strategic retreat
전략적 요충지 strategic location
전략적 가치 strategic worth
전략을 짜다 to organize a strategy
전략을 꾸미다 to plan a strategy

[Example] 전쟁에서 이기고 지는 것은 전략을 얼마나 잘 세우냐에 달려 있다.
Whether you win or lose in a war depends on how well you strategize.

2. a means or a plan to achieve a certain task

[Expression] 판매 전략 sales tactic
전략 상품 strategic product
전략을 펴다 to construct a strategy
전략을 세우다 to build a strategy

[Example] 우리 회사는 제품을 연령층에 따라 다원화하는 판매 전략을 새로 세웠다.
Our business built a new sales strategy focusing on pluralizing products according to age brackets.

006
전망

[전망] 1.view 2. forecast

1. landscape that you can see in the distance

[Expression] 전망대 observatory
전망이 좋다 view is nice
전망이 좋지 않다 view is not nice

[Example] 그 아파트는 큰 건물이 앞을 가리고 있어 전망이 좋지 않다.
Because a big building is in front of that apartment, the view is not good.

2. looking forward into the future

[Usage] N이/가 N으로/로 전망되다
N이/가 N을/를 전망하다

[Expression] 전망이 밝다 future is bright
전망이 어둡다 forecast is gloomy
전망을 살피다 to examine the forecast

[Example] 한국의 국제 수지 전망은 무조건 낙관할 수만은 없다.
Korea's forecast in international revenue and expenditure cannot always be looked upon optimistically.

007
제약

[제약] restriction

restricting by adding conditions to content

[Expression] 제약이 있다 to have a restriction
제약이 많다 to have many restrictions
제약을 하다 to restrict
제약을 받다 to receive restrictions
제약을 가하다 to restrict

[Example] 각국의 보호무역으로 수출에 제약이 많다.
There are many restrictions on exports because of many countries' protective trade.

단체 생활에는 여러 가지 제약이 있기 마련이다.
There are bound to be many restrictions when living in a group.

008
좌절

[좌절] frustration

when goals or energy is broken; also when certain plans or matters do not happen and everything was in vain

[Usage] N이/가 좌절당하다
N이/가 N을/를 좌절시키다

[Expression] 좌절감 sense of frustration
좌절하다 to be frustrated
좌절을 겪다 to endure frustration

[Example] 좌절을 이겨나가는 사람이 인생의 승리자라는 것을 명심해야 한다.
Bear in mind that someone who overcomes frustration is a winner in life.

아버지께서는 경기 침체로 인한 사업의 좌절로 큰 충격을 받으셨다.
My father received a huge shock after the failure of his business due to the economic recession.

009
중독

[중독] 1. poisoning 2. addiction

1. when your life is in danger or there are bad changes in the body due to drugs or poisonous substances

[Usage] N에 중독되다
N이/가 중독을 일으키다

[Example] 구내식당에서 돼지고기를 먹은 사람들이 집단 중독 상태에 빠졌다.
All of the people who ate the pork at the cafeteria on the grounds were mass poisoned.

2. a chronic sickly state when you continue to drink or take alcohol or drugs to the extreme, that you can no longer live or function without it

[Usage] N에 중독되다

[Expression] 중독자 an addict
마약 중독 drug addiction
카페인 중독 caffeine addiction
알코올 중독 alcohol addiction

[Example] 그는 날마다 술을 마시더니 알코올 중독이 되고 말았다.
After drinking alcohol everyday, he eventually became an alcohol addict.

010
지름길

[지름낄] 1. shortcut 2. shortcut

1. a path where you don't have to all the way around and can cut across

[Expression] 지름길로 가다 to take a shortcut
지름길을 이용하여 가다 to use a shortcut to go

[Example] 우리는 가까운 지름길을 놔두고 다른 길로 돌아갔다.
We passed the shortcut closest to us and instead took a different path.

2. a way to achieve something quickly and easily

[Expression] 출세의 지름길 shortcut to advancement
성공의 지름길 shortcut to success

[Synonym] 첩경 shortcut

[Example] 실업 사태를 해결할 수 있는 지름길은 중소기업을 육성하는 것이다.
A shortcut to solving the unemployment situation is promoting small and medium businesses.

011
지원[1]

[지원] support

helping psychologically, materially, or through actions

[Usage] N이/가 지원되다
N을/를 지원하다

[Expression] 지원금 support fund
지원이 끊기다 support is cut off
지원을 아끼지 않다 to be not thrifty with support

[Example] 실업자에 대한 제도적 지원이 필요하다.
There must be institutional support towards unemployment.

정부는 건실한 중소기업에 운영 자금을 지원하기로 하였다.
The government decided to support with working funds for honest and hard working small and medium businesses.

012
지원[2]

[지원] application

hoping and wanting to join a certain work or organization

[Usage] N이/가 N에 지원하다

[Expression] 지원병 volunteer
지원서 application
지원자 applicant

[Example] 회사 지원 자격을 고졸 이상으로 한정하였다.
The business limited the application qualification to above a high school diploma.

내 친구는 교사의 길을 걷겠다며 교대에 지원했다.
My friend wanted to walk the path of a teacher and so applied for Education University.

013
지지

[지지] 1. support 2. support

1. (another person's thoughts) believing that they are right and take their side or help them

[Usage] N을/를 지지하다

[Expression] 지지자 supporter
지지를 받다 to receive support
지지를 얻다 to gain support

[Example] 조합원들은 조합장의 연설을 듣고 열광적인 박수로써 그에 대한 지지를 나타냈다.
The union members showed their support through their enthusiastic applause after hearing the union president's speech.

2. being on the receiving end; supporting a large object

[Usage] N이/가 지지되다
N을/를 지지하다

[Example] 지진 때문에 그 건물을 지지하던 기둥들이 넘어지게 되어 건물이 모두 무너졌다.
The columns supporting that building fell after the earthquake, causing the whole building to collapse.

014
짐작

[짐작] assumption

making a rough estimate about circumstances or conditions

[Expression] 짐작하다 to make an assumption
짐작이 가다 to be able to make an assumption
짐작이 들다 to have an assumption

[Related Words] 추측 speculation
추정 presumption

[Example] 그가 나를 속이고 도망갈 줄은 짐작조차 못했다.
I could never assume that he would lie to me and run away.

경찰은 그를 이번 사건의 범인으로 짐작하고 있는 듯하다.
It seems that the police are assuming that he is the criminal in this crime.

015
찌꺼기

[찌꺼기] 1. sediment 2. remainder

1. things leftover on the ground after the liquid has drained away

[Example] 한약을 짜고 난 찌꺼기를 거름으로 쓰면 식물이 잘 자란다.
If you use the sediments leftover from squeezing out oriental medicine as manure, plants grow well.

2. the remainder after things that are useful or valuable have been already picked out

[Expression] 음식물 찌꺼기 food scraps
기름 찌꺼기 oil sludge

[Example] 날씨가 더워지자 음식 찌꺼기가 썩으면서 악취를 뿜어내기 시작하였다.
As the weather got hotter, the food scraps began to emit a foul odor as they rotted.

016
차원

[차원] level

the basics for entrance for a certain task or thoughts also the degree or level

[Expression] 개인적 차원 personal level
사회적 차원 social level
국가적 차원 national level
차원이 높다 level is high
차원이 다르다 level is different

[Example] 환경오염을 줄이기 위해서는 개개인의 노력도 필요하지만 국가 차원의 정책도 마련되어야 한다.
In order to reduce environmental pollution, the efforts of an individual is needed but national level policies need to be arranged.

생활고를 비관하여 자살하는 사람들의 문제를 개인적 차원의 문제로만 볼 게 아니라 사회 구조적 차원에서의 접근도 필요하다.
Those who commit suicide due to pessimism from hardships must not only be viewed on an individual level but also needs to be approached on a social and structural level.

017
체험

[체험] experience

undergoing something personally; also a similar happening

[Expression] 체험 수기 experience log
체험을 하다 to experience something
체험을 쌓다 to build experience
체험을 살리다 to utilize one's experience

[Example] 이 책은 저자 자신의 체험을 그대로 쓴 것이다.
The author wrote this book exactly based on his personal experiences.

전쟁을 체험한 세대는 전쟁이 얼마나 무서운지 잘 안다.
The generation who experienced war, knows how scary war is.

018
추세

[추세] trend

the tendency for a certain phenomenon to go towards one, fixed direction

[Usage] N 추세를 보이다

[Expression] 증가 추세 increasing trend
세계적 추세 global trend
일반적 추세 general trend
추세를 따르다 to follow the trend

[Example] 결혼을 늦게 하는 것이 요즘의 추세이다.
Marrying late is the trend lately.

올 들어 수출은 계속 증가 추세를 보이고 있다.
There seems to be an increasing trend in exportation.

019
측면

[측면] side

profile; one part or one side of an object or phenomenon

[Expression] 긍정적 측면 positive side
교육적 측면 educational side
실용적 측면 practical side

장기적인 측면 long-term side
측면을 공격하다 to attack the side

[Example] 이번 골은 측면 돌파에 의한 멋진 골이었습니다.
This goal was an amazing goal due to a breakthrough on the side.

너무 한 쪽 측면만 보지 마시고 전체를 봐 주시기 바랍니다.
Please do not only view one side but look at the whole instead.

020
칼럼

[칼럼] column

text written by various experts about their thoughts on current events or customs in society that are in newspapers, magazines, etc.

[Expression] 시사 칼럼 current events column
칼럼니스트 columnist
칼럼을 쓰다 to write a column
칼럼을 기고하다 to contribute to a column

[Example] 나는 신문의 시사 칼럼을 즐겨 읽는다.
I enjoy reading the current events column in the newspaper.

그 칼럼은 어느 기사보다도 주목도가 높고 영향력이 큰 칼럼이다.
That column is a column that is paid attention to and has more influence than any other article.

021
캠페인

[캠페인] campaign

a organizational movement that unfolds continuously with the public as the target

[Expression] 자연보호 캠페인 nature conservation campaign
캠페인을 벌이다 to begin a campaign
캠페인을 전개하다 to spread out a campaign

[Example] 청소년 보호 단체가 폭력 추방 캠페인을 벌이고 있다.
The adolescent protection organization is beginning a campaign to eliminate violence.

여러 단체가 음주 운전 퇴치 캠페인을 펼친 후 음주 운전 사망자가 상당히 줄어들었다.
After many organizations started campaigns to exterminate drunk driving, the death rate from drunk driving has gone down significantly.

022
클럽

[클럽] 1. club 2. club

1. an organization created for hobbies or to create friendships

[Expression] 사교 클럽 social club
봉사 클럽 volunteering club
독신자 클럽 singles club

클럽을 만들다 to make a club
클럽 활동에 참가하다 to participate in club activities

[Example] 이번 클럽 대항 축구 대회에는 50개 클럽이 참가했다.
50 clubs participated in this soccer competition.

2. a place where an organization formed for hobbies or to create friendships can meet

[Expression] 헬스클럽 health club
나이트클럽 night club
클럽에 모이다 to gather at a club

[Example] 나는 요즘 살도 뺄 겸 체력도 기를 겸 집 근처의 헬스클럽에 열심히 운동하러 다닌다.
Lately I've been eagerly going to a health club near my house in order to lose weight and train my fitness.

023
탓

[탇] 1. fault 2. blame

1. a reason or cause for a usually negative phenomena

[Example] 남편은 회사일로 며칠 무리를 한 탓에 과로로 눕고 말았다.
Being forced to work too much during a couple of days caused my husband to fall ill from overwork.

2. using an excuse or pretext to resent or rebuke

[Usage] **N**탓이다
N을/를 탓하다
N탓으로 돌리다

[Example] 어머니는 형과 내가 싸우면 항상 내 탓으로 돌리신다.
When my older brother and I fight, my mother always turns the blame onto me.

024
투기

[투기] speculation

investing one's money at one time and risking danger because one wants to gain a bit profit

[Expression] 투기꾼 speculator
투기과열지구 speculation areas
투기를 하다 to speculate

[Example] 아파트 재개발은 부동산 투기를 조장하는 부작용을 낳았다.
The redevelopment of apartments gave birth to side effects that aggravated real estate speculation.

투기가 투자와 다른 점은 기회를 틈타 부당한 방법으로 큰 이익을 보려고 한다는 점이다.
The difference between speculation and investment is trying to gain a large profit from seizing an opportunity by using unjust ways.

025
투자

[투자] 1. investment 2. investment

1. putting money in advance into a business in order to gain profit

[Usage] N에 N을/를 투자하다

[Expression] 투자자 investor

투자비 investment fee

주식 투자 investment in stocks

[Example] 지금 여러 나라에서 우주 연구에 막대한 연구비를 투자하고 있다.
Many nations are investing enormous amounts of research money into space research.

2. putting in time, effort, or money into something that might create profit

[Usage] N에 N을/를 투자하다

[Example] 최근에는 자녀들의 교육에 엄청난 투자를 하는 사람이 많아졌다.
Recently, there have been many people who invest massive amounts of money to their children's education.

026
틀

[틀] 1. mold 2. frame 3. formality

1. an object that is a guide to making a cast or board

[Expression] 틀로 찍다 to imprint with a mold

틀에 넣다 to put inside a mold

[Example] 어머니는 밀가루 반죽을 틀에 넣어 과자를 구워내셨다.
My mother put the flour dough into the mold and baked some crackers.

2. something that is the border of an object or the structure of an object

[Expression] 창틀 window frame

사진틀 picture frame

틀을 짜다 to make a frame

[Example] 뒷문 윗벽에 걸린 두 개의 사진틀이 장식물의 전부였다.
The two picture frames hung above the door were the only decorations.

3. (in society) a continuous formality or convention. limited structure

[Expression] 틀이 잡히다 to settle into shape

틀을 잡다 to grasp the formality

틀에 맞추다 to adjust to the formality

틀에 갇히다 to be trapped in formality

틀에 박히다 to be stuck in the formality

[Example] 친구와 둘이서 시작한 회사가 이제는 제법 틀이 잡혔다.
The business I started with my friend has now settled into shape.

027
틈

[틈] 1. crack 2. spare time 3. gap 4. chance 5. among the crowd

1. space created from an opening

[Expression] 틈이 생기다 to have a crack form

[Example] 창문 틈으로 햇빛이 들어오고 있다.
Through the window crack, sunshine is coming in.

2. time to spare; time

[Expression] 틈이 있다 to have spare time
틈이 없다 to not have spare time
틈이 나다 to gain time
틈을 내다 to make time

[Example] 그는 틈만 나면 손톱을 깨무는 버릇이 있다.
He has a habit of biting his nails when he has time.

3. (in people's relationships) gap is formed

[Expression] 틈이 생기다 to have a gap form
틈이 벌어지다 to have a gap grow larger

[Example] 여태껏 가깝게 지내던 두 사람 사이에 틈이 벌어지기 시작했다.
The two people who were friendly until now, have had a gap forming in between them.

4. a chance to do a certain action

[Expression] 틈을 타다 to seize an opportunity
틈을 노리다 to watch for a chance
틈을 엿보다 to peek for a chance

[Example] 한 죄수가 감시가 소홀한 틈을 타 도망쳤다.
A prisoner watched for a chance when the surveillance was careless and escaped.

5. inside a crowd

[Expression] 틈에 끼다 to be among the crowd

[Example] 어른들도 아이들 틈에 끼어 인형극을 구경했다.
Adults also joined in the mob of children to watch the puppet play.

028
티[1]

[티] 1. speck 2. flaw

1. an extremely small crumb like dust

[Example] 아이가 눈에 티가 들어갔는지 눈을 계속 깜빡거리고 있었다.
The child blinked as if a small speck was in his eye.

[Related Words] 티끌 speck

2. a small flaw or something trivial

[Expression] 옥에 티
a flaw in the crystal: a phrase where something that is so excellent that no one can rebuke it has a small flaw

[Example] 요즈음에는 기술이 날로 발전해서 얼굴의 티나 흠집 같은 것은 물론 얼굴의 윤곽까지도 마음대로 고칠 수가 있다.
Because techniques are advancing every day, not only can you fix flaws or scratches on the face, but you can also fix the outline of your face freely.

029
티²

[티] look

a certain attitude or expression

[Expression] 촌티 being unsophisticated
어른 티 looking grown up
티가 나다 to have a look
티를 내다 to show a look
티를 벗다 to grow out of a look

[Example] 영수는 몸이 아파도 좀처럼 티를 내지 않는다.
Even though Youngsoo is sick, he hardly looks it.

그 소년은 키는 어른만 하지만 목소리는 아직 어린 티를 벗지 못하고 있다.
That boy is an adult in height but his voice has yet to change out of a child's voice.

030
파견

[파견] dispatch

sending a person who has been given a continuous duty

[Usage] N이/가 N으로/로 파견되다
N을/를 N으로/로 파견하다

[Expression] 파견대 dispatch force
파견 근무 dispatch duty

[Example] 그 사람들은 우리 회사에서 파견한 해외 근로자들이다.
These people are international workers dispatched from our office.

이 문제의 협상을 위해 그 나라로 사절단을 파견하는 것은 현 단계에서는 시기상조이다.
The timing is not yet right to dispatch that nation's delegation in order to negotiate this problem.

031
파괴

[파괴] 1. demolition 2. destruction

1. demolishing something by hitting or breaking it down

[Usage] N이/가 파괴되다
N을/을 파괴하다
N을/를 파괴시키다

[Expression] 파괴력 destructive power

[Antonym] 건설 construction

[Example] 온 나라가 지진으로 파괴된 도시를 복구하는 데 총력을 기울였다.
All energy was focused on restoring cities all over the nation which had been demolished by the earthquake.

2. collapsing or destroying an organization, order, or relationships

[Usage] N이/가 파괴되다
N을/를 파괴하다
N을/를 파괴시키다

[Expression] 파괴력 destructive power
파괴자 destroyer

[Example] 전쟁은 인간의 감정을 황폐화시켜서 인간성을 파괴해 버린다.
War ruins human feelings and destroys humanity.

032
편견

[편견] bias

thoughts that lean to one side, are not objective, and not fair

[Expression] 편견이 심하다 to have a strong bias
편견을 가지다 to be biased
편견을 버리다 to throw away one's biases
편견에 사로잡히다 to be caught by one's bias
편견에서 벗어나다 to break free from biases

[Example] 그 영화는 흑인들을 아주 야만적으로 묘사해 인종적 편견을 드러내었다.
That film showed a ethnic bias through its portrayal of Africans as uncivilized people.

지역감정이란 일정한 지역에 살고 있거나 그 지역 출신의 사람들에게 가지는 좋지 않은 생각이나 편견을 말한다.
Regionalism is a thought or a bias about people who live or are from a certain area.

033
폐쇄

[폐쇄] 1. closing 2. closure

1. closing something that was open or blocking something that was accessible

[Usage] N이/가 폐쇄되다
N을/를 폐쇄하다
N을/를 폐쇄시키다

[Antonym] 개방 opening

[Example] 회사 측의 작업장 폐쇄로 노조원들은 집회를 가질 수가 없었다.
Because the business closed the workplace, the union members were unable to have an assembly.

2. ending an exchange with the outside

[Usage] N이/가 폐쇄되다
N을/를 폐쇄하다
N을/를 폐쇄시키다

[Expression] 폐쇄성 isolation
폐쇄적이다 to be closed off

[Antonym] 개방 opening

[Example] 그 나라는 패쇄성이 강해서 그 나라 국민들의 대부분은 국제 정세에 대해 어두웠다.
Because that nation is extremely isolated, the majority of citizens are in the dark about international state of affairs.

034
피해

[피해] damage

damaging to life, body, wealth, or honor

[Expression] 피해자 victim
피해액 damage (money)
피해를 입다 to suffer damage
피해를 보다 to suffer damage
피해를 주다 to cause damage

[Antonym] 가해 doing harm

[Related Words] 손해 loss

[Example] 이번 비행기 추락으로 많은 인명 피해가 발생했다.
Due to the airplane crashing, there was a loss of many people.

경찰은 화재 원인을 방화로 보고 재산 피해액을 약 수천만 원으로 추산했다.
The police saw that the cause of the fire was arson and estimated the damages to be around tens of millions of won.

035
핑계

[핑계] excuse

avoiding a situation that you are reluctant about or using a different situation to block and hide the truth, or telling a feeble excuse by spinning words about something one has done wrong

[Expression] 핑계삼다 to use as an excuse
핑계를 대다 to state an excuse

[Related Words] 구실 pretense
변명 excuse

[Example] 그는 바쁘다는 핑계로 모임에 참석하지 않았다.
He used the excuse that he was busy and did not participate in the meeting.

발표자는 곤란한 질문을 받으면 적당한 핑계를 대고 대답을 하지 않았다.
The presenter stated an appropriate excuse and did not answer when he received difficult questions.

036
허용

[허용] 1. permission 2. allowance

1. consenting and accepting something

[Usage] N이/가 허용되다
N을/를 허용하다

[Antonym] 금지 prohibition

[Related Words] 허락 permission

[Example] 이 거리는 차량 통행은 안 되고 보행만이 허용되는 번화가이다.
This street is a bustling street where cars are not allowed and only walking is permitted.

2. (usually in various matches) the action one cannot block what they need to block and instead receives a blow

[Usage] N이/가 허용되다
N을/를 허용하다

[Example] 축구 결승전에서 우리 팀은 아깝게도 경기 종료 3분 전에 동점 골을 허용하고 말았다.
In the final match in soccer, our team unfortunately allowed a score-tying goal in the last three minutes of the game.

037
현상[1]

[현상] phenomenon

an object's shape and condition that a human can perceive

[Expression] 노화 현상 symptom of senility
황사 현상 yellow dust phenomena
생리적인 현상 physiological phenomena

현상이 나타나다 phenomenon appears
현상이 일어나다 phenomenon occurs

[Example] 농촌 사회에서는 고령화 현상이 더욱 두드러지고 있다.
In farming societies, the aging phenomenon is becoming more prominent.

이 지점은 두 개 차선으로 줄어드는 곳으로 병목 현상이 심하다.
The spot where the two car lanes become smaller is severely effected by the bottleneck phenomenon.

038
현상² [현상] present situation

current situation; present circumstances

[Expression] 현상을 극복하다 to recover from present situation
현상을 유지하다 to maintain present situation
현상을 파악하다 to understand the situation

[Example] 지금 같은 불경기에는 현상을 유지하는 것만도 힘이 든다.
In this sort of depression, maintaining even the present situation is hard.

관객이 많아야 백 명 정도였으니 악극단의 현상 유지는커녕 단원들의 끼니마저 걱정할 형편이었다.
When the audience was only around one hundred people, the musical troupe's concern was not about maintaining their present situation but worrying about their next meal.

039
협력 [혐녁] collaboration

combining strengths and helping each other

[Expression] 협력자 collaborator
협력 관계 cooperative relations
협력하다 to cooperate
협력을 구하다 to seek for cooperation
협력을 요청하다 to request cooperation

[Related Words] 협동 cooperation

[Example] 두 정상은 양국 간 경제 교류 협력 방안을 모색했다.
The leaders of the two nations began groping for plans to collaboration on economic exchange.

직원들이 모두 협력해서 열심히 일해야 회사가 발전할 수 있다.
All workers must collaborate and work hard so that the business can prosper.

040
혜택

[혜택] benefit

profit or help given to people by social institutions or businesses

[Expression] 할인 혜택 discount benefit
문명의 혜택 civilization's benefits
혜택을 받다 to receive benefits
혜택을 주다 to give benefits
혜택을 누리다 to enjoy benefits

[Example] 우리는 과학의 발달로 인해 많은 문명의 혜택을 누리고 있다.
We are enjoying many of civilization's benefits due to the advancement of science.

훈민정음의 창제로 양반층이 독점해 온 문자의 혜택을 일반 백성들도 누리게 되었다.
The invention of Korean script allowed ordinary people to enjoy the benefits of literacy, which had been previously monopolized by the aristocratic class.

041
화해

[화해] reconciliation

making up and understanding each other after two people have fought

[Usage] N과/와 화해하다

[Expression] 화해를 청하다 to request a reconciliation
화해를 시키다 to make a reconciliation

[Example] 우리는 화해한 후 반에서 둘도 없는 단짝이 되었다.
After we reconciled, we became two peas in a pod in our class.

1991년 소련이 붕괴되면서 냉전이 종식되자 세계는 비로소 냉전 시대에서 화해의 시대로 전환됐다.
After the end of the Cold War due to the collapse of the Soviet Union in 1991, the world has changed from a Cold War era to an era of reconciliation.

042
활기

[활기] vigor

having energy pour out with force; also strength

[Usage] N에 활기를 불어넣다

[Expression] 활기차다 to have vigor
활기가 넘치다 to be overflowing with vigor
활기를 띠다 to have vigor
활기를 되찾다 to regain vigor

[Example] 경기가 회복되어 수출이 활기를 띠고 있다.
Exportation is becoming vigorous after the economic recovery.

봄이 되면 자연은 활기차고 생명감이 넘쳐흐르게 된다.
When it becomes spring, nature is full of vigor and a feeling of vitality is overflowing.

043
회의

[회의/회이] skepticism

having suspicion; also the suspicion that you keep in your heart

[Expression] 회의론자 skeptic
회의적이다 to be suspicious
회의가 들다 to be suspicious
회의를 품다 to have skepticism
회의를 느끼다 to feel suspicious

[Example] 과연 내가 그 일을 해 낼 수 있을까하는 회의가 든다.
I'm skeptic on whether I can complete this task or not.

나의 계획에 대해 회의를 품은 친구들이 많았으나, 난 결국 성공했다.
Although there were many friends who were skeptic about my plans, I eventually succeeded.

044
훼손

[훼손] 1. damage 2. damage

1. damage to dignity, honor, or values

[Usage] N이/가 훼손되다
N을/을 훼손하다
N을/를 훼손시키다

[Expression] 명예훼손 damage of honor

[Example] 전 사원이 훼손된 회사 이미지를 바꾸기 위해 총력을 기울였다.
All of the workers focused their energy into changing the damaged image of the business.

2. breaking or recklessly handling something so you can't use it

[Usage] N이/가 훼손되다
N을/을 훼손하다
N을/를 훼손시키다

[Example] 인류의 무분별한 개발로 원시림이 마구 훼손되어 가고 있다.
Due to mankind's reckless developments, primeval forests are being roughly damaged.

045
흉내

[흉내] imitation

[Usage] N이/가 N을/를 흉내 내다

[Example] 그는 흉내를 잘 낸다고 해서 원숭이라는 별명을 얻었다.
He has the nickname of monkey because he can imitate well.

그 코미디언은 넉살스럽게 바보 흉내를 내서 사람들을 웃긴다.
That comedian makes people laugh by shamelessly imitating a fool.

046
흔적

[흔적] trace

the marks or remains left after a phenomena or substance has disappeared or passed

[Expression] 흔적이 남다 trace is left
흔적을 남기다 to leave a trace
흔적을 없애다 to get rid of any trace
흔적을 지우다 to erase any trace
흔적도 없이 사라지다 to disappear without a trace

[Synonym] 자국 mark
자취 remains

[Example] 그녀의 얼굴에는 눈물을 흘린 흔적이 남아 있었다.
That girl had traces of tears left over on her face.

어젯밤 내린 눈이 아침 햇볕에 녹기 시작하여 흔적조차 없어지고 말았다.
The snow that fell yesterday night began to melt in the morning sunlight and disappeared without a trace.

047
희생

[희생] sacrifice

offering one's body, wealth, profit, or other precious things for someone or a matter

[Usage] N이/가 희생되다
N을/를 희생하다

[Expression] 희생자 victim
희생정신 sacrificial mindset
희생당하다 to be sacrificed

[Example] 이번 폭탄 테러로 인한 희생자 수가 백 명을 넘었다고 한다.
Due to the terror attack of a bomb, the number of victims has gone over one hundred.

대통령은 평화를 위해서는 어떤 희생도 감수하겠다는 의지를 보였다.
The president showed will by stating that for peace, he was willing to put up with whatever sacrifices.

06 연습문제

[1-13] 다음 (　　　)에 알맞은 것을 고르십시오.

Choose the word that fits best in the parenthesis.

1. 내 동생이 늘 어린아이 같았는데 사춘기가 지나더니 이제 제법 어른 (　　　)이/가 난다.

❶ 티　　❷ 분위기　　❸ 향기　　❹ 흉내

2. 정부는 소규모로 농사를 짓는 농민들에게 세금 감면의 (　　　)을/를 주고 있다.

❶ 은혜　　❷ 혜택　　❸ 자유　　❹ 변화

3. 외국 기업과의 기술 제휴가 일반적이지만 국내 기업들 사이의 기술 제휴도 증가하는 (　　　)을/를 보이고 있다.

❶ 현실　　❷ 전망　　❸ 전략　　❹ 추세

4. 어젯밤에 과로를 한 (　　　)인지 몸이 무겁고 머리까지 아파온다.

❶ 덕분　　❷ 탓　　❸ 이유　　❹ 핑계

5. 당국의 지나친 통제로 취재진의 접근이 (　　　)되지 않았다.

❶ 인정　　❷ 수용　　❸ 허용　　❹ 통과

6. 국가나 집단을 위하여 개인을 (　　　)하기란 쉬운 일이 아니다.

❶ 제약　　❷ 희생　　❸ 훼손　　❹ 지지

7. 우리 회사에서는 우수한 신입 사원들을 해외 지사로 (　　　)하여 국제적인 감각을 익히게 하고 있다.

❶ 선발　　❷ 파견　　❸ 전파　　❹ 배송

8. 많은 청소년들이 인터넷 게임에 (　　　)되어 있다고 한다.

❶ 집중　　❷ 구속　　❸ 중독　　❹ 감염

9. 무분별한 개발로 인한 생태계의 (   )으로/로 인류의 생존이 위협을 받고 있다.

❶ 파괴 ❷ 제거 ❸ 파멸 ❹ 피해

10. 대통령의 이번 유럽 순방은 경제적 (   )에 큰 비중을 두고 있다.

❶ 측면 ❷ 방법 ❸ 수단 ❹ 현상

11. 자유로운 공장 설립을 (   )하는 각종 규제가 철폐되었다.

❶ 촉진 ❷ 제약 ❸ 후원 ❹ 공격

12. 대학의 기부금 입학 문제가 요즘 우리 사회의 주요 (   )으로/로 논란의 대상이 되고 있다.

❶ 주제 ❷ 전략 ❸ 쟁점 ❹ 투쟁

13. 작가는 이 소설을 통해 동성애에 대한 (   )을/를 바꿔 보고자 했다.

❶ 제약 ❷ 의견 ❸ 편견 ❹ 가치관

[14-15] 다음 (   )에 들어갈 단어를 순서대로 알맞게 짝지은 것을 고르십시오.

Choose the pair of words that are in the right order to go into the parentheses.

14. 신도시 (   )에 필요한 강모래의 수요가 폭발적으로 증가해 지나친 모래 채취로 인한 환경 (   )이/가 우려되고 있다.

❶ 개발--보호 ❷ 건설--파괴 ❸ 공사--오염 ❹ 공급--붕괴

15. 환경 보호를 위해 (   )되었던 등산로가 다음달부터 (   )된다고 한다.

❶ 폐쇄--개방 ❷ 폐쇄--통제 ❸ 보존--개방 ❹ 복구--공개

[16-18] 다음 (　　　)에 들어갈 말로 알맞지 않은 것을 고르십시오.
Choose the word that does not fit in the parenthesis.

16. 생산성을 높이고 불량률을 낮추는 것이야말로 이윤을 극대화시키는 (　　　)이다.

❶ 첩경　❷ 규칙　❸ 지름길　❹ 가장 쉽고 빠른 방법

17. 말투로 보아 군인으로 (　　　)되는 중년의 남자가 전화를 받고 있었다.

❶ 예상　❷ 추측　❸ 추정　❹ 짐작

18. 우리는 수많은 실패에도 (　　　)하지 않고 다시 일어섰기 때문에 성공의 기쁨을 맛보게 되었다.

❶ 낙심　❷ 좌절　❸ 포기　❹ 기절

[19-23] 다음 밑줄 친 부분과 의미가 비슷한 것을 고르십시오.
Choose the word that is similar to the underlined word.

19. 배낭여행의 좋은 점은 그 나라 사람들의 생생한 생활상을 여행자 자신이 직접 경험할 수 있다는 것이다.

❶ 보험　❷ 실험　❸ 체험　❹ 관람

20. 두 회사는 제품 개발에 긴밀하게 힘을 합하여 서로 돕기로 합의했다.

❶ 협력하다　❷ 협찬하다　❸ 협상하다　❹ 협의하다

21. 그 코미디언의 우스꽝스러운 몸짓과 표정은 아무도 따라할 수 없으리만치 독특하고 기발했다.

❶ 상상하다　❷ 설명하다　❸ 흉내 내다　❹ 인정하다

22. 우연히 발견한 동굴에는 사람이 살았던 자취가 군데군데 남아 있었다.

❶ 체취　❷ 자리　❸ 모습　❹ 흔적

23. 독실한 기독교 신자였던 삼촌은 사고를 당한 후에 신의 존재에 대하여 <u>의심을 갖기</u> 시작했다.

① 믿음을 갖다 ② 회의를 품다 ③ 궁금해 하다 ④ 부정을 하다

[24-25] 다음 중 밑줄 친 명사의 쓰임이 잘못된 것을 고르십시오.

Choose the underlined word that has been used incorrectly as a noun.

24.

① 그 <u>칼럼</u>은 정치적인 쟁점을 날카롭게 분석하고 있다.

② 부모님이 우리의 결혼을 <u>허용</u>해 주실 때까지 기다리기로 했다.

③ 수출입이 자유로워짐에 따라 무역 업계는 <u>활기</u>를 되찾고 있다.

④ 지난해 은행에서 금을 사고 파는 골드뱅킹이 가능해지면서 금이 새로운 <u>재테크</u> 수단으로 떠올랐다.

25.

① 비행기 추락으로 많은 인명 <u>피해</u>가 발생했다.

② 나는 요즘 내가 하고 있는 일에 <u>회의</u>를 느끼고 있다.

③ 범행 현장에는 언제나 범인의 <u>흔적</u>이 남아 있기 마련이다.

④ 돈을 무조건 저축하기보다는 무엇인가 배우고 교양을 쌓는 데에 <u>투기</u>하고 싶다.

[26-28] 다음 중 제시된 단어를 공통적으로 사용할 수 있는 것을 고르십시오.

Choose one word that can be used for all of the given verbs.

26.

검사	맞다	찾다	살리다

① 적성 ② 전공 ③ 경력 ④ 전략

27.

있다	차다	띠다	넘치다

❶ 활력 ❷ 열정 ❸ 열기 ❹ 활기

28.

하다	들다	품다	생기다

❶ 열정 ❷ 생기 ❸ 회의 ❹ 의문

29. 다음에 제시된 단어의 관계가 다른 것을 하나 고르십시오.
Choose the pair of words that has a different relationship from three other pairs.

❶ 할인--혜택 ❷ 노화--현상 ❸ 마약--중독 ❹ 흔적--자국

30. 다음 단어에서 밑줄 친 부분의 의미가 다른 것을 하나 고르십시오.
Choose the word where the underlined part has a different meaning.

❶ 재테크 ❷ 재활용 ❸ 재방송 ❹ 재등록

31. 다음에 제시된 술어를 공통으로 사용할 수 없는 단어를 고르십시오.
Choose one word that cannot be used with the given verbs.

하다	당하다	시키다

❶ 희생 ❷ 파괴 ❸ 좌절 ❹ 화해

[32-36] 다음 (　　)에 공통적으로 들어갈 단어를 쓰십시오.
Find the one word that fits in the parentheses.

32.

❶ 이 카페는 높은 언덕에 자리 잡고 있어서 (　　)이/가 아주 좋다.
❷ 서비스직은 사회가 발달함에 따라 더욱 각광을 받을 것으로 (　　)된다.

33.

❶ 그 회사는 (　　) 자격을 고졸 이상으로 한정하였다.
❷ 이번 입시에서 우리 학교는 (　　)하는 사람이 적어 다른 학교보다 경쟁률이 낮았다.

34.

❶ 농촌 사회에서는 고령화 (　　)이/가 더욱 두드러지고 있다.
❷ 이 세상에는 과학적으로 설명되지 않는 (　　)이/가 많이 존재한다.

35.

❶ 높은 천장은 네 개의 큰 기둥에 의해서 (　　)되고 있다.
❷ 그 교수의 학설은 다른 많은 학자들에 의해 (　　)을/를 받았다.
❸ 그는 국민들의 전폭적인 (　　)을/를 얻어서 대통령에 당선되었다.

36.

❶ 경찰이 방심한 (　　)을/를 노려 범인이 도망쳤다.
❷ 요즘은 너무 바빠서 새벽부터 밤중까지 쉴 (　　)이/가 없다.
❸ 기자 회견장은 취재 기자들로 가득 차서 발 디딜 (　　)도 없었다.
❹ 그는 많은 사람들 (　　)에서 친구를 찾으려고 사방을 두리번거렸다.

[37-39] 다음을 읽고 물음에 답하십시오.

Read the following passage and answer the questions.

18세기 영국의 산업 혁명이래 전 세계적으로 산업화가 급속히 진행되면서 이와 더불어 무분별한 개발도 이뤄지고 있다. 그리하여 그 부작용으로 자연 환경도 심각하게 (㉠)되고 오염되고 있다. 이 문제를 해결하기 위해 정부 (㉡)의 노력도 필요하거니와 국민 각자가 스스로 할 수 있는 다양한 방법도 모색해야 한다. 그 방법 중 대표적인 것은 가정에서 먹을 만큼만 조리해서 음식 쓰레기를 줄이는 것과 병이나 종이 등을 (㉢) 하는 것이다. 아울러 환경 단체들도 환경보호 (㉣)을/를 꾸준히 전개해 나가야 할 것이다.

37. ㉠에 알맞은 것과 그것의 반대말로 짝지어진 것을 고르십시오.

❶ 파멸--회복 ❷ 파괴--건축 ❸ 훼손--보호 ❹ 규제--재생

38. ㉡에 알맞은 것을 고르십시오.

❶ 시도 ❷ 차원 ❸ 기준 ❹ 측면

39. ㉢과 ㉣에 들어갈 알맞은 말로 짝지어진 것을 고르십시오.

❶ 재테크－전략 ❷ 재활용－캠페인 ❸ 투자－지원 ❹ 허용－운동

형용사 I

07

Adjectives I

07 형용사 I

001
각별하다 [각뼈라다] 1. to be particular 2. to be friendly

1. to be extremely special

[Example] 공적인 전화를 주고받을 때는 각별히 예의를 지켜야 한다.
When receiving official phone calls, you must be particular about being well-mannered.

2. to be extremely friendly with each other

[Expression] 사이가 각별하다 relationship is friendly

[Example] 처음부터 각별한 사이는 아니었으나 이웃하여 살면서 가까워지기 시작했다.
Although they were not friendly at first, they became closer while living as neighbors.

002
거창하다 [거창하다] to be enormous

size is big or extremely large

[Expression] 계획이 거창하다 plan is enormous
사업이 거창하다 business is enormous

[Example] 광고는 거창하나 실제로 약의 효과를 보았다는 사람은 별로 없다.
Although the advertisement was enormous, realistically there was no one that said it was effective.

그 사람은 거창하게 자신의 계획을 밝혔는데 현실성은 거의 없는 것 같다.
He revealed his plans in a big way but it seems that he is not very realistic.

003
거칠다 [거칠다] 1. to be rough 2. to be slovenly 3. to be hostile 4. to be rough 5. to be coarse 6. to be vulgar

1. the texture of a surface or skin of an object is not fine and rough

[Expression] 손이 거칠다 hands are rough
피부가 거칠다 skin is rough

[Example] 어머니의 거친 손바닥에 못이 박여 있었다.
There were calluses in my mother's rough palm.

2. not attentive or not being able to do work in a solid way and doing it in a rough and thoughtless way

[Expression] 솜씨가 거칠다 workmanship is slovenly
운전이 거칠다 driving is slovenly

[Example] 그 사람은 일솜씨가 거칠어서 다시 내가 뒷손질을 해야 한다.
Because his task execution is slovenly, I have to go back and review it again.

3. behavior or personality is harsh and possesses a tendency to attack

[Expression] 성격이 거칠다 personality is hostile
행동이 거칠다 behavior is hostile

[Example] 그는 성격이 거칠어 걸핏하면 싸움하기가 일쑤였다.
Because his personality was hostile, he was always quick to fight too readily.

4. current, waves, weather, etc. is harsh and violent

[Expression] 파도가 거칠다 waves are rough
바람이 거칠다 wind is rough

[Example] 날씨가 거칠어 모든 선박의 출입이 금지되었다.
Because the weather was rough, all entrance to the ship was restricted.

5. taste and nutrients of food is small and not soft.

[Example] 우리는 거친 음식으로 간신히 끼니를 이어 갔다.
We barely made a meal from the coarse food.

6. text or words are not refined and are instead vulgar

[Example] 내가 주책을 떨거나 저속하고 거친 말을 쓰면 아버지는 점잖게 나무라셨다.
Whenever I was acting indecent or used offensive and vulgar words, my father gently scolded me.

004
건전하다

[건전하다] to be wholesome

behavior, attitude, heart, etc, is not wrong and is flawless

[Expression] 정신이 건전하다 mind is wholesome

[Example] 적당한 운동은 신체를 발달시키고, 체력을 길러주며, 건전한 정신을 갖게 해 줍니다.
Appropriate exercise develops your body, cultivates stamina, and also helps to give you a wholesome mind.

어른들은 청소년이 올바르고 건전하게 자랄 수 있도록 그들의 세계를 인정해주고 교육적인 환경을 만들어 주어야 한다.
Adults must accept their world and create an educational environment for adolescents so that they can grow correctly into wholesome people.

005
격렬하다

[경녈하다] to be violent

words or behavior is strong and hostile

[Expression] 논쟁이 격렬하다 dispute is violent
싸움이 격렬하다 fight is violent
운동이 격렬하다 exercise is intense

[Example] 권투와 같은 격렬한 격투기를 운동 삼아 하는 사람들이 늘어나고 있다.
There are more and more people doing intense sports like boxing as exercise.

시위가 격렬해짐에 따라 경찰은 시위대를 해산시키려고 최루탄을 사용했다.
Because the protest became violent, the police used tear gas bombs in order to disperse the protestors.

006
경이롭다

[경이롭따] to be marvelous

to be surprising and wonderful

[Expression] 경이로운 사실 marvelous face
경이로운 사건 marvelous event

[Example] 이집트의 피라미드는 경이로운 건축물 중 하나이다.
The pyramids in Egypt are one of the marvelous structures.

'생활의 달인'이라는 TV 프로그램은 한 가지 일을 열심히 해서 경이로운 수준에 도달한 사람들을 보여 준다.
The TV program "Master of Life," shows people who have worked hard in one area and have reached a marvelous level.

007
고소하다

[고소하다] to be pleasing

(after seeing something bad happen to someone one dislikes) feeling refreshed and being amused

[Example] 영수 씨도 이번 시험에 떨어졌다는 말을 듣고 미선 씨는 고소해 하는 표정을 지었다.
After hearing that Youngsoo also failed this test, Misun displayed a pleased expression.

다른 사람들은 내가 소장에게 당하고 있는 것이 고소하다는 듯이 킬킬대고 있었다.
Other people laughed as though it was pleasing to see me be attacked by the manager.

008
곤란하다

[골란하다] to be arduous

situation is extremely hard, difficult, and troubling

[Expression] 곤란한 형편 arduous circumstance
곤란한 질문 arduous question
처지가 곤란하다 situation is arduous

[Example] 병원 응급실에서는 호흡이 곤란한 환자에게 산소마스크를 씌웠다.
At the hospital's emergency room, they gave an oxygen mask to a patient who had difficulty in breathing.

발표자는 곤란한 질문을 받으면 적당한 핑계를 대고 대답을 하지 않았다.
The presenter stated an appropriate excuse and did not answer when he received difficult questions.

009
과감하다

[과감하다] to be daring

becoming determined quickly and is brave

[Expression] 과감한 결정 daring decision

[Example] 남에게 뒤처지지 않으려면 새로운 변화를 받아들이는 데 과감해야 한다.
You must be daring to accept to new changes if you do not want to fall behind others.

선배는 든든한 후원자가 되어 줄 테니 소신을 갖고 과감하게 사업을 시작하라고 나를 격려했다.
My superior encouraged me to daringly start a new business with my own convictions, stating that he would be a solid supporter.

010
굉장하다

[굉장하다] 1. to be great 2. to be amazing

1. to be extremely big

[Expression] 크기가 굉장하다 size is great

[Example] 올림픽 대회를 치르려면 굉장한 규모의 운동 경기 시설이 필요하다.
If you want to hold the Olympics, a sports stadium of a great scale is needed.

2. to be extremely amazing

[Expression] 능력이 굉장하다 ability is amazing
용기가 굉장하다 courage is amazing
비바람이 굉장하다 wind and rain is amazing

[Example] 그 남자의 부인은 소문대로 굉장한 미인이었다.
That man's wife is an amazing beauty as it was rumored.

011
교만하다

[교만하다] to be proud

having a high opinion of yourself, boasting, and being impudent

[Expression] 교만한 태도 proud attitude
교만하게 굴다 to behave proudly

[Example] 재벌 2세인 김 사장은 직원들을 교만한 태도로 대해서 평판이 좋지 않았다.
Mr. Kim, a second-generation chaebol, did not have a good reputation because of his attitude towards his employees.

재주만 뛰어나고 그 재주에 어울리는 덕성을 갖추지 못한 사람은 교만해지기 쉽다.
A person who has talent but no virtue to go along with that talent can become too easily proud.

012
굳다

[굳따] 1. to be steadfast 2. to be tense

1. being strong or having a strong will so that one does not waver or change

[Expression] 굳은 결심 steadfast resolution
굳은 약속 steadfast promise
굳은 의지 steadfast will
굳게 맹세하다 to pledge steadfastly
입을 굳게 다물다 to shut one's mouth steadfastly

[Example] 영수는 다음 달부터 담배를 끊으리라 굳은 결심을 했다.
Young-soo has made a steadfast resolution to quit smoking starting next month.

2. hard and not soft because of anxiety

[Expression] 굳은 표정 tense expression

[Example] 칭찬을 하실 거라고 기대했던 선생님한테서 꾸지람을 듣자 그의 얼굴은 곧 굳어져 버렸다.
His face became tense after hearing a scolding from the teacher he was expecting praise from.

013
귀하다

[귀하다] 1. to be honorable 2. to be exalted 3. to be precious 4. to be rare

1. one's social position or status is high

[Example] 몇년 전까지만 해도 우리는 종종 만나서 한잔하곤 했지만 그가 높은 자리에 올라서 귀한 몸이 된 후부터는 만나기가 아주 어렵다.
Even just a few years ago we used to meet often to drink, but after going up to a higher position and becoming honorable, it is hard to meet at all.

2. (usually used in the form of '귀하게,' '귀한') to be respectable. to be worthy enough to raise up

[Expression] 귀한 손님 exalted guest
귀하게 자라다 to grow up exalted
귀한 걸음을 하다 to make valuable steps

[Example] 귀한 손님이 오셨으니 정성껏 잘 모셔야 된다.
Because he is an exalted guest, we must take care of them with the utmost sincerity.

3. to be extremely valuable and important

[Example] 사람의 생명보다 더 귀한 것이 또 있을까?
Is there anything more precious than a human life?

4. so rare that it is extremely hard to find or acquire

[Example] 할아버지의 말씀에 의하면 우리 집안은 대대로 자손이 귀한 집안이었다고 한다.
If we listen to my grandfather's words, our household has had precious descendants for generations.

014
그윽하다

[그으카다] 1. to be secluded 2. to be deep 3. to be subtle

1. because deep, it is cozy and calm

[Example] 이곳은 바다와 산에 둘러싸여 있고 골짜기는 그윽하여 쉽게 훼손되지 않을 듯싶다.
Because this place is surrounded by an ocean and mountains, and the valley is secluded, it seems as though it will not be damaged easily.

2. having deep thoughts and has a calm feeling

[Expression] 그윽한 눈빛 deep expression of eyes
그윽한 목소리 deep voice

[Example] 그는 아리따운 그녀의 얼굴을 그윽한 시선으로 바라보았다.
He looked at the beautiful woman's face with a deep gaze.

3. the impression or feeling given is implicit

[Expression] 그윽한 향기subtle scent

[Example] 그 꽃은 우아하고 향기도 그윽하다.
That flower is elegant and also has a subtle scent.

015
급급하다

[그끄파다] to be engrossed

being only focused on one task and unable to spare time to do something else

[Usage] N에 급급하다
AV기에 급급하다
AV는 데에 급급하다

[Example] 예전에는 당장 먹고 사는 데에 급급했기 때문에 주위를 돌아볼 여유가 없었다.
Because I was too engrossed with eating and living at that direct moment in my former days, I could not spare time to look around my surroundings.

우리 편 선수는 상대 선수의 공격을 방어하기에만 급급해서 공격을 제대로 펼치지 못하고 있었다.
The athlete on our side was too engrossed with blocking the opponent player's offense that he was unable to play offense correctly.

016
급작스럽다

[급짝스럽따] to be abrupt

(the way a situation changes) extremely quick

[Expression] 급작스러운 사고 abrupt accident

급작스럽게 일어나다 to happen abruptly

[Example] 모든 일이 한꺼번에 급작스럽게 일어나서 당황스러웠다.
Because everything happened so abruptly and at one time, I was caught off-guard.

옛날에는 재해나 일식, 월식 같은 급작스러운 자연 현상의 변화가 보이면 임금의 덕이 부족해서 그런 것이라고 보았다.
In the past, if something in nature changed abruptly like a disaster, solar eclipse, or lunar eclipse, it was blamed on the emperor being deficient.

017
기막히다

[기마키다] 1. to be dumbfounded 2. to be stunning

1. a certain matter is extremely surprising or very ridiculous

[Example] 나는 그의 제안이 너무 기막혀 아무 말도 못했다.
I was so dumbfounded by his proposition that I could not speak.

2. so excited that one cannot speak

[Example] 그들은 동화처럼 기막히게 아름다운 집에 살고 있었다.
They lived in a stunningly beautiful home that looked like it popped out of a children's book.

018
꺼림칙하다

[꺼림치카다] to feel uneasy

your mind is not at ease

[Example] 아이를 그렇게 먼 곳까지 혼자 보내기가 꺼림칙했으나 어쩔 수 없었다.
I felt uneasy about sending my child to such a far place but there was nothing I could do.

얼마 전 드라마에서 거울을 깨뜨린 후 안 좋은 일이 일어나는 장면을 보았는데 아침에 잘못해서 거울을 깨뜨리고 나니 하루 종일 마음이 꺼림칙하다.
My mind felt uneasy all day after breaking the mirror on accident this morning, especially after watching bad things unfold after someone broke a mirror in a drama a couple of days ago.

019
끈질기다

[끈질기다] 1. to be tenacious 2. to be persevering

1. will not break and is very tough

[Example] 호박은 줄기보다 잎사귀가 끈질겨서 쉽게 찢어지지 않는다.
The pumpkin's leaf is more tenacious than the vine and will not easily rip.

2. not easily giving up and hanging onto something in order to achieve a goal

[Expression] 끈질긴 노력 persevering effort
끈질긴 추적 persevering pursuit

[Example] 경찰관의 끈질기고 집요한 추궁에 범인으로 의심을 받던 그 사람이 결국 자백을 했다.
Due to the police man's persevering and stubborn inquiry, the person who was receiving suspicion as the suspect eventually confessed.

020
끊임없다

[끄니멉따] to be continuous

[Expression] 끊임없는 노력 continuous effort
끊임없는 연구 continuous research
끊임없이 continuously

[Example] 그들은 끊임없는 연구와 투자로 신제품을 개발하였다.
With continuous research and investment, they were able to develop a new product.

올해에도 우리 주위에는 크고 작은 사건들이 끊임없이 발생했다.
There were many big and small events that continuously arose around us this year as well.

021
날카롭다

[날카롭다] 1. to be sharp 2. to be sharp 3. to be perceptive 4. to be sensitive 5. to be acute

1. blade is up or sharp so that it can cut or poke

[Expression] 날카로운 칼 sharp knife
이빨이 날카롭다 teeth are sharp
손톱이 날카롭다 nails are sharp

[Example] 호랑이는 날카로운 이빨을 드러내며 으르렁거리고 있었다.
The tiger revealed its sharp teeth and growled.

2. expression of one's eyes are not gentle but hostile

[Expression] 눈매가 날카롭다 expression of one's eyes is sharp
눈빛이 날카롭다 expression of one's eyes is sharp

[Example] 수염이 덥수룩하고 입은 옷은 엉망이었으나 그들의 눈초리는 한결같이 날카로웠다.
Even though their beards were shaggy and the clothes they wore were a mess, the way they gazed at the others was very sharp.

3. skill of recognizing objects is very quick and accurate

[Example] 그의 날카로운 질문에 난 잠시 말문이 막혔다.
I was left at a loss of words at his perceptive question.

4. to be easily irritated because extremely sensitive

[Example] 병상에 있는 사람은 평상시와는 다르게 신경이 날카로우니까 말을 조심해야 한다.
People who are ill are usually more sensitive than other times, so you must be careful with your words.

5. sound is very loud and seems like it will rip open

[Example] 지진으로 건물이 심하게 흔들리자 날카로운 비명과 함께 흩어져 달아나는 사람들의 어지러운 발소리가 들려 왔다.
I heard chaotic footsteps from people dispersing and running away along with acute screams once the building began shaking violently from the earthquake.

022
넉넉하다

[넝너카다] 1. to be sufficient 2. to be well-off

1. enough to fill a certain standard; to be not lacking

[Expression] 시간이 넉넉하다 time is sufficient
먹을 것이 넉넉하다 food is sufficient

[Example] 평일에는 기차의 좌석이 넉넉해서 원하는 자리에 앉을 수 있다.
During the weekdays, there are sufficient seats on the train so you can sit in whatever seat you want.

2. there is allowance in one's lifestyle; to be abundant in physical objects

[Expression] 살림이 넉넉하다 lifestyle is well-off
생활이 넉넉하다 living is well-off

[Example] 그녀는 친정이 넉넉해서 경제적인 도움을 많이 받는다.
Because her parents are well-off, she received a lot of economical help from them.

023
느긋하다

[느그타다] to be relaxed

there is allowance in one's heart so you are not in a hurry

[Expression] 성격이 느긋하다 personality is relaxed
태도가 느긋하다 attitude is relaxed

[Antonym] 조급하다 to be impatient

[Example] 나는 시험이 끝나고 느긋한 마음으로 오랜만에 친구들과 한잔했다.
After I finished my test, I met my friend who I had not seen in awhile for a drink with a relaxed mind.

그 사람은 성격이 워낙 느긋해서 웬만해서는 당황하지 않는다.
His personality is so relaxed that he is not caught off-guard easily.

024
능통하다

[능통하다] to be proficient

to be extremely skillful in techniques, functions, or knowledge in one area

[Expression] 외국어에 능통하다 to be proficient in a foreign language

국제법에 능통하다 to be proficient in international law

[Example] 그 학생은 국제회의에서 통역을 할 수 있을 정도로 영어와 한국어에 능통하다.

That student is proficient enough in English and Korean to interpret in the international relations conference.

조선시대의 학자였던 박지원의 작품은 한문으로 쓰여졌는데 한자에 능통한 한문학자들조차도 그의 작품을 읽기가 매우 어렵다고 한다.

Park Jiwon who was a scholar in the Joseon Dynasty wrote one of his works in Chinese characters, but it is said that even Chinese character scholars who are proficient in Chinese find it hard to read that work.

025
단단하다

[단단하다] 1. to be solid 2. to be firm 3. to be tight 4. to be firm 5. to be solid

1. even if receiving pressure, it is in a state where it does not change its shape easily and does not break

[Expression] 단단한 바위 solid boulder

단단하게 얼다 to be frozen solid

[Example] 나무 재질이 단단해야 가구를 만드는 데 쓸 수 있다.

The quality of the lumber must be solid in order for it to be used to make furniture.

2. not soft or flabby but strong and tough

[Expression] 근육질의 단단한 몸 solid body from muscle

[Example] 그는 최근 몇 년 동안 감기 한 번 안 걸렸을 정도로 단단한 사람이다.

His body is so solid that he hasn't caught a cold for many years.

3. to be not loose or lax but strong

[Example] 나사가 풀어지지 않도록 단단하게 조여라.

Tighten the screw so that it does not come undone.

4. will or thought is strong and does not waver

[Expression] 단단한 결심 firm resolution

[Example] 그렇게 단단하게 마음을 먹고 일을 시작했는데 결국 실패하고 말았다.

Even though I firmly decided to start the task, I eventually failed.

5. the base is strong in studies or business

[Example] 그는 나이 40에 이미 단단한 기반을 갖춘 사업가가 되어 있었다.

At only age 40, he already had become a businessman with a solid base.

026
독특하다

[독트카다] to be peculiar

to be dissimilar from other things and specially different

[Expression] 취향이 독특하다 taste is peculiar
냄새가 독특하다 smell is peculiar
개성이 독특하다 personality is peculiar

[Example] 최근에 세계 각국의 독특한 풍습을 소개하는 책이 많이 출판되었다.
Recently there have been many books that were published introducing peculiar customs of various countries in the world.

그는 현대 물리학을 동양 사상과 접맥해서 독특한 이론을 만들어 내었다.
He connected modern physics and Orientalism to make a peculiar theory.

027
독하다

[도카다] 1. to be poisonous 2. to be strong 3. to be malicious 4. to be vicious

1. a poison that gives injury to a life or health or gives a strong irritation

[Example] 오늘 과학실에서 플라스틱 녹이는 실험을 했는데 그 냄새가 독해서 머리가 어지럽고 속이 메스꺼웠다.
I felt dizzy and was nauseous from the fumes after doing a plastic melting experiment in the science lab.

2. taste or smell is extremely strong and irritating

[Expression] 독한 술 strong alcohol
독한 담배 strong cigarette

[Related Words] 독주 hard liquor
독설 stinging words

[Example] 보드카나 위스키 같은 독한 술을 자주 마시면 간이 손상되기 쉽다.
It is easy to damage your liver if you drink strong liquor like vodka or whiskey.

3. heart or personality is merciless and ruthless

[Expression] 성미가 독하다 disposition is malicious
독하게 마음먹다 to be extremely determined

[Example] 여러 번의 사업 실패를 교훈으로 삼아 이번엔 독하게 마음을 먹고 시작하려고 한다.
I've decided to take lessons from my previous failures in business and start again with extreme determination.

4. to pass an extent and be violent

[Example] 혹독하게 맵고 독한 바람은 줄기차게 불어닥쳤다.
The harsh, severe, and vicious wind blew against us vigorously.

028
드물다

[드물다] 1. to be rare 2. to be uncommon

1. something that does not happen or appear often

[Example] 요즘 눈 코 뜰 새 없이 바빠서 점심을 제때에 먹는 일이 드물다.
It is rare for me to be able to eat lunch on time because I am so busy lately.

2. to be not common and there is not many

[Example] 우리 오빠만큼 여러 분야에서 다재다능한 사람도 드물다.
It is uncommon to find someone who is really talented in various areas as my older brother is.

029
든든하다

[든든하다] 1. to be plentiful 2. to be reliable 3. to be reliable

1. food or clothes are plentiful and there is no sense of emptiness

[Example] 뱃속이 든든해야 무슨 일이든 자신 있게 하는 법이다.
Your stomach must be full in order to complete a task with confidence.

2. content is trustworthy and supporting

[Example] 아버지는 물려받은 재산도 넉넉했고 사업 기반도 든든해서 평생 돈 걱정 없이 살아오셨다.
My father lived his whole life not worrying about money because of the plentiful fortune he inherited and also because of a reliable business foundation.

3. trustworthy enough to not worry and lean against

[Example] 자식 셋이 하나같이 잘 자라서 참으로 든든하고 믿음직스럽다.
Because all of my three children grew up so well, they are reliable and trustworthy.

030
딱딱하다

[딱따카다] 1. to be hard 2. to be stiff 3. to be rigid

1. to be extremely rigid and solid

[Example] 떡을 냉동실에 잠깐 넣어 두었을 뿐인데 돌처럼 딱딱해져서 먹을 수가 없다.
Even though I only placed the rice cake in the freezer for a bit, it got as hard as a rock and I was unable to eat it.

2. (attitude, way of talking, atmosphere) to be not gentle; to be tough and awkward

[Example] 딱딱한 말투와 태도로 고객을 대하는 사람은 결코 영업 사원으로 성공할 수 없다.
People who treat customers with a stiff way of talking and attitude can never succeed as a business employee.

3. (the text) not full of emotion and boring because it is not interesting

[Example] 요즘은 어렵거나 딱딱한 내용을 만화로 만들어 읽기 쉽게 한 책들이 매우 인기가 높다.
Lately, books that made hard or rigid content into comics so that they are easier to read, are extremely popular.

031
떠들썩하다

[떠들써카다] 1. to be noisy 2. to be chaotic 3. to be sensational

1. to be noisy because many are talking at once

[Example] 시장은 사람들이 물건 값을 흥정하는 소리로 떠들썩했다.
The marketplace was noisy with the sounds of people arguing over the price of items.

2. incident or accident makes the atmosphere loud and disorderly

[Example] 정계를 은퇴한다는 그의 폭탄선언 때문에 정치권이 떠들썩하다.
After the explosive announcement of his retirement from politics, the political community was in chaos.

3. rumors are widespread and boisterous

[Example] 자금부의 김 부장이 회사 돈을 횡령했다는 소문에 회사 안이 떠들썩했다.
The rumor of general manager, Mr. Kim in charge of funds, embezzling the company's money made the company noisy.

032
뚜렷하다

[뚜려타다] to be distinct

to be extremely distinct; to be so certain that other people can know

[Expression]
뚜렷한 모습 distinct appearance
뚜렷한 사실 definite truth
뚜렷한 특징 distinct feature
근거가 뚜렷하다 evidence is definite
주관이 뚜렷하다 management is definite

[Example] 큰아버지의 과수원은 공을 들여서 가꾼 흔적이 뚜렷했다.
It is definite that my uncle has put a lot of labor into cultivating the orchard.

그것은 어디까지나 뚜렷한 근거가 없는 짐작일 따름이었다.
That is an assumption without distinct grounds to be based on.

033
마땅하다

[마땅하다] 1. to be suitable 2. to be justifiable 3. to be satisfactory

1. behavior or subject is fitting in the continuous requirement

[Usage] N에/에게 마땅하다

[Example] 식당을 하기에 마땅한 자리를 물색 중이다.
I am looking for an area that is suitable for opening up a restaurant.

대학에 입학한 조카에게 무슨 선물을 할까 고민했지만 마땅한 게 떠

오르지 않았다.
I thought about what to buy for my nephew who had just entered college but could not think of anything suitable.

2. thinking logically that something that was done or happened is right; to be proper, to be appropriate

[Example] 죄를 지은 사람은 벌을 받아 마땅하다.
It is justifiable that someone who has committed a crime, receives punishment.

농사에 절대적으로 필요한 수리 시설은 철도, 지하철 등과 마찬가지로 국가 재정으로 건설하여 운영함이 마땅하다.
Like railroad tracks and subways, it is proper that national finances be used to construct and manage irrigation facilities that are absolutely needed in agriculture.

3. (usually used in the form of '마땅하지, 마땅치') to be satisfied and accepting of something

[Example] 나는 그가 하는 짓이 영 마땅치 않다.
I am just not satisfied with the things that he does.

034
만만하다 [만만하다] to be tractable

handling or treating easily without being scared

[Expression] 만만한 상대 tractable opponent
만만하게 대하다 to treat tractably

[Example] 어리다고 그 아이를 만만하게 대하다가는 큰코 다친다.
If you treat the child tractably just because he is young, you will pay dearly.

이번 축구 대회에서 우리 팀은 만만하다고 생각했던 팀에게 5대 0으로 완패를 당했다.
In this soccer competition, we lost by a big margin of 5 to 0 from a team that we thought was tractable.

035
메마르다 [메마르다] 1. to be arid 2. to be shriveled 3. to be barren

1. no moisture in the ground and not fertile

[Expression] 메마른 땅 arid ground

[Example] 오랜 가뭄으로 인해 땅이 메말라 농부들이 어려움을 겪고 있다.
Due to ground becoming arid from the drought, the farmers were enduring a lot of hardships.

2. skin or lips are lacking in sheen and are rough

[Expression] 메마른 피부 shriveled skin
메마른 입술 shriveled lips

[Example] 그 여자는 메마르고 갈라진 입술에 약을 발랐다.
That girl put medicine on her shriveled and split lips.

3. feelings are dull or lacking in emotion in things like personality or lifestyle

[Expression] 감정이 메마르다 emotions are barren
인정이 메마르다 to be barren in sympathy

[Example] 경쟁이 치열해지고 그로 인해 삶이 각박해짐에 따라 우리 사회에서 인간의 정이 점점 메말라가고 있다.
Heartlessness from competition becoming more intense is making our society more and more barren in human attachment.

036
무분별하다 [무분별하다] to be thoughtless

to be lacking in judgment and reason; no strength to separate

[Example] 무분별한 국토 개발로 자연이 훼손되고 있다.
There is damage to the environment because of the thoughtless land development.

인터넷 언어를 아무 생각 없이 무분별하게 사용하는 학생들이 늘고 있다.
There are a growing amount of students who thoughtlessly use internet slang.

037
미세하다 [미세하다] to be microscopic

[Antonym] 거대하다 to be gigantic

[Example] 이 청소기는 흡인력이 좋아 집안 구석구석의 미세한 먼지까지 빨아들인다.
Because the absorption power on this vacuum is good, even the microscopic dust in the nooks and crannies of my house are sucked up.

거대한 선박에서 미세한 반도체에 이르기까지 한국의 기술력은 세계 수준으 로 발전했다.
From large ships to microscopic semiconductors, Korea's technical skills have developed to be world level.

038
믿음직하다 [미듬지카다] to be trustworthy

[Example] 그가 많은 근로자들과 함께 일하는 모습은 정말 믿음직하고 자랑스러웠다.
Seeing him work with the many laborers showed that he was extremely trustworthy and made me proud.

우리가 다음 세대를 위해서 남겨 줄 수 있는 가장 믿음직한 재산은 근면뿐이다.
The most trustworthy asset we can leave for the next generation is diligence.

039
밀접하다

[밀쩌파다] to be intimate

relationship between each other is very close

[Example] 급변하는 국제 정세는 국가 간의 밀접한 유대와 협력을 필요로 한다.
We need intimate ties and cooperation between the countries in this rapidly changing international situation.

폐암이 담배와 밀접한 관계가 있다는 보고는 애연가들에게 큰 충격을 주었다.
The people who love to smoke were greatly shocked to see that there was an intimate relationship between smoking and lung cancer.

040
배타적이다

[배타저기다] to be exclusive

having a tendency to exclude other people or thoughts

[Expression] 배타적인 성격 closed personality
배타적인 감정 closed feeling
배타적인 태도 exclusive attitude

[Antonym] 포용적이다 to be tolerant

[Example] 국제화를 위해서는 타문화에 대한 배타적인 태도를 지양하고 포용적인 태도를 가져야 한다.
We must reject an exclusive attitude regarding other cultures and instead have a tolerant attitude in order to become more globalized.

다른 종교를 인정하지 않고 자기들만 옳다고 주장하는 종교는 독선적이고 배타적이라는 비판을 받습니다.
Religions that refuse to accept other religions and believe that only they are right are criticized as being self-righteous and exclusive.

041
부담스럽다

[부담스럽따] to be burdened

feeling is present where one feels that they need to complete a duty or take responsibility

[Example] 그는 부담스러울 정도로 나에게 호의적이다.
He is so friendly that it makes me uncomfortable.

부모님의 지나친 관심이 부담스럽고 불편할 때가 있다.
There are times when I'm uncomfortable from my parents' extreme interest.

042
분주하다

[분주하다] to be busy

[Example] 점원은 새로 들어온 상품을 곳곳에 진열하느라 분주했다.
The clerk was busy putting the newly arrived products on display.

각 정당의 대표들은 자기 당 후보를 지원하기 위해 지방 유세를 나서는 등 분주한 모습이었다.
Each party's representatives showed busy images while trying to gather support for their party's candidates by doing campaign swings.

043
불과하다

[불과하다] to be mere

something that remains in a certain state or degree or cannot exceed that standard

[Usage] N에 불과하다

[Example] 말단 직원이 하루아침에 사장이 되길 바라는 것은 한낱 허황된 꿈에 불과하다.
To want a low-level employee to become a president overnight is merely a nonsensical dream.

지난해까지만 해도 여성 수강자들은 20퍼센트에 불과했으나 이제는 절반을 차지하고 있다.
Even just last year, the percentage of females in the class was merely 20 percent but now they are nearly half.

044
불리하다

[불리하다] to be unfavorable

[Expression] 상황이 불리하다 situation is unfavorable
조건이 불리하다 conditions are unfavorable
입장이 불리하다 position is unfavorable

[Antonym] 유리하다 to be favorable

[Example] 그 사람은 상황이 불리함에도 불구하고 끝까지 포기하지 않았다.
Even though his situation was unfavorable, he did not give up until the very end.

그는 자기에게 불리한 얘기가 나오자 화제를 다른 것으로 돌리려고 애를 썼다.
As unfavorable conversations began to come up about him, he tried extremely hard to change the subject.

07 연습문제

[1-7] 다음 밑줄 친 부분과 의미가 가장 비슷한 것을 고르십시오.

Choose the word that is similar to the underlined word.

1. 미국의 수영 선수인 마이클 펠프스는 베이징 올림픽에서 8개의 금메달을 따내는 <u>놀라운</u> 기록을 세웠다.

❶ 드물다 ❷ 든든하다 ❸ 굉장하다 ❹ 경이롭다

2. 공동으로 투자한 사업인데 수익금의 80%를 자기가 갖겠다는 그의 말이 너무 <u>기막혀</u> 말이 안 나올 지경이었다.

❶ 독하다 ❷ 교만하다 ❸ 어이없다 ❹ 무분별하다

3. 어떤 가난한 교사가 박봉을 털어서 <u>어려운</u> 처지에 있는 제자를 도왔다.

❶ 불리하다 ❷ 곤란하다 ❸ 꺼림칙하다 ❹ 부담스럽다

4. 법정 안은 재판의 결과에 불만을 가진 유족들의 거친 항의로 <u>떠들썩했다</u>.

❶ 분주하다 ❷ 격렬하다 ❸ 시끄럽다 ❹ 끊임없다

5. 전력 시설에 과부하가 걸리면 화재가 발생할 수 있으므로 <u>아주 특별한</u> 주의가 필요하다.

❶ 각별하다 ❷ 마땅하다 ❸ 뚜렷하다 ❹ 끈질기다

6. 이번 대선에 출마하는 우리 당 후보자가 만족스럽지는 못했지만 <u>마땅한</u> 대안이 없었다.

❶ 타당하다 ❷ 건전하다 ❸ 적절하다 ❹ 밀접하다

7. 우리 축구 대표팀과 맞붙은 상대팀을 처음에는 <u>수월한</u> 상대라고 생각했었다.

❶ 끈질기다 ❷ 만만하다 ❸ 단순하다 ❹ 까다롭다

[8-12] 다음 밑줄 친 부분과 의미가 반대인 것을 고르십시오.

Choose the word that is the opposite of the underlined word.

8. 우리 오빠는 성격이 느긋해서 그런지 급한 일이 있을 때도 서두르는 법이 없다.

❶ 과감하다　❷ 경박하다　❸ 독특하다　❹ 조급하다

9. 그 부족 사람들은 외부 세계에 배타적이어서 외부와 교류를 차단한 채 살아가고 있다.

❶ 포용적이다　❷ 독립적이다　❸ 개방적이다　❹ 의존적이다

10. 그 술은 너무 독해서 한 잔만 마셔도 취기가 오르고 어지러웠다.

❶ 연하다　❷ 흐리다　❸ 순하다　❹ 간단하다

11. 정성껏 개간한 결과 황무지였던 그 땅이 기름진 옥토로 변했다.

❶ 축축하다　❷ 수수하다　❸ 메마르다　❹ 풍부하다

12. 요즘은 문서 작성에 컴퓨터를 쓰지 않는 사람이 드물다.

❶ 귀하다　❷ 흔하다　❸ 다양하다　❹ 빈번하다

[13-26] 다음 (　　)에 알맞은 것을 고르십시오.

Choose the word that fits best in the parenthesis.

13. 우리의 청소년들이 폭력적이고 자극적인 컴퓨터 게임에만 빠져 있다고 탓하기 전에 (　　　) 놀이 문화의 조성에 힘써야 할 것이다.

❶ 희망찬　❷ 유쾌한　❸ 건전한　❹ 경이로운

14. 경기가 (　　　) 부상과 반칙으로 퇴장하는 선수가 속출했다.

❶ 과감해지자　❷ 격렬해지자　❸ 무식해지자　❹ 무분별해지자

15. 그가 술이 취하니 잘난 척하며 남을 깔보는 (　　　) 본성이 드러났다.

❶ 교만한　❷ 메마른　❸ 날카로운　❹ 배타적인

16. 차가 끓기 시작하자 온 방 안에 (　　　　) 차의 향기가 감돌았다.

❶ 독한　❷ 그윽한　❸ 넉넉한　❹ 뚜렷한

17. 이 세상에는 사사로운 이익 추구에만 (　　　　) 나머지 주위를 돌보지 않는 사람이 있는가 하면 어려운 이웃을 기꺼이 도와주는 사람도 있다.

❶ 급급한　❷ 능통한　❸ 떠들썩한　❹ 급작스러운

18. 대통령의 (　　　　) 경제 정책으로 경제 개혁이 이루어져서 경기가 되살아나기 시작했다.

❶ 단단한　❷ 마땅한　❸ 무모한　❹ 과감한

19. 정부가 수돗물에 대한 안전성을 적극 홍보하고 나서 인식이 많이 개선되기는 했지만 국민들이 여전히 수돗물을 식수로 사용하는 것을 (　　　　) 생각하는 것으로 조사됐다.

❶ 마땅하게　❷ 불리하게　❸ 불가능하게　❹ 꺼림칙하게

20. 경찰관들의 (　　　　) 추적 끝에 도주하던 범인이 결국 잡히고 말았다.

❶ 끈질긴　❷ 격렬한　❸ 밀접한　❹ 든든한

21. 그 사람은 주관이 (　　　　) 남의 말에 쉽게 동요되지 않는다.

❶ 건전해서　❷ 거창해서　❸ 뚜렷해서　❹ 믿음직스러워서

22. 외국 문화의 (　　　　) 수입은 우리 문화의 발전을 저해할 수 있으므로 선별적으로 받아들이자는 목소리가 커지고 있다.

❶ 무분별한　❷ 배타적인　❸ 치밀한　❹ 계획적인

23. 그는 이번 사건과 (　　　　) 관련이 있는 인물이기 때문에 수사 기관의 감시를 받고 있다.

❶ 미세한　❷ 불리한　❸ 밀접한　❹ 굳은

24. 졸업식장은 가족이나 친구들과 사진을 찍는 졸업생들로 (　　　　).

❶ 분주했다　❷ 끊임없었다　❸ 부담스러웠다　❹ 혼잡스러웠다

25. 1850년에 10억에 ( ) 세계 인구가 이제는 60억을 넘게 되었다.

❶ 불과하던 ❷ 만족하던 ❸ 밀접하던 ❹ 넉넉하던

26. 우리는 ( ) 결혼식을 원하지 않는다. 그저 조용한 가족 행사로 식을 치르려고 한다.

❶ 과감한 ❷ 거창한 ❸ 격렬한 ❹ 든든한

[27-29] 다음 중 형용사의 쓰임이 잘못된 것을 고르십시오.

Choose the sentence where the adjective was used incorrectly.

27.

❶ 곱던 아내의 손이 오랜 집안 일로 많이 거칠어졌다.
❷ 험한 일을 오래하다 보면 말과 행동이 거칠어지기 쉽다.
❸ 현미가 많이 든 잡곡밥은 좀 거칠기는 하나 우리 몸의 독소를 없애주는 해독작용을 한다.
❹ 도시화와 산업화로 현대인에게 물질은 많이 풍요로워졌지만 그 만큼 정신은 많이 거칠어졌다.

28.

❶ 콘크리트 벽은 단단해서 못을 박기가 쉽지 않다.
❷ 동네 청년들은 그네를 나뭇가지에 단단하게 묶었다.
❸ 다른 과목과 달리 수학은 기초가 단단해야 잘할 수 있다.
❹ 밥을 잘 먹어 뱃속이 단단해야 무슨 일이든 잘 할 수 있다.

29.

❶ 처음에는 불리하던 상황이 유리하게 역전되었다.
❷ 우리 편은 선수층이 두꺼워서 불리한 경기를 펼쳤다.
❸ 전세가 불리해지자 많은 군인이 최전방으로 증파되었다.
❹ 눈치가 빠른 그는 사태가 자기에게 불리한 것을 곧바로 눈치챘다.

[30-35] 다음 (　　)에 공통적으로 들어갈 단어의 기본형을 쓰십시오.

Find the one word that fits in the parentheses and write the most basic form.

30.

❶ 나물을 무칠 때 참기름을 넉넉하게 넣는 것이 (　　)은/ㄴ 맛을 내는 비결이다.

❷ 날마다 나를 괴롭히던 영수가 선생님께 야단을 맞는 걸 보니 (　　)은/ㄴ 기분이 들었다.

31.

❶ 전혀 어울릴 것 같지 않던 가야금과 드럼의 합주가 (　　)게 아름다웠다.

❷ 그렇게 믿었던 사람이 배신을 하다니 너무나 (　　)어/아/여 말이 안 나온다.

32.

❶ 날씨가 쌀쌀해져서 옷을 (　　)게 입고 나왔다.

❷ 보통 바빠서 아침을 거르기가 일쑤였는데 오늘은 아침밥을 잘 먹으니 속이 (　　).

❸ 처음에 유학 왔을 때는 아는 사람이 없어 외롭고 힘들었는데 이제는 친한 친구들이 많이 생겨서 마음이 (　　).

33.

❶ (　　)은/ㄴ 손님이 오셨으니 잘 모셔야 한다.

❷ 사람의 생명보다 더 (　　)은/ㄴ 것이 또 있을까?

❸ 구하기 힘든 산삼이니 (　　)게 여기는 것은 당연한 일이다.

❹ 옛날부터 우리 집안은 아들이 (　　)어서/아서/여서 아들이 태어나면 동네 사람들을 불러 잔치를 벌인다.

34.

❶ 그는 화가 났는지 시종일관 입을 (　　)게 다물고 있었다.

❷ 큰 충격을 받은 후 그의 표정은 돌처럼 (　　)어져/아져/여져 있었다.

❸ 꼭 다시 돌아오리라는 그의 (　　)은/ㄴ 약속은 끝내 지켜지지 않았다.

❹ 그 아이는 나이가 어린데도 의지가 참 (　　)어/아/여 끝까지 포기하지 않았다.

35.

❶ 나와 시선이 마주치자 그의 표정은 (　　　)게 굳어졌다.

❷ 이 나무 의자는 (　　　)어서/아서/여서 오래 앉아 있기가 힘들다.

❸ 우리 사무실 사람들은 사이가 안 좋아서 분위기가 (　　　)은/ㄴ 편이다.

❹ 이 글은 번역문이라서 그런지 문체가 좀 (　　　)고 문맥도 부자연스러운 데가 많다.

형용사 Ⅱ

08

Adjectives Ⅱ

08 형용사 II

001
불합리하다 [불함니하다] to be irrational

to be not rational or doesn't match with logic

[Expression] 불합리한 제도 irrational system

불합리한 조건 irrational condition

[Antonym] 합리적이다 to be rational

[Example] 이 작품은 당시 사회 제도가 안고 있었던 불합리한 면을 드러내고 있다.
This work exposes the irrational regime that was in that era.

단지 전통이라는 이유로, 모든 사람들에게 똑같은 행동을 요구하는 것은 불합리하다.
It is irrational to demand the same behavior from everyone just because it is traditional.

002
빈틈없다 [빈트멉따] 1. to be tight 2. to be astute

1. no empty space in between

[Example] 너무 빈틈없이 빡빡하게 하루 계획을 세우면 지키기 힘들다.
If you plan everything too tight, it is hard to keep up with all of it.

2. not shabby or lacking in anything

[Example] 그는 일처리가 빈틈없기 때문에 사장님의 신임을 얻었다.
Because his task management skills are astute, he earned the president's trust.

003
빠듯하다 [빠드타다] 1. to be tight 2. to be barely enough

1. reaching a limit or fitting just enough so that there is no space

[Example] 하루 작업 일정이 빠듯하게 짜여졌다.
The work plans for one day were organized tightly.

2. (if you want to meet a limit or quantity) extremely hard, you can barely do it

[Usage] AV기에 빠듯하다

[Expression] 빠듯한 생활비 living expenses are barely enough

시간이 빠듯하다 time is barely enough

[Example] 지금 받는 월급으로는 저축은 고사하고 학자금 대출 갚느라고 한 달 한 달 생활하기도 빠듯하다.
It is barely enough to live from month to month with the salary I receive right now because I am paying back my school loans which makes saving money out of the question.

004
빡빡하다

[빡빠카다] 1. to be dry and hard 2. to be tight 3. to be rigid 4. to be tight

1. amount of moisture is small so it is not soft

[Example] 반찬도 없이 맨밥만 먹으려니 빡빡해서 잘 넘어가지 않는다.
Eating plain rice without any side dishes was too dry and hard, and made it hard to eat.

2. no allowance; very tight

[Expression] 빡빡한 스케줄 tight schedule
용돈이 빡빡하다 allowance is tight

[Example] 일정이 빡빡하여 우리는 시내 구경은 꿈도 못 꾸었다.
We couldn't even dream of looking around the city because the day's schedule was too tight.

3. no flexibility and a bit too serious

[Example] 사람이 너무 빡빡하게 굴면 인심을 얻지 못한다.
If a person is too rigid, they are unable to gain people's hearts.

4. something is firmly stuck, or will not turn or move easily

[Example] 이 선풍기는 빡빡하여 잘 안 돌아가니 기름을 좀 쳐야겠다.
It seems that I will have to oil the fan because it is too tight and will not turn.

005
뿌듯하다

[뿌드타다] to be satisfied

a sense of satisfaction fills you

[Expression] 마음이 뿌듯하다 heart is satisfied
가슴이 뿌듯하다 heart is satisfied

[Example] 3년 동안 고생한 끝에 한 권의 책이 나왔을 때 나는 무척 뿌듯했다.
I was extremely satisfied when one book was published after suffering difficulty for three years.

장애인을 돕는 봉사활동을 하고 나니 나도 뭔가 보람 있는 일을 했다는 생각에 가슴이 뿌듯했다.
After feeling rewarded by doing volunteer work to help the disabled, my heart felt satisfied.

006
색다르다

[색따르다] to be unusual

different from the average in the same variety

[Expression] 색다른 맛 unusual flavor
색다른 느낌 unusual feeling
색다른 디자인 unusual design
분위기가 색다르다 atmosphere is unusual

[Example] 그 식당은 색다른 맛을 즐기려는 젊은 층에게 그만일 것이다.
I feel that the restaurant will be the best for the younger people who want to experience unusual flavors.

이 책은 한국역사를 독일 사람의 시각에서 색다르게 서술했다.
This book unusually described Korean history to fit the German people's perspective.

007
선명하다 [선명하다] to be clear

to be definite and distinct

[Example] 그 남자는 안경을 쓰지 않았으나 콧등에 안경 자국이 선명했다.
Although the man didn't wear his glasses, the marks left by his glasses were clear on the bridge of his nose.

외국 국기와 나란히 펄럭이고 있는 태극기가 매우 선명하게 보였다.
You could clearly see the Korean flag flying next to the other foreign flags.

008
성숙하다 [성수카다] 1. to be mature 2. to be mature

1. body and mind grows like an adult

[Example] 새로 신입 회원이 된 여대생들은 작년에 여고생이었다고는 도저히 생각되지 않을 정도로 성숙한 모습들을 하고 있었다.
The college girls who were new members were so mature looking that it was hard to believe that they were mere high school students just last year.

2. something that has fully developed and reached maturity

[Example] 토론을 통해서만이 진정한 민주주의가 이루어지고 보다 성숙한 사회가 만들어질 수 있다.
Only from debate can a true democracy be achieved and also a mature society made.

009
소박하다 [소바카다] to be simple

to be not elaborate but plain

[Expression] 소박한 행복 simple happiness
소박한 생활 simple lifestyle
소박한 옷차림 simple outfit

[Example] 고려자기가 귀족적인 데 비하여 조선의 백자는 서민적이며 소박하다.
If you compare the nobility of Goryeo ceramics, the white porcelain of the Chosun dynasty are for the masses and simple.

비록 선생님의 옷차림은 소박했으나 태도와 말투에서는 품위가 느껴졌다.
Even though the teacher's outfit was simple, I can feel the grace from his attitude and the way he spoke.

010
소중하다

[소중하다] to be important

to be extremely precious

[Example] 나 못지않게 남도 소중하게 여길 줄 알아야 한다.
Not only should I regard myself as important, but I should know to also regard other people as important as well.

날이 갈수록 그녀가 내게는 더 사랑스럽고 소중한 존재가 되었다.
As the days passed, she became a more lovely and important existence in my life.

011
속상하다

[속쌍하다] to be bothered

mind is uncomfortable or depressed because you are angry or worried

[Example] 나름대로 공을 들였는데, 일이 제대로 되지 않아 속상하다.
Because I had put in so much effort but everything didn't work out, I was bothered.

내 동생은 이번 시험에서 일 등을 놓친 것 때문에 속상해서 집에 돌아와서는 시무룩해 있었다.
My younger sibling sulked around after she returned home because she was bothered by the fact that she was not first place for this test.

012
수월하다

[수월하다] to be easy

to be not picky or hard to do

[Usage] AV기가 수월하다

[Expression] 수월한 일 easy task

[Example] 컴퓨터를 십분 활용하면 문서 정리가 훨씬 수월하다.
The organization of documents will be much easier if you can use the computer fully.

이 도서실은 정리가 잘 되어 있어서 자료 찾기가 수월하다.
It is easy to find documents because this library is organized so well.

013
순진하다

[순진하다] 1. to be innocent 2. to be naive

1. heart is not made up but simple-hearted

[Example] 착하고 순진한 사람을 등쳐먹고 사는 파렴치한 인간도 있다.
There are shameless people who scam kind and innocent people.

2. not worldly-wise but naive instead.

[Example] 내 친구 영희는 사기꾼의 허풍도 곧이곧대로 믿을 만큼 순진한 사람이다.
My friend Younghee is such a naive person that she would honestly believe the talk of a scammer.

014
순하다 [순하다] 1. to be gentle 2. to be gentle 3. to be light

1. temperament or attitude is soft

[Expression] 순한 사람 gentle person
순하게 생긴 얼굴 gentle-looking face
마음이 순하다 mind is gentle

[Example] 아이가 순해서 좀처럼 떼를 쓰거나 고집을 부리지 않는다.
The child is so gentle that he is barely fussy or stubborn.

2. wind or current or a pitch is soft

[Expression] 물살이 순하다 the flowing water is gentle
바람이 순하게 불다 the wind is blowing gently

[Example] 순한 바람을 안고 배는 미끄러지듯 달렸다.
The ship sailed as if it were gliding over the water with a gentle breeze.

3. flavor is not strong

[Expression] 순한 술 light alcohol
순한 담배 light cigarette

[Example] 아무리 순한 담배라도 기관지가 약한 사람에게는 해를 끼칠 수 있다.
No matter how light the cigarette, if your bronchial tube is weak, damage can be done.

015
시끌벅적하다 [시끌벅쩌카다] to be boisterous

to be terribly disordered and loud

[Example] 항구는 방금 잡은 생선들을 놓고 많은 사람들이 가격을 흥정하느라 시끌벅적했다.
The harbor was boisterous because many people were buying and selling the fish that were just caught.

개학날이 되자 학교 운동장은 오랜만에 등교한 아이들이 삼삼오오 모여서 웃고 떠들어대는 소리로 시끌벅적했다.
The school sports arena was noisy on the day school started again with the sounds of children in twos and threes laughing and talking.

016
신중하다 [신중하다] to be cautious

when doing something, you think very deeply and are also careful

[Expression] 신중한 자세 cautious attitude
신중한 태도 cautious attitude
신중하게 검토하다 to examine cautiously
신중하게 대처하다 to cope cautiously

[Example] 출제 위원들은 시험 문제의 적정성을 여러모로 신중하게 검토하였다.
The people who made the exam questions cautiously examined the test questions for appropriateness.

우리 부장님은 매사에 빈틈없고 신중하기 때문에 실수를 별로 하지 않으신다.
Because my director is prepared and cautious in each matter, he does not make many mistakes.

017
썰렁하다

[썰렁하다] 1. to be chilly 2. to be lonely 3. to be awkward

1. to be slightly chilly or cold because you are in a bad mood

[Example] 난방이 들어오지 않는 방안은 썰렁하게 추웠다.
Because the heater didn't work, the inside of my room was chilly.

2. to be empty and desolate with a chill

[Example] 식구들이 모두 외출하고 나자 집이 썰렁하고 허전하게 느껴졌다.
After all of my family members left the house, the house felt empty and lonely.

3. the atmosphere is suddenly cold and awkward

[Example] 아버지가 벌컥 화를 내시자 방안 분위기는 다시 썰렁해졌다.
As soon as my father suddenly got angry, the atmosphere inside the room became awkward again.

018
쓸데없다

[쓸떼업따] to be useless

to have no use. to have no worth

[Expression] 쓸데없는 말 useless words
쓸데없는 소리 useless words
쓸데없는 걱정 useless worries
쓸데없는 생각 useless thoughts
쓸데없이 uselessly

[Example] 쓸데없이 모여서 시간만 낭비하지 말고 하던 일을 계속하자.
Instead of uselessly gathering and wasting time, let's continue the work that we were doing.

중학교 때 같은 반 친구였던 철수는 수업 시간에 쓸데없는 말을 많이 해서 선생님께 야단을 맞기 일쑤였다.
During junior high, my friend Chulsoo who was in the same class, was always the first to get scolded because he uselessly talked to much during class.

019
쓸쓸하다

[쓸쓸하다] 1.to be lonely 2. to be dreary

1. to be lonely and deserted

[Example] 혼자 사는 노인들은 명절 때 한층 더 쓸쓸함을 느낀다.
Elderly people who live by themselves feel even more lonely during the holidays.

2. (weather) causes chills and is gloomy

[Example] 내 남자친구는 찬바람이 부는 쓸쓸한 늦가을에 입대했다.
My boyfriend enlisted into the army during the windy and dreary late fall.

020
씁쓸하다

[씁쓸하다] 1. to be bitter 2. to be bitter

1. to have a bit of a bitter taste

[Example] 인삼차는 조금 씁쓸한 맛이 나지만 건강에는 아주 좋은 차입니다.
Although ginseng tea has a bitter taste, it is very good for your health.

2. to feel disagreeable or to have a feeling of dislike because something is not desirable

[Expression] 씁쓸한 표정 dissatisfied expression
씁쓸하게 웃다 to smile bitterly

[Example] 며칠 전에 퇴직한 회사 앞을 지나오자니 씁쓸한 기분이 들었다.
After I passed by the front of the office that I had resigned from a couple of days ago, I felt bitter.

021
아깝다

[아깝따] 1. to feel regretful 2. to feel regretful 3. to be regretful

1. to have a feeling of sadness or longing because you lost something that was precious to you

[Example] 사업이 실패로 끝나서 그동안 투자한 돈이 무척 아까웠다.
I was extremely regretful of all of the money I had invested when the business failed.

2. to not want to throw or put out something because an object has value

[Example] 그가 사 준 케이크는 너무 예뻐서 먹기가 아까웠다.
I felt regretful because the cake that he bought me was too pretty to eat.

3. to feel regretful because an object that has value is not properly used or handled

[Example] 경치가 너무 아름다워 나만 혼자 보기가 아깝다.
I felt regretful being the only one able to see the beautiful scenery.

022
아쉽다

[아쉽따] 1.to feel the lack of 2. to feel sad

1. a feeling of suffocating or regret because someone or something that should be present is not or lacking

[Example] 실업자가 되면 당장 아쉬운 것이 돈이다.
When you become unemployed, the first thing you feel the lack of is money.

2. to regret and feel sad

[Example] 우리 팀은 지나친 체력 소모로 인해 아쉽게도 우승 문턱에서 주저앉고 말았다.
Unfortunately we collapsed at victory's doorstep because of our team's extreme emaciation.

023
아슬아슬하다

[아슬아슬하다] to be a close call

to be fearful and nervous because you feel a matter or situation will go wrong or will exceed the limit

[Expression] 아슬아슬한 장면 a breathtaking scene
아슬아슬한 순간 a close call

[Example] 아슬아슬한 공중서커스는 보는 이들에게 무더위를 잊게 했다.
Watching the breathtaking aerial circus made them forget the stifling heat.

그가 찬 공이 아슬아슬하게 골문을 빗겨 나가자 관중석에서는 아쉬움의 탄성이 일었다.
Exclamations of disappointment were heard from the spectators when the ball he kicked missed the goal by an inch.

024
안쓰럽다

[안쓰럽따] to be pitiable

to feel upset or pity because one's junior or someone who is weaker than you are is experiencing pitiful circumstances

[Example] 그녀는 처자식 부양에 피곤해하는 남편이 안쓰러웠다.
She felt pity for her husband who was exhausted from providing for their family.

내 병간호를 하느라 고생에 찌든 아내의 얼굴과 거친 손을 보니 안쓰러워 눈물이 났다.
I felt so much pity for my wife whose face was worn and hands had become rough from attending to me when I was sick, that I cried.

025
안타깝다

[안타깝따] to feel regrettable

to feel upset and stuffy because something did not go the way you planned

[Example] 어렵게 차린 가게를 경영난으로 폐점할 수밖에 없는 것이 안타깝다.
I felt regrettable that I had to close the shop I had worked so hard to set up because of financial problems.

아직 자신의 역량을 어디로 집중해야 할지 몰라 헤매는 젊은 사람이 많아 안타깝다.
I feel regrettable to the young people who are still lost because they do not know where to focus there abilities.

026
알차다

[알차다] to be rich in content

when insides are full, there is substance, and the content is very thorough

[Expression] 내용이 알차다 substance is rich in content
프로그램이 알차다 program is rich in content

[Example] 읽고 싶었던 책도 많이 읽고 아르바이트도 하면서 방학을 알차게 보냈다.
My vacation was spent meaningfully, reading many books that I had wanted to read while also having a part-time job.

벼이삭들은 지난 여름 동안의 햇볕으로 속속들이 알차게 자라서 모두 황금빛으로 물들어 가고 있었다.
The ears of rice had become fruitful under the past summer sun so they were all turning into a golden color.

027
애매하다

[애매하다] to be ambiguous

to be vague and not clear

[Example] 내 질문에 애매하게 대답하지 말고 명확한 대답을 해라.
Do not answer my question ambiguously and instead give me a clear answer.

그 남자는 비웃음 같기도 하고 미소 같기도 한 애매한 표정으로 나를 바라보았다.
He stared at me with an ambiguous expression which could have been a sneer but also a smile.

028
얄밉다

[얄밉따] to be odious

someone else's actions or words are not likable

[Expression] 얄미운 말 odious words
얄미운 짓 odious acts
얄미운 행동 odious behavior
얄미운 사람 odious person

[Example] 그를 막상 만나게 되자 얄미운 생각보다는 반가운 생각이 먼저 들었다.
When I actually met him, instead of getting angry or feeling that he was odious, I felt happy to see him.

내가 그렇게 가족을 위해 희생했는데 고마워하지 않는 식구들이 얄미웠고 심지어 배신당한 느낌마저 들었다 .
I felt that my family was odious and even felt betrayed when they were not grateful for my sacrifice.

029
어리둥절하다

[어리둥절하다] to be bewildered

to be dazed because of a sudden occurrence or something that does not follow logic

[Expression] 어리둥절한 표정 bewildered expression
어리둥절한 얼굴 bewildered expression

[Example] 난데없는 개발 소식에 동네 사람들은 어리둥절한 표정이었다.
The people in the neighbored had bewildered expressions when they heard the sudden news of development.

갑자기 웃음을 터뜨리는 나를 가족들은 어리둥절한 눈으로 바라보았다.
My family looked at me with bewildered eyes when I suddenly began laughing.

030
어리석다

[어리석따] to be foolish

to be not wise but dense

[Expression] 어리석은 행동 foolish behavior
어리석은 생각 foolish thoughts
어리석은 사람 foolish person

[Example] 나는 어리석게도 어머니가 내 거짓말에 속을 거라고 생각했다.
Foolishly, I believed that my mother would believe my lies.

늘 자기가 못났다는 열등감에 빠져 있는 사람은 어리석은 사람이다.
People who feel inferior because they think that they are unattractive are foolish.

031
어마어마하다

[어마어마하다] to be enormous

to be large and tremendous in size, quantity or degree

[Example] 야당 후보의 선거 유세에 어마어마한 인파가 몰려들었다.
An enormous amount of people flocked to the opposite candidate's campaign.

지금까지 밝혀진 시장의 비리가 어마어마해서 모두 할 말을 잃었다.
The revealing of the corruption of the mayor until now was so enormous that everyone was at a loss for words.

032
어설프다

[어설프다] 1. to be clumsy 2. to be clumsy 3. to be clumsy 4. to be half asleep

1. because your body is not experienced in doing a certain an act, it is very clumsy and not familiar

[Example] 오늘 처음 식당의 주방 일을 시작한 그 여자의 칼질이 어설프고 느렸다.
The woman who started her first day in the kitchen of the restaurant had slowly and clumsily cut with a knife.

2. organization, knowledge, behavior is not totally well-knit so there is something clumsy

[Expression] 어설픈 지식 clumsy knowledge
어설픈 계획 clumsy plans

[Example] 이번 여행은 기대를 많이 하고 떠났지만 어설픈 계획으로 여행 도중 고생이 많았다.
Although I left to the vacation with high expectations, I suffered many hardships during the vacation due to clumsy planning.

3. to act out rashly without extensive preparation or careful thought

[Example] 잘 알지도 못하면서 남의 일에 어설프게 나서지 마라.
Do not clumsily meddle in someone else's business if you do not know the whole situation.

4. not deeply asleep or not dreaming clearly

[Example] 어설프게 잠이 들었는데 인기척에 잠이 깼다.
I woke up from being half-asleep because I sensed someone's presence.

033
어수룩하다

[어수루카다] 1. to be naive 2. to be naive

1. words or behavior is not clever but instead simple and generous

[Example] 그 사람은 어수룩한 시골 사람들을 상대로 장사를 해서 많은 돈을 모았다.
He made a lot of money doing business with naive country people.

2. to be impudent and foolish

[Example] 김 과장은 첫인상은 어수룩해 보였지만 알고 보니 결코 만만한 사람이 아니었다.
Mr. Kim had a first impression of being naive but now I know that he is never an easy person to deal with.

034
어지럽다

[어지럽따] 1. to be dizzy 2. to be chaotic 3. to be disorganized

1. the mind is in a blur and in a daze to the point where one cannot keep themselves steady

[Example] 몇 바퀴나 돌았는지 아이는 다 돌고 나서도 어지러워서 바로 서지를 못했다.
The child must have spun in many circles because even after he stopped spinning, he was so dizzy that he could not stand up right away.

2. society is chaotic and there is no order

[Example] 세상이 어지러우면 이상향을 제시하는 예언서가 많이 나돈다.
When the world becomes chaotic, there are prophetic writings that go around suggesting a utopia.

3. things are messy because they are not in their rightful place and instead are dispersed

[Example] 길거리에는 사람 하나 없이 낙엽만이 어지럽게 굴러다닐 뿐이었다.
There were not people out in the streets, only leaves messily rolling around.

035
억울하다

[억울하다] to feel wronged

to feel angry and stifled because one is forced to cope with a vague matter

[Example] 잘못도 없이 아버지에게 꾸중을 듣는 게 너무 억울했다.
I felt so wronged, getting a scolding from my father when I did nothing wrong.

영문도 모른채 감옥에 갇힌 그 남자는 모든 수단을 동원해서 억울한 누명을 벗고 진실을 밝히려고 애를 썼다.
That man used all means available to try and reveal the truth because he was wrongly charged and locked up in jail for no reason.

036
엄격하다

[엄껴카다] to be strict

words, attitude, rules are very severe and thorough

[Expression] 엄격한 규율 strict rules
엄격한 심사 strict evaluation
엄격한 통제 strict regulations
엄격하게 말하다 to speak strictly
엄격하게 시행하다 to enforce strictly

[Example] 옛날의 혼례는 그 격식이 매우 엄격하였다.
In the olden times, formalities concerning nuptials were very strict.

아이들을 너무 엄격하게 다루면 오히려 역효과가 날 수 있다.
There could be rather the opposite effect if you handle children too strictly.

037
엄숙하다

[엄수카다] 1. to be serious 2. to be solemn

1. atmosphere or ceremony is solemn and silent

[Example] 운동장에는 애국가가 엄숙하게 울려 퍼지고 있었다.
The Korean national anthem solemnly played throughout the sports arena.

2. words or attitude are dignified and respectful

[Example] 아버지는 슬픔을 겨우 참아 내며 엄숙한 자세로 할아버지 영정에 절을 올렸다.
My father barely contained his sadness and solemnly bowed to my grandfather's picture.

038
엄청나다

[엄청나다] to be tremendous

the level or amount is much more extreme than one's assumption or thoughts

[Example] 정부에서 벌이는 이번 사업의 규모가 엄청나다.
The size of the business that the government is starting is tremendous.

이번 홍수 피해는 이루 말할 수 없이 엄청났다.
The damages from the flood were so tremendous that they were indescribable.

039
역동적이다

[역똥저기다] to be dynamic

to move with strength and energy

[Expression] 역동적 현상 dynamic phenomenon
역동적인 삶 dynamic life
역동적으로 활동하다 to act dynamically

[Example] 개인의 발전과 사회의 발전은 항상 역동적으로 영향을 주고받는다.
Personal growth and social evolution are always dynamically influencing each other.

세계 여러 나라 축제 중 가장 역동적인 축제는 브라질의 삼바 축제라고들 한다.
Out of all nations' festivals, it is said that the Brazilian Samba festival is the most dynamic festival.

040
엷다

[열따] 1. to be pale 2. to be light 3. to be faint

1. color is not dark but is instead slightly pale

[Expression] 엷은 색 pale color
엷은 화장 light makeup

[Example] 엷은 분홍색 저고리에 연두색 치마를 입은 언니는 마치 새색시 같았다.
My older sister looked just like a new bride in her pale pink jeogori, a Korean traditional jacket, and yellow-green skirt.

2. concentration or density is not heavy

[Example] 새벽이 조금씩 밝아 옴에 따라서 엷은 안개가 천천히 피어올랐다.
As the dawn became brighter and brighter, light fog began to slowly rise.

3. (usually used in the '엷은, 엷게' form) laughter, sleep, feeling, etc. is light and almost there but not quite

[Example] 할아버지께서는 내 얘기를 들으시더니 입가에 엷은 미소를 지으셨다.
My grandfather had a faint smile on his face after he listened to my story.

041
올바르다

[올바르다] to be proper

words, thoughts, behavior, etc. does not break free from logic or rules and is correct and right

[Expression] 올바른 말 proper words
올바른 생각 proper thoughts
올바른 정신 proper mind
올바른 태도 proper attitude

[Example] 그는 지금까지 부정한 재물을 탐하지 않고 올바르게 살아왔다.
He has lived his life properly without desiring dishonest wealth.

내 생각이 옳고 내 행동이 올바르다고 해서 세상이 그대로 받아들이는 것도 아니다.
Just because my thoughts and behavior are correct doesn't mean that the world will accept it.

042
우습다

[우습따] 1. to be humorous 2. to be ludicrous 3. to be laughable 4. to be laughable

1. because it is funny, it is something that people can laugh at

[Example] 나는 그의 행동이 우스워서 웃음을 참을 수가 없었다.
His actions were so humorous that I could not hold back my laughter.

2. so dissatisfied that it is uncomfortable to see

[Example] 사장님의 비위를 맞추려고 그 앞에서 알랑대는 김 대리의 모습은 정말 우습다.
Seeing Deputy Kim flattering our boss in order to adulate him was ludicrous.

3. to be not grand or insignificant

[Example] 그의 태도는 마치 나를 우습게 생각하는 것 같아서 기분이 나쁘다.
I felt angry because his attitude was almost as if he thought I was laughable.

4. coincidental and strange

[Example] 뭐가 잘못되었는지는 몰라도 일이 의도한 대로 되지 않고 아주 우스워졌다.
Although I don't know what went wrong, that matter did not go the way I attended and instead became laughable.

043
우아하다

[우아하다] to be elegant

[Expression] 우아한 자태 elegant figure
우아한 차림새 elegant attire
우아하게 걷다 to walk elegantly

[Example] 그녀는 우아하고 기품 있는 중년의 여인이 되어 있었다.
She had become an elegant and graceful middle-aged woman.

박물관에 전시된 도자기에서 우아하고 아름다운 곡선미를 느낄 수 있었다.
I was able to feel the elegant and beautiful curves of the ceramic put on display at the museum.

044
원만하다

[원만하다] 1. to be easygoing 2. to be smooth 3. to be amicable

1. personality is not difficult but is instead gentle and generous

[Expression] 원만한 성품 easygoing character
성격이 원만하다 personality is easygoing

[Example] 직장생활에서는 업무능력뿐만 아니라 원만한 대인관계도 아주 중요하다.
In the workplace, not only is job performance important, but also are easygoing personal relationships.

2. the course of things are smooth

[Expression] 원만하게 처리하다 to handle smoothly

[Example] 국민들은 여당과 야당이 경색된 정국을 대화를 통해 원만하게 풀어 나가기를 기대한다.
The citizens are hoping to amicably solve the political deadlock through talks between the ruling party and the opposition party.

3. relationship between people is good

[Expression] 원만한 부부 생활 amicable married life
원만한 관계를 유지하다 to maintain an amicable relationship

[Example] 그 사람은 워낙 성격이 모가 나서 주위 사람들과의 사이가 원만하지 못하다.
He personality is so difficult that his relationship with people around him is not amicable.

08 연습문제

[1-12] 다음 밑줄 친 부분과 의미가 비슷한 것을 고르십시오.

Choose the word that is similar to the underlined word.

1. 나는 세계 최고의 대학에 합격했다는 합격 통지서를 받고 내 자신이 너무 자랑스러운 나머지 가슴이 벅찼다.

❶ 기쁘다 ❷ 알차다 ❸ 뿌듯하다 ❹ 엄청나다

2. 해가 뜨자 건물의 윤곽이 점차 선명해졌다.

❶ 뚜렷해지다 ❷ 완전해지다 ❸ 화려해지다 ❹ 날카로워지다

3. 그 아이는 자기 또래에 비해 아주 성숙하다.

❶ 어설프다 ❷ 든든하다 ❸ 어른스럽다 ❹ 믿음직스럽다

4. 그 방들은 수수하지만 깔끔하게 단장이 되어 있었다.

❶ 단순하다 ❷ 썰렁하다 ❸ 소박하다 ❹ 우아하다

5. 한번 저지른 실수는 되돌릴 수가 없으니 매사에 신중해야 한다.

❶ 성숙하다 ❷ 원만하다 ❸ 과감하다 ❹ 조심스럽다

6. 한창 뛰어 놀아야 할 어린 나이에 힘든 노동을 하는 아이들을 보니 너무 가엽고 불쌍했다.

❶ 서글프다 ❷ 안쓰럽다 ❸ 억울하다 ❹ 우울하다

7. 운전자의 사소한 부주의로 대형 사고가 발생해 참으로 속이 타고 가슴이 아팠다.

❶ 괴롭다 ❷ 안타깝다 ❸ 씁쓸하다 ❹ 기막히다

8. 지난 2개월 동안 외국 친구와 언어교환을 통해 언어와 문화를 교류하면서 방학을 알차고 보람 있게 보냈다.

❶ 실속 있다 ❷ 색다르다 ❸ 뿌듯하다 ❹ 역동적이다

9. 인색하기로 소문난 우리 사장님이 연말 보너스를 200% 준다는 소식에 회사 직원들은 모두 얼떨떨한 표정을 지었다.

❶ 어설프다 ❷ 씁쓸하다 ❸ 어수룩하다 ❹ 어리둥절하다

10. 나는 그가 왜 어렵게 들어간 회사를 그만두는 바보같은 짓을 했는지 이해할 수가 없다.

❶ 엄청나다 ❷ 얄밉다 ❸ 어리석다 ❹ 안타깝다

11. 그는 이번 시합에 우승함으로써 1,000만 불이라는 굉장한 돈을 상금으로 받게 되었다.

❶ 불합리하다 ❷ 어마어마하다 ❸ 급작스럽다 ❹ 부담스럽다

12. 나는 네가 심사숙고해서 옳은 결정을 내리기를 바란다.

❶ 알차다 ❷ 귀하다 ❸ 소중하다 ❹ 올바르다

[13-16] 다음 밑줄 친 부분과 의미가 반대인 것을 고르십시오.

Choose the word that is the opposite of the underlined word.

13. 이번 판결로 국제간의 범죄자 인도 절차가 한결 수월해질 것이다.

❶ 완전해지다 ❷ 만만해지다 ❸ 까다로워지다 ❹ 부담스러워지다

14. 우리의 빈틈없는 판매 계획은 사업을 성공으로 이끌었다.

❶ 허술하다 ❷ 성숙하다 ❸ 순진하다 ❹ 어리석다

15. 깊고 고요한 밤공기에 실려 어디선지 모르게 엷은 꽃향기가 흘러왔다.

❶ 진하다 ❷ 순하다 ❸ 독하다 ❹ 선명하다

16. 그는 첫인상은 어수룩해 보였지만 막상 일을 같이 해보니 매사에 빈틈없는 사람이었다.

❶ 신중하다 ❷ 교만하다 ❸ 단단하다 ❹ 치밀하다

[17-31] 다음 (　　)에 알맞은 것을 고르십시오.

Choose the word that fits best in the parenthesis.

17. 국가인권위원회가 국회에 제출한 공식 보고서는 인터넷 게재물에 실명을 써야 한다는 정부의 결정은 (　　　)고 주장하고 있다.

❶ 불공평하다　❷ 불가능하다　❸ 불합리하다　❹ 불필요하다

18. 시의 (　　　) 예산 때문에 빈곤층에게 무료로 의료 서비스를 제공하려던 계획은 잠정적으로 연기되었다.

❶ 빠듯한　❷ 넉넉한　❸ 무분별한　❹ 아슬아슬한

19. 그 요리 연구가는 땅콩 버터와 두부, 딸기를 이용해서 아주 (　　　) 맛의 아이스크림을 개발해 냈다.

❶ 과감한　❷ 씁쓸한　❸ 건전한　❹ 색다른

20. 우리 아이는 지난번 축구 경기에서 상대팀에게 4 대 0으로 패한 것에 대해 아직도 (　　　) 하고 있다.

❶ 두려워　❷ 곤란해　❸ 쓸쓸해　❹ 속상해

21. 그 아이가 처음에는 (　　　) 보였지만 시간이 조금 지나자 버릇없는 행동을 해서 다른 사람들을 불쾌하게 만들었다.

❶ 교만해　❷ 순진해　❸ 얄미워　❹ 날카로워

22. 추석 대목을 맞은 시장은 발 디딜 틈도 없이 사람들로 (　　　).

❶ 어지러웠다　❷ 빈틈없었다　❸ 아슬아슬했다　❹ 시끌벅적했다

23. 아무리 화려하고 웅장한 궁궐도 주인을 잃으면 폐허처럼 (　　　).

❶ 쓸쓸해진다　❷ 느긋해진다　❸ 아까워진다　❹ 엄숙해진다

24. 그날의 농구 경기는 처음부터 끝까지 쫓고 쫓기는 (   ) 경기여서 시합이 끝날 때까지 한시도 긴장의 끈을 놓을 수 없었다.

❶ 무모한 ❷ 안타까운 ❸ 어지러운 ❹ 아슬아슬한

25. 박 과장은 어렵고 곤란한 문제가 생기면 늘 핑계를 대고 자기만 교묘히 빠져 나갔기 때문에 회사 사람들이 모두 그를 (   ) 한다.

❶ 얄미워 ❷ 아쉬워 ❸ 아까워 ❹ 꺼림칙해

26. 피겨 스케이트 선수들이 유연하고 힘을 들이지 않는 듯이 (   ) 동작으로 얼음판 위를 누비고 다녔다.

❶ 끈질긴 ❷ 우아한 ❸ 그윽한 ❹ 역동적인

27. 목격자의 증언으로 결국 무죄인 것이 밝혀졌지만 그녀는 그때 일을 생각하면 (   ) 아직도 속이 부글부글 끓는다고 한다.

❶ 억울해서 ❷ 고소해서 ❸ 어리석어서 ❹ 불합리해서

28. 그의 익살맞은 태도는 (   ) 할 장례식에는 전혀 걸맞지 않았다.

❶ 치밀해야 ❷ 엄격해야 ❸ 엄숙해야 ❹ 빈틈없어야

29. 오늘날 우리는 인터넷을 통해 (   ) 양의 정보를 손쉽게 수집할 수 있다.

❶ 빽빽한 ❷ 엄청난 ❸ 미세한 ❹ 끊임없는

30. 요즘에 나오는 뮤지컬은 다양한 스토리와 (   ) 안무로 그 지평을 넓혀가고 있습니다.

❶ 순진한 ❷ 분주한 ❸ 역동적인 ❹ 시끌벅적한

31. 회사 생활을 잘 하려면 상사와 (   ) 관계를 유지하는 것이 매우 중요하다.

❶ 원만한 ❷ 색다른 ❸ 소중한 ❹ 마땅한

[32-33] 다음 중 형용사의 쓰임이 잘못된 것을 고르십시오.

Choose the sentence where the adjective was used incorrectly.

32.

❶ 우리 아이는 양처럼 순해서 좀처럼 보채지도 않고 말도 잘 듣는다.

❷ 요즘은 장마철인데도 비가 순하게 와서 아직까지 홍수 피해가 나지 않았다.

❸ 가벼운 상처를 입었을 때는 순한 비누와 물로 그 부위를 부드럽게 씻어내는 게 좋다.

❹ 카페인은 우리 몸에 들어오면 심장 박동, 혈류, 호흡, 그리고 신진대사를 몇 시간 동안 가속화시키는 순한 흥분제의 역할을 한다.

33.

❶ 모두 퇴근하고 썰렁한 사무실을 나 혼자 지키고 있다.

❷ 아직 초가을이지만 아침저녁으로는 썰렁해서 보일러를 조금씩 돌린다.

❸ 친구 생일 파티가 처음에는 사람이 적어서 썰렁했지만 시간이 지날수록 차츰 분위기가 살아났다.

❹ 혼자 고향에 남아 썰렁하게 살고 계신 어머니를 생각하자 가슴이 저미는 듯 아팠다.

[34-36] 다음 (　　)에 공통적으로 들어갈 단어의 기본형을 쓰십시오.

Find the one word that fits in the parentheses and write the most basic form.

34.

❶ 그는 허탈감에 빠져 혼자 (　　)게 웃었다.

❷ 나는 (　　)은/ㄴ 맛을 싫어해서 커피에는 꼭 설탕이나 시럽을 넣어 마신다.

❸ 능력도 없고 비전도 없어 내가 차버렸던 옛날 남자 친구가 출세해서 엄청나게 잘 사는 걸 보니 기분이 (　　).

35.

❶ 나는 어머니께 (　　)은/ㄴ 변명을 늘어놓다가 야단만 더 맞았다.

❷ 내 친구는 돈이 된다는 소문만 믿고 (　　)게 그 사업에 뛰어들었다가 돈만 날렸다

❸ 그 배우는 충분한 연습 없이 무대에 올라 (　　)은/ㄴ 연기로 극장에서 웃음거리가 되었다.

36.

❶ 현관문이 너무 (　　)어서/아서/여서 기름을 좀 칠했더니 많이 부드러워졌다.

❷ 3박 4일의 여행 일정이 다소 (　　)다는 의견이 많아 하루를 더 늘리기로 했다.

❸ 죽을 끓일 때 물을 적게 넣으면 (　　)어지니/아지니/여지니 물을 넉넉하게 넣으세요.

❹ 남편 월급으로는 아이들 과외비 대기도 (　　)어서/아서/여서 시간제로 할 수 있는 일을 찾고 있다.

형용사 Ⅲ

09

Adjectives Ⅲ

09 형용사 Ⅲ

001
웬만하다

[웬만하다] 1.to be acceptable 2. to be tolerable

1. level or circumstances are close to the average or a little less than that

[Example] 그 학생은 평소 성실했으며, 성적도 웬만했다.
Not only was that student sincere, but also his grades were acceptable.

2. used as '웬만하면', '웬만한', '웬만해서는', a state that does not break free too far from the permitted range

[Example] 나는 그동안 여러 가지 사건을 경험해서 웬만한 일에는 눈 하나 깜짝하지 않는다.
Because I have experienced so many situations, almost none of them cause me to even blink an eye.

002
유리하다

[유리하다] to be advantageous

to be beneficial or a gain to someone

[Usage] N에/에게 유리하다

[Synonym] 이롭다 to be beneficial

[Antonym] 불리하다 to be unfavorable

[Example] 기온이 높고 비가 많은 여름 계절풍은 벼농사에 특히 유리하다.
It is particularly advantageous to do rice farming when temperatures are high, and there is a lot of rain along with summer seasonal wind.

약속을 이미 했다면 그 약속이 자기에게 유리하건 불리하건 간에 반드시 지켜야 한다.
If you have already promised something, you must keep your promise no matter if it is advantageous or disadvantageous to you.

003
유사하다

[유사하다] to be similar

[Usage] N과/와 유사하다

[Expression] 유사품 imitation
유사성 similarity
유사 단체 kindred organization

[Example] 유사한 사건들이 연일 꼬리에 꼬리를 물고 발생했다.
Similar situations happened one after another.

나는 얼마 전에도 오늘 꾼 꿈과 유사한 꿈을 꾸었었다.
I had a similar dream from today a couple of days ago as well.

004
익살스럽다

[익쌀스럽따] to be humorous

to be deliberately trying to be funny with words or behavior in order to make other people laugh

[Expression] 익살스러운 말 humorous words
익살스러운 표정 humorous expression
익살스러운 행동 humorous behavior

[Example] 무대 위에서 광대가 익살스러운 표정을 짓자 관객들이 폭소를 터뜨렸다.
As soon as the entertainer made a humorous expression, the audience burst out laughing.

시골 장터에서 재미있고 익살스러운 노래가 길게 이어지는 동안 구경꾼들의 박장대소도 끊이지 않는다.
The observers' laughter did not cease while the fun and humorous sound kept playing at the countryside market.

005
잔인하다

[잔인하다] to be cruel

[Example] 이토록 잔인하고도 무자비한 학살을 누가 지시했는가?
Who ordered this cruel and merciless massacre?

이제 그만 헤어지자는 그의 말은 나에게 너무나도 잔인했다.
His words saying that we should break up were too cruel to me.

006
잔잔하다

[잔잔하다] 1.to be tranquil 2.to be calm 3.to be calm 4.to be quiet

1. wind or wave has settled and is calm

[Expression] 잔잔한 호수 tranquil lake
잔잔한 바다 tranquil ocean
잔잔한 수면 ranquil water surface

[Example] 화창한 봄철이어서 바람은 따뜻하고 파도는 잔잔하였다.
Because it was a clear spring day, the wind was warm and the waves were tranquil.

2. atmosphere is silent and peaceful

[Example] 잔잔하던 집안에 한바탕 큰 소동이 일어났다.
A sudden disturbance arose in the otherwise calm house.

3. attitude is relaxed and peaceful

[Expression] 잔잔한 눈빛 calm gaze
잔잔한 미소 calm smile

[Example] 어머니는 품에 안긴 아기를 바라보며 부드럽고 잔잔한 미소를 지으셨다.
My mother gave the baby she was holding in her arms a soft and calm smile.

4. sound is quiet and low

[Example] 그는 눈을 지그시 감고 잔잔한 목소리로 이야기를 시작했다.
He closed his eyes softly and began his story with a quiet voice.

007
저렴하다

[저렴하다] to be inexpensive

price of things are cheap

[Expression] 저렴한 물건 inexpensive item
값이 저렴하다 price is inexpensive
가격이 저렴하다 price is inexpensive

[Example] 이 시장은 물건 값이 저렴하여 늘 많은 사람이 모인다.
This market always has many people that come to it because its' prices are inexpensive.

라디오가 저렴한 가격으로 전국에 보급된 것은 60년대 초반부터였다.
It was in the early 60's when radios were supplied across the nation at an inexpensive price

008
절실하다

[절씰하다] to be desperate

something is very urgent or your heart desires it greatly; feelings or thoughts are in such a strong state that you can feel it in your bones

[Expression] 절실한 눈빛 desperate gaze
절실한 과제 urgent task
절실한 그리움 desperate longing
절실하게 와 닿다 to reach desperately
대책 마련이 절실하다 measures are desperate

[Example] 최근 들어 강한 태풍이 한반도에 자주 영향을 미치므로 이에 대한 대책 마련이 절실하다.
Urgent measures are needed on how to combat the effects of the recent, strong typhoons that hit the Korean peninsula.

그 학생은 입학 시험에 벌써 두 번이나 떨어졌기 때문에 이번 시험에 합격하기를 절실히 원한다.
That student desperately wanted to be accepted on this test because he had already failed the entrance exam twice before.

009
정직하다

[정지카다] to be honest

heart is righteous

[Expression] 정직한 사람 honest person
정직한 행동 honest behavior
정직한 마음 honest heart
정직하게 살다 to live honestly

[Antonym] 부정직하다 to be dishonest

[Example] 그는 비록 가난했지만 정직하고 바르게 살려고 노력했다.
Although he was poor, he made an effort to live an honest and correct life.

부정을 저질러 부자가 되기보다는 가난하더라도 명예롭고 정직하게 살고 싶다.
Instead of becoming rich through illegal ways, I would rather be poor but honorable and honest.

010
조급하다

[조그파다] to be impatient

to be without any patience but instead in a hurry

[Expression] 조급한 성격 impatient personality
조급히 서두르다 to hurry impatiently

[Example] 그는 시험 날짜가 다가오면서 마음이 점점 조급해지기 시작했다.
As the test day came closer, he began to become more and more impatient.

나는 교통사고로 길이 막혀 비행기를 놓칠까봐 조급한 마음에 택시에서 내려서 공항까지 뛰기 시작했다.
I got out of the taxi and began running towards the airport with an impatient mind because I could've missed my plane due to the traffic jam caused by a car accident.

011
주요하다

[주요하다] to be major

to be the main and most important

[Example] 이것들은 모두 제품 생산에 주요한 시설들이다.
Theses are all major facilities for the production of products.

이 시점에서 우리에게 무엇보다 주요한 것은 단결이다.
At this time, nothing is more major to us than unity.

012
중대하다

[중대하다] to be crucial

something that is very important, large, and should not be taken lightly

[Expression] 중대한 결정 crucial decision
중대한 문제 crucial problem

[Example] 그는 순간의 실수로 중대한 과오를 범하고 말았다.
Due to an error made in an instant, he committed a crucial mistake.

천문학자 허블이 발명한 허블망원경은 천문학 연구에 획기적인 발전을 가져온 매우 중대한 발견이었다.
The Hubble telescope invented by the astronomer Hubble, was a crucial discovery that brought on innovative development in astronomical research.

013
지겹다

[지겹따] to become boring

the same act repeats itself and becomes dislikable and not fun

[Example] 방학동안 너무 놀았더니 이제 노는 것이 지겹다.
Because I played so much during the break, playing has become boring now.

힘들게 취직했는데 회사에서 매일 똑같은 일을 반복하자니 지겨워 죽겠다.
Even though it was difficult to get hired , I am bored to death because I do the same task continuously everyday.

014
진실하다

[진실하다] to be truthful

to be truthful and sincere

[Expression] 진실한 벗 a truthful friend
진실한 태도 truthful attitude
진실을 감추다 to hide the truth
진실을 밝히다 to reveal the truth
진실성이 있다 to have truthfulness

[Example] 이번 사건의 진실이 언젠가는 드러나고 말 것이다.
Sooner or later, the truth will be revealed in this incident.

진실한 대화를 통해 서로를 이해하고 더욱 더 가까워질 수 있다.
Through truthful conversations, you can understand each other and become much closer.

015
진지하다

[진지하다] to be serious

attitude or behavior is sincere

[Expression] 진지한 대화 serious conversation
진지한 태도 serious attitude
진지하게 논의하다 to discuss seriously

[Example] 사장은 사원들의 제안을 진지하게 받아들였다.
The boss seriously accepted the employees' suggestions.

그는 전혀 농담하는 기색이 없이 진지한 얼굴로 말했다.
He spoke with a serious face that contained no trace of joking.

016
짜다

[짜다] to be stingy

to be incredibly stingy when it comes to using money

[Example] 씀씀이가 짜면 그 주변으로 사람이 안 모이는 법이다.
If you are stingy with your money, people will not flock to you.

내 친구 민철이는 부자인데도 돈을 내는 일에는 굉장히 짜게 군다.
Even though my friend Minchul is a wealthy man, when it comes to using money he is incredibly stingy.

017
차분하다

[차분하다] 1. to be calm 2. to be calm 3. to be calm

1. mind is at ease and quiet

[Expression] 차분한 성격 calm personality

차분한 태도 calm attitude

마음이 차분하다 mind is calm

[Example] 산을 오르면 마음이 차분하게 가라앉으면서 세속적이고 이기적인 생각들이 다 없어진다.

When you climb a mountain, your mind becomes calm and more at ease while secular and selfish thoughts disappear.

2. voice is not excited but low

[Example] 시험에 또 떨어진 나는 불호령이 떨어질 것이라 예상했지만 의외로 아버지께서는 차분한 목소리로 나를 위로해 주셨다.

I predicted that I would be scolded severely after failing the test again, but surprisingly, my father consoled me in a calm voice.

3. atmosphere is not excited but quiet

[Example] 올해 송년회는 시끌벅적하고 요란했던 작년의 송년회와는 달리 차분한 분위기에서 진행되었다.

This year's year-end party was progressing calmly compared to the boisterous and noisy year-end party last year.

018
창피하다

[창피하다] to be embarrassed

(due to a matter or truth) to be extremely embarrassed

[Synonym] 창피스럽다 to be ashamed

[Example] 나는 여드름이 잔뜩 난 얼굴이 창피해서 고개를 들지 못했다.

I was so embarrassed of my face covered in pimples that I could not lift my head.

그녀는 다른 사람들 앞에서 창피한 줄도 모르고 바닥에 주저앉아 엉엉 소리 내어 울었다.

She had no shame in front of others but just sank to the floor and began crying.

019
철저하다

[철쩌하다] to be thorough

when doing a task, one is very careful and meticulous

[Usage] N에 철저하다

[Example] 이번에 당선된 시장님은 정해진 원리 원칙엔 누구보다 철저하고 예외가 없으셨다.

The elected mayor was chosen thoroughly according to the fixed rules and principles without any exception.

당국은 그 사업의 계획과 시행에 철저하지 못했음을 시인하고 시민들에게 사과하였다.
The authorities apologized to the citizen after acknowledging that they were not thorough with the business plan and its enforcement.

020
초조하다

[초조하다] to be nervous

heart is nervous because of anxiousness

[Expression] 초조한 기색 nervous expression
초조한 얼굴 nervous face

[Example] 그 사람은 말로는 큰소리를 치면서도 초조한지 자꾸 시계를 들여다 보았다.
He must have been nervous even with all of the big talk because he kept looking at his watch.

초조해하거나 불안해하거나 하지 않고 하루하루를 느긋하게 지내는 것이 가장 좋은 장수의 비결이라고들 한다.
The best secret to longevity is to live every day relaxed without feeling nervous or anxious.

021
촉박하다

[촉빠카다] to be tight

deadline or time is close

[Example] 행사 일정이 너무 촉박하게 잡혀 준비를 철저히 하지 못했다.
Because the event schedule was too tight, there was no way to prepare thoroughly.

국가 대표 축구팀은 대회 개최 일주일 전에 소집되어 대회를 준비하기에는 시간이 촉박했다.
Time was too tight to prepare for the competition with the national soccer team only being summoned a week before the opening of the competition.

022
충실하다

[충실하다] to be faithful

to be loyal and sincere

[Usage] N에 충실하다
N에게 충실하다

[Expression] 가정에 충실하다 to be faithful to the family
직장에 충실하다 to be faithful to one's job
자기 자신에게 충실하다 to be faithful to oneself

[Example] 그는 가정에 충실할 뿐만 아니라 애처가로도 소문이 나 있다.
Not only was he rumored to be faithful to his family but he was also known to be a devoted husband.

자신에게 맡겨진 임무를 충실히 수행하고 매사에 최선을 다 하며 살아가다 보면 언젠가는 꼭 성공할 날이 올 것이다.
A day where you succeed will happen without fail if you faithfully carry out the duty given to you and work hard in every matter.

023
치명적이다 [치명저기다] 1.to be lethal 2. to be pernicious

1. when a disease or injury can be life-threatening

[Usage] N이/가 N에/에게 치명적이다

[Example] 그 사람은 자동차 사고로 치명적인 뇌손상을 입어 사망하고 말았다.
He suffered lethal brain damage from the car crash and eventually passed away.

2. irreversibly bad effects are given

[Usage] N이/가 N에/에게 치명적이다

[Example] 한창 감수성이 예민한 나이의 학생들에겐 정학이나 퇴학 같은 조치가 치명적일 수도 있다.
Actions like suspension or expulsion can be pernicious to students who are are particularly sensitive at that age.

024
침착하다 [침차카다] to be poised

to not be excited by getting caught up in one's emotions but instead behaving correctly

[Expression] 침착한 성격 poised personality
침착하게 행동하다 to behave in a poised way

[Example] 우리 형은 침착해서 무슨 일에 맞닥뜨려도 당황하지 않는다.
My older brother is so poised that he never gets flustered when he is suddenly encountered with something.

지진으로 무너진 건물 더미에 갇힌 상황에서도 그들은 서로를 위로하며 침착하게 구조대가 오기를 기다렸다.
Even in the situation where they were trapped in the building rubble from the earthquake, they consoled each other and waited calmly for the rescue team to come.

025
캄캄하다 [캄캄하다] 1. to be pitch-black 2. to be hopeless 3. to not be familiar

1. so dark that one is not able to see anything

[Example] 여름날에도 캄캄한 지하실의 방문을 열면 초겨울의 밤기운과 같은 이상한 한기가 맴돌았다.
Even on a summer night, when the door to the pitch-black basement was opened, a chill akin to early winter hovered around.

2. to be hopeless; there are no means to do anything

[Example] 전 재산을 투자한 회사가 부도가 났다는 말을 듣고 나는 눈앞이 캄캄해져 맥없이 주저앉았다.

I sank down dejectedly and without any hope after hearing that the business in which I had invested all of my assets into had gone bankrupt.

3. to have absolutely no knowledge about something

[Example] 그 여자는 세상 물정에 캄캄해서 여러 번 사기를 당했다.

Because that woman did not know much of the world, she was scammed multiple times.

026
타당하다

[타당하다] to be valid

[Expression] 타당한 처사 valid treatment

타당한 방법 valid method

타당성이 없다 to lack in validity

논리가 타당하다 reasoning is valid

주장이 타당하다 opinion is valid

[Example] 너의 주장은 이 상황에서는 타당하지 않다.

Your opinion is not valid in this situation.

그는 말도 안 되는 논리로 자기 행동이 타당했다고 주장했다.

He used ridiculous logic to insist that his actions were valid.

027
탁월하다

[타궐하다] to be outstanding

skills or ability are exceptional compared to other people

[Expression] 탁월한 선택 outstanding choice

[Example] 그림을 보는 그의 안목은 듣던 대로 탁월했다.

His discerning eye for drawings was as outstanding as rumored.

그는 이야기를 재미있게 하는 데 탁월한 능력을 가지고 있다.

He had an outstanding ability to tell stories in an entertaining way.

028
투박하다

[투바카다] 1. to be crude 2. to be crude

1. appearance looks shabby and is slow, only solid

[Example] 그 제품은 숙련된 기술자가 아닌 견습생이 서툰 솜씨로 만든 것이어서 거칠고 투박했다.

That product was rough and crude because it was not made by an experienced technician but by a probation worker's unexperienced skills.

2. words or actions are rough and not refined

[Example] 그 여자는 조금 전에 쓰던 투박한 사투리 대신 상냥하고 부드럽게 말을 건네고 있었다.
That woman did not use her crude dialect from before but instead was speaking now in a kind and gentle way.

029
특이하다

[트기하다] to be unusual, unique

to be noticeably different from the norm

[Expression] 특이체질 diathesis
특이한 점 unique feature
특이한 성격 unusual personality
특이한 현상 unusual phenomenon

[Example] 고등학교 동창인 민수는 특이한 행동을 자주해서 친구들이 그를 괴짜라고 불렀다.
Friends called my high school alumnus Minsoo a freak because he always exhibited unusual behavior.

손잡이는 보통 나무나 뿔로 되어 있는 것이 많은데 이것은 특이하게도 양쪽을 은으로 장식했다.
Although handles are usually made from wood or antlers, this is unusually decorated on both sides with silver.

030
포근하다

[포근하다] 1. to be warm 2. to be cozy

1. the feeling when something touches the skin is soft and warm

[Example] 아직 2월인데 햇살이 포근하고 바람도 잔잔해서 벌써 봄이 온 것 같다.
Although it is only February, because the sunshine is warm and the wind is calm it already feels like spring has come.

2. emotions or atmosphere is soft and warm which gives a comfortable feeling

[Example] 어머니가 계신 집은 언제나 따뜻하고 포근하다.
The house where my mother stays is always warm and cozy.

031
폭넓다

[퐁널따] 1. to be extensive 2. to be wide

1. the territory of a range concerning a matter is big and wide

[Expression] 폭넓은 활동 extensive activities
폭넓은 교제 extensive association
폭넓게 다루다 to handle extensively

[Example] 내 동생은 어렸을 때부터 책을 많이 읽어 폭넓은 지식과 깊이 있는 사고력을 지녔다.
Because my younger sibling read many books since he was young, he has extensive knowledge and thinking skills with depth.

2. to be broad-minded with tolerance

[Expression] 폭넓은 마음 broad mind

[Example] 선생님은 무례한 학생들의 행동에 처음에는 화가 났지만 폭넓은 마음으로 그들을 용서하기로 했다.
At first, the teacher became angry due to the disrespectful students' behaviors but decided to forgive them with a broad mind.

032
하찮다

[하찬타] 1. to be insignificant 2. to be unimportant

1. to be not exactly excellent

[Expression] 하찮은 솜씨 insignificant skill

[Example] 내가 다니고 있는 직장은 남들 눈에는 하찮아 보이겠지만 내게는 삶의 터전이고 가족을 부양할 수 있게 해 주는 소중한 일터이다.
Although the job I have may seem insignificant to other people, it is a precious workplace that gives me my livelihood and is a way to support my family

2. to be trivial; not important

[Expression] 하찮은 일 unimportant matters
하찮게 여기다 to consider unimportant

[Example] 어떤 경우에도 사람의 생명을 하찮게 여겨서는 안 된다.
No matter the circumstance, you must not regard a human life as unimportant.

033
한결같다

[한결간따] 1. to be unchanging 2. to be constant

1. to continue without change from start to finish

[Expression] 한결같은 태도 unchanging attitude
한결같은 마음 unchanging mind

[Example] 슬플 때나 화날 때나, 한결같은 모습으로 떡 버티고 있는 저 산을 바라보면 조금은 마음이 가라앉곤 하였다.
Whether I am sad or mad, when I look at that unchanging mountain, my mind becomes more at ease.

2. many things seem like they are one

[Expression] 한결같은 반응 constant reactions

[Example] 사람들의 표정은 한결같이 밝았고 흥분에 들떠 있었다.
People's expressions were constantly bright and excited.

034
한심하다

[한심하다] to be pathetic

to be pitiful and worrisome because something is past or short from a limit

[Example] 중학생이 구구단도 못 외우다니 참으로 한심스럽다.
It is pathetic that a junior high school student cannot memorize the times tables.

대학생이랍시고 공부는 안하고 술이나 마시고 다니다니 정말 한심한 일이다.
It is pathetic that you do not study and just drink when you are a university student.

035
해롭다

[해롭따] to be harmful

[Usage] N이/가 N에/에게 해롭다

[Expression] 인체에 해로운 물질 harmful substance to the human body
건강에 해롭다 to be harmful to health

[Example] 너무 살이 찌면 움직임이 둔할뿐더러 건강에도 해롭다.
When you gain weight, not only does it make your body move slower but it is also harmful to your health.

잠을 지나치게 많이 자는 것은 잠을 적게 자는 것만큼 해롭다는 연구결과가 발표되었다.
Research results were presented showing that sleeping too much was just as harmful as sleeping too little.

036
황당하다

[황당하다] to be absurd

words or actions are not sincere but instead unreasonable

[Expression] 황당한 말 absurd words
황당한 일 absurd matter

[Example] 너무 황당한 일이라 그의 말이 사실로 믿기지 않았다.
Because it was such an absurd matter, I did not believe his words as the truth.

공원에서 만난 어떤 노인이 들려준 옛날이야기는 허황되고 황당한 것이었다.
The old story told to me by an elderly man I met at the park was hollow and absurd.

037
흔하다

[흔하다] 1. to be common 2. to be common

1. to be not rare and to be large in quantity

[Expression] 흔한 일 common matter
흔한 사건 common incident
흔한 이름 common name

[Antonym] 드물다 to be rare

[Example] 아이들끼리 놀다 싸우는 것은 흔한 일이다.
Fighting while playing is a common incident amongst children.

2. easy to obtain because there is a lot in quantity

[Antonym] 귀하다 to be rare

[Expression] 흔한 물건 common item

[Example] 휴대 전화는 이제 너무 흔해서 웬만한 학생은 다 하나씩 가지고 있다.
Cellphones are so common that mostly all students have one.

038
흡사하다

[흡사하다] to be similar

to be almost at the same limit or resemble

[Usage] N과/와 흡사하다

[Example] 그 두 사람은 마치 쌍둥이인 것처럼 생김새가 매우 흡사했다.
Those two people's appearance was so similar that they were almost like twins.

이 병은 초기 단계에서는 증상이 감기와 아주 흡사해 사람들이 대수롭지 않게 여겨서 병을 더 키우는 경향이 있다.
This disease in its early stages has such similar symptoms to the cold that people shrug it off and instead tend to let the disease progress.

039
흥미롭다

[흥미롭따] to be interesting

[Expression] 흥미로운 이야기 interesting story
경기가 흥미롭다 game is interesting

[Example] 이 신문에서 연재되고 있는 북한의 문화재에 대한 기사문이 흥미롭다.
This article published in the newspaper about North Korea's cultural assets is interesting.

어제 치러진 월드컵 결승전은 역전에 역전을 거듭하여서 매우 흥미로웠다.
Yesterday's World Cup final match was interesting because there was a repeated turn in the game.

040
희귀하다

[히귀하다] to be rare

[Expression] 희귀한 병 rare illness
희귀한 일 rare matter
희귀한 동물 rare animal

[Example] 이 보석은 좀처럼 보기 힘든 희귀한 것이다.
This jewel is so rare that you hardly see it around.

그 골동품은 너무 희귀하기 때문에 가격을 따질 수가 없다.
That antique is so rare that it is priceless.

041
희박하다

[히바카다] 1. to be thin 2. to be slim 3. to be weak

1. gas or liquid's concentration or density is not thick but instead is low or light

[Example] 사막과 같은 건조 지역, 산지가 많은 지역, 극지방과 같은 추운 지역 등은 인구 밀도가 매우 희박하다.
Areas that are dry like the desert, areas that have a lot of producing districts, and areas that are cold like the polar regions have a very thin population density.

2. hope or probability that something will happen is very low

[Expression] 확률이 희박하다 probability is slim
가능성이 희박하다 possibility is slim
성공률이 희박하다 rate of success is slim

[Example] 공군은 사고 발생 후 실종된 그의 생존 가능성이 희박하다는 결론을 내리고 수색 작업을 중지시켰다.
The air force stopped the search after deciding that the probability of him being alive was slim when he disappeared after the accident.

3. state of emotions or will is not strong but instead weak

[Expression] 의욕이 희박하다 desire is weak
자립심이 희박하다 sense of independence is weak

[Example] 희생정신이 희박한 사람에게 남을 위해 봉사하는 일을 맡겨서는 안 된다.
You must not give the work of volunteering to someone who has a weak sense of sacrifice.

042
희한하다

[히한하다] to be strange

to be very rare and amazing

[Expression] 희한한 일 strange matters
희한한 물건 strange object
희한한 소문 strange rumors

[Example] 황학동 벼룩시장에서는 별의별 희한한 물건을 많이 볼 수 있다.
At the Hwanghak-dong flea market, you can see many various kinds of strange objects.

바다에서 아주 희한하고도 괴상한 모습을 한 물고기가 발견되어 생물학자들의 비상한 관심을 끌었다.
There was extraordinary interest from biologists when a very strange and peculiar-looking fish was discovered from the ocean.

043
힘겹다

[힘겹따] to be difficult

to be lacking physical or mental strength to accomplish a task

[Usage] AV기가 힘겹다

[Example] 몇 년 동안 물가는 자꾸 오르고 월급은 안 올라 먹고 살기가 힘겹다.
Due to the rise in prices over the past few years but no rise in salary, living has become difficult.

나는 요즘 회사에서 맡은 일을 해 내기가 너무 힘겨워서 회사를 그만둘까하는 생각까지 했었다.
I was thinking about quitting my job because the work that I was managing recently was too difficult.

09 연습문제

[1-10] 다음 밑줄 친 부분과 의미가 비슷한 것을 고르십시오.

Choose the word that is similar to the underlined word.

1. 병사들은 실제 전투와 비슷한 상황에서 훈련을 받는다.

❶ 일치하다 ❷ 한결같다 ❸ 유사하다 ❹ 완전하다

2. 우리 회사 제품의 가격은 타 회사 제품에 비해 30%나 쌉니다.

❶ 알차다 ❷ 저렴하다 ❸ 수월하다 ❹ 정직하다

3. 나는 부모님께 형편없는 성적표를 내놓기가 부끄러웠다.

❶ 어설프다 ❷ 초조하다 ❸ 캄캄하다 ❹ 창피하다

4. 방사능 누출은 환경에 돌이킬 수 없을 만큼 나쁜 영향을 미친다.

❶ 잔인하다 ❷ 중대하다 ❸ 절실하다 ❹ 치명적이다

5. 그는 뛰어난 외교술을 발휘하여 협상을 유리하게 이끌었다.

❶ 탁월하다 ❷ 희귀하다 ❸ 타당하다 ❹ 철저하다

6. 오늘은 날씨가 꽤 포근해서 두꺼운 겨울옷 대신 얇은 봄옷으로 바꿔 입고 나온 사람들이 많다.

❶ 선명하다 ❷ 잔잔하다 ❸ 희한하다 ❹ 따뜻하다

7. 그 모조품은 원그림과 거의 같아서 전문가도 감정해 내기가 어려웠다고 한다.

❶ 상이하다 ❷ 흡사하다 ❸ 빈틈없다 ❹ 대조적이다

8. 다른 사람들은 이성을 잃고 있었던 반면에, 그는 차분하게 평정을 유지했다.

❶ 한결같다 ❷ 원만하다 ❸ 냉정하다 ❹ 침착하다

9. 이번 답사에서 보기 드물고 귀한 식물과 곤충이 다수 채집되었다.

❶ 흥미롭다 ❷ 희박하다 ❸ 희귀하다 ❹ 주요하다

10. 그 책은 터무니없는 내용 때문에 관심을 끌었으나, 그 책을 처음부터 끝까지 읽은 사람은 많지 않을 것이다.

❶ 충실하다 ❷ 황당하다 ❸ 흥미롭다 ❹ 희한하다

[11-17] 다음 밑줄 친 부분과 의미가 반대인 것을 고르십시오.
Choose the word that is the opposite of the underlined word.

11. 그는 자기에게 유리한 쪽으로 말을 하였다.

❶ 이롭다 ❷ 하찮다 ❸ 불리하다 ❹ 불합리하다

12. 개인용 컴퓨터가 저렴한 값으로 전국에 보급된 것은 90년대 초반부터였다.

❶ 비싸다 ❷ 타당하다 ❸ 엄청나다 ❹ 희한하다

13. 내가 농담으로 한 말을 그는 진지하게 받아들였다.

❶ 절실하다 ❷ 초조하다 ❸ 흥미롭다 ❹ 장난스럽다

14. 그는 준비를 철저히 한 덕에 시합 전에 느긋하고 자신 있어 보였다.

❶ 초조하다 ❷ 차분하다 ❸ 창피하다 ❹ 캄캄하다

15. 담당 형사는 사건 현장에서 중요한 단서를 찾아냈다.

❶ 어설프다 ❷ 어리석다 ❸ 하찮다 ❹ 투박하다

16. 의사들은 급격한 체중 감소가 건강에 해롭다며 지나친 다이어트에 대해 경고하고 있다.

❶ 이롭다 ❷ 절실하다 ❸ 탁월하다 ❹ 치명적이다

17. 국민들은 선수들의 4년간의 <u>힘겨웠던</u> 훈련이 이번 올림픽에서 보상을 받기를 바라고 있다.

❶ 폭넓다 ❷ 촉박하다 ❸ 수월하다 ❹ 철저하다

[18-29] 다음 ( )에 알맞은 것을 고르십시오.

Choose the word that fits best in the parenthesis.

18. 사람들은 그의 ( ) 행동에 폭소를 터뜨렸다.

❶ 신중한 ❷ 차분한 ❸ 흥미로운 ❹ 익살스러운

19. 그는 평생 일하지 않고 놀고먹겠다는 내 말을 듣고 ( ) 듯 내 얼굴을 물끄러미 쳐다보았다.

❶ 한심한 ❷ 조급한 ❸ 희귀한 ❹ 불합리한

20. 그녀는 눈이 높아서 ( ) 남자는 거들떠보지도 않는다.

❶ 진실한 ❷ 웬만한 ❸ 특이한 ❹ 빈틈없는

21. 어떤 이들은 ( )고 말하지만 그래도 동물 실험은 의학에 상당한 발전을 가져왔다.

❶ 과감하다 ❷ 타당하다 ❸ 억울하다 ❹ 잔인하다

22. 대개의 부모들은 자신들의 자녀가 ( ) 사려 깊은 사람으로 성장하기를 희망한다.

❶ 정직하고 ❷ 황당하고 ❸ 중대하고 ❹ 익살스럽고

23. 거래처 사장님과의 약속 시간은 다가오는데 길이 막혀서 늦을까봐 마음이 ( ).

❶ 빠듯했다 ❷ 촉박했다 ❸ 조급했다 ❹ 아슬아슬했다

24. 해외로 이주할지 말지를 결정하는 것은 그 가족에게 매우 ( ) 일이었다.

❶ 흔한 ❷ 해로운 ❸ 한심한 ❹ 중대한

25. (　　　) 사랑을 막을 수 있는 것은 아무것도 없다.

① 느긋한　② 진실한　③ 희귀한　④ 철저한

26. 그의 (　　　) 목소리는 감정적으로 흥분한 사람들의 마음을 가라앉히는 효과가 있었다.

① 차분한　② 투박한　③ 어지러운　④ 역동적인

27. 개는 인간에게 고양이보다 (　　　). 이는 고양이가 장소에 애착을 갖는 반면에 개는 사람에게 애착을 갖기 때문이라고 한다.

① 얄밉다　② 충실하다　③ 아깝다　④ 꺼림칙하다

28. 그의 의견이 (　　　) 때문에 나는 그의 의견에 전적으로 동의하였다.

① 끈질겼기　② 특이했기　③ 타당했기　④ 희한했기

29. 회사는 그 소문에 대해 즉각적이고 (　　　) 조사를 하겠다고 발표했다.

① 철저한　② 침착한　③ 엄숙한　④ 주요한

[30-31] 다음 중 형용사의 쓰임이 잘못된 것을 고르십시오.

Choose the sentence where the adjective was used incorrectly.

30.

① 이 영화는 잔잔하면서도 깊은 감동을 준다.
② 난 잠자기 전에 잔잔한 음악을 즐겨 듣는다.
③ 파란색은 나를 잔잔하게 해주기 때문에 나는 이 색깔을 좋아한다.
④ 수상비행기는 잔잔한 호수 위를 미끄러져 가다가 천천히 솟아올랐다.

31.

❶ 그 제품이 내년 말 이전에 출시될 가능성은 희박하다.

❷ 사막여우는 매우 희박한 동물이라서 세계적으로 보호를 받고 있다.

❸ 지상의 온도가 섭씨 -20도 이하로 떨어지면 눈이 내릴 확률은 희박하다고 한다.

❹ 고도가 높아질수록 산소가 희박해져서 높은 산을 오르는 산악인들은 산소 마스크를 쓰기도 한다.

[32-33] 다음 (　　)에 공통적으로 들어갈 단어의 기본형을 쓰십시오.

Find the one word that fits in the parentheses and write the most basic form.

32.

❶ 저녁이 (　　)었는지/았는지/였는지 계속 갈증이 난다.

❷ 그 교수님은 학점이 (　　)기로 소문이 나서 수강생이 매우 적다.

❸ 눈물의 (　　)은/ㄴ 성분은 안구 안팎의 염분 농도가 균형을 유지하도록 돕는다.

33.

❶ 실업자가 되니 어떻게 살아야 할지 앞날이 (　　).

❷ 그는 (　　)은/ㄴ 동굴 속을 기어가다가 박쥐에 놀라 움찔했다.

❸ 나는 언제나 일에 파묻혀 지냈기에 집안에서 일어나는 일에 대해서는 (　　).

❹ 시험에 떨어졌다는 말을 듣고 나는 눈앞이 (　　)어져/아져/여져 맥없이 주저앉았다.

[34-35] 다음 (　　)에 들어갈 말의 기본형으로 알맞은 것을 고르십시오.

Choose the basic form of the word that fits in the parentheses.

34.

김철수연구소의 최홍선 대표는 디도스 대란이 발생한 지 1년이 지났지만 각종 보안 위협은 더 지능화된 방법으로 현재에도 진행되고 있다고 경고했다. 그는 이어 돈을 벌기 위해 혈안이 된 프로 해커들이 신형 악성 도구를 유통시키고 청부 공격도 자행하고 있다면서 보안 전문가의 역할과 존재는 아주 (　　　)기 때문에 가장 큰 투자는 사람에 대한 투자임을 다시 한 번 (　　　)게 호소한다고 말했다.

❶ 이롭다-침착하다　　❷ 절실하다-진지하다

❸ 진실하다-엄숙하다　　❹ 조급하다-철저하다

35.

부산역 건너편 초량동은 '상해거리'이다. 항구와 가까워 한 세기 전에 중국인과 일본인이 많이 살았던 곳으로 지금은 화교와 러시아인들이 주인공이다. 그래서 차이나타운의 상징물인 붉은 문을 지나면 간판마다 한자는 물론 러시아 문자도 적혀 있다. 들려오는 언어가 다양하고, 거리의 경관도 독특하다. 이 상해거리는 고풍스럽지만 질그릇 같은 (　　　) 느낌이 있다. 1884년 청나라 영사관이 들어섰던 자리에는 화교 학교가 대신 서 있고, 1950년대부터 대를 이어 장사를 하는 중국 음식점도 많다.

❶ 투박하다　　❷ 잔잔하다　　❸ 차분하다　　❹ 희한하다

부사 I

10

Adverbs I

10 부사 I

001
가급적

[가급쩍] as possible

if possible; if circumstances allow

[Synonym] 되도록 as much as possible

[Example] 예산은 가급적 적게 편성하십시오.
Please organize the budget so that it is small if it is possible.

가급적 빠른 시일 안에 보고서를 작성해서 제출하겠습니다.
I will write the report and submit it as soon as possible.

002
가까스로

[가까스로] 1. barely 2. narrowly

1. take great pains to do something and do it barely

[Synonym] 겨우 barely
간신히 barely

[Example] 실업자 생활을 몇 년 하다가 가까스로 지금의 일자리를 구했다.
I was barely able to obtain this job after living unemployed for many years.

2. narrowly and barely

[Synonym] 겨우 narrowly
간신히 narrowly

[Example] 그 법안은 야당의 반대로 처리에 어려움을 겪다가 임시 국회 막판에 가까스로 국회를 통과했다.
That bill barely passed at the last moment during a temporary session of the National Assembly after encountering a lot of obstacles due to the opposition party opposing it.

003
가령

[가령] 1. assuming 2. for example

1. saying by assumption

[Example] 가령 내일 세상의 종말이 온다면 지금 뭘 하고 싶습니까?
Assuming that tomorrow the world will end, what would you want to do now?

2. for example

[Synonym] 이를테면 for example

[Example] 사람은 누구나 소망을 가지고 있는데, 가령 나는 아주 부자가 되고 싶은 소망이 있다.
Everyone has a wish, for example, my wish is to become very wealthy.

004
간신히

[간신히] barely

extremely hard and narrowly doing something

[Example] 노인은 숨을 거두기 직전에 간신히 몇 마디 유언을 남겼다.
Before the elderly man passed away, he barely said his last testament.

지난번에 큰 지진이 났을 때 우리 가족은 간신히 몸만 빠져 나왔다.
Last time there was the big earthquake, our family barely were able to escape with just our bodies.

005
간혹

[간혹] occasionally

from time to time

[Synonym] 가끔 from time to time

[Example] 아무리 치밀한 사람이라도 간혹 실수할 때가 있다.
No matter how detailed you are, occasionally you will make mistakes.

후문 쪽 길은 좁긴 하지만 지름길이기 때문에 급할 때 간혹 이용하곤 한다.
Although the path towards the back gate is narrow, I use it occasionally because it is a shortcut.

006
감히

[감히] 1. daringly 2. daringly

1. to risk fear or hardship

[Example] 신하가 감히 임금의 명을 거역하다니 죽음을 각오하지 않고서는 있을 수 없는 일이다.
Without daring to die, a liege disobeying the emperor's command is something that could never happen.

2. (usually used with '못하다') words or behavior are presumptuous and thoughtless

[Example] 작은 섬마을에서 자란 나에게 올림픽 출전이라는 것은 감히 상상도 못할 일이었다.
Having grown up in a small island village, I wouldn't dare dreaming of participating in the Olympics.

007
거듭

[거듭] 1. repeatedly 2. repeatedly

1. constantly doing something over and over again; doing something multiple times over

[Example] 그는 이번 사업 계획을 꼭 성공시키리라고 거듭 다짐했다.
He repeatedly made a resolution to succeed in this business.

2. for the second time

[Example] 거듭 말하지만 같은 실수를 되풀이하지 않도록 만전을 기해 주십시오.
I repeatedly say this but make doubly sure that you do not make the same mistakes.

008
걸핏하면

[걸피타면] easily

even if there is a little incident

[Synonym] 툭하면 easily

[Example] 요즘 누나는 신경이 예민한지 걸핏하면 화를 낸다.
It seems that my older sister is sensitive lately because she is easily angered.

깡패들은 걸핏하면 그녀를 찾아와서 돈을 달라고 괴롭혔다.
The gangsters often came around to the girl and bothered her, asking for money.

009
고스란히

[고스란히] remaining intact

remaining intact in its entirety without anything bothering it and without any change

[Example] 나는 봉급 외의 수입은 고스란히 저축했다.
Aside from my salary, I kept my income intact and saved it.

대통령의 생가에는 생전에 쓰던 물건들이 고스란히 남아 있다.
At the birthplace of the president, the items that he used in during his life are left remaining intact.

010
고이

[고이] 1. carefully 2. peacefully 3. peacefully 4. calmly

1. with sincerity; preciously

[Example] 친구는 내가 빌려준 손수건을 고이 접어서 돌려주었다.
My friend carefully folded the handkerchief I lent him and returned it to me.

2. comfortably and smoothly

[Example] 가족의 품에 안겨 떠나신 할머니는 고이 눈을 감으셨으리라 믿습니다.
I believe that my grandmother peacefully closed her eyes when she passed away amongst her family.

3. unimpaired and remaining intact.

[Example] 세월도 많이 지났거니와 전쟁까지 치렀는데 고향집이 고이 남아 있을 리가 만무하다.
It is hardly possible that my house in my hometown has been peacefully left after not only a lot of time has passed but also the war that happened.

4. temperament or attitude is docile

[Example] 아이의 고이 잠든 얼굴을 보니 하루의 피로가 다 사라지는 듯 했다.
After looking at the calmly sleeping face of my child, the day's exhaustion seemed to disappear.

011
고작

[고작] only

barely having enough at best or when counting. means that no matter how much you try to appraise it as good and big, it is not much

[Example] 대학 때 1년 동안 공부했던 스페인어 단어 중에 기억나는 건 고작 인사말뿐이다.
The only things I remember from studying Spanish for a year in college are greetings.

시장 출마에 앞서 행해진 김 의원의 후원회에는 고작 10명의 후원자가 참석했을 뿐이다.
There were only ten people who participated as sponsors in the supporters association for Mr. Kim, the assembly man, that took place before the elections for mayor.

012
곧잘

[곧짤] 1. fairly well 2. frequently

1. doing something fairly well

[Example] 동생은 운동 신경이 발달한 것 같지도 않은데 운동을 곧잘 한다.
Although it seems my younger sibling hasn't developed his athleticism, he plays sports fairly well.

2. often, frequently

[Example] 집 앞 공원은 공부하다 지칠 때면 곧잘 들르던 곳이다.
I used to frequently visit the park in front of my house when I got tired of studying.

013
구태여

[구태여] not necessarily

(used with words that deny or used in a sentence that makes a retort) deliberately trying

[Synonym] 굳이 obstinately

[Example] 네가 혼자서 해결하겠다면 나는 구태여 나서지 않겠다.
If you say that you will solve it by yourself, I will not necessarily interfere.

아무리 범죄자라 해도 구태여 이름과 얼굴까지 공개할 필요는 없다고 본다.
Even if you are a criminal, I do not think it is necessary to reveal a name and face.

014
기꺼이

[기꺼이] readily

with a happy heart

[Expression] 기꺼이 승낙하다 to consent readily
기꺼이 받아들이다 to accept readily

[Example] 남편은 나라를 위해서라면 목숨까지도 기꺼이 내던질 사람이었어요.
My husband was someone who would readily give his life away if it was for our country.

평소에 가장 존경하던 은사님께 결혼식 주례를 부탁드렸는데 기꺼이 승낙해 주셨다.
I asked the teacher who I had respected to be the officiant to my wedding and he readily consented.

015
기껏

[기껃] 1. at most 2. at best

1. (a certain act's or condition's limit) at the max

[Synonym] 겨우 barely
고작 only

[Example] 손님이 많다 한들 기껏 20명인데 무슨 걱정을 그렇게 많이 해요?
At most there are only twenty guests so why are you worrying so much?

2. putting in a lot of effort and doing something purposely but not receiving anything in return

[Example] 기껏 숙제를 도와 줬더니 영수는 고맙다고 하기는커녕 엉터리라고 화를 내더군요.
Even though I tried my best to help Youngsoo with his homework, instead of thanking me he got mad saying that it was unreliable.

016
기껏해야

[기꺼태야] 1. only 2. at most

1. the work you do or the level of it is worthless

[Example] 내가 방송국에서 하는 일이란 기껏해야 소품을 챙기고 정리하는 것이 다였다.
Although I work at the broadcasting station I only gathered the props and organized.

2. (used in front of something that shows quantity) no matter how high or many you have; at the most

[Synonym] 겨우 barely
고작 only
기껏 at most
많아야 at most

[Example] 승용차 한 대의 수송 능력은 기껏해야 네댓 명에 불과하다.
The transportation capacity of a compact car is at most four or five people.

017
기어이

[기어이] 1. surely 2. finally

1. no matter the task, surely

[Synonym] 기어코 by all means

기필코 without fail

[Example] 저들의 속셈이 무엇인지 기어이 밝혀내고야 말겠어.

I will surely reveal what their intentions are.

2. eventually in the end; finally

[Synonym] 기어코 by all means

결국 eventually

마침내 in the end

[Example] 하늘이 잔뜩 흐리더니 기어이 비가 오는구나.

It finally rains after the sky was quite cloudy.

018
기필코

[기필코] without fail

no matter the difficulties, surely; without fail

[Synonym] 반드시 surely

기어이 surely

[Example] 이번 계약은 기필코 성사시켜야 한다.

We must achieve this contract without fail.

지난해의 대선 실패를 거울삼아 이번 선거에서는 기필코 승리합시다.

After taking a lesson from losing last year's presidential election, let's win this election without fail.

019
끝내

[끋내] 1. until the end 2. in the end

1. (usually used with a phrase that negates) until the very end; until the end is reached

[Usage] 끝내 AV지 않다

끝내 AV지 못하다

[Example] 경찰은 공개수사까지 펼쳤으나 범인을 끝내 찾지 못했다.

Even though the police even had an open criminal investigation, in the end they were unable to find the criminal.

2. after arriving at the end; finally

[Usage] 끝내 AV고 말다

끝내 AV어/아/여 버리다

[Example] 나오는 울음을 참다못해 끝내는 엉엉 울고 말았다.

I couldn't suppress my tears and in the end bawled loudly.

020
난데없이

[난데업씨] suddenly

appear suddenly so that you don't know where it came from

[Expression] 난데없이 나타나다 to appear suddenly

[Example] 공원에 난데없이 멧돼지 두 마리가 나타나서 큰 소동을 빚었다.
There was a large disturbance at the park when two boars suddenly appeared.

싸움에서 제삼자가 난데없이 끼어들 때는 울화가 치미는 법이다.
When a third party suddenly interferes in an argument, you can't help but get angry.

021
낱낱이

[난나치] fully

not lacking in anything; everything

[Expression] 낱낱이 밝히다 to reveal fully
낱낱이 드러나다 to be fully exposed
낱낱이 기억하다 to remember fully

[Example] 경찰의 수사가 진행됨에 따라 피의자의 죄과가 낱낱이 드러났다.
Following the police's investigation, the suspect's crime was fully exposed.

형은 어찌나 기억력이 좋은지 내가 한 말을 낱낱이 기억하고 있었다.
My older brother's memory was so good that he could fully remember all of the things I have said.

022
누누이

[누누이] repeatedly

(same words) constantly, many times; repeated many times

[Expression] 누누이 말하다 to say repeatedly
누누이 강조하다 to emphasize repeatedly
누누이 당부하다 to request repeatedly

[Example] 영수는 그 일은 우리 둘만의 비밀이라고 누누이 강조했다.
Youngsoo repeatedly emphasized that this was a secret between us two.

사장이 누누이 당부했음에도 불구하고 직원들이 문단속을 철저히 안 해서 도둑이 들고 말았다.
Even with our boss repeatedly requesting us to lock the door, we ended up having a robber because the employees forgot to lock the door.

023
다만

[다만] 1. merely 2. only

1. at the least. the minimum; barely

[Synonym] 오직 solely
단지 only

[Example] 그는 아무 말도 하지 않고 다만 고개만 끄덕였다.
He didn't say anything but merely shook his head.

2. (added to the subject of one's speech where it speaks about exceptions or requirements) only; however

[Synonym] 단 simply

[Example] 기회는 누구에게나 있다. 다만 잡지 못할 뿐이다.
Chances are given to anyone. It's only that people don't grasp them.

024
더불어

[더부러] along with

along with; together; as one

[Synonym] 아울러 combined

[Example] 우리 향토의 역사와 문화재를 찾아내고 더불어 그 소중함을 인식해야 합니다.
We must find the rural area's history and cultural artifacts along with realizing the importance of them.

이번 청문회의 목적은 쓰레기 소각장 설치의 필요성을 인식하고 더불어 여러분과 솔직한 의견을 나누는 데 있습니다.
The purpose of this hearing is to realize the necessity of building a garbage incineration plant along with discussing your truthful opinions.

025
덩그러니

[덩그러니] by itself

alone and forlornly

[Example] 좀 늦게 학교 운동장에 갔더니 아이가 덩그러니 혼자 앉아 있었다.
When I went to the schoolyard late, my child was sitting all alone and forlornly.

세 평쯤 되는 직원실에는 직원들은 보이지 않고 난로만 덩그러니 놓여 있었다.
The faculty room which looked to be about three pyeong only had a heater by itself with no employees in sight.

026
덮어놓고

[더퍼노코] blindly

without nitpicking about the circumstances or reason

[Synonym] 무조건 unconditionally
무작정 thoughtlessly
무턱대고 blindly

[Example] 아버지는 내가 사업 얘기만 꺼내면 덮어놓고 화를 내신다.
When I bring up the subject of business, my father blindly becomes angry at me.

몸에 좋다고 덮어놓고 아무거나 섭취하면 오히려 건강을 해칠 수 있다.
If you blindly ingest things just because they are said to be good for you, it can actually harm your health.

027
도대체

[도대체] 1. on earth 2. at all

1.(usually used with words that question) in one word; asking something you are extremely curious about

[Example] 도대체 어딜 갔다 이제 오니?
Exactly where are you just coming from?

2. (usually used with words that negate) at all

[Example] 박 작가의 글은 너무 난해해서 무슨 말인지 도대체 이해할 수가 없다.
The author, Mr. Park's, text is so difficult to understand that I can not understand what he is trying to say at all.

028
도리어

[도리어] 1. instead 2. on the contrary 3. rather

1. different or opposite from what you first expected or thought

[Example] 큰돈을 벌겠다고 주식에 손을 대었다가 도리어 파산한 사람이 하나 둘이 아니다.
There are many people who tried their hands at stocks because they wanted to gain a large profit but instead went bankrupt.

2. opposite from the norm or average

[Example] 내가 질문했던 것을 도리어 나에게 되묻는 그가 말할 수 없이 얄미웠다.
The person whom I asked the question to was so odious when he asked me the same question instead.

3. (used after '보다') instead

[Example] 저희 회사에서는 경험이 많다고 자신만만해하는 사람보다는 도리어 겸허하고 성실한 자세로 임하는 사람을 선호합니다.
Our office prefers people who is willing to experience with a sincere attitude rather than someone who is confident because they say that they are experienced.

029
도무지

[도무지] 1. at all 2. at all

1. (usually used with words that negate) no matter what

[Synonym] 도통 at all

[Example] 모르는 사람들뿐인 자리에 나를 불러낸 그 사람의 속셈을 도무지 모르겠다.
I cannot understand his intentions at all for calling me to a gathering where I knew no one.

2. at the least ; entirely

[Synonym] 도통

[Example] 바람은 밤이 되어도 도무지 누그러질 줄 모르고 매섭게 불어 왔다.
Even when it became night, the wind wouldn't soften at all and kept blowing fiercely.

030
도저히

[도저히] no way

(usually used with words that negate) no matter how you try, not at all

[Synonym] 도무지 no way

[Example] 너무 화가 나서 도저히 진정을 할 수 없다.
I am so angry that there is no way I can calm down.

작품들이 너무나 명작이어서 도저히 가격을 매길 수 없다고 한다.
It is said that there is no way to name a price for these works because they are all masterpieces.

031
드디어

[드디어] finally

(after experiencing many hardships) arriving at the end; in the end; eventually

[Synonym] 마침내 eventually

[Example] 꿈에 그리던 내 집을 드디어 마련했다.
I finally arranged to buy the house of my dreams.

차가 험난한 산굽이를 돌아들자 눈앞에 드디어 작은 마을이 나타났다.
After the car went around a rugged mountain bend, the small village finally appeared.

10 연습문제

[1-10] 다음 밑줄 친 부분과 의미가 비슷한 것을 고르십시오.

Choose the word that is similar to the underlined word.

1. 과거가 그대로 보존되어 있는 고대 도시에서의 여행은 꿈만 같았다.

❶ 기필코 ❷ 간신히 ❸ 덩그러니 ❹ 고스란히

2. 이 서류 작성을 가능한 한 빨리 끝내고 보고서를 수정하도록 하세요.

❶ 가급적 ❷ 구태여 ❸ 낱낱이 ❹ 도저히

3. 예를 들어 우리가 무인도에 있다고 치면 가장 필요한 것이 무엇일까요?

❶ 다만 ❷ 가령 ❸ 거듭 ❹ 감히

4. 내 동생은 툭하면 넘어져서 다리가 상처투성이이다.

❶ 난데없이 ❷ 가까스로 ❸ 기껏해야 ❹ 걸핏하면

5. 그녀는 눈치가 빨라서 일부러 말하지 않아도 금방 알 거야.

❶ 구태여 ❷ 기필코 ❸ 누누이 ❹ 낱낱이

6. 공항에서 잃어버린 가방은 끝내 돌아오지 않았다.

❶ 다만 ❷ 결국 ❸ 오직 ❹ 고작

7. 아이가 잘못했다고 무조건 벌을 주어서는 안 되며 아이의 이야기를 먼저 들어보아야 한다.

❶ 덮어놓고 ❷ 난데없이 ❸ 고스란히 ❹ 걸핏하면

8. 치밀한 설계를 바탕으로 세운 백화점 건물이 갑자기 붕괴한 원인을 도무지 알 수가 없다.

❶ 가급적 ❷ 기어이 ❸ 도리어 ❹ 도대체

9. 친구와 싸우게 된 상황을 <u>하나도 빠짐없이</u> 선생님께 말씀드렸다.

❶ 거듭 ❷ 감히 ❸ 낱낱이 ❹ 도무지

10. 시험을 잘 보려고 밤을 새웠는데 시험시간에 잠들어 버려 <u>도리어</u> 시험을 망치고 말았다.

❶ 반대로 ❷ 기꺼이 ❸ 드디어 ❹ 도저히

[11-20] 다음 ( )에 들어갈 말로 알맞은 것을 고르십시오.

Choose the word that fits best in the parenthesis.

11. 동생 앞에서 내가 꼭 그렇게 해야만 하는 이유를 어머니께서 ( ) 강조하셨다.

❶ 반드시 ❷ 기꺼이 ❸ 누누이 ❹ 더불어

12. 검찰은 지위고하를 막론하고 조사해서 뇌물수수 사건의 전말을 ( )밝히겠다고 했다.

❶ 드디어 ❷ 낱낱이 ❸ 도대체 ❹ 간신히

13. 쌍둥이 형제가 하도 닮아서 할머니도 ( ) 혼동하셨다.

❶ 간혹 ❷ 기껏 ❸ 감히 ❹ 가령

14. 책상 위에는 편지 한 장만이 ( ) 놓여 있었다.

❶ 잔뜩 ❷ 더불어 ❸ 덮어놓고 ❹ 덩그러니

15. 영수는 거절당할까 봐 영희에게 ( ) 가까이 가지도 못했다.

❶ 감히 ❷ 고이 ❸ 당장 ❹ 괜히

16. 구청장은 소각장 설치의 필요성을 ( ) 강조했다.

❶ 푹 ❷ 하도 ❸ 제발 ❹ 거듭

17. 나는 슬픔을 참지 못해 ( ) 울고 말았다.

❶ 특히 ❷ 끝내 ❸ 주로 ❹ 점점

18. 고속도로 휴게소에 (　　) 멧돼지가 나타나 여행객들이 대피하는 등 소동이 일어났습니다.

❶ 덩그러니　　❷ 무턱대고　　❸ 난데없이　　❹ 나름대로

19. **가 :** 제임스 씨, 바쁘신데 죄송합니다만 이 영어 문장 좀 해석해주실 수 있어요?
나 : 죄송하기는요. 이런 일이라면 (　　) 도와드리고말고요.

❶ 기꺼이　　❷ 기어이　　❸ 도저히　　❹ 다행히

20. **가 :** 정말 고마워요. 이렇게 위로를 받으니 힘이 나네요.
나 : 뭘요. 제가 할 수 있는 일이라야 (　　) 위로해 드리는 것뿐인데요.

❶ 괜히　　❷ 끝내　　❸ 고작　　❹ 원래

[21-23] 다음 밑줄 친 부분의 의미가 다른 셋과 다른 것을 고르십시오.
Choose the sentence where the underlined word has a different meaning from the other three.

21.

❶ 일주일 동안 땀 흘려서 번 돈이 겨우 십만 원이다.
❷ 어제는 시험 공부하느라고 고작 두 시간밖에 못 잤다.
❸ 옷을 싸게 산다는 것이 도리어 만원을 더 준 셈이 됐다.
❹ 기껏 한 시간 운동했는데 이렇게 힘들다니 정말 운동부족인 모양이다.

22.

❶ 나는 실패를 거듭한 끝에 결국 목표를 달성했다.
❷ 이번에는 기필코 우승하리라는 각오로 훈련에 임했다.
❸ 동생은 그 가방을 갖고 싶어하더니 기어이 사고 말았다.
❹ 그는 그렇게 열심히 노력하더니 마침내 원하던 학교에 합격했다.

23.

❶ 오랫동안 사귀었지만 그의 성격을 도무지 알 수가 없다.

❷ 그 사람이 무슨 말을 하는 건지 도대체 이해를 못 하겠다.

❸ 친구를 상대로 사기를 치려하다니 도저히 용서할 수 없다.

❹ 이번 문제를 해결하기 위해 구태여 제도를 바꿀 필요는 없다고 본다.

[24-25] 다음 밑줄 친 두 단어의 관계가 다른 것을 고르십시오.

Choose the number where the two underlined words have a different relationship.

24.

❶ **가 :** 방학 내내 쉬지도 못하고 일해서 등록금을 간신히 마련했어요.
나 : 그 정도라면 괜찮은 거예요. 전 그것도 모자라서 은행에서 대출받아 겨우 낸 걸요.

❷ **가 :** 그 친구는 걸핏하면 저한테 와서 숙제를 도와 달라고 해요.
나 : 그래요? 저한테는 난데없이 돈을 빌려 달라고 하던데요.

❸ **가 :** 고작 1시간 공부했을 뿐인데 벌써 머리가 아프네요.
나 : 1시간 공부했다면 기껏해야 한 과쯤 공부했을 텐데 그 정도로 머리가 아프면 어떡해요?

❹ **가 :** 덮어놓고 화부터 내시지 말고 제 말씀을 들어 보세요.
나 : 내가 무턱대고 화를 내는 게 아니고 네가 한 일이 어이없어서 그러는 거야.

25.

❶ **가 :** 걱정이 돼서 한 말이 오히려 친구 기분을 상하게 한 것 같아요.
나 : 친구를 위해서 한 일이 도리어 오해를 산 모양인데 오해는 곧 풀릴 거예요.

❷ **가 :** 이 시는 아무리 읽어 봐도 무슨 말인지 도무지 모르겠어.
나 : 난 선생님의 설명까지 들었는데도 도저히 이해가 안 되더라.

❸ **가 :** 세탁기가 고장 났는데 가급적 빨리 와서 수리해 주셨으면 좋겠어요.
나 : 네, 알겠습니다. 될 수 있는 대로 빨리 방문하도록 하겠습니다.

❹ **가 :** 디자인이랑 크기는 마음에 드네요. 다만 값이 좀 비싼 게 흠이군요.
나 : 거듭 말씀드리지만 이만한 제품을 이 가격에 구입하시기는 어렵습니다. 가령 타 회사의 유사한 제품은 값이 2배 쯤 되거든요.

[26-27] 다음 중 부사의 쓰임이 잘못된 것을 고르십시오.

Choose the sentence where the adverb was used incorrectly.

26.

❶ 세 살밖에 안 된 아이가 말을 곧잘 한다.

❷ 몰라도 될 일을 기꺼이 말해서 걱정하게 할 필요는 없다.

❸ 어렸을 때 친구에게서 받은 편지들을 지금도 고이 간직하고 있다.

❹ 우리 팀은 주장 선수의 활약으로 동점을 만든 뒤 연장전에서 승리하며 가까스로 1승을 챙겼다.

27.

❶ 포기하고 나니 도리어 마음은 편해졌다.

❷ 친구의 부탁을 도저히 거절할 수 없었다.

❸ 무리하더니 드디어 그는 몸이 아프기 시작했다.

❹ 그 사람의 얼굴이 지금은 도무지 생각나지 않는다.

[28-30] 다음 (　　)에 들어갈 말로 알맞지 않은 것을 고르십시오.

Choose the word does not fit in the parenthesis.

28.

잉크 카트리지로 위장된 소포 폭탄 2개가 공항 두 군데에서 발견돼 전 세계가 테러 공포에 휩싸였다. 소포 폭탄 중 하나는 다행히 폭발 17분전에 (　　) 분해됐다.

❶ 겨우　　❷ 간신히　　❸ 난데없이　　❹ 가까스로

29.

부모들은 자녀의 이성교제 사실을 알게 되면 성적이 떨어질까 봐, 혹은 잘못된 행동을 할까 봐 걱정부터 한다. 그러나 자녀의 이성교제 문제는 자녀를 부모와 동등한 인격체로 여기는 데에서부터 출발해야 한다.

(　　) '안돼'라고 하기보다 아이가 자라면서 거치는 자연스러운 발달단계로 받아들이고 올바른 조언을 해주어야 한다는 것이다.

❶ 무조건　　❷ 무작정　　❸ 덮어놓고　　❹ 걸핏하면

30.

> 설렁탕 식당의 박 사장은 21세기 경영의 모델이 될 만한 성공한 기업인중의 한명이다.
>
> 박 사장과 함께 일하는 직원들은 존경할 수 있는 사장님을 모시고 일하는 기쁨에 대해 (　　) 이야기한다. 직원 교육에 대한 열정은 대기업 못지않으며 투명한 재무는 이 회사의 가장 큰 장점이자 자랑거리다. 하급 직원에게까지 기업 카드가 제공되고 협력업체의 접대를 받아서는 안 된다는 엄명이 내려져 있다고 한다.

❶ 자주 ❷ 곧잘 ❸ 툭하면 ❹ 이따금

부사 Ⅱ

11

Adverbs Ⅱ

11 부사 II

001
마냥 [마냥] 1. continuously 2. to one's heart's content 3. endlessly

1. continuously; constantly

[Example] 우리는 아무 말 없이 마냥 걷기만 하였다.
We continuously walked without any words being said.

2. not lacking in anything and as much as one wants

[Example] 모처럼 친구들을 만나 마냥 웃고 떠드느라고 시간 가는 줄도 몰랐다.
I didn't know that time was passing because I met my friends after a long period of not seeing them and just laughed and talked to our heart's content.

3. extremely past the level of average

[Example] 분홍 스웨터 소매를 걷어 올린 팔과 목덜미가 마냥 희었다.
The arm and nape that was exposed after the sleeve of the pink sweater was pulled up was endlessly white.

002
마지못해 [마지모태] inevitably

even though you were reluctant to do it, you had no choice but to do it

[Example] 친구가 하도 사정하는 바람에 마지못해 부탁을 들어주었다.
Because my friend pleaded so much, I inevitably granted his favor.

부모님의 권유로 마지못해 의과대학에 들어 왔지만 공부가 적성에 안 맞아서 후회하고 있다.
Although I inevitably went to medical school by my parents' suggestion, I am regretting it because the studies do not fit my aptitude.

003
막상 [막쌍] actually

(different from what you had thought or guessed previously) actually; really

[Example] 나는 집을 떠나려고 나서긴 했지만 막상 갈 곳이 없었다.
Although I left my house trying to run away, I actually had no where to go.

친구가 많다고 생각했는데 막상 고민이 생기니 터놓고 얘기할 수 있는 친구는 별로 없는 것 같다.
Although I thought I had many friends, when I actually had a problem I felt there was not many friends I could talk to without reserve.

004
모조리

[모조리] altogether

everything without missing anything

[Synonym] 모두 everything

전부 everything

몽땅 all

[Example] 집 안에 있는 시계가 모조리 고장 났다.
All of the clocks in the house are completely broken.

나는 도서관의 철학 책을 모조리 독파하겠다는 거창한 계획을 세웠다.
I made the grandiose plans to completely read all of the philosophy books in the library.

005
모쪼록

[모조록] as much as one can

as possible; earnestly hoping for something

[Synonym] 아무쪼록 as much as one can

[Example] 출세도 중요하지만 모쪼록 몸조심하여라.
Although success is important as well, please take care of your body as much as you can.

이번에는 제가 도움을 드릴 차례이니 모쪼록 이를 거절하지 마십시오.
Since it is now my turn to help you, please don't reject me if you can.

006
무려

[무려] as many as, as much as, as long as

(used with words that show quantity) words that show that the quantity is a lot larger than previously predicted

[Usage] 무려 N이나/나

[Synonym] 자그마치 no less than

[Example] 며칠 사이에 물가가 무려 갑절이나 올랐다.
Within a few days, the price of objects has gone up as much as double.

나는 약속 장소에서 무려 두 시간이 넘도록 기다렸지만 그녀는 끝내 나오지 않았다.
I waited as long as two hours for her at the place we promised to meet but in the end she did not come.

007
무턱대고

[무턱때고] thoughtlessly

without any special reason or plans

[Expression] 무턱대고 화를 내다 to get angry thoughtlessly

[Synonym] 무작정 blindly

[Example] 동생은 무슨 일만 생기면 무턱대고 나에게 달려온다.
Whenever something happens to my younger sibling, he thoughtlessly comes running to me.

친구는 나를 보자 전후 사정을 제대로 듣지도 않고 무턱대고 화를 냈다.
My friend got angry thoughtlessly at me without properly hearing the full content as soon as he saw me.

008
미처

[미처] not yet to a point

(used with words that negate) behavior or thoughts before they reach a certain level or situation

[Usage] 미처 AV지 않다
미처 AV지 못하다

[Expression] 미처 모르다 couldn't know yet

[Example] 한국 김치의 종류가 이렇게 많은지 미처 몰랐어요.
I didn't know that there was so much variety in Korean Kimchi.

아침 일찍 집을 나섰기 때문에 우산을 미처 챙기지 못했는데 갑자기 비가 내리는 바람에 무척 당황스러웠다.
I was caught off-guard when it suddenly began raining with me being unable to pack an umbrella because I had left the house early that morning.

009
바야흐로

[바야흐로] at the height of

at the height of; just; soon

[Example] 때는 바야흐로 만물이 소생하는 봄이다.
This moment in spring is when creativity is at the height of revival.

여기저기 붙기 시작한 후보자 홍보 포스터는 바야흐로 본격적인 선거철이 임박했음을 느끼게 해 준다.
The candidate promotion posters getting posted everywhere made me feel the imminent and full-scale of election time.

010
별안간

[벼란간] suddenly

abruptly

[Example] 별안간 벌어진 일이라 잘 기억이 나질 않는다.
Because it happened so suddenly, I can't really remember it.

잠자리에 들었을 때 별안간 밖에서 큰 고함 소리가 들려 왔다.
After I fell asleep, I heard a sudden scream from outside.

011
본래

[볼래] originally

from the beginning; at the beginning

[Synonym] 원래 originally

본디 originally

본시 originally

[Example] 남편은 본래 말이 없고 점잖은 사람이다.
My husband is originally a quiet person who is of a few words.

설렁탕은 본래 서울 지방의 겨울철 전통 음식이다.
Seolleongtang is originally a traditional winter food from Seoul.

012
부쩍

[부쩍] 1. remarkably 2. remarkably

1. a certain object or force increases, grows, or advances forcibly and without reserve

[Expression] 부쩍 늘다 to increase a lot remarkably

부쩍 자라다 to grow a lot rapidly

부쩍 오르다 to rise suddenly

[Example] 한두 해 못 본 사이에 아이는 부쩍 자라 있었다.
Within about two years, the child had grown suddenly.

2. form where you suddenly strain or are anxious

[Expression] 부쩍 긴장하다 to be anxious a lot

[Example] 직원들은 사장님의 안색을 살피며 부쩍 긴장한 모습들이다.
The employees appear to be anxious a lot after studying their boss' face.

013
불과

[불과] only

(usually used in front of words that show quantity) shows that it doesn't pass the quantity

[Usage] 불과 N밖에 없다

불과 N에 지나지 않다

[Synonym] 고작 only

기껏해야 at the most

[Example] 사내에서 부장의 공금 횡령 사실을 아는 사람은 불과 몇 명뿐이었다.
In the office, there are only a few people who know the truth of the head of the department's embezzlement of public money.

불과 한두 시간만 차를 타고 나가면 오염되지 않은 자연이 우리를 기다리고 있다.
Nature which has not yet polluted is only a two-hour car ride away.

014
비로소

[비로소] for the first time

for the first time after an incident only then.happens

[Expression] 비로소 알다 to know for the first time

비로소 깨닫다 to realize for the first time

[Example] 2년 전에 시작한 사업이 비로소 정상 궤도에 올랐다.

The business that started two years ago went on the right track for the first time.

집을 떠나 봐야 비로소 가정의 편안함을 실감하게 된다.

In order to realize for the first time the comforts of home, you must leave your house.

015
사뭇

[사묻] 1. quite 2. continuously

1. (although you didn't think it to be in that state) quite over the average

[Example] 교장 선생님은 평소와는 사뭇 다른 어조로 우리들에게 훈계를 시작하셨다.

The principal started his lessons with us in quite a different tone from the usual.

2. the same from beginning to end

[Synonym] 줄곧 continuously

[Example] 사뭇 조용하기만 하던 병실 분위기가 젊은 환자의 입원으로 갑자기 떠들썩해지며 생기를 되찾은 듯 했다.

It seemed that the constantly quiet hospital room has suddenly become more boisterous and lively along with the hospitalization of a younger patient.

016
새삼

[새삼] anew

(even though you had already felt or known it) it seems like it's new again

[Expression] 새삼 놀라다 to be surprised again

새삼 깨닫다 to realize again

새삼 느끼다 to feel anew

[Related word] 새삼스럽게 anew

[Example] 김 교수님의 말솜씨가 좋다는 것은 전부터 알고 있었지만 오늘 좌담회에서 거침없는 달변을 듣고 새삼 놀랐다.

I knew since long ago that Professor Kim was good at speaking but after hearing his eloquent flow of words during today's symposium I was surprised again.

나는 역사박물관을 관람하면서 선조들의 청동기 주조 기술의 수준이 얼마나 높은 것이었던가를 새삼 느낄 수 있었다.

While viewing the Historical museum, I was able to feel again how advanced our ancestors' skills were in casting bronze .

017
서서히 [서서히] gradually

no in a rush but slowly; little by little; slowly

[Example] 날씨가 따뜻해지면서 서서히 눈이 녹고 있다.
As the weather gets warmer, the snow is gradually beginning to melt.

입대하는 오빠를 태운 기차는 서서히 고향 역을 출발하고 있었다.
The train that was taking my older brother who had enlisted, was gradually departing from our hometown's station.

018
설사 [설싸] even though

(usually used in a negative sentence) used in an assumption

[Usage] 설사 AV/DV는다/ㄴ다/다 하더라도
설사 AV/DV는다/ㄴ다/다 할지라도
설사 AV/DV는다고/ㄴ다고/다고 하여도

[Synonym] 설령 even if
설혹 even if

[Example] 사막에는 거의 비가 오지 않는다. 설사 온다 하더라도 극히 소량에 지나지 않는다.
It barely rains in the desert. Even if it were to rain, it would be an extremely small amount.

그가 너를 속였다는 것도 믿기 어렵지만, 설사 그랬다손 치더라도 그를 원망해서는 안 된다.
As hard as it is to believe that he deceived you, even if he did do that, you must not resent him.

019
소위 [소위] so-called

what people usually say

[Synonym] 이른바 so-called

[Example] 백화점에 가 보니 소위 '명품' 가방 매장에 사람들이 줄을 서 있었다.
Once I got to the department store, there was a line of people at the so-called designer bag store.

아기는 탄생한 지 21일이 되어서 소위 '삼칠일'을 지낸 후에야 외부인과 접촉하는 것이 전통이다.
It is tradition that only after the so-called baby's twenty-first day of life is celebrated after the baby's twenty first day of being born, can outsiders come into contact.

020
손수

[손수] personally

without relying on someone else, doing something personally

[Expression] 손수 만들다 to personally make

손수 돌보다 to personally look after

[Synonym] 몸소 personally

친히 in person

[Example] 어머니는 명절 때면 손수 옷을 만들어 우리에게 입히시곤 했다.
When it was a holiday, my mother would personally make clothes and have us wear them.

할아버지는 성품이 부지런하시고 빈틈이 없으셔서 만 평의 과수원을 손수 돌보셨다.
Because my grandfather's nature was to be hard-working and irreproachable, he personally looked after an orchard that was ten thousand pyeongs.

021
수북이

[수부기] in a heap

shape that objects are stacked in or filled in is quite high and ample

[Expression] 수북이 쌓이다 to be stacked in a heap

수북이 담기다 to be filled in a heap

[Example] 이틀 사이에 마당에 낙엽이 수북이 쌓였다.
For two days, the leaves in the yard were stacked in a heap.

소쿠리에 수북이 담긴 달걀을 안고 나올 때는 대단한 부자가 된 것 같은 흐뭇함을 느꼈다.
When I walked out with the basket filled in a heap of eggs, I felt such satisfaction as if I were incredibly wealthy.

022
슬쩍

[슬쩍] 1. stealthily 2. slightly 3. secretly 4. slightly

1. calmly while no one knows

[Expression] 슬쩍하다 to steal

슬쩍 훔치다 to stealthily

[Example] 다들 술에 취해 정신이 없는 사이에 나만 슬쩍 빠져 나와 집으로 돌아 왔다.
While everyone was so drunk that they could not think straight, I stealthily escaped and returned home.

2. lightly without using too much strength

[Expression] 슬쩍 치다 to slightly hit

슬쩍 건드리다 to slightly nudge

[Example] 그는 내 옆을 지나갈 때 어깨를 슬쩍 부딪치며 눈짓을 했다.
When he passed by me, he slightly hit my shoulder and gave me a glance.

3. elusively without a trace

[Expression] 슬쩍 떠보다 to secretly feel out

[Example] 나는 그 사람이 내 이야기에 관심이 있는지 슬쩍 떠 보려고 찾아 갔다.
I went to find him in order to secretly feel out if he was interested in my story.

4. not particularly worrying about something, not putting effort into something and doing it quickly

[Expression] 슬쩍 훑어 보다 to slightly skim

[Example] 그는 책을 한 번 슬쩍 훑어보더니 재미없다는 듯 곧 던져 버렸다.
After he slightly skimmed the book, he threw it in an instant as if it was not interesting .

023
실컷

[실컫] 1. to one's heart's content 2.without restraint

1. as much as you want; as much as one likes; enough

[Synonym] 마음껏 as much as one likes.

[Example] 어렸을 때 우리 집은 제과점을 했기 때문에 다른 것은 몰라도 빵은 실컷 먹었다.
Because my family owned a bakery when I was young, although I couldn't get to eat anything else enough but I ate bread to my heart's content.

2. very extreme; very

[Example] 그 아이는 실컷 맞고 돌아와서도 다음날 또 싸움을 걸었다.
Even after he got beat without restraint, he picked another fight the next day.

024
썩

[썩] 1. quite 2. quickly

1. enough to catch one's fancy

[Expression] 썩 잘 하다 to do very well
썩 내키지 않다 to be very halfhearted

[Synonym] 상당히 considerably

[Example] 처음 만들어 본 음식치고는 맛이 썩 괜찮았다.
The taste was quite alright considering the fact that it was a dish I made for the first time.

2. quickly without delay

[Example] 썩 나오지 못하고 뭐하고 있는 거야?
What are you doing that you won't come out quickly?

025
아예

[아예] 1. from the beginning 2. never 3. might as well

1. before something happens; from the beginning

[Synonym] 애당초 from the start

[Example] 그 문제에 대해서는 김 선생님이 모르실 수도 있으니 아예 사무실에 가서 문의해 보세요.
Mr. Kim may not even know about that problem so you should go inquire directly in his office from the beginning.

2. absolutely not; not at all

[Usage] 아예 AV지 않다
아예 AV지 말다

[Example] 같은 반 학생들이 모두 어찌나 우수한지 장학금은 아예 꿈도 꿀 수 없었다.
I could never even dream of receiving a scholarship because all the students in my class were so outstanding.

3. (if done that way) rather; entirely

[Synonym] 차라리 rather

[Example] 혼자서 걱정만 하느니 아예 속 시원히 털어 놓겠다.
Instead of worrying by myself, I might as well spit it out.

026
아울러

[아울러] 1. also 2. additional

1. (usually used in the form of '-과/와 아울러') plus or added on to whatever is in front

[Synonym] 함께 together
더불어 along with

[Example] 경찰은 교통사고 사망을 줄이기 위해 지속적인 교통지도단속과 아울러 사고다발지역에 대한 시설 개선에 힘써 왔다.
In order to decrease the percentage of deaths from car accidents, the police enforced traffic and also worked on improving accommodations in places of frequent accidents.

2. along with many

[Example] 그처럼 지혜와 용기를 아울러 갖춘 사람은 보기 드물다.
It is hard to find someone who has wisdom in addition to courage like he does.

027
어김없이 [어기멉씨] certainly

without fail; surely

[Example] 그는 자기가 약속한 것은 어김없이 지킨다.
He is certain to keep all the promises that made.

자연의 순리대로 올해도 가을은 어김없이 찾아왔다.
Following the laws of nature, fall came without fail this year as well.

028
어느덧 [어느덛] before one knows

while you didn't even know it happened; something that already happened while you were unaware

[Synonym] 어느새 before one knows

[Example] 외국 생활을 시작한 것이 엊그제 같은데 어느덧 20년이란 세월이 지났다.
It seems like just yesterday when I started my life abroad, but before I knew it, 20 years have already passed.

10년 만에 고향에 돌아와 보니 코흘리개였던 조카가 어느덧 고등학생이 되어 있었다.
After returning to my hometown for the first time in ten years, little kid who was my relative had become a high school student before I knew it.

029
어련히 [어련히] undoubtedly

(usually used in question form) showing that something will obviously play out well so there is no need to worry; nothing will go wrong

[Example] 선생님께서 직접 하신 일인데 어련히 알아서 잘 하셨겠습니까?
Isn't it undoubtable that the task has been done well by our teacher?

아우들이 그런 인사는 어련히 잘 챙겼을라고요. 걱정하실 필요 없어요.
There is no need to worry. Our younger siblings have undoubtedly taken care of those greetings.

030
어차피 [어차피] anyway

to do either way; either way it happens; no matter how you do it. however it happened

[Example] 어차피 이 일은 성사되기 힘들테니 준비하느라고 괜히 헛수고할 필요는 없네.
In any case, this task will be hard to achieve so there is no need to uselessly put in your effort into preparing for it.

하나라도 틀리면 어차피 다시 해야 하니까 기한을 지키지 못하는 한이 있더라도 이 서류를 완벽하게 작성하겠어요.
Because I have to do it all over anyway if I even make one mistake, I will draw up these documents perfectly even if I miss the deadline.

031
억지로

[억찌로] against one's will

to the point where it is by force; by force even when it doesn't match with reason or requirements

[Expression] 억지로 참다 to suppress against one's will
억지로 시키다 to force against one's will

[Example] 나를 무시하는 듯한 그 사람의 태도에 화가 치밀었으나 억지로 참았다.
Even though anger flared when it seemed like he disregarded me, I suppressed it against my will.

하기 싫은 일을 억지로 하면 능률도 오르지 않고 금방 싫증나기 마련이에요.
If you are forced against your will to do something you didn't want to do, efficiency does not increase and it is sure thing that you will grow tired of it.

032
언뜻

[언뜯] 1. by chance 2. in an instant

1. (without planning beforehand) by chance; in a moment

[Expression] 언뜻 보다 to catch a glimpse of by chance

[Synonym] 얼핏 in accident

[Example] 그는 언뜻 보아도 점잖은 사람이라는 것을 알 수 있었다.
Even if you catch a glimpse of him by chance, you can tell that he is a gentle person.

2. when thoughts or memories suddenly are recalled

[Expression] 언뜻 떠오르다 to rise in an instant
언뜻 깨닫다 to realize in an instant

[Synonym] 문득 suddenly
별안간 suddenly

[Example] 차창 밖으로 황금색 들판이 보이자 요 몇 년간 돌아가지 못한 시골 고향이 언뜻 떠올랐다.
Thoughts of the hometown in the country I couldn't return to for a few years rose in an instant as soon as I saw the gold fields outside the car window.

033
여지없이 [여지업씨] beyond anything

mercilessly, without necessity for more; there is no other way or possibility

[Example] 올해 지방선거에서 여당은 여지없이 참패했다.
In this year's local elections, the ruling party totally crushed.

신상품의 높은 수수료가 증권사들의 새로운 수익원이 될 것이란 기대는 여지없이 빗나갔다.
The expectations that the high charge on the new products would be the new source of revenue for the stock firm was beyond wrong.

034
오로지 [오로지] only

without any other probability; only

[Synonym] 오직 solely

[Example] 그 당시에는 교통수단이라고는 오로지 나룻배뿐이었다.
At that time, the only means of transportation was by boat.

동화 작가가 기획하고 그림 작가와 출판사가 동참하여 출간한 이 책은 오로지 기부를 목적으로 쓰인 것이라고 한다.
The book that was published from planning by a children's book author along with an artist and publishing company participating, is said to be written only for donations.

035
온통 [온통] wholly

everything

[Usage] 온통 N으로/로 차다
온통 N으로/로 덮이다
온통 N에 휩싸이다

[Example] 골짜기는 온통 초록색으로 덮여 있었다.
The valley was wholly covered in green.

오랜 시간 기다리던 아기가 태어나자 집안은 온통 웃음소리로 꽉 찼다.
The whole house was filled wholly with the sounds of laughters after the baby we had been waiting a long time for was finally born.

036
워낙 [워낙] 1. by nature 2. very

1. by nature; originally

[Synonym] 원래 originally
원체 originally

[Example] 이곳은 워낙 한겨울에도 얼음이 어는 법이 없이 봄날같이 따뜻한 고장이다.
This place is a region where it's as warm springtime by nature, so ice doesn't form even in the middle of winter.

2. (fundamentally) very

[Example] 아버지는 성격이 워낙 느긋하셔서 작은 일에는 좀처럼 당황하는 일이 없으시다.
Because my father's personality is very relaxed, he rarely becomes flustered at small incidents.

037
의외로

[의외로] unexpectedly

different from thoughts or expectations or even predictions

[Synonym] 뜻밖에 surprisingly

[Example] 주머니는 커다란 부피에 비해 의외로 가벼웠다.
Compared to the large volume of the pocket, it was unexpectedly light.

그 남자는 몸집은 큰데 성격은 의외로 소심했다.
Although he had a large frame, his personality was unexpectedly timid.

038
이따금

[이따금] 1. occasionally 2. once in awhile

1. often in a period of time

[Example] 심심할 때면 이따금 산에 올라가 달을 바라보곤 한다.
When I have time, I occasionally go up the mountain and look at the moon.

2. sometimes once in awhile

[Example] 유학생활에 적응하지 못해 도중에 포기하고 귀국하는 학생이 이따금 있다.
Once in awhile, there are students who cannot adjust to the study abroad lifestyle and give up during it to return home.

11 연습문제

[1-10] 다음 밑줄 친 부분과 의미가 비슷한 것을 고르십시오.

Choose the word that is similar to the underlined word.

1. 외로울 때면 가끔 산에 올라가서 하늘을 바라보다 내려오곤 했다.

   ❶ 언제나 ❷ 여전히 ❸ 기필코 ❹ 이따금

2. 하기 싫은 일을 억지로 하면 좋은 결과가 나오기 어렵다.

   ❶ 절대로 ❷ 어차피 ❸ 마지못해 ❹ 엄청나게

3. 소나무 숲에 나 있는 산책로는 언제까지나 걷고 싶은 오솔길이다.

   ❶ 마냥 ❷ 미처 ❸ 온통 ❹ 아예

4. 교내 독창대회에서 상이란 상은 다 우리 반 친구들이 휩쓸었다.

   ❶ 아울러 ❷ 모조리 ❸ 일부러 ❹ 오로지

5. 집필 중이던 작품이 채 완성되기도 전에 그는 세상을 떠나고 말았다.

   ❶ 미처 ❷ 설사 ❸ 이미 ❹ 언뜻

6. 회식 모임이 너무 길어져서 피곤해진 나는 슬쩍 자리에서 빠져 나와 집으로 돌아왔다.

   ❶ 슬슬 ❷ 얼른 ❸ 급하게 ❹ 말없이

7. 수업이 없는 토요일인 이른바 '놀토'(노는 토요일)의 취지는 학생들이 학습에서 벗어나 창의적 활동이나 체험학습 등을 할 수 있도록 하자는 데에 있다.

   ❶ 그저 ❷ 소위 ❸ 마냥 ❹ 널리

8. 요즘은 결혼을 해서 생활에 얽매이기보다는 자유를 실컷 누릴 수 있는 독신으로 살겠다는 젊은이가 늘고 있다고 한다.

   ❶ 당당히 ❷ 공연히 ❸ 골고루 ❹ 마음껏

9. 평일이어서 백화점이 한산할 줄 알고 구경하러 갔는데 의외로 쇼핑객이 많아서 깜짝 놀랐다.

❶ 가급적 ❷ 구태여 ❸ 뜻밖에 ❹ 별안간

10. 대기 중의 공기를 이용해서 열을 발생시키는 신형 난방 기구는 폭발이나 화재 위험과 더불어 유해가스 발생까지 막는 이점이 있다.

❶ 아울러 ❷ 긴밀히 ❸ 따라서 ❹ 상관없이

[11-20] 다음 ( )에 알맞은 것을 고르십시오.

Choose the word that fits best in the parentheses.

11. 그가 돌아왔다는 사실을 아는 사람은 ( ) 몇 명뿐이었다.

❶ 불과 ❷ 설마 ❸ 차마 ❹ 무려

12. 지붕마다 눈이 ( ) 쌓여 있는 모습은 마치 한 폭의 그림 같았다.

❶ 어찌나 ❷ 수북이 ❸ 줄줄이 ❹ 함부로

13. 신입생 환영회에서 내가 술을 못 마신다고 했는데도 선배는 ( ) 폭탄주를 마시게 했다.

❶ 억지로 ❷ 의외로 ❸ 비로소 ❹ 어차피

14. 가족과 떨어져 외국에서 생활하다 보니 가족의 소중함을 ( ) 깨닫게 되었다.

❶ 막상 ❷ 새삼 ❸ 마침 ❹ 하필

15. 친구에게서 곤란한 부탁을 받고 한참을 고민한 끝에 ( ) 그 부탁을 들어주었다.

❶ 일부러 ❷ 모처럼 ❸ 마지못해 ❹ 틀림없이

16. 흰 수염을 기른 그 할아버지는 오늘도 ( ) 공원에 나타나 새들에게 모이를 주고 있었다.

❶ 어찌나 ❷ 어느덧 ❸ 더욱이 ❹ 어김없이

17. 학생으로서 공부가 ( ) 피할 수 없는 일이라면 즐기면서 할 수 있는 방법을 찾아보자.

❶ 어련히 ❷ 어차피 ❸ 뜻밖에 ❹ 소홀히

18. 평소엔 4시간이면 갈 수 있는 곳을 폭설로 인해 ( ) 10시간이나 걸려서 가야 했다.

❶ 불과 ❷ 미처 ❸ 무려 ❹ 기껏

19. 정부가 국민을 위해서 ( ) 알아서 잘 해 줄까 하고 안이하게 생각할 게 아니라 국민은 국민으로서의 정당한 요구를 해나가야 할 것이다.

❶ 막연히 ❷ 모쪼록 ❸ 어련히 ❹ 어설피

20. 운동이 꼭 필요하다는 걸 알면서도 ( ) 시작하려고 하면 어떤 운동을 해야 할지, 어떻게 시간을 내야 할지 몰라서 주저앉은 적이 한 두 번이 아니다.

❶ 새삼 ❷ 막상 ❸ 다만 ❹ 고작

[21-23] 다음 밑줄 친 부분의 의미가 다른 셋과 다른 것을 고르십시오.

Choose the sentence where the underlined word has a different meaning from the other three.

21.

❶ 학교에서 집까지 무려 두 시간이나 걸린다.
❷ 한 시간쯤 지난 줄 알았더니 기껏 십 분밖에 안 지났다.
❸ 그렇게 어려운 문제를 불과 일 분만에 풀었다니 정말 놀랍다.
❹ 하루 종일 고생한 대가로 고작 이 만원을 받고 보니 좀 어이가 없었다.

22.

❶ 친구들을 만나면 이따금 노래방에 가기도 한다.
❷ 오늘은 구름이 많이 끼고 때때로 비가 오겠습니다.
❸ 춥고 지루했던 겨울이 가고 바야흐로 만물이 소생하는 봄이 왔다.
❹ 한국어의 높임법이 복잡해서 간혹 한국인조차 잘못 사용하는 경우가 있다.

23.

❶ 해안 사구는 풀로 덮여 있어 얼핏 보기에는 모래 언덕 같지 않다.

❷ 연수와 민수는 너무 닮아서 언뜻 보면 형제라고 착각하기 쉽다.

❸ 김 교수님에 대해서 이야기만 듣다가 막상 만나 보니까 느낌이 완전히 달랐다.

❹ 이번에 적발된 위조지폐는 잠깐 봐서는 식별할 수 없을 만큼 진짜 화폐와 똑같다.

[24-25] 다음 밑줄 친 두 단어의 관계가 다른 것을 고르십시오.

Choose the number where the two underlined words have a different relationship.

24.

❶ **가 :** 여기만 해도 공기가 도심과는 사뭇 다르군요.
나 : 네, 도심에서 1시간 거리인데도 분위기가 꽤 다르지요.

❷ **가 :** 차에 시동을 걸고 천천히 출발해 보세요.
나 : 그럼 서서히 출발하도록 하겠습니다.

❸ **가 :** 그녀는 오늘도 어김없이 나를 면회하러 와 주었어.
나 : 난데없이 면회를 오다니, 무슨 일이야?

❹ **가 :** 이 한복은 어머니가 손수 만들어주신 것이에요.
나 : 어머니께서 이 한복을 직접 지으셨다고요? 솜씨가 정말 훌륭하시군요.

25.

❶ **가 :** 큰일 났어. 지갑과 돈, 여권을 모조리 잃어버렸어.
나 : 가방에 들어 있던 걸 전부 잃어버렸다는 거야?

❷ **가 :** 갑자기 좋은 기회가 생겨서 중국으로 유학을 가게 됐어.
나 : 별안간 유학을 간다고? 무슨 공부를 할 거야?

❸ **가 :** 그 황당한 소식 듣고 어찌 해야 할지 몰라서 무작정 너한테 달려 왔어.
나 : 무턱대고 나를 찾아온다고 해결되는 것도 아닌데 뭐.

❹ **가 :** 영수 씨는 본래 제주도 출신이에요.
나 : 역시 그렇군요. 제주도 사투리를 워낙 잘 해서 신기하게 생각했었거든요.

[26-27] 다음 중 부사의 쓰임이 잘못된 것을 고르십시오.

Choose the number where the adverb was used incorrectly.

26.

① 케이크는 언뜻 딸기로 뒤덮여 있었다.
② 어머니는 오로지 나만을 위해서 지금껏 살아오셨다.
③ 우리 팀은 농구대회 본선에서 강팀을 만나 여지없이 지고 말았다.
④ 항상 꼴찌였던 그 팀이 이번 대회에서 의외로 좋은 성적을 거두었다.

27.

① 이 아이는 피아노를 썩 잘 치는군요.
② 학교를 졸업하고 어느덧 이십 년이란 세월이 흘렀다.
③ 아이를 낳고서 비로소 부모님의 은혜를 알게 되었어요.
④ 하기 싫은 일을 어차피 시켜서 사고가 난 거 아니에요?

[28-30] 다음 (   )에 들어갈 말로 알맞지 않은 것을 고르십시오.

Choose the word that does not fit in the parenthesis.

28.

학벌지상주의를 깨고 당당하게 실력으로 성공을 거둔 화제의 인물이 있다. 그 주인공은 중학교만 졸업하고 대리운전기사로 시작해 연매출 200억을 올리는 국내 최대 대리운전업체의 사장이 된 김동근 대표다. 8년 전 대리운전기사로 시작한 그는 (   ) 젊은 열정과 패기만으로 한 회사의 대표 자리까지 올랐다고 한다.

① 단지 ② 오직 ③ 오로지 ④ 아울러

29.

한 유명 커피 전문점이 지난달부터 가요를 포함한 다양한 장르의 음악방송을 시작했다. 고객은 휴대 전화 문자나 인터넷 홈페이지로 노래를 신청을 할 수 있는데 처음에 이 의견을 냈을 때는 옛날 음악다방 분위기가 될 거라며 반대하는 의견이 많았지만, 시작해 보니 (　　) 20–30대 손님들의 호응이 뜨겁다고 한다. 그래서 현재 하루 2시간으로 제한되어 있는 음악 방송 시간을 더욱 늘릴 계획이라고 한다.

❶ 뜻밖에　　❷ 우연히　　❸ 의외로　　❹ 놀랍게도

30.

우리 지역에서 가정보육교사제도가 시행된 지 2년째다. 전문 보육교사가 36개월 미만의 아동이 있는 가정을 직접 방문해 1대 1로 돌보는 이 제도는 부모의 보육선택권을 존중하고 보육의 질을 높였다는 평가를 받고 있다.

처음엔 남한테 아이 양육을 맡기는 게 (　　) 내키지 않았다는 한 부모는 "전문교육을 받고 양육 경험이 많은 가정보육교사가 아이들을 잘 돌보는 모습을 보면서부터 마음이 놓였다"며 가정보육교사가 없었더라면 직장생활을 계속하기 어려웠을 것이라고 매우 만족해했다.

❶ 썩　　❷ 별로　　❸ 여간　　❹ 그다지

부사 Ⅲ

12

Adverbs Ⅲ

12 부사 III

001
저절로

[저절로] automatically

without using the strength of something else; also naturally without using the strength of artificiality

[Expression] 저절로 나오다 to automatically come out

저절로 생기다 to automatically happen

[Synonym] 절로 naturally

[Example] 약도 안 먹었는데 감기가 저절로 나았다.
Even though I didn't take any medicine, my cold got better automatically.

나이가 든다고 해서 저절로 성숙해지는 것은 아닌 듯싶다.
It seems that just because you get older doesn't mean you automatically mature.

002
제대로

[제대로] 1. properly 2. properly 3. properly

1. fitting into the standard or formality

[Example] 경제 문제 때문에 가족이 기능을 제대로 못하는 가족 해체 현상이 나타났다.
The phenomenon where families were dissolving were appearing because family's couldn't properly carry out their functions due to economic problems.

2. the way that you have decided

[Example] 여행 일정이 빡빡하여 제대로 구경을 못했다.
Because the vacation schedule was so tight, I couldn't properly sightsee.

3. appropriate degree

[Example] 한식 상차림을 제대로 배우기 위해 요리학원에 다니고 있다.
In order to learn how to properly set a Korean meal, I am attending a culinary school.

003
죽

[죽] 1. in a row 2. in a row 3. rapidly 4. into shreds 5. stretch out 6. gulp down 7. drain out

1. to draw a line or row straight

[Example] 나는 중요한 부분에 줄을 죽 그으면서 책을 읽었다.
I read the book while underlining the important parts.

2. many things are evenly or lined in uniformly

[Example] 옷장을 열어 보니 한 번도 입지 않은 듯한 옷들이 죽 걸려 있었다.
When I opened the closet, clothes that I seem to have not even wore once were all hung in a row.

3. to read, recite, or say without hesitation

[Example] 철수는 큰 소리로 구구단을 죽 외워 나갔다.
Chul Soo recited the times tables rapidly.

4. to rip or strip off paper or fabric in one movement without stopping

[Example] 편지 봉투를 죽 찢더니 서둘러 편지를 꺼내 읽었다.
As soon as he ripped open the envelope, he hurriedly took out the letter and read it.

5. to open up straight or spread

[Example] 어른들이 나가기가 무섭게 그는 다리를 죽 펴고 앉았다.
As soon as the adults left, he spread his legs wide and sat.

6. to drink water or liquids in one take

[Example] 갈증이 나서 사발에 있는 물을 죽 마셨다.
Because I was thirsty, I gulped down the water in the bowl.

7. to have liquid or energy flow out all at once

[Example] 거기서 철민은 갑자기 온몸의 힘이 죽 빠져 버리는 듯 했다.
It seemed as if all of the strength in Chulmin's body drained out there suddenly.

004
줄곧

[줄곧] continuously

to follow after something happens; continuously

[Example] 그는 아침부터 줄곧 나를 기다리고 있었다고 했다.
He said that he continuously waited for me since the morning.

나는 태어나서부터 줄곧 섬에서 살아서 육지 사람에게 시집가는 것이 소원이었다.
Because I continuously lived on the island since I was born, it was my wish to get married to someone who lived on main land.

005
차라리

[차라리] rather

showing that one is relatively better than the other even when both things being compared are inconvenient.

[Example] 비서에게 하나하나 설명하느니 차라리 내가 하는 게 빠르겠어요.
Doing it by myself would be rather faster than explaining it one by one to the secretary.

기껏 도와주고도 이런 말을 들을 바에야 차라리 도와주지 말 걸.
I would rather not help if it means helping to the best of my ability and yet hearing these words.

006
차마

[차마] cannot bear

(used in the context where it negates the verb that comes after) pitiful and regrettable so you dare not

[Usage] 차마 AV지 않다
차마 AV지 못하다
차마 AV을/ㄹ 수 없다

[Synonym] 도저히 no way

[Example] 공포 영화의 장면들이 너무 끔찍해서 차마 눈 뜨고 볼 수 없었다.
Because the scenes in the horror movie were so gruesome, I couldn't bear to open my eyes and watch.

회사 상황이 아무리 어렵다고 해도 직원들 생각을 하면 차마 회사 문을 닫을 수는 없다.
No matter how hard the circumstances for the business, I cannot bear closing the doors if I think of my employees.

007
턱없이

[터겁씨] 1. absurdly 2. outrageously 3. unreasonably

1. whimsical and not fitting with common sense; very different from the average

[Example] 턱없이 넓은 목욕탕은 마치 수영장 같았다.
The absurdly extensive bath tub almost seemed like a swimming pool.

2. too much; greatly

[Expression] 턱없이 모자라다 outrageously lacking

[Example] 환자 수에 비해 간호사의 수는 턱없이 모자랐다.
Compared to the number of patients, the number of nurses was outrageously insufficient.

3. not fitting with level or fraction

[Synonym] 무턱대고 blindly

[Example] 물가가 턱없이 올라가니 서민들은 앞날이 캄캄할 뿐이라고들 한다.
The future is said to be bleak for the ordinary people as the price of objects unreasonably rise.

008
툭하면

[투카면] easily

(not a desirable act) even at the smallest excuse; like a habit, often

[Synonym] 걸핏하면 readily

[Example] 형은 툭하면 말을 안 듣는다고 동생을 쥐어박기 일쑤다.
At the slightest provocation, my older brother is quick to hit my younger sibling saying that he was not listening.

그는 툭하면 전화해서 자기 사업에 투자하라고 나를 꼬인다.
He habitually calls me trying to get me to invest in his business

009
하긴

[하긴] actually

(used to speak positively about something that happened before or a story) to speak the truth

[Example] 하긴 이 더운 여름날에 공사장에서 일하려니 덥기도 하겠지.
Well, of course it would be hot to work at a construction site on a hot, summer day like this.

하긴 직장을 옮긴다는 건 간단한 일은 아니니 좀 더 신중을 기하는 게 좋지요.
Well, moving jobs is not a simple task so it's important to use discretion.

010
하마터면

[하마터면] nearly

(after barely breaking free from a dangerous situation) if you even faltered a bit

[Usage] 하마터면 AV을/ㄹ 뻔하다

[Synonym] 까딱하면 easily

[Example] 형의 사고 소식에 아버지는 하마터면 쓰러지실 뻔했다.
My father nearly fainted after hearing the news about my older brother's accident.

길이 안 막혔기에 망정이지 하마터면 기차를 놓칠 뻔했다.
Fortunately there was no traffic otherwise we could have nearly missed the train.

011
하물며

[하물며] much more

(compared to the truth mentioned before and showing more positivity for the truth said after) moreover; furthermore

[Usage] N도 AV/ DV는데 /은데 /ㄴ데 하물며 N은/는 AV/ DV으랴/랴

[Example] 집안일도 내 마음대로 잘 안 되는데 하물며 나라 일은 오죽하랴.
Things in my house don't go my way, let alone the affairs of the country.

짐승도 제 새끼는 귀한 줄 아는데 하물며 사람이야 말해서 무엇하겠습니까?
If even a beast knows how to treasure its child, how do you think a human would be?

012
하염없이

[하여멉씨] 1. endlessly 2. blankly

1. without an end

[Example] 그는 두 주먹을 불끈 쥐고 하늘을 쳐다보며 하염없이 눈물을 흘렸다.
He clenched his two fists and stared at the sky while endlessly crying.

2. without any thought

[Example] 그녀는 노을이 지는 창가에 앉아 바다를 하염없이 바라보고 있었다.
She sat at the window where the sun was setting and blankly stared at the ocean.

013
하필

[하필] of all occasions

(used in a sentence when you are displeased or disappointed) not differently and in just that way

[Expression] 하필이면 of all things

[Example] 하필 버스가 고장 나는 바람에 예정보다 2시간이나 늦게 서울에 도착했다.
Of all occasions, I arrived in Seoul two hours later than expected because the bus broke down.

밀린 빨래를 하려고 마음먹었는데 하필이면 왜 오늘 단수가 된다는 거야?
Why does there have to be an outage of all things when I finally made up my mind to do the accumulated laundry?

014
한껏

[한껃] to the utmost limit

until the level that you can do something; to the maximum; very much, extremely

[Expression] 한껏 즐기다 enjoy to the utmost limit

[Example] 젊음은 한번 가면 돌아오지 않는 것이니만큼 한껏 즐기고 싶어요.
I want to enjoy to the utmost limit my youth which will not return once it has gone.

봄 기분을 만끽하려고 한껏 멋을 부리고 친구들과 꽃구경을 갔다.
I went to view the flowers with my friends after prettifying myself to the utmost limit, because I wanted to fully enjoy the spring.

015
한사코

[한사코] to the death

to be constantly stubborn; to use all energy

[Expression] 한사코 우기다 to insist to the death

한사코 말리다 to dissuade to the death

한사코 거절하다 to reject to the death

[Example] 막내는 겨울 방학을 시골 큰댁에서 지내겠다고 한사코 우겼다.
The youngest sibling insisted to the death that he would spend his winter break at the country home of the head of the family.

가족들이 한사코 말렸으나 그는 아프리카로 난민 의료 활동을 하러 떠났다.
Although the family dissuaded him to the death, he left to Africa to start his activities for medical treatment for refugees.

016
한창

[한창] at the prime

when something is with the most energy or the best condition

[Example] 요즘의 우리 딸은 한창 피어나는 꽃처럼 곱고 예쁘다.
Lately, my daughter is as pretty and beautiful as a flower that is blooming at its prime.

학교 급식은 한창 자라는 어린이들에게 공급되는 것인 만큼 영양의 균형이 잘 잡힌 식사가 제공되어야 한다.
A nutritiously balanced meal must be offered as the school lunch to the children who are growing at their prime.

017
한층

[한층] all the more

one level up from the present state; especially

[Example] 꽃잎을 장식한 녹두전이 봄의 입맛을 한층 더 해 준다.
The flower petals decorating the mung bean pancake serves to all the more enhance the flavor of spring.

음주운전 사고율이 10년 새 2배로 급증하자 경찰은 음주운전 단속을 한층 강화하기로 했다.
The police have decided to all the more strengthen the crackdown on drunk driving as the accident rate for drunk driving doubled in ten years.

018
함부로

[함부로] 1. thoughtlessly 2. impolitely

1. roughly without thought; at random

[Synonym] 무턱대고 blindly

[Example] 전문가가 아닌 사람의 말을 듣고 함부로 약을 쓴다는 건 위험한 일입니다.
Thoughtlessly taking medicine ofter listening to someone who is not an expert is a dangerous act.

2. ill-mannered

[Synonym] 감히 to dare

[Example] 이 분 연세가 자네보다 한참 위인데 함부로 이름을 부르면 안 되지.
You cannot impolitely call his name when he is much older than you are.

019
행여

[행여] possibly

possibly while doing something

[Usage] 행여 AV을/ㄹ까
행여 AV을/ㄹ까봐

[Synonym] 행여나 possibly
혹시 perhaps

[Example] 행여 복권에 당첨이라도 될까 하고 매주 5장씩 복권을 사요.
Because I could possibly win the lotto, I buy five lottery tickets weekly.

사업에 실패하고 나서는 행여 누구 아는 사람이라도 만나게 될까봐 외출도 자제했던 때가 있었다.
There was a time after my business failed, where I restrained myself from leaving the house because I could possibly meet someone I knew.

020
혹시

[혹씨] 1. possibly 2. possibly 3. possibly

1. although not concrete, from what I guess

[Synonym] 혹시나 possibly
혹시라도 possibly

[Example] 혹시 어제 저에게 전화하셨어요?
Did you possibly call me yesterday?

2. possibly; (that something will happen) there seems to be a possibility

[Synonym] 혹시나 possibly
혹시라도 possibly

[Example] 그는 혹시 자기에게도 뭔가 이득이 있을까 하여 자리를 떠나지 않고 있었다.
He did not leave his spot because he thought that there could possibly be a profit for him as well.

3. in case of; (if something happens) in that case

[Synonym] 만약 if
혹시나 possibly
혹시라도 possibly

[Example] 혹시 제가 없는 사이에 그 분이 오시거든 잠시만 기다려 달라고 전해 주세요.
If by some chance he comes while I'm not present, can you tell him to wait for a moment.

021
혹여

[호겨] 1. possibly 2. unexpectedly

1. although you're not sure, it could happen; doesn't exceed a guess or presumption

[Synonym] 혹시 possibly

[Example] 혹여 오해하실 분이 계실까 봐 다시 한 번 설명을 해 드리겠습니다.
Because there are people who could possibly misunderstand, I will explain one more time.

2. unexpectedly

[Example] 혹여 그 분을 만나시더라도 제 이야기는 하지 말아 주세요.
Even if you unexpectedly happen to meet him, please do not speak of me.

022
흔쾌히

[흔쾌히] readily

with a satisfied and happy heart; (without hesitation) happily

[Expression] 흔쾌히 받아들이다 to readily accept
흔쾌히 허락하다 to readily consent
흔쾌히 승낙하다 to readily consent
흔쾌히 수락하다 to readily agree

[Example] 시민단체 대표는 구청과 주민 간 협의의 중재자 역할을 흔쾌히 수락했다.
The representative of the civic group readily consented to the role of being the intermediary to the deliberation between the district office and the residents.

은사님은 오랜만에 찾아온 제자의 결혼식 주례 부탁을 흔쾌히 들어주셨다.
The former teacher to the student who had come to seek him readily accepted his favor to officiate his wedding.

023
흠뻑

[흠뻑] 1. fully soaked 2. fully 3. fully 4. fully

1. (water) fully soaked in, very wet

[Expression] 흠뻑 젖다 to be fully soaked

[Example] 운동을 한 시간쯤 하고 나면 땀으로 옷이 흠뻑 젖는다.
After I exercise for an hour, my clothes are fully soaked in sweat.

2. (in a certain situation or feeling) to be deeply pulled in or to sink into

[Expression] 흠뻑 빠지다 to fully sink into

[Example] 그 남자는 잠에 흠뻑 빠져 주위가 시끄러워도 일어날 줄 모른다.
He is so fully asleep that no matter how loud his surroundings are, he doesn't wake up.

3. (with powder or dust) to have a lot stuck on your body or to breathe in a lot

[Example] 아이는 놀이터에서 놀다가 모래를 흠뻑 뒤집어쓰고 집으로 돌아왔다.
My child returned home covered fully in sand after playing at the playground.

4. (from alcohol) extremely drunk

[Example] 그의 손엔 술병이 들려 있었고 그는 벌써 흠뻑 취해 있었다.
There was already a bottle of alcohol in his hand, and he was already fully drunk.

12 연습문제

[1-10] 다음 밑줄 친 부분과 의미가 비슷한 것을 고르십시오.

Choose the word that is similar to the underlined word.

1. 초등학생이 긴 영어 문장을 죽 읽어나가는 것을 보고 모두들 감탄했다.

❶ 난데없이　❷ 거침없이　❸ 끊임없이　❹ 아낌없이

2. 영수는 외교관인 아버지를 따라 계속 외국에서만 생활해서 한국어가 서투르다.

❶ 거듭　❷ 그저　❸ 줄곧　❹ 곧잘

3. 이번에 개발에 성공한 신약이 혹여 부작용이라도 있을까 봐 임상 실험에 신중을 기하고 있다.

❶ 설사　❷ 혹시　❸ 절대　❹ 다만

4. 아이들은 엄마가 해 주는 밥이 건강에 좋다는 걸 알면서도 툭하면 외식을 하자고 한다.

❶ 걸핏하면　❷ 대수롭게　❸ 쓸데없이　❹ 하필이면

5. 대통령은 남미의 한 국가를 방문하여 공동선언문을 채택하고 경제협력을 한층 강화하기로 합의했다.

❶ 아예　❷ 거듭　❸ 감히　❹ 더욱

6. 내년부터 병원과 철도, 항공사들이 함부로 파업할 수 없도록 제한하는 법이 시행된다.

❶ 갑자기　❷ 임시로　❸ 절대로　❹ 제멋대로

7. 숲속을 맨발로 한참 걷고 나니 마음을 억누르고 있던 분노와 스트레스가 자연적으로 사라졌다.

❶ 구태여　❷ 우연히　❸ 저절로　❹ 갈수록

8. 유명 연예인 친구에게 내 결혼식의 사회를 맡아 달라고 부탁했는데 그 친구는 주저하지 않고 내 부탁을 들어주었다.

❶ 한사코　❷ 공연히　❸ 흔쾌히　❹ 도리어

9. 그 영화에서 학도병들이 전쟁에 끌려가 사투를 벌이는 모습을 보면서 나는 하염없이 눈물을 흘렸다.

❶ 계속 ❷ 한창 ❸ 희미하게 ❹ 진심으로

10. 친구의 권유로 요가를 시작했는데 한 달쯤 되니까 한결 몸이 가볍고 유연해졌다.

❶ 일단 ❷ 한층 ❸ 한껏 ❹ 차츰

[11-20] 다음 ( )에 들어갈 말로 알맞은 것을 고르십시오.

Choose the word that fits best in the parenthesis.

11. 경주에서 신라 시대의 유적을 ( ) 구경하려면 최소한 3박 4일은 필요하다.

❶ 고이 ❷ 결코 ❸ 제대로 ❹ 수시로

12. 한약은 맛이 써서 조금씩 천천히 먹으면 더 먹기 힘드니까 단숨에 ( ) 마시는 게 좋다.

❶ 죽 ❷ 푹 ❸ 꽉 ❹ 썩

13. 아무리 명품이라 해도 ( ) 비싼 제품을 보면 입이 다물어지지 않는다.

❶ 억지로 ❷ 턱없이 ❸ 갈수록 ❹ 제대로

14. 참기 어려운 굴욕감까지 느끼면서 일을 할 바에야 ( ) 그만두는 게 낫겠어.

❶ 차라리 ❷ 도대체 ❸ 아무리 ❹ 아무튼

15. 갑자기 비가 쏟아지는 바람에 물에 빠진 생쥐처럼 ( ) 젖고 말았다.

❶ 줄줄 ❷ 깜짝 ❸ 깜빡 ❹ 흠뻑

16. 하루아침에 빚더미에 앉은 동창생을 ( ) 모른 척 할 수 없어서 대출 보증을 서 주었다.

❶ 미처 ❷ 미리 ❸ 이왕 ❹ 차마

17. 감사의 뜻으로 선물을 드리고 싶었지만 선생님께서 (　　) 사양하시는 바람에 전하지 못하고 돌아 왔다.

❶ 오히려　❷ 마침내　❸ 한사코　❹ 도저히

18. 이번에 발표된 사진집 속에서 그 여배우는 분위기 있는 눈빛과 청순한 얼굴이 절묘한 조화를 이루며 매력을 (　　) 표출하고 있다.

❶ 힘껏　❷ 한껏　❸ 무려　❹ 기껏

19. 가끔은 내 발 씻기도 귀찮건만 (　　) 남의 발은 오죽할까 싶은데 어느 성당의 신부님은 신도들의 발을 손수 씻겨주신다고 한다.

❶ 막연히　❷ 모쪼록　❸ 어련히　❹ 하물며

20. 개장 첫날에 (　　) 비가 오고 기온이 떨어지는 바람에 해수욕장은 피서객이 없어 썰렁했다.

❶ 자칫　❷ 온통　❸ 하필　❹ 실컷

[21-23] 다음 밑줄 친 부분의 의미가 다른 셋과 다른 것을 고르십시오.

Choose the sentence where the underlined word has a different meaning from the other three.

21.

❶ 어머니가 조기에 암을 발견했으니 망정이지 하마터면 큰 일 날 뻔했다.
❷ 영희는 불면증 때문에 잘 수 없다면서 걸핏하면 한밤중에 전화를 걸어 나를 깨운다.
❸ 어제 밤에 지하철이 끊기는 것도 모르고 놀다가 잘못하면 집에 못 갈 뻔했다.
❹ 오늘은 집에서 일찍 나왔는데 도중에 버스가 고장 나서 까딱하면 지각할 뻔했다.

22.

❶ 사장님께 결혼식 주례를 부탁드렸더니 흔쾌히 수락해 주셨다.
❷ 교수님께서는 입사 시험에 필요한 추천서를 기꺼이 써 주셨다.
❸ 친구에게 대출 보증을 부탁했는데 두말 않고 들어 주어서 얼마나 고마웠는지 모른다.
❹ 오랜만에 만난 후배가 한사코 저녁 값을 치르겠다고 해서 나는 본의 아니게 얻어먹게 됐다.

23.

❶ 입학원서는 우편으로 보내거나 혹은 인터넷으로 직접 접수할 수 있다.
❷ 그들은 혹여 들통이 나더라도 서로 모르는 사이라고 말하기로 약속했다.
❸ 식당 사장은 음식을 나르랴 손님들이 혹시 불편한 것이라도 있나 살피랴 분주했다.
❹ 공장 종업원들의 파업으로 행여 생산에 차질이 생길까 봐 염려했으나 임시직원들 덕분에 큰 문제는 없었다.

[24-26] 다음 중 부사의 쓰임이 잘못된 것을 고르십시오.
Choose the sentence where the adverb was used incorrectly.

24.

❶ 처음엔 거절했지만 그의 끈질긴 권유를 못 이겨 차마 받아들이고 말았다.
❷ 아내는 수저를 들려고 하다가 문득 상 위에 놓인 남편의 쪽지를 발견했다.
❸ 내 앞에 아무리 시련과 역경이 닥친다 해도 다 헤치고 나갈 각오가 되어있다.
❹ 나는 아이가 놀이터에서 놀 때는 맨발로 흙장난을 할 수 있도록 구태여 신발을 신기지 않는다.

25.

❶ **가 :** 어머니, 오늘 친구가 이사해서 도와주고 왔어요.
나 : 그러니? 도와준다면서 차라리 방해를 한 건 아니겠지?

❷ **가 :** 아직 6월인데도 한여름 같은 더위 때문에 에어컨이 날개 돋친 듯 팔린대요.
나 : 하긴 요즘엔 밤에도 너무 더워서 선풍기만으로는 견딜 수가 없더라고요.

❸ **가 :** 기말시험 날짜가 발표되었습니다. 좋은 결과를 얻도록 준비하시기 바랍니다.
나 : 아! 기말 시험 날짜가 내 생일과 겹쳤어. 왜 하필 그 날이지?

❹ **가 :** 직원들의 친목 도모를 위해 단합대회를 겸한 야유회를 다음 달 5일에 서울 공원에서 갖도록 하겠습니다.
나 : 저… 그날 혹시 비가 오면 야유회는 취소되는 건가요?

26.

❶ **가 :** 갑자기 소나기가 와서 우산이 없는 친구들은 비를 맞고 집에 갔어요.
나 : 넌 우산을 챙겨 갔으니 망정이지 하마터면 너도 비를 맞을 뻔 했구나.

❷ **가 :** 그런 부탁이라면 제가 쉽게 해결해 드릴 수 있습니다. 염려 마십시오.
나 : 정말이십니까? 제 부탁을 함부로 들어 주셔서 뭐라고 감사의 말씀을 드려야 할지 모르겠습니다.

❸ **가 :** 동생분이 외국에서 유학하고 계시다고 했지요? 부모님께서 많이 보고 싶어하시겠어요.
나 : 물론이죠. 누나인 저도 이토록 보고 싶은데 하물며 부모님은 어떠시겠어요?

❹ **가 :** 너는 뛰어난 외국어 실력에다가 인턴 경험까지 풍부하니까 취업은 문제 없을 거야.
나 : 아니에요. 요즘처럼 경쟁이 치열한 때에 제가 과연 취업할 수 있을까 걱정이 돼요.

[27-30] 다음 (　　)에 들어갈 말로 알맞은 것을 고르십시오.
Choose the word that fits best in the parenthesis.

27.

가: 옆집 중학생은 여름 방학을 이용해서 어학연수를 간대요.
나: 어학연수? 영어를 배우러 가는 건가?
가: 맞아요. 아무래도 연수를 다녀오면 자신감도 생길뿐더러 외국문화도 접해 볼 수 있어서 일석이조일 것 같아요.
나: (　　) 요즘은 입시에서나 취업에서 영어가 차지하는 비중이 워낙 크니까…….

❶ 하긴　❷ 하필　❸ 설마　❹ 설사

28.

최근 경제 악화로 인해 신용 불량자나 실업자가 늘어나면서 자살하는 사람이 급증하고 있다. 희망 없이 하루하루를 힘들게 살 바에야 (　　) 죽음을 택하겠다는 극단적인 생각에 의한 것이다. 그러나 모든 것은 마음먹기에 달려 있다고 하지 않는가? 죽을 용기로 도전한다면 못할 일이 무엇이 있겠는가?

❶ 뜻밖에　❷ 무조건　❸ 차라리　❹ 되도록

29.

어젯밤에 내린 집중호우로 실종자와 재산 피해가 속출하고 있다. 인근 군부대 군인들이 구조 작업에 나섰으나 인원이 (　　　) 부족한 상황이다. 정부도 수해 복구를 지원할 대책을 마련 중이며 구조작업에 참여할 인원도 대폭 늘리겠다고 발표했다.

❶ 간신히　　❷ 턱없이　　❸ 제대로　　❹ 충분히

30.

'신이 내린 웰빙 과일'로 불리는 블루베리가 요즘 제철을 맞아 수확이 (　　)입니다.

최근에 세계 10대 장수식품으로 선정되면서 건강식품으로 인기를 얻고 있는 블루베리가 까만 포도송이처럼 탐스럽게 익어 나무에 주렁주렁 달렸습니다. 귀농한 한 농가가 시범재배에 성공하면서 지난해부터 본격적으로 출하되고 있습니다.

❶ 한창　　❷ 부쩍　　❸ 물론　　❹ 활짝

의성어 · 의태어

13

Onomatopoeias Mimetic words

13-1 의성어

001
깔깔 [깔깔]

(usually a child or girl) the sound when you laugh with a high sound as if you cannot contain your laughter

[Heavy word] 껄껄

[Example] 그녀는 내가 무슨 말만 하면 재미있다는 듯이 깔깔 웃었다.
She laughed "깔깔" whenever I said something, as if it were funny.

002
껄껄 [껄껄]

the sound when you laugh refreshingly loud

[Example] 아버지는 내 대답이 마음에 드셨는지 기분 좋게 껄껄 웃으셨다.
My father must have liked my answer because he laughed "껄껄".

003
꽝 [꽝]

1. the sound when something heavy and solid falls to the ground or crashed into another object

[Synonym] 쾅

[Example] 직원들이 의견의 일치를 보지 못하고 우왕좌왕하자 사장은 책상을 꽝 치며 벌떡 일어났다.
Because the employees' opinions didn't form a consensus and kept going back and forth, the boss hit his desk with a "꽝" sound and stood up rigidly.

2. the sound when a gun or a canon is fired or a bomb explodes

[Synonym] 쾅

[Example] 꽝 소리와 함께 공사장의 발파 음이 천지를 진동했다.
With a "꽝" sound, the land shook from the blasting of the construction site.

004
둥둥 [둥둥]

the sound as if one is continuously hitting a large drum

[Example] 우리 학교 응원단들이 일제히 북을 둥둥 치며 한껏 기세를 올리기 시작했다.
Our school cheerleaders hit the drums "둥둥" all at once and raised the spirit with all their might.

005
빵빵 [빵빵]

1. the sound where balloons or bombs suddenly explode one after another

[Example] 할머니는 아이들이 길에서 고무풍선을 빵빵 터뜨릴 때마다 깜짝깜짝 놀라신다.
My grandmother is very startled every time children pop rubber balloons "빵빵" out on the street.

2. the sound when a car honks its horn continuously

[Example] 새벽이면 빵빵 울려 대는 트럭들의 경적 소리에 자꾸 잠을 깨게 된다.
When it becomes morning, I keep waking from my sleep because of the sounds of trucks honking their horn "빵빵".

006
삐걱삐걱 [삐걱삐걱]

the rough, continuous sound made when two big and solid objects keep touching each other and grind or rub against each other

[Example] 아무리 살금살금 걸어도 복도의 마룻바닥에서 삐걱삐걱 소리가 났다.
No matter how silently I walked, the wood floor in the hallway made a "삐걱삐걱" sound.

007
쨍그랑 [쨍그랑]

the clear sound when a thin metal object or glass falls or crashes into something

[Example] 어머니를 돕는답시고 설거지를 하다가 접시를 떨어뜨리는 바람에 접시가 쨍그랑 하고 깨졌다.
I was doing the dishes in order to help my mom but because I dropped a plate, it went "쨍그랑" and broke.

008
쯧쯧 [쯛쯛]

the light clucking sound your tongue makes because something looks miserable or pitiful

[Example] 어머니는 내가 하는 일들마다 마음에 안 차시는지 그저 혀만 쯧쯧 차고 계셨다.
It seemed that my mom did not like any of my actions because all she did was cluck her tongue "쯧쯧".

009
찰칵

[찰칵]

1. the sound made when a small and solid object lightly crashes into something

[Example] 그는 재빨리 호주머니에서 라이터를 꺼내 찰칵 불을 켜서 내 코앞으로 내밀었다.
He quickly took out a lighter from his pocket, lit it with a "찰칵" sound, and stuck it in front of my nose.

2. the sound made when you press the shutter on a camera

[Example] 요즘 휴대전화의 카메라는 찍을 때 찰칵 소리가 나도록 되어 있다.
Cellphones nowadays are made so that when you use the camera, a "찰칵" sound is made.

010
찰싹찰싹

[찰싹찰싹]

1. (things like water) the sound when a solid object roughly hits something

[Example] 물결이 밀려 와서 나룻배의 뱃전을 찰싹찰싹 때린다.
Because the waves came in, it hit the sides of the ferry "찰싹찰싹".

2. the sound when a small object sticks hard or hits something hard

[Heavy word] 철썩철썩

[Example] 우리 어머니는 내가 어렸을 때 예의에 어긋난 행동을 하면 바지를 걷게 하시고 회초리로 찰싹찰싹 때리셨다.
When I was younger and behaved in a way that went against manners, my mother would make me roll up my pants and cane me "찰싹찰싹".

011
콜록콜록

[콜록콜록]

the sound of coughing that comes out of the chest due to a cold or asthma

[Example] 할머니는 가슴이 답답하고 괴로운 듯 기침을 계속 콜록콜록 했다.
It seems as if my grandmother's chest is stifled and painful because she keeps coughing "콜록콜록".

012
퉁탕퉁탕

[퉁탕퉁탕]

the sound when a solid object recklessly and noisily beats continuously or the sound made when stamping one's foot

[Example] 노인 분들만 사시는 위층에서 퉁탕퉁탕 아이들의 발 구르는 소리가 들리는 걸 보니 손자들이 놀러 왔나 보다.
Since I hear the "퉁탕퉁탕" sound of children stamping their feet from upstairs where only the elderly live, it seems as if their grandchildren have come to visit.

13-1 연습문제 (의성어)

[1-5] 다음 (   )에 알맞은 말을 〈보기〉에서 찾아 쓰십시오.

Find the word that fits in the parenthesis from the word bank and write it in.

보기	찰칵	껄껄	둥둥	찰싹찰싹	통탕통탕

1. 빙그레 미소 짓는 것보다 (   ) 소리 내면서 크게 웃을 때 암세포를 제거하는 면역 세포의 능력이 더 향상된다고 한다.

2. 고수가 북을 (   ) 치자 동네 사람들이 덩실덩실 춤을 추기 시작했다.

3. 5살짜리 아들이 사진기 셔터의 (   ) 소리가 재미있는지 계속 눌러대고 있다.

4. 할 일이 산더미 같이 쌓였는데 너무 졸리기에 내 뺨을 (   ) 때렸다.

5. 중앙 공원 근처에서는 공사가 한창인지 100m 밖에서부터 망치 소리가 (   ) 들렸다.

[6-7] 의성어의 의미가 잘못 연결된 것을 고르십시오.

Choose the onomatopoeia where the meaning has been incorrectly linked.

6. (   )

❶ 빵빵 - 풍선이 터지는 소리
❷ 깔깔 - 여자 아이가 웃는 소리
❸ 둥둥 - 큰북을 두드리는 소리
❹ 쨍그랑 - 비가 많이 내리는 소리

7. (   )

❶ 콜록콜록 - 기침하는 소리
❷ 똑딱똑딱 - 시계가 잇달아 돌아가는 소리
❸ 보글보글 - 적은 양의 액체가 끓는 소리
❹ 통탕통탕 - 물 따위가 단단한 물체에 부딪치는 소리

[8-9] 다음 중 의성어의 쓰임이 잘못된 것을 고르십시오.
Choose the sentence where the onomatopoeia was used incorrectly.

8. (　　)

❶ 움직일 때마다 낡은 의자에서 삐걱삐걱 소리가 났다.
❷ 점심을 걸렀더니 뱃속에서 자꾸 꼬르륵 소리가 난다.
❸ 친구들은 내 농담을 듣고 배꼽이 빠지도록 쯧쯧 웃었다.
❹ 그 사람은 자기 이야기를 하는 줄도 모르고 쿨쿨 잠만 자고 있었다.

9. (　　)

❶ 고양이 목에 달린 방울 소리가 딸랑딸랑 들린다.
❷ 오빠는 내가 깔깔 울면 사탕을 주며 달래주곤 했다.
❸ 아이들은 개울 쪽으로 달려가서는 풍덩 물속에 뛰어 들었다.
❹ 사고 차량 때문에 정체가 심해지자 차들은 경적을 빵빵 울려 대기 시작했다.

[10] 다음 (　　)에 공통적으로 들어갈 말을 쓰십시오.
Find the one word that fits in the parentheses..

❶ 가정용 가스통이 (　　　　)하는 소리와 함께 폭발하면서 인근 주민들이 대피하는 소동이 벌어졌다.
❷ 학생이 대답을 머뭇거리자 선생님은 교실바닥을 발로 (　　　　) 차며 대답을 재촉하셨다.

13-2 의성의태어

013
앙앙 [앙앙]

the sound or form in which a small child cries loudly

[Heavy word] 엉엉

[Example] 아기가 앙앙 우는 건 배 고프니 젖 달라는 뜻 아니면 어딘가 몸이 안 좋다는 표시이다.
If a baby cries "앙앙", it is a sign that he is either hungry and wants to breast-feed or he is not feeling good.

014
엉엉 [엉엉]

the sound made when crying loudly and unrestrainedly

[Example] 두 사람은 맨땅에 주저앉아 엉엉 울음을 터뜨리고 말았다.
The two people ended up falling to the bare ground and crying "엉엉".

015
똑똑 [똑똑]

1. the sound made when a small object or drops of liquid lightly fall to the ground continuously

[Heavy word] 뚝뚝

[Example] 물받이에서 똑똑 물 떨어지는 소리가 들려온다.
I can hear the "똑똑" sound of water falling from the waterspout.

2. the sound made when a small and solid object continuously breaks or snaps

[Heavy word] 뚝뚝

[Example] 손에 쥐는 연필마다 심이 똑똑 부러지니 공부할 마음이 사라졌다.
My motivation to study disappeared after the lead in every pencil I held broke "똑똑".

3. the sound made when a solid object lightly and continuously beats

[Example] 누군가 문을 똑똑 두드리는 소리가 났다.
I heard the sound of someone knocking on the door "똑똑".

016
뚜벅뚜벅 [뚜벅뚜벅]

the sound made when the sound of foot steps is clear and continuously walking

[Example] 어둠 속에서 발자국 소리가 뚜벅뚜벅 들리더니 곧이어 사람의 형체가 희미하게 드러났다.
Right after hearing the "뚜벅뚜벅" sound of foot steps from inside the darkness, the form of a person faintly appeared.

017
짝짝[1]

[짝짝]

1. the sound when a line or stroke is drawn rashly

[Example] 그는 뭔가 언짢은 일이 있는지 바닥에 분필로 줄을 짝짝 긋고 있었다.
It seems that something happened which upset him because he is drawing lines "짝짝" on the ground with chalk.

2. the sound where paper or fabric is violently being ripped

[Example] 순이는 그가 보낸 편지를 뜯어보지도 않고 짝짝 찢어 버렸다.
Sooni didn't even open the letter that he sent to her and ripped it "짝짝" apart.

3. the sound when shoes are lightly being dragged while walking

[Example] 조용히 책을 읽고 있을 때 슬리퍼를 짝짝 끌면서 복도를 지나가는 소리는 신경에 거슬린다.
The sounds of slippers being dragged "짝짝" through the hallway grate on my nerves when I'm quietly reading a book.

018
짝짝[2]

[짝짝]

the sound when you repeatedly hit the palms of your hands together

[Example] 유치원생들이 선생님의 율동에 따라 손뼉을 짝짝 치며 노래하는 모습은 귀엽기 짝이 없다.
The appearance of the preschool children following their teacher's dance routine and clapping their hands "짝짝" while singing, is extremely cute.

13-2 연습문제 (의성의태어)

[1-3] 다음 (　　)에 알맞은 말을 〈보기〉에서 찾아 쓰십시오.

Find the word that fits in the parenthesis from the word bank and write it in.

보기	앙앙	짝짝	뚜벅뚜벅

1. 딸아이는 인형을 사 달라며 (　　　　) 울었다.
2. 아이들이 박자를 맞추어 손뼉을 (　　　　) 치는 모습이 마치 천사 같았다.
3. 어젯밤에 집에 돌아오는데 뒤에서 누군가 (　　　　) 걸어오는 소리가 들려서 정말 무서웠다.

[4] 다음 중 의성어의 의미가 잘못 연결된 것을 고르십시오.

Choose the onomatopoeia where the meaning has been incorrectly linked.

❶ 쯧쯧 - 혀를 차는 소리
❷ 짝짝 - 종이나 천을 마구 찢는 소리
❸ 똑똑 - 물방울이 연달아 떨어지는 소리
❹ 찰칵 - 높은 데서 물건이 떨어지는 소리

[5] 다음 중 의성어의 쓰임이 잘못된 것을 고르십시오.

Choose the sentence where the onomatopoeia was used incorrectly.

❶ 어린 아이가 뚜벅뚜벅 걸어가는 모습이 참 귀여웠다.
❷ 너무 힘을 주면서 글씨를 써서 그런지 분필마다 뚝뚝 부러졌다.
❸ 아이가 밤새도록 기침을 콜록콜록 하더니 기운이 다 빠진 모양이다.
❹ 영화를 보던 친구는 남녀주인공이 헤어지는 장면에서 엉엉 울기 시작했다.

[6] 다음 (　　)에 공통적으로 들어갈 말을 쓰십시오.

Find the one word that fits in the parentheses.

❶ 사무실 문을 (　　　　) 두드려 보았지만 아무 대답도 없었다.
❷ 나뭇잎에 맺혀 있던 물방울이 (　　　　) 떨어지는 소리가 참 듣기 좋았다.

13-3 의태어

019
갈팡질팡 [갈팡질팡]

the form shown when you don't know what to do and are wandering hurriedly and aimlessly

[Example] 날이 어두워지자 우리는 길을 잃고 갈팡질팡하였다.
As soon as the day grew dark, we got lost and were "갈팡질팡".

020
글썽글썽 [글썽글썽]

the form shown when tears pool up in the eyes as if tears will fall

[Example] 거짓말한 것이 들통 나자 아이는 눈물을 글썽글썽하며 잘못을 빌었다.
As soon as his lie was detected, the child begged for forgiveness with tears "글썽글썽".

021
꼬깃꼬깃 [꼬긷꼬긷]

(piece of paper) the form shown when creases are extremely deep because it was extremely crumpled

[Example] 남편은 꼬깃꼬깃한 만 원짜리 몇 장을 양말 속에서 꺼내 나에게 내밀었다.
My husband took out a couple of "꼬깃꼬깃" 10,000won bills from his sock and held it out to me.

022
꿈틀꿈틀 [꿈틀꿈틀]

the form shown when one part of the body repeatedly curves or moves while twisting

[Example] 아이는 애벌레가 꿈틀꿈틀 나무에 오르는 것을 호기심에 찬 눈으로 관찰하고 있었다.
The child was observing the caterpillar go up the tree "꿈틀꿈틀" with eyes ful of curiosity.

023
뒤죽박죽 [뒤죽빡쭉]

the form shown when many things are recklessly jumbled and tangled

[Example] 여행에서 돌아와 보니 도둑이 들었었는지 집안이 온통 뒤죽박죽이었다.
There must have been a thief in my house because after I returned from my vacation, the whole household was "뒤죽박죽".

024
들썩들썩 [들썩뜰썩]

1. (an object) the form shown when something moves up and down

[Example] 마룻바닥이 들썩들썩하도록 아이들이 뛰어다닌다.
The children ran around so that the floor moved "들썩들썩".

2. (shoulders or buttocks) the form when it is repeatedly lifted and laid down

[Example] 흥겨운 탈춤을 보고 있으니 나도 모르게 어깨가 들썩들썩했다.
Because I was watching an exciting mask dance, my shoulders went "들썩들썩" without me knowing.

3. (heart or atmosphere) the form shown where things are disorderly or unstable and moving

[Example] 새로 태어날 손자를 기다리는 할머니는 마음이 들썩들썩하는 모양이었다.
It seemed that my grandmother's heart was "들썩들썩" while waiting for the new born grandson.

025
들쭉날쭉 [들쭝날쭉]

1. the form where similar things that are a line have some parts of it that are in and some parts of it where it is out and not even

[Synonym] 들쑥날쑥
[Example] 아이들이 줄을 선다고 선 것이 들쭉날쭉 제멋대로였다.
Although the children tried standing in a line, it was "들쭉날쭉" as they pleased.

2. the form shown when things that you always do or things that usually are fulfilled are not fixed

[Synonym] 들쑥날쑥
[Example] 버스가 오는 시간이 들쭉날쭉해서 지각하기 일쑤였다.
I was always late because the times when the bus came were "들쭉날쭉".

026
듬성듬성 [듬성듬성]

the form where it is not fine but instead loose

[Example] 아침나절이라 버스 안에는 듬성듬성 비어 있는 자리가 많았다.
Because it was the forenoon, there were empty seats "듬성듬성" inside the bus.

027
띄엄띄엄

[띠엄띠엄]

1. (the space between repeated tasks or objects) the form shown when things are not close but instead spread out

[Example] 여울의 얕은 곳을 따라 디딤돌이 띄엄띄엄 놓여 있었다.
Steppingstones were placed "띄엄띄엄" around where the rapids are shallow.

2. (words or behavior) the form when things are not continuous but instead often break and are slow

[Example] 창밖에서는 가을을 알리는 벌레 울음소리가 띄엄띄엄 들려왔다.
Outside my window, I heard "띄엄띄엄" the crying of birds that let me know that autumn was here.

028
모락모락

[모랑모락]

(steam, smell, smoke) the form when it rises in small quantities

[Example] 어머니는 김이 모락모락 나는 밥을 그릇에 담으며 아이를 불렀다.
The mother called the child while putting rice that was steaming "모락모락" into a bowl.

029
무럭무럭

[무렁무럭]

the form when something grows powerfully and smoothly

[Example] 아이가 세 살 때 한 번 심하게 앓고 난 후로는 탈 없이 무럭무럭 잘 자랐다.
My child safely grew "무럭무럭" and well after seriously falling ill at age three.

030
바짝바짝

[바짝빠짝]

1. the form where there is barely any moisture or something dries or shrinks to the extreme

[Example] 가뭄으로 강물이 바짝바짝 말라가고 있다.
Due to the drought, the river water is drying "바짝바짝".

2. the form where something clings even more or becomes even closer

[Example] 5만 명의 일본군사들이 남원성을 겹겹이 에워싸며 바짝바짝 다가오고 있었다.
The 50,000 Japanese soldiers came "바짝바짝", surrounding Namwon fortress in multiple rows.

031
부랴부랴 [부랴부랴]

the form shown when one is hurrying very quickly

[Example] 기차를 놓치지 않으려고 부랴부랴 달려갔지만 기차는 이미 떠난 뒤였다.
Although I ran "부랴부랴" because I didn't want to miss the train, it had already left.

032
사뿐사뿐 [사뿐사뿐]

the form where you continuously walk lightly

[Example] 학교의 복도나 실내에서 걸을 때에는 쿵쿵거리며 뛰지 말고 사뿐사뿐 걸어야 한다.
In the school hallways or interior, you should not run around while stomping but instead walk "사뿐사뿐".

033
싱글벙글 [싱글벙글]

the form where you keep smiling gently while also moving your eyes and mouth big as if you are very satisfied

[Example] 친구는 복권이라도 당첨이 되었는지 싱글벙글거리며 입을 못 다물었다.
My friend could not close his mouth as he smiled "싱글벙글", as if he had won the lotto.

034
아장아장 [아장아장]

the form when a small child walks totteringly and carefully with its small body

[Example] 예쁜 여자아이가 엄마 뒤를 따라 아장아장 걷고 있었다.
The pretty girl was walking "아장아장" behind her mother.

035
알록달록 [알록딸록]

the form where a differently colored small spot or pattern is mixed up or alternated on a certain background

[Example] 꽃 전시장의 꽃들이 알록달록 저마다의 빛깔을 뽐내고 있다.
In the flower displays, each of the flowers is "알록달록" showing off their colors.

036
엉금엉금 [엉금엉금]

the form where you are crawling or walking slow

[Example] 폭설이 내린 도로 위를 차들이 엉금엉금 지나가고 있다.
Cars are passing "엉금엉금" on the road where heavy snow had fallen.

037
와들와들

[와들와들]

(when cold, scared, or angry) the form where your body severely shakes

[Example] 아이가 악몽을 꾸었는지 얼굴이 새파랗게 질려서 와들와들 떨고 있었다.
The child must have had a nightmare because his face was pale and he was shaking "와들와들".

038
우물쭈물

[우물쭈물]

the form where words or behaviors are not done distinctly but instead done hesitantly

[Example] 그녀는 무엇인가 말하려다 말고 계속 우물쭈물 더듬거리고만 있었다.
She was about to say something but instead continuously stammered "우물쭈물".

039
주렁주렁

[주렁주렁]

(something like fruit) the form where something is dangling

[Example] 사과 나뭇가지에 사과가 먹음직스럽게 주렁주렁 달려 있다.
On the branches of the apple tree, apples were appetizingly hanging "주렁주렁".

040
허둥지둥

[허둥지둥]

the form where you are extremely hurried or something is urgent to the point where you have no time to recover consciousness

[Example] 늦잠을 잔 딸아이는 밥도 먹지 않고 허둥지둥 책가방을 메고 학교로 뛰어간다.
My daughter who had overslept, didn't even eat breakfast and is instead running to her school after slinging on her book bag "허둥지둥".

13-3 연습문제 (의태어)

[1-8] 다음 (　　)에 알맞은 말을 〈보기〉에서 찾아 쓰십시오.

Find the word that fits in the parenthesis from the word bank and write it in.

보기				
	갈팡질팡	꼬깃꼬깃	뒤죽박죽	듬성듬성
	모락모락	사뿐사뿐	알록달록	와들와들

1. 한 소녀가 우리 앞을 발걸음도 가볍게 (　　　　) 걸어가고 있다.
2. 어느새 나도 (　　　　) 흰 머리카락이 보이는 나이가 되었다.
3. 아이들이 집을 (　　　　)으로/로 만들어 놓았기 때문에 그녀는 몹시 화가 났다.
4. 동물원에 온 어린이들이 공작의 (　　　　)한 깃털을 신기한 듯 쳐다보고 있었다.
5. 날씨가 너무 추운데 난방이 안 되니 손이 (　　　　) 떨려서 글을 쓸 수가 없었다.
6. 병사들이 요란한 총성에 놀라 (　　　　)하며 방향을 못 찾고 어둠 속을 헤매고 있다.
7. 모닥불의 연기가 (　　　　) 피어오르고, 어디선가 "찌르륵 찌르륵" 풀벌레 소리가 들려왔다.
8. 아버지는 내가 가방 속에 숨겨 두었던 (　　　　)한 시험지를 찾아내셔서 죽 펴 놓으셨다.

[9-13] 다음 (　　)에 알맞은 말을 고르십시오.

Choose the word that fits best in the parenthesis.

9. 점점 불어오는 강물에 위험을 느낀 우리는 (　　　) 텐트를 접었다.

❶ 갈팡질팡　❷ 꿈틀꿈틀　❸ 부랴부랴　❹ 우물쭈물

10. 아기는 아직 채 돌이 안 됐는데 벌써 (　　　) 걸음마를 시작하였다.

❶ 살금살금　❷ 허둥지둥　❸ 들쭉날쭉　❹ 아장아장

11. 많은 사람들 앞에서 발표를 하려니 긴장이 되어 입술이 (　　　) 탄다.

❶ 주룩주룩　❷ 바짝바짝　❸ 와들와들　❹ 들썩들썩

12. 비가 그치자 어디선가 나타난 지렁이가 마당을 (　　　) 기어 다녔다.

❶ 듬성듬성　❷ 꿈틀꿈틀　❸ 띄엄띄엄　❹ 무럭무럭

13. 기다랗고 가는 나뭇가지에는 탐스러운 열매들이 (   ) 달려 있었다.

❶ 싱글벙글 ❷ 뒤죽박죽 ❸ 방실방실 ❹ 주렁주렁

[14-15] 다음 중 의태어의 의미가 잘못 연결된 것을 고르십시오.

Choose the mimetic word where the meaning has been incorrectly linked.

14.

❶ 와들와들 - 비가 계속해서 내리는 모양

❷ 사뿐사뿐 - 계속해서 가볍게 걷는 모양

❸ 무럭무럭 - 힘차고 순조롭게 잘 자라는 모양

❹ 글썽글썽 - 눈에 눈물이 넘칠 듯이 자꾸 그득하게 고이는 모양

15.

❶ 꼬깃꼬깃 - (물건이) 자꾸 위아래로 움직이는 모양

❷ 뒤죽박죽 - 여럿이 함부로 뒤섞이고 엉클어져 있는 모양

❸ 갈팡질팡 - 어떻게 할지를 모르고 이리저리 급히 헤매는 모양

❹ 알록달록 - 어떤 바탕에 다른 빛깔의 작은 얼룩이나 무늬가 뒤섞여 있든가 번갈아 나 있는 모양

[16-17] 다음 중 의태어의 쓰임이 잘못된 것을 고르십시오.

Choose the sentence where the mimetic word was used incorrectly.

16.

❶ 감자 줄기에 감자알들이 주렁주렁 매달려 있다.

❷ 나는 오늘 늦잠을 자서 허둥지둥 학교로 뛰어갔다.

❸ 지금 하는 일은 마음에 드는데 수입이 꿈틀꿈틀거려서 생활의 안정이 되지 않는다.

❹ 면접시험을 잘 보려면 시험관 앞에서 우물쭈물하지 말고 자신 있게 대답해야 한다.

17.

❶ 뱃속의 태아는 하루가 다르게 모락모락 자랐다.

❷ 결혼식장에서 신랑은 예쁜 신부를 보고 좋아서 싱글벙글했다.

❸ 어머니께서는 어제 콩을 듬성듬성 섞어 옥수수빵을 쪄 주셨다.

❹ 등산객들은 해가 지자 어두컴컴한 등산로를 엉금엉금 기다시피하며 갔다.

[18-20] 다음 (　　)에 공통적으로 들어갈 말을 쓰십시오.

Find the one word that fits in the parentheses.

18.

❶ 그 위원회는 정기적으로 모이는 게 아니라 (　　) 불규칙하게 모인다.

❷ 별로 유명하지 않은 팀들이 하는 야구 경기라서 그런지 경기장에는 몇 안 되는 사람들이 여기저기에 (　　) 앉아 있었다.

19.

❶ 자식들 걱정에 잠이 오지 않으시는지 어머니는 밤새 이불을 (　　)하며 뒤척이셨다.

❷ 아이들이 이리저리 뛰어다닐 때마다 바닥이 (　　) 움직였다.

20.

❶ 연말 결산 때라서 요즘은 퇴근 시간이 (　　)하다.

❷ 손재주 없는 내가 뜬 털목도리는 가장자리가 (　　)해서 모양이 형편없었다.

접두사 · 접미사

14

Prefixes · Suffixes

14-1 접두사

001
군–

군말, 군소리, 군침, 군식구, 군살

extra words, extra sounds, extra saliva, extended family, extra fat meaning 'unnecessary' or 'in addition'

[Example] 군말하지 말고 제발 시키는 대로 해라.
Please do as I say without complaining.

002
날–

날고기, 날생선, 날계란, 날고구마

raw meat, raw fish, raw egg, raw sweet potato meaning 'food or fruit is not ready or ripe'

[Example] 여름에는 날생선을 먹으면 탈이 날 수도 있으니 반드시 조리해서 드세요.
Because you can get sick from eating raw fish during the summer, you must eat after cooking it.

003
덧–

덧니, 덧저고리, 덧나다, 덧붙이다, 덧입다

snaggletooth, overwear, to add, put on something else over a garment meaning 'once again,' 'something extra on top of something that was originally there'

[Example] 웃을 때마다 살짝 살짝 드러나는 덧니가 그 여자 아이의 귀여움을 더해 주었다.
The snaggletooth that slightly showed every time she smiled, made the little girl even cuter.

004
되–

되찾다, 되돌아가다, 되묻다, 되풀이하다

to recover, to return, to ask again, to repeat meaning 'again,' 'once more'

[Example] 실패가 되풀이되어서는 안 되니까 이번에 확실하게 그 원인을 밝히고 대책을 세웁시다.
Let us reveal the definite cause and raise some countermeasures because we cannot revert back to failure.

005
맨–

맨손, 맨발, 맨주먹, 맨얼굴, 맨바닥

bare hands, bare feet, bare fist, bare face, bare ground meaning 'not adding anything extra but instead just the present object'

[Example] 맨바닥에 앉으면 옷이 더러워지니까 의자에 앉으세요.
Since your clothes will get dirty if you sit on the bare ground, please sit on a chair.

006
외–

외나무다리, 외길, 외톨이, 외아들, 외며느리

single log bridge, single path, loner, only son, only daughter-in-law
meaning 'only one,' 'alone'

[Example] 원수는 외나무다리에서 만난다더니 거래처 대표로 나온 사람이 지난번에 크게 싸웠던 사람이었다.
They say that you'll run into your enemy on a single log bridge and sure enough, the person who came in as the transaction representative was the person whom I fought big with.

007
풋–

풋사과, 풋고추, 풋사랑, 풋내기

unripe apple, green chili, puppy love, rookie
meaning 'fruit or vegetable is not quite ripe,' something is not familiar so one is callow'

[Example] 영수는 이쪽 방면에 아직 풋내기이니 자네가 잘 가르쳐 주게.
Youngsoo is still a rookie in this field so you must teach him well.

008
한–

한복판, 한낮, 한여름, 한겨울, 한밤중

the center, middle of the day, middle of summer, middle of winter, middle of the night
meaning 'the middle' for space, and 'now' for time

[Example] 한여름에는 너무 더워서 아무 것도 할 수가 없다.
Because it is so hot during the middle of summer, I cannot do anything.

009
헛–

헛기침, 헛걸음, 헛소리, 헛소문, 헛수고

dry cough, fool's errand, nonsense, false rumor, vain attempt
meaning 'empty inside,' 'nothing will work,' or 'having no satisfaction'

[Example] 어차피 이 일은 성사되지 않을 테니 준비하느라고 괜히 헛수고할 필요까지는 없네.
There is no need to make a vain attempt at preparing for this task because it will not be accomplished anyway.

010
휘–

휘감다, 휘날리다, 휘몰아치다, 휘젓다

to twist, to fly, to rage, to stir
meaning 'very,' 'extremely severe'

[Example] 우승국의 선수들이 국기를 휘날리며 위풍당당하게 운동장에서 퇴장했다.
The athletes from the winning country left the sports arena majestically with their flag flying.

14-1 연습문제 (접두사)

[1-10] 다음을 읽고 알맞은 단어를 넣어 대화를 완성하십시오.

After reading the conversation, write in the word that fits best and complete the conversation.

1. **가 :** 미선 씨가 영수 씨하고 보통 사이가 아니라던데 사실이에요?

   나 : 아, 그거요? 모두 ______________이에요/예요. 행사 준비 때문에 두 사람이 함께 있는 걸 보고 누가 만들어 낸 이야기예요.

2. **가 :** 어떻게 오셨습니까?

   나 : 약을 발랐는데도 상처가 낫기는커녕 오히려 ________________어서/ 아서/여서 왔어요.

   가 : 그럼 이 약을 바르고 가능하면 손을 대지 마세요.

3. **가 :** 교통경찰까지 온 걸 보니 큰 사고라도 났나 봐요.

   나 : 아니에요, 가벼운 접촉사고가 난 것 같은데 다투느라고 길 __________________에서 10분째 저러고 있어요.

4. **가 :** 왜 이렇게 늦었어? 30분이나 기다렸잖아.

   나 : 미안해. 네게 줄 책을 깜박 잊고 안 가져와서 집에 다시 __________________어서/아서/여서 가져 오느라고 늦었어.

5. **가 :** 와! 많이 잡으셨네요. 이걸 모두 ______________으로/로 잡으셨어요?

   나 : 아니에요, 여기 있는 뾰족한 작대기로 잡았어요.

6. **가 :** 아니 이렇게 늦은 시간에 웬 운동이에요?

   나 : 요즘 바쁘다고 운동을 통 안 했더니 ______________이/가 많이 늘어서 몸이 둔해요.

7. **가 :** 이 영화는 예매를 하지 않으면 볼 수 없을 정도라면서요?

   나 : 네, 요즘 10대 소년 소녀의 어설프지만 순수한 __________________과/와 기상천외한 모험담들이 많은 사람들의 공감을 얻고 있대요.

8. **가 :** 이번 올림픽에서 우리 선수들이 역대 최고의 성적을 올렸다지요?
나 : 네, 현지 교민들도 태극기를 ________________으며/며 우리 선수들을 열렬히 응원을 해서 그곳 사람들의 부러움을 사기도 했답니다.

9. **가 :** 저 남자는 이제 아무도 없고 아무 데도 갈 곳이 없는 ________________ 이/가 되었대.
나 : 참 안 됐구나. 그러니 가족이 곁에 있을 때 좀 잘하지, 쯧쯧.

10. **가 :** 소시지는 어떻게 만드는지 알아요?
나 : ____________ 을/를 갈아서 양념을 한 후에 동물의 창자 속에 넣어 여러 가지 방법으로 가공해서 만드는 거예요.

14-2 접미사

011
–거리다

반짝거리다, 방실거리다, 출렁거리다, 비틀거리다, 울렁거리다
to glitter, to smile at someone, to slop, to stumble, to feel sick
meaning 'a certain state is continuous'

[Example] 그는 술에 취했는지 몸을 비틀거리며 걷는다.
He must be drunk off of alcohol because he is walking while staggering.

012
–나다

별나다, 맛나다, 엄청나다
to be strange, to be delicious, to be massive
meaning 'to have a certain temperament'

[Example] 우리 아이는 하는 짓이 별나서 다음에 어떤 사람이 될지 몹시 궁금하다.
Because my child's actions are strange, I am extremely curious as to see what kind of person he becomes.

013
–답다

남자답다, 사람답다, 정답다, 참답다, 학생답다, 선생님답다
to be manly, to be like a human being, to be friendly, to be truthful, to act like a student, to act like a teacher
meaning 'having a personality or trait'

[Example] 이제는 저도 사람답게 살고 싶어요.
Now I also want to live like a human being.

014
–롭다

명예롭다, 신비롭다, 자유롭다, 풍요롭다, 향기롭다
to be honorable, to be marvelous, to be free, to be rich, to be fragrant
meaning 'to be,' 'seems to be'

[Example] 부정을 저질러 부자가 되기보다는 정직하고 명예롭게 살고 싶어요.
Instead of becoming rich by cheating, I want to live truthfully and honorably.

015
–스럽다

복스럽다, 걱정스럽다, 자랑스럽다, 자연스럽다
to be pleasantly plump, to be worrisome, to be proud, to be natural
meaning 'having a type of personality'

[Example] 아이들이 어른들의 행동을 흉내내는 것은 자연스러운 일이니 걱정하지 마세요.
Because it is a natural thing for children to copy the behaviors of adults, do not worry.

016
–꾸러기

장난꾸러기, 욕심꾸러기, 잠꾸러기, 말썽꾸러기, 심술꾸러기
mischievous person, greedy person, sleepyhead, troublemaker cynic
cutely expressing someone who has a lot of something.

[Example] 너 같은 잠꾸러기가 이렇게 일찍 일어나다니, 해가 서쪽에서 뜨겠다.
The sun will probably rise from the west if a sleepyhead like you woke up this early.

017
–꾼

나무꾼, 노름꾼, 사기꾼, 사냥꾼, 구경꾼, 일꾼, 누리꾼
lumberjack, gambler, swindler, hunter, bystander, worker, netizen
meaning 'someone who does something as an expert,' 'someone who does something as a habit,' or 'people who have gathered because of a certain task'

[Example] 그는 사기꾼에게 걸려들어 재산을 다 날렸다.
Because he got caught by a swindler, his entire assets are now gone.

유명한 배우가 출연하는 영화 촬영지에는 늘 구경꾼들이 몰려든다.
Bystanders always swarm to the location for the filming of the movie a famous actor was participating in.

018
–뱅이

가난뱅이, 게으름뱅이, 주정뱅이
poor man, lazybones, drunkard
meaning 'someone who has something as a unique trait'

[Example] 워낙 식구가 많고 가진 것 없이 시작해서 언제 이런 가난뱅이 신세를 면할 수 있을지 막막하기만 하네요.
It is bleak thinking about when I can escape this poor life because I have so many family members and started without any possessions.

019
–쟁이

겁쟁이, 고집쟁이, 멋쟁이, 무식쟁이, 욕심쟁이, 심술쟁이
coward, stubborn person, sharp dresser, ignorant person, greedy person, grumpy person
meaning 'person that shows that they have a lot of a certain attribute'

[Example] 옷도 세련되게 입고 어디를 가도 꼭 분위기를 따져보는 그는 멋쟁이로 소문나 있다.
He is rumored to be a sharp dressed because he wore his clothes in a polished way and always considered the atmosphere no matter where he went.

020
–투성이

흙투성이, 피투성이, 먼지투성이, 거짓말투성이

being covered in dirt, being covered in blood, being covered in dust, being a web of lies

meaning 'when having too much of something,' or 'object or person's state'

[Example] 청소를 끝내고 보니 옷이 온통 먼지투성이였다.
My clothes were covered in dust after finishing cleaning.

14-2 연습문제 (접미사)

[1-10] 다음을 읽고 알맞은 단어를 넣어 대화를 완성하십시오.

After reading the conversation, write in the word that fits best and complete the conversation.

1. **가 :** 학교에 가는데 옷차림이 그게 뭐니? ________________지 못하게.
   나 : 다들 이렇게 입고 다니는데…….

2. **가 :** 아직도 잘잘못이 밝혀지지 않은 거야?
   나 : 말도 마. 다들 하는 말마다 ________________이야/야. 이야기를 듣다 보면 도무지 앞뒤가 안 맞아.

3. **가 :** 기사님, 죄송한데요. 차 좀 잠깐만 세워주세요. 속이 ____________ 어서/아서/여서 토할 것 같아요.
   나 : 네, 잠깐만 기다리세요.

4. **가 :** 선생님, 이번 토론은 주제를 정하지 않고 ________________게 하면 어떨까요?
   나 : 그러면 진행이 너무 산만해지지 않을까요?

5. **가 :** 우리 선수가 이번 대회에서 세계 신기록을 세웠다면서요?
   나 : 네, 대한민국 국민으로서 정말 가슴 뿌듯하고 ______________어요/ 아요/여요.

6. **가 :** 지난 주말에 민속촌에 가서 외줄타기를 봤어요.
   나 : 어땠어요?
   가 : 외줄 타는 묘기를 보고 저 뿐만 아니라 모든 ______________이/가 환호를 지르기도 하고 가슴을 졸이기도 하면서 재미있게 봤어요.

7. **가 :** 형제가 어떻게 돼요?
   나 : 욕심이 많아 뭐든지 다 자기가 가지려고 하는 ________________ 남동생하고 저 이렇게 둘이에요.

8. **가 :** 이제 좀 일어나지? 그러다가 소가 되겠다.
나 : 소가 되다니, 그게 무슨 말이에요?
가 : 옛날에 꼼짝도 하기 싫어하는 ________________이/가 소가 되었다는 얘기가 있지. 한 번 들어볼래?

9. **가 :** 와! 드디어 완성했다.
나 : 뭔데?
가 : 비가 올 때 쓰는 모자 우산인데 너도 한번 써 봐.
나 : 넌 언제나 기발하고 ________________는/은/ㄴ 물건들을 만들어 내는 구나.

10. **가 :** 이 책은 어떤 책이에요?
나 : 이 책은 상식과 불가능을 과감하게 뒤집으며 무농약 사과 재배에 최초로 성공한 ________________ 농부의 도전과 역경, 눈물과 성취의 감동 실화예요.

속담

15

Proverbs

15-1 속담 1

001
같은 값이면 다홍치마

an expression that shows if you are required to pay the same price or put in the same effort, but given a choice, you would rather choose the option that is better and is to your liking

[Example] 같은 값이면 다홍치마라고 이왕 소개팅 시켜주실 거면 젊고 잘생긴 사람을 소개해 주세요.
Saying "같은 값이면 다홍치마", if you're going to set me up on a blind date, set me up with someone who is young and good looking.

002
개구리 올챙이 적 생각 못 한다

an expression used when one is boasting after doing well for oneself, without thinking of thinking of the past when one did not do so well or had a hard time

[Example] 김 과장, 개구리 올챙이 적 생각 못 한다고 자네도 신입사원 시절에는 똑같은 실수를 했었잖나. 그러니 너무 나무라지 말게.
Section chief Mr. Kim, they say "개구리 올챙이 적 생각못한다", when you made the same mistake when you were a new employee as well. So do not scold too much.

003
개똥(쇠똥)도 약에 쓰려면 없다

an expression used to show that no matter how trivial or commonplace an object is, when you actually need it, it is nowhere to be found

[Example] 개똥도 약에 쓰려면 없다고 지갑 속에 늘 가득 차 있던 동전들이 오늘 따라 없네. 커피 좀 마시려고 했더니.
They say "개똥도 약에 쓰려면 없다" when my wallet which is usually full of coins, is empty today. Just when I was about to buy some coffee.

004
과부 사정 홀아비가 안다

an expression saying that someone who has directly experienced or is in the same circumstances as someone else's' difficult circumstances, understand the best

[Example] 과부 사정은 홀아비가 안다고 소아 백혈병 환자를 둔 부모들의 모임에 나가 이야기를 나누면서 위로를 많이 받아요.
They say "과부 사정 홀아비가 안다" so I received a lot of consolation by going to a gathering of parents who have children who are patients of childhood leukemia and talking with them.

005
남의 떡이 커 보인다

an expression where you think that someone else's task or someone else's possession looks better than your task or your possession

[Example] 남의 떡이 커 보인다고 친구가 시킨 음식이 늘 더 맛있어 보인다.
They say "남의 떡이 커 보인다" when the food that my friend had delivered always looked delicious.

006
떡 본 김에 제사 지낸다

an expression that means that when a coincidental and good chance comes along, you do something that you were thinking of

[Example] 약속 때문에 찻집에 갔는데, 찻집 옆에 카센터가 있길래 떡 본 김에 제사 지낸다고 2주 전부터 바빠서 못 고치고 있던 자동차 창문을 손봤다.
They say "떡 본 김에 제사 지낸다" so when I went to a teahouse for an appointment, I fixed the car door that I had been wanting to fix for two weeks but couldn't because I was too busy since there was a car center right next to the teahouse.

007
똥 묻은 개가 겨 묻은 개 나무란다

an expression where someone who has a big flaw or mistake actually scolds someone else's mistake that is not as big

[Example] 똥 묻은 개가 겨 묻은 개 나무란다고 너는 네 방 청소도 안 하면서 책상 좀 지저분한 걸 가지고 동생한테 잔소리를 하니?
They say "똥 묻은 개가 겨 묻은 개 나무란다" so how can you nag your younger sibling about his messy desk when you don't even clean your room?

008
등잔 밑이 어둡다

an expression that states that someone who is close to the subject on the contrary does not know much about the subject; also an expression that states that you don't know more about something that happened close to you compared to something that happened far away

[Example] 내가 아끼는 볼펜을 허락도 없이 가져간 사람을 한참 찾았는데 등잔 밑이 어둡다고 범인은 바로 내 동생이었다.
They say "등잔 밑이 어둡다" when I searched for a long time for the person who took my prized pen and the culprit ended up being my own younger sibling.

009
매도 먼저 맞는 게 낫다

an expression where it states that if it is a deed that you must already endure, no matter how hard or painful, it is better to do it first

[Example] 매도 먼저 맞는 게 낫다고 내가 첫 번째로 예방주사를 맞겠다고 나섰다.
They say "매도 먼저 맞는 게 낫다" so I volunteered to be the first one to get the vaccination.

010
벼는 익을수록 고개를 숙인다

an expression used as a metaphor meaning the more you are cultured and educated, the more you need to be humble and not boast about yourself to other people

[Example] 화려한 수상 경력과 고소득으로 자칫 거만해 보일지 모르는 김 팀장은 벼는 익을수록 고개를 숙인다는 말처럼 항상 검소한 옷차림과 단정한 자세로 고객과 동료들로부터 존경을 받고 있다.

Like they say "벼는 익을수록 고개를 숙인다", Mr. Kim could possibly look arrogant because of all of the prizes he won as well as his high income but instead he is receiving a lot of respects from his colleagues and customers because of his simple attire and graceful position.

15-1 연습문제 (속담 1)

[1-10] 다음을 읽고 알맞은 속담을 넣어 대화를 완성하십시오.

After reading the conversation, write in the proverb that fits best and complete the conversation.

1. **아 들 :** 엄마, 진수는 네 살인데 아직도 오줌을 못 가리네요.
   어머니 : ______________________ 네. 넌 일곱 살까지 이불에 지도 그렸어.

2. **선생님 :** 인터뷰조사 발표 순서를 정해야 하는데, 첫 번째로 누가 발표할 거예요?
   리 에 : ______________________는다고/ㄴ다고/다고 제가 먼저 할게요. 먼저 하고 나야 마음이 편하지요.

3. **아 들 :** 엄마, 선생님이 내일 미술 시간에 쓸 빈 깡통 준비해 오래.
   어머니 : 빈 깡통? 쓰레기통에서 찾아 봐. 많이 있을 거야.
   아 들 : 엄마, 아무리 찾아봐도 없는데.
   어머니 : ______________________는다고/ㄴ다고/다고 그렇게 많던 깡통이 필요할 때는 하나도 없구나.

4. **김감독 :** 박 감독님, 선수들이 정말 잘 치더군요. 타자들 폼도 좋고 타격도 좋고. 지난번에 보니까 다들 훈련에 정말 열심이던데요. 탐나는 선수들이에요.
   박감독 : ______________________어/아/여 보이는 거예요. 내가 보기엔 김 감독 팀 선수들이야말로 최고던데요.

5. **희정 :** 다음 주에 있는 발표 준비 다 했어? 사진 자료도 많이 찾았잖아.
   지영 : 사진 편집을 아직 못해서 내일 친구한테서 프로그램을 받기로 했어.
   희정 : 지금 이 프로그램도 사진 편집 프로그램인데.
   지영 : 그래? ______________________ 는다고/ㄴ다고/다고 이 컴퓨터 잠깐 써도 될까? 한 30분이면 될 것 같아.

6. **명숙 :** 경제가 어려운 가운데에서도 개인들의 기부가 늘었대.

은희 : 글쎄 말이야. 요즘 경제가 너무 안 좋아서 모금액 목표를 낮춰 잡았다는데.

명숙 : ______________________는다고/ㄴ다고/다고 넉넉지 않은 사람들이 오히려 어려운 이웃에게 애정과 관심을 더 쏟기 때문일 거야.

은희 : 그런 얘기를 들으니 마음이 훈훈해지네. 아직은 우리 사회가 건강하고 희망이 있다. 그렇지?

7. **제이슨 :** 에리 씨는 왜 자주 지각해요? 선생님께서 교실에 늦게 들어오면 다른 학생들에게 방해가 되니까 일찍 오라고 하셨잖아요.

에 리 : ______________________는다고/ㄴ다고/다고, 그러는 제이슨 씨는 왜 수업시간마다 몇 번 씩 전화기 들고 들락날락 해요?

8. **어머니 :** 민수야, 여기 있는 휴대폰 중에서 마음에 드는 걸 골라 봐. 이번 생일 선물로 네가 그토록 갖고 싶어하던 휴대폰 한 대 사 줄게.

민 수 : 어머니, 저 휴대폰은 다른 것과 값은 비슷한데 디자인이 아주 예쁘네요. ______________________이라고/라고 저 걸로 사 주세요.

9. **박부장 :** 김 과장, 우리 팀의 김미선 씨에게 소개해 줄 마땅한 남자 없을까? 싹싹하고 상냥한데다가 외모도 괜찮은 편인데 아무리 찾아 봐도 소개할 사람이 없네.

김과장 : 부장님, 우리 팀의 최 대리 어때요? 능력도 있고 성격도 좋은 것 같던데요.

박부장 : 아, ______________________는다고/ㄴ다고/다고 바로 옆에 두고도 내가 왜 여태 그 생각을 못 했는지 모르겠네.

10. **영수 :** 김 회장님은 국내에서 손꼽을만한 기업의 대표인데도 불구하고 아랫사람들을 늘 배려하고 편안한 모습으로 대해 주세요.

미선 : ______________________ 는다는/ㄴ다는/다는 말처럼 교양이 쌓인 분들일수록 겸손한 모습을 보이는 것 같아요.

15-2 속담 2

011
사공이 많으면 배가 산으로 간다

an expression stating that if there is not one person to be the center and lead people, but instead many people each saying this or that, tasks will not be done properly

[Example] 사공이 많으면 배가 산으로 간다는 말처럼 '토요일 밤에'의 집단 MC 체제는 진행이 산만하고 방송집중력이 떨어진다는 역효과를 낳았다.

Like how they say "사공이 많으면 배가 산으로 간다," there was an adverse reaction of a distracting progression and decline in concentration on the broadcast because of the system of group MC's on "토요일 밤에".

012
선무당이 사람 잡는다

an expression about a task that was ruined because of someone who talked knowingly of something they actually had no knowledge about and meddled

[Example] 정부의 서투른 금융 정책은 선무당이 사람 잡는다는 속담처럼 은행과 중소 기업이 환율 변동에 대처하는 것을 방해하여 이로 인해 은행과 중소 기업이 큰 손실을 입었다.

Like the sating "선무당이 사람 잡는다" says, because of the government's clumsy financial policy, banks and small businesses suffered a great loss because the policy interfered with the small businesses trying to handle exchange fluctuations.

013
수박 겉핥기

an expression where someone doesn't know the inside substance of an object and only roughly nudges the outside

[Example] 이 박물관의 유물들을 수박 겉 핥기로 둘러보자면 두어 시간이면 되겠지만 제대로 다 보자면 11시간 이상 걸린다.

If we look around the museum's relics "수박 겉 핥기로", it would take around two hours but if we were to properly look at everything, it would take more than eleven hours.

014
십 년이면 강산도 변한다

an expression stating that even things that don't seem to change have no choice but to change as time goes on

[Example] 올해로 데뷔 10년째를 맞은 윤두현! 십 년이면 강산도 변한다는데 윤두현의 음악을 사랑하는 팬들의 마음은 변함이 없는 것 같습니다.

Yoon Doohyun who has reached his ten year anniversary since his debut! Even though they say "십 년이면 강산도 변한다", it seems as though the hearts of fans who love Yoon Doohyun's music haven't changed.

015
열 길 물속은 알아도 한 길 사람 속은 모른다

an expression stating that although you can measure the depth of water, it is hard to measure someone's heart

[Example] '관상'은 과학적 근거는 없는 것이지만 호기심을 자극하기에는 충분한 소재다. 열 길 물속은 알아도 한 길 사람 속은 모른다는데, 얼굴만 읽어 사람 속을 알 수 있다니 그 비결이 궁금하다.

Although physiognomy has no scientific basis, it is a subject matter that sufficiently stimulates curiosity. Since they say " 열 길 물속은 알아도 한 길 사람 속은 모른다", I'm curious of the secret to knowing someone's heart by just reading their face.

016
오르지 못할 나무는 쳐다보지도 마라

an expression stating that it is not good to prematurely attempt an impossible task that is outside of your ability

[Example] 나희의 어머니는 상현을 찾아가 오르지 못할 나무는 쳐다보지도 말라며 한 번만 더 회사 밖에서 사적으로 나희를 만났다가는 그땐 큰일 날 줄 알라는 반 협박까지 퍼부었다.

Nahee's mother sought out Sanghyun and told him "오르지 못할 나무는 쳐다보지도 마라" and if he ever met Nahee in private outside of the office, that would be when there would be a lot of trouble and basically poured on the threat.

017
우물을 파도 한 우물을 파라

an expression saying that you must do one task consistently and continuously in order to succeed instead of spreading out too many tasks or changing the task frequently

[Example] 건설업으로 한 우물만 파 온 '연세건설'은 창립 후 지난 50년간 한 번도 적자를 내지 않았다.

"Yonsei Construction" which only "한 우물만 판다" in the construction business, never had a deficit in the fifty years after it was founded.

018
웃는 낯에 침 뱉으랴

an expression stating that you can't treat someone badly if they are treating you well

[Example] 웃는 낯에 침 못 뱉는다고 오바마의 거듭된 러브콜에 이란도 호의적 반응을 보이면서 두 나라 간 30년 불화의 빙벽이 조금씩 녹아내릴 조짐을 보이고 있다.

Like the saying "웃는 낯에 침 못 뱉는다" with the favorable response from Iran due to Obama's repeated attention, there seems to be an indication of the melting of the ice wall of discord that happened for thirty years between the two countries

019
쥐구멍에도 볕들 날 있다

an expression stating that even someone who is suffering severely will also have their good day as well when the time comes

[Example] 쥐구멍에도 볕들 날 있다고 십여 년간 무명의 설움을 겪어온 가수 서운도의 새 앨범이 대박을 터뜨렸다.

Like they say "쥐구멍에도 볕들 날 있다", the singer Seo Woondo who endured the sorrow of ten years as a nobody finally hit the jackpot with his new album.

020
짚신도 짝이 있다

an expression stating that no matter who it is, everyone has a partner that they will marry

[Example] 짚신도 짝이 있다더니 저렇게 성격 나쁜 사람도 결혼을 하네.

Like they say "짚신도 짝이 있다", even someone with such a bad personality is marrying.

15-2 연습문제 (속담 2)

[1-10] 다음을 읽고 알맞은 속담을 넣어 대화를 완성하십시오.

After reading the conversation, write in the proverb that fits best and complete the conversation.

1. **아버지 :** 이번 피서 여행은 어디로 갈까?
   어머니 : 제주도에 갔으면 좋겠어요.
   딸 : 아빠, 남해안으로 가요.
   아 들 : 안 돼. 아빠, 설악산으로 가요.
   아버지 : ______________________ 더니 안 되겠다. 아빠가 정하는 대로 따라 와.

2. **지영 :** 25년 만에 서울에 와 보니 너무 변해서 어디가 어딘지 하나도 모르겠어요.
   명숙 : ______________________ 는데/은데/ㄴ데 당연한 일이지요.

3. **영준 :** 철민이는 요즘 뭐 한대?
   윤수 : 건설 사업하다가 잘 안 돼서 무역업으로 바꿨잖아?
   영준 : 그래? ______________________ 으라고/라고 잘 안 되더라도 참고 끝까지 해 봐야 될 텐데.

4. **영준 :** 이번에 회사 기밀을 경쟁사에 팔아 넘긴 사람이 김 부장이라면서?
   수연 : 신망도 두텁고 인격적으로 훌륭한 분인 줄 알았는데.
   영준 : 그러니까 ______________________ 는다고/ㄴ다고/다고 하잖아.

5. **부인 :** 여보, 우리는 언제쯤 저런 멋진 집에서 살아 볼까?
   남편 : ______________________ 는다고/ㄴ다고/다고 언젠가 그렇게 될 날이 있겠지.

6. **윤 수 :** 할머니, 이제 저는 결혼 포기할까 봐요. 선을 그렇게 많이 보는데도 저 좋다는 사람이 없네요.
   할머니 : 너무 조급하게 생각하지 말아라. 아직 확실한 직장을 못 잡아서 그럴 거야.
   ______________________ 는다는데/ㄴ다는데/다는데 기다리면 좋은 짝이 나타날 거야.

7. **김부장 :** 이 과장, 박 대리는 아침회의 때마다 늦던데, 한 마디 하지 그래?
이과장 : 저도 한 번 따끔하게 야단 좀 치려고 몇 번 기회를 봤는데요. ______________________________을/ㄹ 수가 없더라고요. 박 대리가 워낙 싹싹하고 밝잖아요.

8. **영수 :** 나는 꼭 한국대학교에 갈 거야.
미선 : 네 실력으로 어떻게 거길 가니? ______________________________ 으라고/라고 했어. 꿈도 꾸지 마.

9. **교수 :** 자네 에리히 프롬을 아나?
학생 : 잘 모르겠는데요.
교수 : 그럼 앨빈 토플러는 누구인지 아나?
학생 : …
교수 : 자네 전공이 사회학이라면서 그런 것도 모른단 말이야? ______________________________ 으로/로 공부한 모양이군.

10. **선우 :** 승탁아, 너 위염으로 고생한다더니 좀 괜찮아졌니?
승탁 : 아니, 삼촌이 지난 번 산에서 뜯어 온 약초가 위염에 좋다고 하도 먹어 보라고 해서 먹었다가 속이 더 쓰려서 혼났어.
선우 : ______________________________ 는다고/ㄴ다고/다고 잘 알지도 못하는 삼촌 말을 믿으면 어떻게 해?

15-3 속담 3

021
친구 따라 강남 간다

used to describe an instance of following a friend but not because of something important or used to describe the instance where although one does not want to do something, one has to do it unavoidably due to someone else's suggestion

[Example] 미국프로골프(PGA) 챔피언십 대회에서 우승을 한 양용은은 우연히 친구와 함께 골프 연습장에 갔다가 골프를 알게 되었다고 한다. 친구 따라 강남 간 것이 성공에 이르는 첫 출발이었던 셈이다.

Yang Yongeun who is the winner of the PGA Championship Competition, stated that he came to know golf after he followed a friend to a golfing range by chance. It seems as though it is a case of "친구 따라 강남 간다" where it was the start of his success.

022
가지 많은 나무 바람 잘 날 없다

an expression showing that parents who have a lot of children never have a day where they can stop worrying or be concerned

[Example] 가지 많은 나무에 바람 잘 날 없다고 자식이 많은 부모는 항상 노심초사하며 마음 편할 날이 없다.

Like they say "가지 많은 나무 바람 잘 날 없다", parents who have many children are constantly worrying and do not have a day where they feel easy.

023
개천에서 용 났다

meaning someone excellent came out of a household that had difficult circumstances or was not decent

[Example] 어려운 가정형편에도 불구하고 피나는 노력을 하여 변호사가 된 지선에게 사람들이 개천에서 용 났다고 하며 뒷이야기를 했다.

People spoke behind Jisun's back, stating that "개천에서 용 났다" when even with difficult family circumstances, she became a lawyer through strenuous effort.

024
공든 탑이 무너지랴

meaning that a task you put your effort into will not be in vain; meaning that if you put all of your effort into something, there will surely be good results

[Example] 이 보고서는 거의 6개월이 넘도록 착실하게 준비한 자료를 바탕으로 만든 계획 안이니까 틀림없이 통과될 거예요. 공든 탑이 무너지겠어요?

Because this report is a schedule made from a background of documents prepared throughout a period of six months, it will certainly pass. 공든 탑이 무너지겠어요?

025
달면 삼키고 쓰면 뱉는다

meaning that one only does things that are profitable to oneself and there is an act of sticking to something if it is beneficial to an interest or if it not beneficial, he or she will turn away from it

[Example] 달면 삼키고 쓰면 뱉는다고 간 쓸개 다 빼줄 것처럼 나한테 잘 하던 김 과장이 내 형편이 좀 어려워졌다고 모르는 척하더라.

Like they say "달면 삼키고 쓰면 뱉는다", Mr. Kim who treated me so nice that he was almost willing to give me his gall bladder and liver, ignored me once my circumstances got harder.

026
백지장도 맞들면 낫다

meaning no matter how easy a task, doing it by combining strengths rather than doing it alone is much more efficient

[Example] 백지장도 맞들면 낫다고 아이들이 청소를 도와 줘서 생각보다 일찍 끝낼 수 있 었어요.

Because the children helped me with the cleaning like it is said "백지장도 맞들면 낫다", I was able to get done faster than I expected.

027
비 온 뒤에 땅이 굳어진다

an expression meaning the strengthening of someone after enduring an ordeal and comparing it the hardening of mud created from the rain

[Example] 이명우 선수도 한 때 부상과 스캔들로 많은 어려움을 겪었지만 비 온 뒤에 땅이 굳어진다고 그런 어려움이 오늘의 최고의 선수로 성장할 수 있었던 밑거름이 되었다고 생각해요.

Although the athlete Lee Myungwoo at one time endured a lot of hardship because of his injury and scandals, like they say "비 온 뒤에 땅이 굳어진다", I believe that those hardships became the foundation so that he could grow into the best player that he is today.

028
서당 개 삼 년에 풍월을 한다(읊는다)

meaning no matter how knowledge-less or experience-less you are in a certain area, if you stay in that field you will gain a number of knowledge and experiences, which is compared to if a dog lived in a village school for three years and heard the sounds of words being read, even the dog can make the sounds of words

[Example] 친구들과 같이 노래방에 자주 가다 보니 서당 개 삼년이면 풍월을 한다고 음치인 나도 이제는 유행하는 노래 몇 곡쯤은 따라 할 수 있게 되었답니다.

Like they say "서당 개 삼 년에 풍월을 한다", after going often to karaoke with my friend, even a tone-deaf person like me can now sing a couple popular songs.

029
소문난 잔치에 먹을 것 없다

an expression showing an instance where a noisy rumor doesn't live up to its reputation and is washy or does not line up with the truth

[Example] 어제 일간지마다 가보라고 추천한 딸기 축제에 갔다 왔는데 소문난 잔치에 먹을 것 없다고 볼만한 구경거리도 체험 행사도 거의 없어서 아주 실망했어.

I was very disappointed after going to the strawberry festival that all of the daily newspapers recommended because like the expression "소문난 잔치에 먹을 것 없다", there was nothing to eat, nothing to see, and nothing to experience.

030
송충이는 솔잎을 먹어야 산다

an expression stating that people must live according to their budget and if they attempt to not or try to go over it, they will have a problem

[Example] 도시로 나간 친구들이 성공했다는 소식이 들려오기도 하지만 송충이는 솔잎을 먹어야 산다고 나 같이 농사일밖에 모르는 농부는 물 맑고 공기 좋은 시골이 최고야.

Although I do hear news about my friends succeeding after moving to the city, like the expression "송충이는 솔잎을 먹어야 산다", for a farmer who knows nothing but farming, the countryside where the water is clear and the air is good is the best for me.

15-3 연습문제 (속담 3)

[1-10] 다음을 읽고 알맞은 속담을 넣어 대화를 완성하십시오.

After reading the conversation, write in the proverb that fits best and complete the conversation.

1. **교수 :** 자네는 왜 영문과를 선택했나?

   학생 : 제일 친한 친구가 영문과를 지원해서 저도 영문과를 지원했습니다.

   교수 : ______________________________더니 바로 자네 같은 경우를 보고 하는 말이군.

2. **가 :** 성윤 씨가 권고사직을 당했다는 소식 들었어요?

   나 : 금시초문이에요. 아니, 언제는 우수사원이라고 표창까지 하더니 건강이 나빠졌다고 사표를 내라고 하다니요.

   가 : 그러게 말이에요. 아무리______________________________ 는/은/ㄴ 세상이라고 하지만 너무하는 거 아니에요?

3. **가 :** 이번에 사법고시에서 수석을 한 사람에 대해서 이야기 들었어요?

   나 : 네, ______________________________었다고/았다고/였다고 하더군요.

   가 : 집안 형편이 어려워서 고생을 많이 했던 사람이니 그렇게 이야기할 만하지요.

4. **가 :** 옆집이 요즘은 잠잠하지요?

   나 : 네. 정말 다행이에요. 한동안 부부 간의 불화로 조용한 날이 없었잖아요. 사네 마네 하더니 요즘은 신혼부부가 따로 없어요.

   가 : ______________________________고 갈등을 겪고 난 후에 오히려 두 사람이 더 가까워졌나 봐요.

5. **가 :** 실패를 거듭하면서도 꿋꿋하게 10년을 연구 개발에만 매진하더니 드디어 국내외에서 특허를 받았대요. 이제 돈방석에 앉는 것은 시간문제예요.

   나 : ______________________________겠어요? 오랜 시간 동안 엄청난 노력과 정성을 쏟았으니 좋은 결실을 맺게 된 것은 당연하지요.

6. **가 :** 옆집 영훈이가 축구하다가 넘어졌는데 다리가 부러졌대요.
   나 : 아이고, 영훈이 엄마가 많이 놀랐겠네요.
   가 : ______________________고 얼마 전에는 그 집 셋째가 교통사고가 나서 영훈이 엄마가 많이 고생했잖아요.

7. **가 :** 어머니, 봉사활동 다녀오시느라 힘드실 텐데 오늘은 그냥 쉬세요. 저녁 준비는 서툴지만 제가 할게요…….
   나 : 그래, 그럼 내가 콩나물만 다듬어 줄게. ______________________고 내가 이거라도 해 주면 식사 준비를 빨리 끝낼 수 있을 거야.

8. **가 :** 선생님, 이거 제가 만들었는데 한 번 드셔 보세요.
   나 : 와, 정말 맛있다! 제임스 씨, 한국요리를 배우신 적이 있으세요?
   가 : 아니에요. 그냥 같이 사는 친구가 한국요리를 할 때마다 도와 줬더니______________ ______________ 고 간단한 요리 정도는 만들 수 있게 되었어요.

9. **가 :** 박찬명 감독의 영화에 출연한다고 기자회견하시는 것을 봤습니다. 우리들은 정계에 남으실 줄 알았는데요.
   나 : ______________________ 고 하지 않습니까? 국회의원은 제가 할 일이 아닌 것 같습니다. 의원생활 내내 배우 시절이 그리웠습니다.

10. **가 :** 주말에 아이들과 같이 '피카소 특별전'에 다녀왔어요.
    나 : 그러셨어요? 안 보면 후회할 금세기 최고의 전시회라고 신문, 방송에서 하도 떠들어대서 저도 시간을 내서 한 번 가보려고 해요.
    가 : 글쎄요, 가보라고 별로 권해드리고 싶지는 않네요. ______________________ 고 피카소가 그린 그림은 단 두 점뿐이었어요. 나머지는 들어본 적도 없는 무명 현대 화가들의 그림들이었어요. 돈이 아깝더라고요.

15-4 속담 4

031
새 술은 새 부대에

meaning that you need to establish new content and one formality and daringly throw away old customs and regulations in order to establish a new institution or system

[Example] 새 술은 새 부대에 담아야 하듯이 경제적 · 정치적 변화가 필요한 시대에는 민족과 국가를 개혁할 수 있는 새로운 지도자가 필요하다.

Like they say "새 술은 새 부대에," a society that needs a change in economics and politices needs a new leader who will reform the people and country.

032
안 되면 조상 탓 잘 되면 제 탓

meaning if something goes right, you think it is because you did it well, but if something goes wrong, you will resent someone else

[Example] 함께 일을 하다가 실패로 끝나니까 안 되면 조상 탓 잘 되면 제 탓이라고 사태의 책임을 서로에게 돌리면서 반목하기 시작했다.

Like they say "안 되면 조상 탓 잘 되면 제 탓," after the task they did together ended in failure, they started spinning the responsibility on each other and hostility was started.

033
열 번 찍어 안 넘어가는 나무 없다

meaning that no matter hard the task, with constant effort, it will be achieved

[Example] 영미가 내 데이트 신청을 거절했지만 나는 열 번 찍어 안 넘어가는 나무 없다는 믿음을 가지고 계속 도전해 보련다.

Although Youngmi rejected my request for a date, I will continue trying with the belief that "열 번 찍어 안 넘어가는 나무 없다."

034
옥에도 티가 있다 / 옥에 티

meaning no matter how great a person or object, if you closely nitpick over it, there are small flaws

[Example] 새로 이사한 하숙집은 주인 아주머니도 친절하시고 음식도 입에 맞고 집도 깨끗하고 다 좋은데 도로변이라 시끄러운 게 옥에 티예요.

Although the boarding house I just moved to has a nice land lady, the food fits my taste, and it is clean, the "옥에 티" is that it is loud because it is by the wayside.

035
입이 열 개라도 할 말이 없다

meaning that because the mistake is clearly shown, there is no chance for excuses

[Example] 연쇄 살인범을 눈앞에서 놓친 것에 대해서 경찰은 입이 열 개라도 할 말이 없다며 사죄했다.

The police apologized saying "입이 열 개라도 할 말이 없다" after losing the serial killer right in front of their eyes.

036
잘 자랄 나무는 떡잎부터 알아본다

meaning that someone who will become someone great in the future shows an extraordinary future from since they are young

[Example] 잘 자랄 나무는 떡잎부터 알아본다고 노벨 물리학상을 받은 김 박사는 어릴 때부터 선생님도 풀지 못한 수학문제를 척척 풀곤 했다고 합니다.

Like they say "잘 자랄 나무는 떡잎부터 알아본다", it's said that Professor Kim who received the Nobel Peace Prize in Physics was able to solve math problems that his teacher wasn't able to solve easily.

037
종로에서 뺨 맞고 한강에서 화풀이 한다

meaning that although you are humiliated at a certain place you cannot say anything and instead go to off place to show your grumbling

[Example] 형은 종로에서 뺨 맞고 한강에서 화풀이한다고 엄마한테 야단맞고는 죄 없는 나한테 계속 짜증을 내고 있다.

Like they say "종로에서 뺨 맞고 한강에서 화풀이 한다", my older brother who has gotten scolded by my mother, keeps showing his irritation to me when I am blameless.

038
중이 제 머리 못 깎는다

an expression showing that you must borrow the strength of others, in order for a personal matter to be easy to achieve although you wanted to personally solve it

[Example] 내가 학교에서 아이들을 가르치고는 있지만 중이 제 머리 못 깎는다고 내 자식은 직접 못 가르치겠더라.

Although I am teaching children at school, I am unable to personally teach my own kids like when it is said "중이 제 머리 못 깎는다".

039
첫 술에 배부르랴

an expression stating that no matter the task, you can not be satisfied in one try

[Example] 배우기 시작한 지 얼마 되지는 않았지만 한국어 실력이 빨리 늘지 않아서 마음이 조급하다. 하지만 첫 술에 배부르겠냐는 마음으로 차근차근 계속 노력해 봐야겠다.

Although it hasn't been long since I've been learning Korean, I have gotten impatient because my Korean skills haven't been improving. However, with a "첫 술에 배부르랴" mindset, I will have to make a continuous effort in a calm and orderly way.

040
한 번 엎지른 물은 다시 주워 담지 못 한다

an expression stating that a mistake already made is hard to recover from

[Example] 그렇게 입이 가벼운 친구에게 얼떨결에 비밀얘기를 한 걸 백 번 천 번 후회했지만 이미 한 번 엎지른 물은 다시 주워 담지 못하니 가슴만 칠 뿐이야.

Although I regretted telling my loose-tongued friend the secret a hundred times over, the situation was already as they say "한 번 엎지른 물은 다시 주워 담지 못 한다" and I was left to hit my chest.

15-4 연습문제 (속담 4)

[1-10] 다음을 읽고 알맞은 속담을 넣어 대화를 완성하십시오.

After reading the conversation, write in the proverb that fits best and complete the conversation.

1. **가 :** 관객 1,000만을 넘긴 영화 '경포대'를 드디어 어제 봤어요.
   나 : 1,000만을 넘길 만하던가요?
   가 : 네, 이야기도 재미있고 특수효과도 대단하고 배우들 연기도 훌륭했는데, 배우들의 사투리가 좀 어색한 것이 ______________________________이었어요/였어요.

2. **가 :** 영숙아, 아까 엄마가 왜 그렇게 우리에게 화를 내셨지? 보통 때 같으면 그냥 넘어가실 일인데…….
   나 : 엄마가 오늘 아침에 할머니께 크게 혼나서 그래.
   가 : ______________________________고 할머니께 야단맞았는데 우리한테 그러시면 안 되지.

3. **가 :** 시장님, 지하철 9호선이 시운전 때 발견된 결함 때문에 개통이 세 번이나 지연된 것에 대해서 어떻게 생각하십니까?
   나 : 사전에 철저히 대비하지 못한 것은 저희들의 불찰입니다. ______________________________습니다/ㅂ니다.

4. **가 :** 드디어 계약을 성사시키셨다면서요? 축하해요.
   나 : 감사합니다. 사실 이번 계약 건은 좀 힘들었습니다.
   가 : 보험은 절대 들 일이 없을 거라는 고객의 마음을 어떻게 바꾸셨어요?
   나 : 고객의 냉대와 무시 때문에 마음 상한 일도 많았지만 포기하지 않고 자주 고객과 접촉하면서 보험의 필요성을 강조했더니 마음을 돌리던데요. ______________________________고 하지 않습니까?

5. **가 :** 선생님, 조선시대 사회를 지배하던 이념이 불교였나요?
   나 : 아니야, 조선시대는 고려시대와는 달리 유교였어.
   가 : 왜 불교를 버리고 유교를 택했을까요?
   나 : 그거야 ______________________________이라는/라는 말이 있듯이 새로운 나라 조선은 친불교 정책을 폈던 고려와는 차별화되는 새로운 이념이 필요했겠지.

6. **가 :** 어휴, 이 일을 어떡하지? 큰일 났네.
   나 : 무슨 일인데 그래?
   가 : 아, 글쎄, 친구에게 문자를 보낸다는 것이 그만 과장님께 보내버렸어. 그것도 과장님 욕이 잔뜩 쓰인 내용을 말이야. 시간을 10분 전으로 되돌릴 수는 없을까?
   나 : ______________________________고 후회한다고 해결될 일도 아니니 내 생각에는 내일 회사에 가서 진심으로 사과드리는 것이 최선인 것 같다.

7. **가 :** 진희야, 네가 맺어준 부부가 10쌍이 넘는다면서 너는 왜 노처녀 소리를 듣고 다니니?
   나 : ______________________________는 말이 있잖아요. 제 일은 이상하게 제 뜻대로 풀리지를 않네요.

8. **가 :** 초등학교에 다니는 제 조카 희수가 서울에서 열리는 '세계 어린이 환경회의'에 한국대표로 참가해요.
   나 : 와, 대단하군요. ______________________________고 커서 큰 인물이 되겠는데요.

9. **가 :** 여보, 개업하고 한 달 동안 입이 부르트도록 열심히 일했는데 왜 수입은 이것밖에 안되지요? 이러다 식당 문 닫는 거 아니에요?
   나 : 좀 더 기다려 봅시다. 전단지도 돌리고 했으니 입소문이 나면 손님도 점점 늘고 수입도 많아지겠지요. ______________________________겠어요?

10. **가 :** 운동경기 심판들은 동네북 신세를 면하기 어려운 것 같아요.
    나 : 동네북이라니요? 그게 무슨 말이에요?
    가 : ______________________________이라고/라고 선수들이나 감독들은 경기에서 이기면 자기들의 실력이 좋아서 이겼다고들 하고, 지면 심판의 판정이 잘못됐기 때문이라고들 하니까요.

관용어

16

Idioms

16-1 관용어 1

001
가려운 곳을 긁어 주다

to do something absolutely needed on behalf of someone else without being asked to do it

[Example] '대통령과의 대화'에서 한 시민의 날카로운 질문은 국민들의 가려운 곳을 긁어 주었다.

When a citizens asked a sharp question during "A Talk with the President," he "가려운 곳을 긁어 주었다" for the citizens.

002
간에 기별도 안 가다

the amount eaten is so small that it feels like one hasn't eaten

[Example] 2인분을 넷이서 나눠 먹었더니 간에 기별도 안 간다.

Since four people divided and ate portions for two, "간에 기별도 안 간다".

003
간이 콩알만 해지다

an expression showing that you're very scared because there is something to fear, or that you're very surprised

[Example] 아무도 없는 숲길을 밤늦게 걷다 보니까 마치 귀신이 나올 것 같아서 간이 콩알만 해졌다.

Because it seemed like a ghost would come out while I was walking on the forest path late at night with no one around, my "간이 콩알만 해졌다".

004
개미 새끼 한 마리 얼씬하지 않다

nothing (or no one) appears

[Example] 부동산 시장이 얼어붙어서 부동산 중개소에 개미 새끼 한 마리 얼씬하지 않는다.

Because the real estate market froze, not even "개미 새끼 한 마리 얼씬하지 않는다" to the real estate agency.

005
검은 머리가 파뿌리가 되도록 살다

to live until your hair grows white from becoming old

[Example] 결혼식에서 신랑과 신부는 어떤 어려움이 있더라도 검은 머리가 파뿌리가 되도록 살겠다고 했다.

At the wedding, the groom and bride said that they would live "검은 머리가 파뿌리가 되도록 살겠다" no matter what difficulties come.

006
걸 다르고 속 다르다

an expression used for someone who thinks bad about something inside but on the outside, shows behaviors like they like something; the outside and inside is different

[Example] 걸 다르고 속 다른 사람을 표리부동한 사람이라고 하는데, 그런 사람들은 믿을 수 없다.

They say people that "걸 다르고 속 다른" are double-faced people, and you can't trust people like that.

007
굶기를 밥 먹듯 하다

to starve often

[Example] 김영수 씨는 굶기를 밥 먹듯 하더니 결국 영양실조에 걸렸다.

Ultimately after "굶기를 밥 먹듯 하다", Youngsoo Kim eventually was diagnosed with malnutrition.

008
그 사람(놈)이 그 사람(놈)이다

an expression saying that when comparing between two or more people or objects, there is no estimated difference between the two

[Example] 그 사람이 그 사람이라는 생각으로 선거에 참여하지 않는 유권자도 있지만 투표권을 정당하게 행사해서 국민을 위해 일해 줄 진정한 일꾼을 뽑아야 한다고 본다.

Although there are voters that do not participate in the elections due to thinking "그 사람이 그 사람이다", I feel that we must properly use the right to vote in order to choose someone who will work hard for the nation's people.

009
꿀 먹은 벙어리

someone who does not express their inner thoughts

[Example] 회의 시간에 다른 사람들이 자신들의 생각을 너무나 강력하게 주장하는 바람에 나는 꿀 먹은 벙어리처럼 듣고 있을 수밖에 없었다.

I could only listen like a "꿀 먹은 벙어리" during the meeting because the other people asserted their own thoughts so strongly.

010
다람쥐 쳇바퀴 돌 듯 하다

an expression when you have to continuously repeat the same task without it ending.

[Example] 우리는 오랜 시간 토의를 했지만 다람쥐 쳇바퀴 돌 듯 같은 말을 반복하기만 했을 뿐 결론은 나지 않았다.

Although we had a debate for a long time, we only talked about the same topics like "다람쥐 쳇바퀴 돌 듯 하다" and were not able to reach a conclusion.

16-1 연습문제 (관용어 1)

[1-10] 다음을 읽고 알맞은 관용어를 넣어 대화를 완성하십시오.

After reading the conversation, complete it by putting in the idiom that fits best.

1. **가 :** 배고파 죽겠다.

   나 : 책상 위에 과자가 있으니까 먹으렴.

   가 : 아이고, 이것 갖고는 ______________________

2. **가 :** 골프 연습장에서 만난 허 사장하고 동업할까 해. 인상도 좋고 사업 경험도 많은 것 같던데…….

   나 : 그래도 ______________ 는/은/ㄴ 사람이 많으니까 조심해야지......

3. **가 :** 지난주에 개봉한 공포 영화 봤어? 너무 무섭다던데.

   나 : 응. 공포영화를 즐기는 나조차도 무서워서 ______________ 더라.

4. **가 :** 오늘도 가게에______________는군요/군요.

   나 : 그래. 오늘도 손님이 한 사람도 오지 않는구나...

   가 : 이렇게 경기가 나빠서야 어디 살 수 있겠어요?

5. **가 :** 지난번에 얘기한 그 일, 믿고 맡길 만한 사람을 골랐나?

   나 : 글쎄, 우리 부서 사람들은 다______________ 고 마땅한 사람이 없네.

6. **가 :** 아까 외국인하고 같이 있던데, 그동안 쌓은 영어 실력 발휘 좀 했어?

   나 : 아니, 막상 외국인을 만나니까 너무 긴장이 돼서 ______________ 처럼 아무 말도 못했어.

7. **가 :** 너 그 신문 만평 봤니?

   나 : 이번에 나온 교육 정책의 문제점을 정확히 꼬집었더라. 정말 ______________었어/았어/였어.

8. **가 :** 전 세계에서 8억 5천만 명 정도가 기아에 시달리고 있대.
   나 : 우리는 한 끼만 굶어도 힘든데 ______________________________ 는 사람들은 얼마나 괴로울까.

9. **가 :** 여보, ______________________________자더니 왜 이렇게 병원에 누워만 있소? 어서 털고 일어나구려.
   나 : 나 때문에 당신과 아이들이 고생이 많네요. 빨리 일어나야 할 텐데...

10. **가 :** 오랜만이네, 자네 요즘 어떻게 지내나?
    나 : 매일 매일이 ______________________________ 똑같지, 뭐. 자넨 어떤가?

16-2 관용어 2

011
두 다리 쭉 뻗고 자다

to sleep comfortably without any concerns

[Example] 이제 시험도 다 끝났으니 두 다리 쭉 뻗고 자야겠다.

Now that my tests are all over, I'm going to "두 다리 쭉 뻗고 자다".

012
둘이 먹다가 하나가 죽어도 모르다

to be extremely delicious

[Example] 이 음식은 둘이 먹다가 하나가 죽어도 모를 만큼 맛있다.

This food is so delicious that "둘이 먹다가 하나가 죽어도 모르겠다".

013
도마 위에 오르다

where an object becomes the object of criticism

[Example] 그 대선 후보의 비리가 여론의 도마 위에 오르면서 지지율이 하락했다.

After that presidential candidate's corruption was "도마 위에 오르다" of public sentiment, his approval rating decreased.

014
마음은 굴뚝같다

in your heart, there is an action that you want to do very much

[Example] 친구들과 여행을 가고 싶은 마음은 굴뚝같았지만 중요한 시험이 가까워서 포기할 수밖에 없었다.

Although my desire to go on a vacation with my friends was "마음은 굴뚝같다", because an important test was coming up, I had no choice but to abandon those plans.

015
모기 소리만 하다

a sound is extremely small and weak

[Example] 그 지원자는 면접시험을 볼 때 얼마나 긴장을 했는지 대답하는 목소리가 모기 소리만 해졌다.

It seemed as though the application was extremely tense during the interview because the voice he responded in was "모기 소리만 했다".

016
물 쓰듯 하다

to use a lot of money with no purpose

[Example] 그렇게 돈을 물 쓰듯 하다가는 금방 거지가 될 것이다.

If you keep using money like "물 쓰듯 하다", you will become a beggar.

017
물거품이 되다

to go down the drain; effort is fruitless

[Example] 자원봉사자들의 수고가 물거품이 되지 않도록 바닷가 주민들은 수거된 쓰레기를 깨끗이 처리하고 바다 오염방지에 적극적으로 참여하고 있다.
The residents along the seaside cleanly disposed of the collected trash and are actively participating in the prevention of pollution of the ocean so that the efforts of the volunteers do not become "물거품이 되다".

018
바닥이 나다

to run out of money or an object

[Example] 그 사람의 많은 재산은 그의 낭비벽 때문에 바닥이 나 버렸다.
Because of his spendthrift habits, all of his numerous assets are "바닥이 났다".

019
손때가 묻다

plates or furniture are broken in or one is affection of it because they've been used for a long time

[Example] 어머니는 할머니의 손때가 묻은 바느질 상자를 소중하게 여기신다.
My mother regards my grandmother's "손때가 묻은" sewing kit preciously.

020
양다리를 걸치다

to have relationships with both sides because one is trying to see the benefits to each side

[Example] 알고 보니 남자친구가 이제까지 나와 내 친구 사이에서 양다리를 걸치고 있었다.
It turned out that my boyfriend was "양다리를 걸쳤다" between my friend's and mine relationship until now.

16-2 연습문제 (관용어 2)

[1-10] 다음을 읽고 알맞은 관용어를 넣어 대화를 완성하십시오.

After reading the conversation, complete it by putting in the idiom that fits best.

1. **가 :** 요즘 모델 활동에 전념하고 계신데, 영화에 출연하실 생각은 없으신가요?
   나 : ________________________지만 너무 바빠서요.

2. **가 :** 너, 엄마 말 또 안 들을 거야? 앞으로 말 잘 들을 거지.
   나 : 네, 잘 들을게요.
   가 : ________________________게 말하지 말고 좀 크게 말해.

3. **가 :** 요즘 회사 분위기가 말이 아니야......
   나 : 지난 번 회의에서도 해고할 사람에 대해 얘기했대.
   다 : 누구누구에 대해 이야기했대? 설마 우리가________________________
   는/은/ㄴ 것은 아니겠지?

4. **가 :** 어, 오늘은 얼굴이 아주 밝은데... 뭐 좋은 일이라도 있어?
   나 : 응. 두 달 동안 준비해 온 기획안 발표가 어제 잘 끝나서 오랜만에____________
   __________ 었어/았어/였어.

5. **가 :** 아니, 계산서가 잘못 된 거 아니야? 여보.
   나 : 아니. 맞아...... 그건 지난달에 백화점 세일 때......
   가 : 이렇게 돈을 ________________________ 으면/면 어떻게 해?

6. **가 :** 그 선수가 갑자기 부상을 당해서 이번 올림픽 대회에 참가를 못하게 됐다면서요?
   나 : 지난 4년 동안 그렇게 열심히 연습을 했다는데, 모두 ________________
   었군요/았군요/였군요.

7. **가 :** 이번 여행 같이 가는 거지?
   나 : 아니, 나는 못 갈 것 같아. 이번 달 용돈이 벌써 ________________________
   어서/아서/여서 지금 한 푼도 없거든.

8. **가 :** 유명세 감독이 다른 팀으로 갔다면서?

   나 : 재계약을 앞두고 ______________________________고 협상을 하다가 유리한 조건을 제시한 다른 팀으로 갔대.

9. **가 :** 방이 이렇게 좁은데 오래된 물건들을 버리지 않고 쌓아 놓고 사는구나.

   나 : 어머니의 ______________________________ 는/은/ㄴ 것들이라 도저히 버릴 수가 없어서...

10. **가 :** 어제 간 식당 음식은 어땠어?

    나 : 너무 맛있어서 ______________________________ 겠더라.

16-3 관용어 3

021
가지를 치다

1. branches are propagating; an offshoot forms from one basis

[Example] 소문이 가지를 쳐서 크게 부풀었다.
The rumors inflated largely because they "가지를 쳤다".

2. to cut off branches; to get rid of useless things

[Example] 교수는 학생에게 논문 주제와 직접적인 관계가 없는 내용은 가지를 치라고 지시했다.
The professor directed the student to "가지를 치다" content that had no direct relationship to the paper topic.

022
값을 치르다

to give the appropriate amount of money or price

[Example] 잘못을 저질렀으면 그만한 값을 치러야 한다.
If you have made a mistake, you must give the proper "값을 치르다".

023
거울삼다

to model oneself or be vigilant by looking at someone else's matters or reflecting on past matters

[Example] 지난 해 대통령 선거의 실패를 거울삼아 이번 총선에서는 기필코 승리합시다.
Let us "거울 삼다" last year's failure in the presidential elections and without fail ,win this general election.

024
걸음마 단계

the beginning steps to a certain task or process

[Example] 인공 장기 이식 분야의 연구는 아직 걸음마 단계이다.
The research in the area of transplanting artificial organs is still in the "걸음마 단계".

025
고개를 돌리다

to ignore a certain person, task, or situation

[Example] 이번 여름 극장가에 많은 공포 영화들이 개봉되었지만 지루한 스토리 전개와 미숙한 연기는 관객들의 고개를 돌리게 했다.
Although many horror films opened in the theater district, due to the boring plot development and unskilled acting, it made the audience "고개를 돌리다".

026
기를 죽이다

to dampen someone else' enthusiasm

[Example] 링 위에 오른 두 선수는 서로 상대방의 기를 죽이려고 눈싸움을 하고 있다.
The two athletes in the ring are staring each other down trying to "기를 죽이다" each other.

027
등을 돌리다

to sever and ostracize relationships with people or groups that had the same goals

[Example] 그 배우의 경솔한 행동이 보도되자 그의 팬들마저 등을 돌렸다.
After that actor's careless behavior was reported, even his fans "등을 돌렸다".

028
무릎을 꿇다

to surrender or submit

[Example] 세계 최고를 자랑하는 축구팀이 상대편의 철통같은 수비 앞에 무릎을 꿇고 0대 1로 지고 말았다.
The soccer team considered the best in the world lost 0 to 1 after "무릎을 꿇다" in front of the opposite team's iron-like defense.

029
발목이/을 잡히다
발목을 잡다

1. to be caught tightly from a task and being unable to break free from it

[Example] 요즘은 아버님께서 시키신 일에 발목을 잡혀서 다른 일은 전혀 못하고 있다.
Lately because I am "발목을 잡히다" by the tasks ordered by my father, I am totally unable to do any other task.

2. to be caught by your weak point

[Example] 사장은 전과 사실을 빌미로 그의 발목을 잡고 협박을 했다.
The boss used the excuse of his criminal record to "발목을 잡다" and threaten him.

030
발을 맞추다

to fall into step with

[Example] 경제 발전에 발을 맞추어 정치도 발전을 해야 한다.
Politics must "발을 맞추다" along with the development of the economy.

16-3 연습문제 (관용어 3)

[1-10] 다음을 읽고 알맞은 관용어를 넣어 문장을 완성하십시오.

After reading the conversation, complete it by putting in the idiom that fits best.

1. 시대의 변화에 ________________________ 어/아/여 낡은 제도를 개선해야 한다.

2. 남편이 들어왔는데도 아내는________________________고 앉아서 말도 하지 않았다.
   성공할 수 있도록 도와주고 뒷받침해 준 사람에게 ________________________다니!

3. 이번 인사 조치는 불필요한 인원을________________________기 위한 조치이다.
   생각이 자꾸 ________________ 다 보니 지금 생각할 필요가 없는 것까지 신경 쓰게 되어 머리가 복잡했다.

4. 친환경 자동차와 바이오 에너지 개발은 아직________________________ 이다/다.
   중국어를 배우기는 하지만 아직 ____________________ 이어서/여서 겨우 인사 정도 밖에 할 수 없다.

5. 물건을 고른 뒤________________________으려고/려고 계산대에 갔다.
   사회적 도덕적으로 물의를 일으킨 사람은 반드시 ____________________어야/아야/여야 한다.

6. 우리나라 대표팀은 결승전에서 혈전을 벌였지만 결국 상대팀에____________________ 고 말았다.
   대통령은 들끓는 국민의 반대 여론에____________________ 어야/아야/여야 했다.

7. 현재 벌어지고 있는 참혹한 현실에 ____________________ 고 싶었다.
   요즘 외국 드라마에 빠진 20대가 국내 드라마에____________________자 중년층을 겨냥한 드라마들이 계속 방송되고 있다.

8. 지나친 규제가 지방 자치 발전의____________________ 고 있다.
   꾸준히 성장해 오던 우리 회사의 수출이 최근에 벌어진 노사 갈등으로 인해____________
   _________________________ 었다/았다/였다.

9. 자라는 아이의 _________________________ 지 않도록 잘못을 타이르는 것이 바람직한 교육방법이라고 생각한다.
   이번 합창대회에서 일등을 노리던 우리 반은 다른 반의 월등한 합창 실력에 ____________
   __________고 말았다.

10. 체력 부족으로 패배한 지난 번 경기의 실패를 _________________어/아/여 그 선수는 체력 보강 훈련에 돌입했다.
    아이들은 부모를 _________________어서/아서/여서 행동하기 때문에 부모의 말씨나 행동은 매우 중요하다.

16-4 관용어 4

031
빛을 보다

achievements or benefits emerge

[Example] 그의 작품은 오랫동안 세상에 알려지지 않았으나 이번에 빛을 보게 되었어요.
Although his works were not known to the world for a long time, they have now "빛을 보다".

032
배가 부르다

to be satisfied

[Example] 부모님께서는 아이들이 잘 먹는 모습을 지켜보시면서 보기만 해도 배가 부르다고 하셨다.
As the parents observed their children eat well, they said that by just watching them they were "배가 부르다".

033
뿌리를 뽑다

to get rid of the root of something that can cause something to appear and grow

[Example] 무엇보다도 먼저 우리 사회에 깊이 자리하고 있는 부정부패를 뿌리 뽑아야 한다.
More than anything, we must first "뿌리를 뽑다" the deeply rooted corruption in our society.

034
손이 가다

a lot of effort goes into doing a certain task

[Example] 한지를 만드는 일은 손이 많이 가는 일이지만 완성되면 그만큼 곱고 아름다워요.
Although making hanji, traditional Korean paper, is a task that "손이 많이 가다", it is that much more beautiful and gorgeous.

035
손발이 맞다

while doing a task together, mindset or opinions, or behavior patterns etc. are the same

[Example] 같이 일하는 사람들끼리 손발이 맞으면 일의 능률이 오를뿐더러 즐거운 마음으로 일할 수 있다.
When people who work together "손발이 맞다", not only does efficiency go up but they can work with a pleasant feeling.

036
시치미를 떼다

to pretend like you didn't do anything after doing it or pretending like you don't know even though you know

[Example] 그 사람은 모든 사실을 알고 있으면서도 모른다고 시치미를 뗐다.
That person said that he didn't know and "시치미를 뗐다" even though he knew all of the facts.

037
얼굴 깎이다

to lose face

[Example] 밖에 나가서 부모 얼굴 깎이는 짓은 하지 마라.
Do not go out into the world and do anything that will "얼굴 깎이다" your parents.

038
입을 모으다

to speak uniformly; to speak the same opinions

[Example] 그 사람이 이번 프로젝트의 팀장을 맡아야 한다고 모두 입을 모았다.
Everyone "입을 모았다" saying that he needs to be the team leader of this project.

039
마침표를 찍다

to end, to finish

[Example] 아버지께서는 내일 퇴임식을 끝으로 35년에 걸친 직장생활에 마침표를 찍으신다.
After his retirement ceremony is over tomorrow, my father will "마침표를 찍다"on his working life spanning across 35 years.

040
찬물을 끼얹다

to jump into something that is moving along fine and interrupt it by spoiling the atmosphere or unnecessarily finding fault with it

[Example] 사장이 갑자기 회식 자리에 나타나서 직원들끼리의 즐거운 분위기에 찬물을 끼얹었다.
The boss suddenly appeared at the office get-together and "찬물을 끼얹었다" on the pleasant atmosphere amongst the employees.

16-4 연습문제 (관용어 4)

[1-10] 다음을 읽고 알맞은 관용어를 넣어 문장을 완성하십시오.

After reading the conversation, complete it by putting in the idiom that fits best.

1. 구절판은 만들 때 ________________ 는/은/ㄴ 음식이다.
   유기농산물은 일반 농산물을 재배할 때보다 ________________ 는다/ㄴ다/다.

2. 절대로 부모님________________는/은/ㄴ 일을 해서는 안 된다.
   상대방이 잘못했다하더라도 네가 그렇게 심한 욕을 하면 네 ________________ 는/은/ㄴ거야.

3. 그 아나운서와 해설자는 미리 입을 맞추지 않아도 ________________ 어요/아요/여요.
   그 사람하고는 ________________ 지 않아 같은 팀에서 일하기가 힘들어요.

4. 살아있을 때는 인정을 받지 못하다가 사후에 ________________ 는/은/ㄴ 예술가도 있다.
   방송이 금지되었던 가요 837곡도 이 조치 이후 다시 ________________ 을/ㄹ 수 있게 되었다.

5. 뇌물 수수는 워낙 은밀하게 이루어지는 것이라 완전히________________ 는/은/ㄴ 것은 쉽지 않은 일이다.
   부정 선거를________________기 위해 정부와 시민 단체 그리고 온 국민이 나섰다.

6. ________________으면/면 누가 모를 줄 알아? 틀림없이 네가 한 짓이지?
   증거를 들이대자 계속 ________________ 고 있던 그 피의자는 사실을 인정했다.

7. 그에 대한 이야기를 꺼내자 모든 사람들이________________어/아/여 칭찬을 했다.
   축구장의 관중들이________________어/아/여 '박지성'을 연호했다.

8. 대형 비리 사건에 연루된 그 국회의원은 정치인으로서의 생활에 ________________ 게 되었다.

새로운 증거가 발견됨에 따라 검사와 변호사의 치열한 논전에 ______________________ 게 되었다.

9. 반찬 투정을 하자 엄마가 ____________________는/은/ㄴ 소리를 한다고 꾸중을 하셨다.
의젓하게 자란 아이를 보노라면 먹지 않아도 ______________________어요/아요/여요.

10. 실업률 상승이 경기 회복에 ____________________________________ 었다/았다/였다.
국경선 근처에서 발생한 분쟁 소식은 올림픽으로 들떠 있던 축제 분위기에 ___________ ____________________었다/았다/였다.

16-5 관용어 5

041
발 벗고 나서다

to actively do a task

[Example] 김 부장은 남을 돕는 일에는 항상 발 벗고 나선다.
Mr. Kim always "발 벗고 나선다" when it comes to helping others.

042
뒤끝이 없다

to not have hard feelings

[Example] 우리 사장님은 화가 나면 바로 표현을 하지만 그만큼 뒤끝이 없어서 좋다.
Although our boss immediately expresses his anger, it is nice that he "뒤끝이 없다".

043
내 코가 석자다

because one's own circumstances are urgent, you can't afford to look after others

[Example] 도와주고 싶지만 할 일이 쌓여서 내 코가 석자니 네 문제는 네가 해결해라.
Although I want to help, because all of these tasks have piled up so "내 코가 석자다", you need to figure out your own problems.

044
난다 긴다 하다

talent or ability is more outstanding than others

[Example] 이번 외국어 경시대회에는 각 학교에서 난다 긴다 하는 아이들이 다 나왔다더라.
They said that all of the "난다 긴다 하는" students from each school have come out to participate in the foreign language competition.

045
날개 돋친 듯이 팔리다

an expression that figuratively shows when items sell at a fast rate

[Example] 이번에 내놓은 신상품은 날개 돋친 듯이 팔려 나갔다.
The new products that were released "날개 돋친 듯이 팔려나갔다".

046
꼬리를 물다

thoughts or incident happen one after another

[Example] 잠자리에 누워서도 여러 생각들이 꼬리에 꼬리를 물고 떠올라서 잠을 이루지 못했다.
Although I laid down to sleep, I couldn't sleep due to various thoughts "꼬리에 꼬리를 물고" emerged.

047
눈독을 들이다

to set one's mind on something because you want it

[Example] 고양이가 밥상 위에 놓인 생선에 눈독을 들이고 있다.
The cat was "눈독을 들이고 있다" the fish set on the dinner table.

048
트집을 잡다

to find out small flaws or make a flaw

[Example] 내가 별로 잘못한 것도 없는데 부장님은 사사건건 트집을 잡는 걸 보니 뭔가 기분 나쁜 일이 있으신가 보다.
Seeing that my general manager is "트집을 잡다" every little thing even when I haven't done anything wrong, there must have been something that put him in a bad mood.

049
발 등에 불이 떨어지다

tasks approach with extreme urgency

[Example] 저는 늘 발등에 불이 떨어져야 일을 시작하는 습관이 있어요.
I always have a habit of starting everything when "발등에 불이 떨어지다".

050
베일에 가리다

something is covered secretively

[Example] 그 여배우의 사생활은 철저히 베일에 가려져 있다.
That actress' private life is thoroughly "베일에 가려져 있다".

16-5 연습문제 (관용어 5)

[1-10] 다음을 읽고 알맞은 관용어를 넣어 대화를 완성하십시오.

After reading the conversation, complete it by putting in the idiom that fits best.

1. **가 :** 미선 씨는 내가 마음에 안 드나 봐요.
   나 : 왜요?
   가 : 내가 하는 일마다 ______________________ 어서/아서/여서 잔소리를 하니 정말 힘들어요.

2. **가 :** 요즘 잘 팔리는 책이 뭐예요?
   나 : 재테크에 관한 책이 나왔는데______________________고 있어요.

3. **가 :** 너______________________ 는/은/ㄴ 모양이구나. 밤을 새워서 보고서 쓰는 걸 보니.
   나 : 응, 내일까지 내지 않으면 성적을 받을 수 없거든.

4. **가 :** 경기 북부 지역에 홍수로 피해를 입은 지역이 많아졌다면서요?
   나 : 네, 그래서 저희 학생회에서도 ______________________어서/아서/여서 그분들을 돕기로 했어요.

5. **가 :** 도저히 혼자서는 할 수 없는데 지금 좀 도와 줄 수 있어?
   나 : 미안해. ______________________ 이야/야. 나도 할 일이 산더미야.

6. **가 :** 이번에도 기계 조립 분야에서 김영수 씨가 우승을 하겠지?
   나 : 글쎄요, 결과가 나와 봐야겠지만 그 분야에서 ______________________는/은/ㄴ 사람들이 다 참가해서 쉽지는 않을 거예요.

7. **가 :** 김 선생님은 어떤 분이세요?
   나 : 아주 직선적인 분이지만 ______________________어서/아서/여서 저는 더 좋아해요.

8. **가 :** 이번 유괴 사건의 범인은 찾았나요?
   나 : 아니요, 사건을 파헤치면 파헤칠수록 의문점이______________________고 생기는 바람에 아직까지 오리무중이에요.

9. **가 :** 언니가 새로 산 구두 정말 예쁘다. 내가 찾던 바로 그 디자인이야.
   나 : ______________________________지 마. 절대로 안 빌려 줄 테니까.

10. **가 :** 이번 뇌물수수 사건의 전모가 꼭 밝혀졌으면 좋겠어요.
    나 : 워낙 배후 세력이 ______________________________ 어서/아서/여서 밝혀내기 쉽지 않을 거예요.

16-6 관용어 6

051
사서 고생이다

to suffer hardship from a task that doesn't usually cause hardship because you made it so

[Example] 택시를 타면 금방 갈 곳을 걸어서 가느라고 사서 고생이다.

Because I am walking to the place where I could've easily gotten there by taxi, "사서 고생이다".

052
불똥이 튀다

harm goes to someone who is unrelated

[Example] 임원급 이상만 구조조정을 한다더니 말단 직원인 우리에게까지 불똥이 튈 줄은 몰랐다.

We didn't know that "불똥이 튀다" to low-ranking employees like us because they said that they would only restructure executive level employees.

053
얼굴에 먹칠을 하다

to be put to shame so that your face or honor is dirtied

[Example] 나 때문에 부모님 얼굴에 먹칠하는 일은 만들고 싶지 않아서 지금까지 늘 성실히 생활해 왔다.

Because I didn't want to "얼굴에 먹칠을 하다" on my parents due to my actions, I always lived a sincere life.

054
재미를 보다

obtain good results from a certain task and gain benefits

[Example] 내가 투자한 주식의 값이 배로 올라서 재미를 좀 봤다.

Because the price of the stock I invested in doubled, "재미를 좀 봤다".

055
죽이 맞다

two people are like-minded

[Example] 일할 때도 놀 때처럼 죽이 잘 맞으면 일도 빨리 끝나고 결과도 좋을 텐데.

If we "죽이 잘 맞다" when working like we do when playing, our work would end quicker and the result would be good as well.

056
싼 게 비지떡이다

an expression used metaphorically to show that the cheaper the price, the lower the quality is as well

[Example] 다른 회사 제품보다 싸서 구입했는데 싼 게 비지떡이라고 금방 고장이 나고 말았어요.

Like they say "싼게 비지떡이다", the product I bought quickly broke after I bought it due to it being cheaper than other business' products.

057
열을 올리다

to be extremely absorbed in something or to show enthusiasm

[Example] 최근 자동차 업체들이 새로운 해외 시장 개척에 열을 올리고 있다.
Recently, automobile businesses are "열을 올리고 있다" in pioneering the overseas markets.

058
눈 밖에 나다

to lose trust and receive dislike

[Example] 그는 여러 번 약속을 지키지 않아 직장 상사의 눈 밖에 나고 말았다.
Because he broke his promises numerous times, he "눈 밖에 나고 말았다" from our supervisor.

059
코가 납작해지다

to feel discouraged because you are put to shame

[Example] 자신만만해하던 과목에서 낙제를 한 후 영수는 코가 납작해졌다.
After failing the subject that he was confident in, Youngsoo's "코가 납작해졌다".

060
눈살을 찌푸리다

to furrow one's brow because of something that you dislike

[Example] 공공장소에서의 지나친 애정 표현은 사람들의 눈살을 찌푸리게 한다.
Couples who display deep affection in public areas make people "눈살을 찌푸리다".

16-6 연습문제 (관용어 6)

[1-10] 다음을 읽고 알맞은 관용어를 넣어 대화를 완성하십시오.

After reading the conversation, complete it by putting in the idiom that fits best.

1. **가 :** 네가 우리 ______________________다니. 어떻게 그런 부끄러운 일을 저지를 수 있니?
   나 : 죄송해요. 제가 잠시 돈에 눈이 멀었나 봐요.

2. **가 :** 준비는 잘 돼 갑니까?
   나 : 잘 돼 가기는요. 두 사람이 __________________어야/아야/여야 일을 신나게 하지요. 서로 눈치만 살피느라 진행이 더뎌요.

3. **가 :** 지난 대회의 우승 팀이 이번 대회에서는 본선 진출도 못했다면서?
   나 : 그러게요. 준결승까지는 자신 있다고 큰 소리 치더니 이번 대회 첫 출전팀에게 0대1로 지면서 ________________________어졌어/아졌어/여졌어.

4. **가 :** 식당에 손님이 많아요?
   나 : 네, 장사가 잘 돼서 톡톡히 ______________________고 있어요.

5. **가 :** 공금을 유용한 사건으로 온 회사가 시끄럽다면서요?
   나 : 네, 이번 사건으로 누구에게 __________________________을지/ㄹ지 몰라서 모두들 쉬쉬하고 있어요.

6. **가 :** 너희 집은 여유 있는 것 같은데 왜 날마다 아르바이트 하느라고 __________________?
   나 : 그게 뭐 내 돈이니? 우리 아버지 돈이지.

7. **가 :** 미선 씨가 좌담회에서 상대팀에게 반말로 이야기한 건 좀 심했던 것 같아.
   나 : 그래요. 좌담회를 본 사람은 모두 너무 무례한 행동이라면서 ______________________었어요/았어요/였어요.

8. **가 :** 첫 출근이라 많이 떨리네요.
   나 : 무엇보다도 신입 사원 때에는 선배들 _________________지 않도록 행동을 잘 해야 해.

9. **가 :** 지난번에 백화점에 갔다가 하도 싸서 가방을 하나 샀더니 벌써 고장이 났지 뭐야.
나 : ______________________이라고/라고 하나를 사더라도 제값을 주고 사는 게 나아.

10. **가 :** 요즘 미선 씨가 노래방에서 산다며?
나 : 응, 이번 대회에서는 꼭 수상을 하겠다며 연습에 ______________________ 고 있어.

한자성어

17

Chinese character phrases

17-1 한자성어 1

001
감언이설 [가먼니설]

enticing someone by adulating them to the point where they are tempted or raising favorable terms

[Example] 떼돈을 벌게 해주겠다는 감언이설에 속아 장사 밑천을 떼이고 말았어요.

I was deceived by the "감언이설" stating that I would be able to gain a large fortune and instead was swindled out of my business funds.

002
견물생심 [견물생심]

when you see something in person, you become greedy and want it

[Example] 견물생심이라고 그 여자가 무심코 서랍을 열었는데 안에 있는 돈을 보고 자기도 모르게 손이 갔대.

Like they say "견물생심," the girl said that when she casually opened the drawer and saw the money, her hand automatically went to it.

003
과대망상 [과대망상]

a symptom where you exaggerate the truth or think ridiculously

[Example] 어렸을 때 아무래도 내가 천재인 것 같다는 과대망상에 빠지곤 했다.

When I was younger, I used to fall into "과대망상" thinking that I was a genius.

004
구태의연 [구태의연]

in the previous state without any change or any development

[Example] '두발규제'가 학생들로 하여금 공부에 집중할 수 있게 해준다는 학교 측의 주장은 구태의연한 발상입니다.

The opinion of the school stating that the regulation on hair will help the students focus more on their studies is a "구태의연" idea.

005
금시초문 [금시초문]

hearing for the first time just now

[Example] 이 지역에 신도시가 조성된다고요? 저는 금시초문입니다.

They're going to build a new city in this area? That is "금시초문" for me.

006
당연지사 [당연지사]

when judging a matter with all of the details laid out, you perceive it to have to happen in a certain way or it will happen in a certain way

[Example] 비록 적은 액수라고는 하나 뇌물을 받은 경찰관이 해직되는 건 당연지사야.

No matter how small an amount the bribe the police officer received, it is "당연지사" for him to be dismissed.

007
동고동락 [동고동낙]

suffering hardship and experiencing happiness together

[Example] 삼십 년 동안 동고동락해 온 부인과 사별한 후 아직도 마음을 잡지 못하고 있어요.

After being separated by death from his wife, the man who had spent thirty years "동고동락" still can't settle.

008
동분서주 [동분서주]

running around here and there extremely rushed

[Example] 요즘 결혼과 유학을 앞두고 결혼식장 알아보랴 서류 보내랴 동분서주하고 있어요.

Lately having my wedding and study abroad ahead, I am "동분서주" trying to find out about wedding halls and also trying to send documents.

009
마이동풍 [마이동풍]

meaning like even when the east wind will blow into a horse's ear and it doesn't care, words that you do not listen to and instead let just flow out

[Example] 자금을 한 곳에 집중투자하지 말라고 수차 권고했는데도 마이동풍이니 걱정이네요.

Although I repeatedly advised to not invest all of the funds into one concentrated area, I'm worried because it is "마이동풍".

010
무궁무진 [무궁무진]

an expression saying that there is so much that you can see no end to it

[Example] 대통령은 양국 간 협력 가능성은 무궁무진하다며 에너지, 정보통신, 첨단 기술 분야 등에서의 협력 증진을 거듭 강조했습니다.

The president stated that the potential collaboration between the two nations was "무궁무진" and again emphasized that energy, information technology, and other cutting edge areas would promote further collaboration.

17-1 연습문제 (한자성어 1)

[1-10] 다음을 읽고 알맞은 한자성어를 넣어 대화를 완성하십시오.

After reading the conversation, complete it by putting in the Chinese character phrase that fits best.

1. **박대리 :** 김 대리가 입사동기들 중에 자기만한 실력을 가진 사람도 없고, 윗분들에게 신임을 얻었으니 다음 번 승진 1순위는 자기라고 하더라.

   이대리 : 나 참, 완전히 ____________________에 빠져 있구나. 정신 차리라고 그래라.

2. **언니 :** 오늘 심심한데 백화점에나 갈까?

   동생 : 지난달에 돈을 많이 써서 아무것도 못 사.

   언니 : 그럼, 가서 안 사고 구경만 하면 되지. 구경도 즐겁잖아.

   동생 : ____________________이라고/라고 일단 보면 사고 싶어져서 안 돼. 아예 보지도 않는 편이 나아.

3. **동생 :** 바쁘다 바빠. 오늘은 거래처에도 가야 하고, 사장님한테 결재도 받아야 하고, 내일까지 보고서도 내야 하고... 몸이 10개라도 모자라겠다.

   언니 : 그렇게 ____________________ 하는 네가 오히려 부럽다. 어디 괜찮은 자리 있으면 하나 소개해줘.

4. **박과장 :** 김 과장, 얘기 들었어? 내년에 해외영업부를 철수하기로 했대.

   김과장 : 그게 무슨 말이야? 어디에서 들었어? 나는 ____________________이야/야. 헛소문 아니야? 아무 공고도 없이 갑자기 그런 일이 있겠어?

5. **가 :** 어! 너, 김 일병 아냐? 김 일병 맞지?

   나 : 누구신지……. 혹시, 이 병장님? 진짜 이 병장님이십니까? 아이고, 정말 반갑습니다.

   가 : 우리 오뚜기 부대에서 ____________________ 하던 때가 엊그제 같은데 이게 몇 년 만이야?

   나 : 함께 울고 웃던 그때가 벌써 10년 전이군요!

6. **가 :** 이제는 그 드라마를 안 볼래요.

   나 : 왜요? 아줌마들에게 인기가 많던데요. 꽃미남들도 여럿 나오고요.

   가 : 소재와 이야기 전개가 ____________________ 해서 식상해요. 예전이나 지금이나 크게 달라진 게 없어요. 사회는 하루가 다르게 변해 가는데 드라마 소재는 너무 뻔해요.

7. **가** : 여보, 웬 옷들을 이렇게 많이 샀어? 오늘 무슨 날이야?

나 : 아휴, 내가 미쳤지. 백화점에 바지 한 벌 사러 갔다가 '아가씨 같다', '학생인 줄 알았다'는 ______________에 속아서 입을 일도 없는 정장에다가 코트까지 사고 말았지 뭐예요.

8. **가** : 요즘 정치인들이 하는 꼴들 좀 봐. 우리 서민들의 생활에 관심이나 있는지 원.

나 : 그 사람들이 우리말을 귀담아 듣겠어요? 그동안 수없이 정치권을 향해 싸우지 말고 민생을 챙기라고 주문했건만 늘 ______________이었잖아요/였잖아요.

9. **가** : 줄리아 씨가 유학생활에 적응하지 못해 우울증에 시달리더니 요즘엔 감기다, 소화불량이다, 하루가 멀다 하고 병원을 찾네요.

나 : 마음이 아프니 몸이 아픈 건 ______________지. 마음이 병이 들었는데 몸인들 온전하겠어?

10. **가** : 박사님, 요즘 집중적으로 연구하시는 분야는 무엇입니까?

나 : 우리 연구소는 요즘 대체 에너지 개발 작업이 한창인데 그 중에서도 가장 많은 공을 들이고 있는 분야가 바로 2차 전지입니다.

가 : 2차 전지란 새로운 형태의 건전지인가요?

나 : 음, 2차 전지는 쉽게 말해 한 번 쓰고 버리는 건전지와 달리 재충전해서 쓸 수 있는 건전지를 말합니다. 그 활용 분야도 ______________하고 경제성도 높기 때문에 세계 여러 나라들이 이 연구에 큰 관심을 보이고 있습니다.

17-2 한자성어 2

011
무용지물 [무용지물]

useless object or person

[Example] 무인주차관리기가 잦은 고장과 이용률 저하로 무용지물이 되고 있다.

Because of the frequent breakdowns and decline in utilization, unmanned parking managing machines are becoming "무용지물".

012
무위도식 [무위도식]

idling away wastefully without doing any work

[Example] 옆집 아저씨는 아내가 벌어다 주는 돈으로 무위도식하고 있다.

The middle-aged man next door is "무위도식" with the money that his wife earns.

013
반신반의 [반신바니]

even though you trust a bit, you also are suspicious

[Example] 미선이는 그 영업사원의 말을 반신반의 하면서도 결국 물건을 사고 말았다.

Although Miseon was "반신반의" about what the salesperson was saying, she eventually bought the product.

014
비일비재 [비일비재]

an expression saying that the same phenomenon does not only happen once or twice but many times

[Example] 실제로 국내 수입업체들 가운데는 외국기업에 선수금을 지불해 놓고 국제법을 잘 알지 못해서 돈을 떼이는 경우가 비일비재하다.

In reality, it is "비일비재" that there are many domestic import businesses that give advances to foreign companies and then get swindled out of that money because they do not know of the international law very well.

015
산전수전 [산전수전]

an expression literally meaning fighting in the mountains and also fighting on water, but also meaning that one has already endured all of the hardships and suffering in the world

[Example] 강력계 형사 생활 십오 년, 김 형사는 이 방면에서 산전수전 다 겪은 몸이었다.

Detective Kim is someone who has endured "산전수전" while living as a detective in charge of violent crime for fifteen years.

016
새옹지마 [새옹지마]

an expression meaning that because there are so many changes in the fortune of our lives that it is hard to predict

[Example] 투자를 할 때 호재와 악재에 관심을 가지는 것은 좋지만 부화뇌동할 필요 없습니다. 인생사 새옹지마라고 당장의 호재가 미래의 악재일지, 아니면 지금의 악재가 미래의 호재일지 모르기 때문입니다.

It is good to be interested in both favorable factors and unfavorable factors when investing but there is no need to follow others blindly. Like they say, life is "새옹지마" and we don't know if favorable factors will be unfavorable factors in the future, or presently unfavorable factors will become favorable factors in the future.

017
속수무책 [속쑤무책]

as if your hands are tied, there are no plans and you can't move

[Example] 가방을 빼앗아 오토바이를 타고 도망가는 남자를 속수무책으로 쳐다볼 수밖에 없었다.

I could only stare "속수무책" at the man who grabbed my bag and was running away on his motorcycle.

018
시기상조 [시기상조]

an expression saying that it is not quite the moment

[Example] 우리나라의 형편 상 전면적인 농산물 시장 개방은 아직 시기상조다.

With the circumstances of our nation, it is still "시기상조" to open an overall agricultural market.

019
심사숙고 [심사숙꼬]

thinking well and deeply

[Example] 중요한 문제이니만큼 며칠만 여유를 주시면 심사숙고해서 결정을 내리겠습니다.

Because this problem is important, if you give me a couple more days, I will "심사숙고" and make a decision.

020
애지중지 [애지중지]

loving something a lot and considering it precious

[Example] 동생은 새로 산 옷을 애지중지하며 만지지도 못하게 하였다.

My younger sibling "애지중지" the clothes he newly bought and didn't even let me touch it.

17-2 연습문제 (한자성어 2)

[1-10] 다음을 읽고 알맞은 한자성어를 넣어 대화를 완성하십시오.

After reading the conversation, complete it by putting in the Chinese character phrase that fits best .

1. **지연 :** 이번 독감이 꽤 무서운가 봐. 사망자도 있다던데.

   희정 : 빨리 예방주사를 맞아야 할 텐데. 예전에 전 세계를 휩쓸었다는 독감 얘기 알지? 그런 일이 또 일어나지는 않겠지?

   지연 : 그때는 발병의 원인이 정확히 파악이 안 된 상태여서 ____________________이었지만/였지만 이번엔 다르잖아. 백신도 있고 치료제도 있다잖아.

2. **은희 :** 다른 나라에서는 요즘 동성애를 법적으로 인정하려는 움직임이 일고 있대요.

   명숙 : 우리나라도 곧 그렇게 되지 않을까요?

   은희 : 그렇지만 우리의 현실로는 아직 ____________________인 것 같은데.

3. **진수 :** 전 벌써 대학 졸업 후 3년 째 집에서 놀고 있어요.

   민호 : 그래요? 저하고 비슷하군요.

   진수 : 그럼, 그쪽도 ____________________ 한 지 3년째라는 얘긴가요?

   민호 : 아니오, 전 아직 2년밖에 안 됐어요. 제가 좀 낫죠?

4. **희정 :** 요즘은 사전 사용하는 사람이 별로 없는 것 같아.

   지영 : 그래, 집에 있는 사전도 자리만 차지하고 ____________________이/가 된 지 오래야.

   희정 : 하긴. 전자 사전도 있고 인터넷으로 찾아도 되고.

5. **아버지 :** 와, 정말 경치가 좋구나.

   네 말을 처음 들었을 때는 ____________________ 했는데, 와 보니까 설악산 봄 경치도 아름답네. 가을만 아름다운 줄 알았는데.

   아　들 : 그것 보세요. 여기 안 오셨으면 섭섭하실 뻔했죠?

6. **김과장 :** 이 과장이 아침에 사직서를 냈대. 벌써 영국의 MBA 과정 합격 허가를 받은 상태라고 하데. 부럽긴 한데 이제 공부를 시작하기엔 좀 늦은 거 아닌가?

박과장 : 공부는 벌써 몇 년 전부터 뜻이 있었다더군. 이번에 밀어붙이지 않으면 앞으로 공부할 기회가 없을 것 같아서 ____________________ 끝에 결정을 한 모양이야.

김과장 : 송별회 겸 한잔 하면서 얘기를 들어봐야겠네.

7. **손 녀 :** 할아버지, 옆집 할아버지께서 많이 편찮으신가 봐요.

할아버지 : ____________________ 하던 도자기를 ____________________하는 손자가 깼으니 어떻게 하겠니? 혼자 끙끙 앓을 수밖에.

8. **가 :** 부모 욕심으로 조기 유학을 보낸 아이들이 객지에서 몸 고생, 마음 고생만 하다가 귀국하는 경우가 많다면서?

나 : 그렇다네요. 유학생 중 10%만이 명문대에 진학할 뿐이고 낙제 후에 학업을 포기하고 귀국하는 경우도 ____________________ 하대요.

9. **가 :** 큰 수술 앞두고 많이 걱정되시지요?

나 : 걱정은 무슨… 살아가면서 볼 것, 안 볼 것 다 보고 ____________________다 겪은 사람이 뭘 두려워하겠나?

10. **가 :** 연기력 부족으로 평론가들에게 혹평을 받던 배우 박명신이 최근에 감독으로 큰 성공을 거두었다면서요?

나 : 인생이란 ____________________ 이라더니/라더니 배우로 주목받지 못했던 것이 진로를 바꾸는 계기가 되어 오히려 큰 성공을 거두게 되었군요.

17-3 한자성어 3

021
약방감초 [약빵감초]

literally meaning that licorice must always be present in a herbal medicine shop because licorice is used a lot in oriental medicine, it also means that in a matter a certain person always interferes or an object that is a necessity must be present

[Example] 자네는 어느 일에나 끼어들어 약방감초처럼 행동하는데 이번에는 조용히 있는 것이 더 나을 거야.

You always interfere in every matter and behave like "약방감초" but I think it's best that you just stay quietly·

022
양자택일 [양자태길]

choosing one out of two

[Example] 내각이 불신임결의를 받으면 스스로 총사퇴하거나 국회를 해산하거나 양자택일해야 한다.

When there is a passage of a vote of non-confidence in the Cabinet, there must be "양자택일" of either mass resignation of one's own accord or a dissolution of the National Assembly.

023
어부지리 [어부지리]

a third party doesn't make a great effort and yet earns a benefit because of two people quarreling over a concern

[Example] 여당 후보와 야당 후보의 다툼 속에서 무소속 후보가 어부지리로 당선되었다.

The independent candidate was elected "어부지리" from the ruling party candidate and the opposition party candidate fighting.

024
오리무중 [오리무중]

literally meaning being stuck inside a thick fog, it also means that you can not grasp a direction or heads or tails of a situation

[Example] 무장단체에 의해 납치된 것으로 추정되는 한국인 여성 등 외국인 9명의 소재가 여전히 오리무중이라고 합니다.

The whereabouts of nine foreigners including the korean woman suspected to have been kidnapped by militants are still "오리무중".

025
오십보백보 [오십뽀백뽀]

an expression meaning although there is a slight difference in superiority and level, there is essentially no difference

[Example] 45등이나 50등이나 오십보백보다.

Being 45th or 50th is "오십보백보".

026
왈가왈부 [왈가왈부]

saying if a certain matter is correct or incorrect

[Example] 이번 구조조정 결정에 대해서는 이미 결정된 사안이니 더 이상 왈가왈부하지 맙시다.

Because the decision to restructure is an issue that has already been decided, let us not "왈가왈부" any more.

027
의기양양 [의기양양]

showing satisfaction on one's face because something has happened the way you wanted

[Example] 난생 처음 잠자리 한 마리를 잡은 꼬마는 의기양양하게 뛰어왔다.

The child ran over "의기양양" after catching a dragonfly for the first time in his life.

028
이구동성 [이구동성]

many people say the same thing

[Example] 한국말을 배우려면 어디가 제일 좋냐고 물어봤더니 모두들 이구동성으로 연세대 한국어학당이 최고라고 하던데요.

When I asked where the best place to learn Korean is, everyone said in "이구동성" that Yonsei University's Korean Language Institute was the best.

029
일구이언 [일구이언]

literally meaning that one mouth says two different things, it also means that one blows hot and the cold on one issue

[Example] 그는 일구이언을 밥 먹듯 해서 아무도 그를 믿지 않게 되었다.

Because he "일구이언" like he ate food, it happened that no one believed him anymore.

030
일사천리 [일싸철리]

literally meaning river water that flows a long distance quickly, it also means that a certain matter progresses quickly and without a hitch

[Example] 그 법안은 국회에서 일사천리로 통과되었다.

That bill passed "일사천리"through the National Assembly.

17-3 연습문제 (한자성어 3)

[1-10] 다음을 읽고 알맞은 한자성어를 넣어 대화를 완성하십시오.

After reading the conversation, complete it by putting in the Chinese character phrase that fits best.

1. **지영 :** 그래서 그 집 사기로 했어? 안 사기로 했어? 부동산 가격이 이렇게 자꾸 떨어지면 지금 사는 거 손해 아니야?

은희 : 응, 그런데 어제 집주인한테 전화해 봤는데, 벌써 계약금을 건넸으니까 계약조건대로 사든지, 아니면 계약금 날리고 계약 취소하든지 ________________ 하래.

2. **학　생 :** 설문 조사를 했는데요, 이상하게도 모두 같은 대답이었습니다. 한국어학당에서는 5급이 제일 재미있다는군요.

선생님 : 모두 ________________ 으로/로 그렇게 얘기하는 걸 보니 사실인가 본데요.

3. **동생 :** 형, 정말 다음 달 월급 타면 내 돈 갚을 거지?

형 : 물론이지. 내가 언제 약속 안 지키는 거 봤어?

동생 : 그래도 다음 달에 딴 소리 할까 봐...

형 : 뭐? 넌 내가 그렇게 ________________ 하는 사람으로 보이냐? 날 믿어.

4. **김과장 :** 박 대리, 이번 달 판매 실적이 이게 뭐야? 한 달 동안 한 대가 뭐냐고?

이대리 : 맞아, 박 대리, 다음 달엔 더 뛰어다녀야겠어.

김과장 : 두 사람 ________________ 이야/야. 이 대리도 두 대는 계약만 한 거고, 확실하게 판건 한 대밖에 없잖아.

5. **아버지 :** 뭘 그렇게 웃고 있니?

딸 : ________________ 으로/로 아까 도서상품권이 생겼어요. 언니하고 오빠가 서로 갖겠다고 싸우는 바람에 엄마가 저한테 주셨거든요.

6. **남편 :** 어? 당신 일찍 왔네. 오늘 저녁에 회의가 있어서 좀 늦을 거라더니.

아내 : 부장님이 바쁜 일이 있으신지 회의를 ________________ 으로/로 진행하시더라고. 적어도 두 시간은 걸릴 줄 알았는데, 30분도 안 돼서 끝났어.

7. **앵커 :** 인천공항에 나가있는 박명수 기자를 연결하겠습니다. 박명수 기자.
기자 : 네, 여기는 인천공항입니다. 지금 올림픽 메달을 목에 건 우리 국가대표 선수들이 ______________________ 한 모습으로 입국장을 빠져나오고 있습니다.

8. **가 :** 뺑소니사건 용의자가 경찰이 한 눈을 파는 사이에 도망갔대.
나 : 그래, 어디로 도망갔대?
가 : 아직은 ______________________ 인가 봐.

9. **가 :** 깻잎은 느끼한 맛을 없애줘서 삼겹살과 같은 고기를 먹을 때는 절대 빠질 수 없는 ______________________ 같은 존재야.
나 : 비타민C와 철분도 풍부해 훌륭한 건강식품이기도 하지.

10. **가 :** 우리가 보기에는 분명히 상대팀이 먼저 반칙을 했는데 다시 한 번 항의해 봅시다.
나 : 이미 심판의 결정이 난 이상______________________ 해 봐야 소용없잖아요.

17-4 한자성어 4

031
일편단심 [일편단심]

one piece of a heart that is red. a heart that comes from sincerity and does not change

[Example] 처음 만난 순간부터 지금까지 일편단심 당신만을 사랑해 왔어요.

Since the first time we met until now, I have only loved you "일편단심".

032
자급자족 [자급짜족]

supplying or producing needed supplies by oneself

[Example] 농경 사회는 필요한 대부분의 것을 자급자족하는 사회였다.

The agrarian society was a society that mostly "자급자족" everything that they needed.

033
자화자찬 [자화자찬]

literally meaning complimenting oneself on the picture that he drew, it also means boasting about something that you did yourself

[Example] 자화자찬으로 들리겠지만 이 작품은 내가 심혈을 기울인 것으로 비평가들도 한국 현대 미술을 대표할 만한 작품이라고 극찬을 한 바 있다.

Although this may sound "자화자찬," this piece of work is something I threw my heart and soul into and is a work that even critics highly praised as something that could be representative of Korean Modern Art.

034
전무후무 [전무후무]

there was nothing before and there will be nothing in the future

[Example] 장수란 선수는 역도에서 올림픽 5연패라는 전무후무의 대기록을 세웠다.

The athlete Jang Sooran raised the "전무후무" record of five consecutive victories in weightlifting.

035
전전긍긍 [전전긍긍]

trembling while being careful because you are extremely fearful

[Example] 세계 금융 업계는 미국의 유명 투자 회사의 파산으로 겪을 후폭풍에 전전긍긍하고 있다.

The world's banking industry was "전전긍긍" from the storm that would follow the bankruptcy of a famous American investment company.

036
주객전도 [주객쩐도]

literally meaning that the positions of an owner and guest will switch, it also means the change of an object's order and importance

[Example] 공교육과 사교육의 주객전도 현상이 일어나서 학생들이 학교 공부는 소홀히 하고 밤늦게까지 학원을 전전하는 일이 벌어지고 있다.

Because of the "주객전도" phenomenon that happened between public education and private education, the matter of students carelessly studying at school and then wandering to private educational institutes late at night is happening.

037
죽마고우 [죽마고우]

literally meaning riding a horse made from bamboo and playing as friends, it also means a friend that you grew up and played with since you were young

[Example] 오늘 처음 만난 두 사람은 술이 들어가자 마치 죽마고우처럼 흉금을 터놓고 이야기하기 시작했다.

As soon as they started drinking, the two people that just met today bared their souls and spoke as if they were "죽마고우".

038
차일피일 [차일피일]

pushing the time limit while saying today or the next day

[Example] 영수는 돈을 빌려간 지 벌써 2년이나 지났는데도 빚을 갚겠다고 얘기만 하고 차일피일 돈 갚기를 미루고 있다.

Although two years have already passed since Young-soo borrowed money, he only says that he will repay me and is instead pushing off repaying me "차일피일".

039
포복절도 [포복쩔또]

laughing a lot while holding one's stomach to the point of falling over

[Example] 웃음 다이어트의 기본은 '미소'가 아닌 '포복절도'. 무조건 소리 내어 배꼽이 빠지도록 웃는다.

The basis of the laughter diet is not 'smiling' but "포복절도". No matter what, one must laugh out loud and laugh oneself into convulsions.

040
학수고대 [학쑤고대]

waiting earnestly while sticking out your neck so far that it is like a crane's neck

[Example] 어머니는 전쟁터에서 실종된 아들이 무사히 돌아오기를 학수고대하고 있다.

The mother is waiting "학수고대" for her son to return safely after he went missing on the battlefield.

17-4 연습문제 (한자성어 4)

[1-10] 다음을 읽고 알맞은 한자성어를 넣어 대화를 완성하십시오.

After reading the conversation, complete it by putting in the Chinese character phrase that fits best.

1. **아내 :** 당신 요즘 좀 이상해. 변한 거 같아. 결혼 전엔 나만을 사랑한다더니.
   남편 : 어허, 그런 말은 생각하지도 마. 아직도 당신을 향한 ________________ 은/는 변함 없다오.

2. **희정 :** 요즘 계속 기분이 가라앉는데, 어디________________ 할 만한 영화 없을까?
   명숙 : 나는 '가문의 영광' 하고 '두사부일체' 보고 배꼽이 빠지는 줄 알았어.

3. **가 :** 오늘도 정희는 하루 종일 휴대전화만 바라보고 있니?
   나 : 응, 일주일 전에 만난 남자가 자기 이상형이라나?
   그래서 전화가 오기만 ________________ 하고 있어.

4. **가 :** 왜 그 사람과 동업을 하세요? 좀 더 경험도 많고 능력 있는 사람도 많을 텐데요.
   나 : 그 친구는 어린 시절부터 한 동네에서 친형제처럼 지내온 ________________ 이어서/여서 믿을 수 있거든.

5. **가 :** 요즘 뉴스에서 보험회사 직원들의 비리 사건들이 연일 크게 보도되고 있던데 보셨어요?
   나 : 네, 보험회사의 얼굴인 보험설계사들의 비리가 속속 드러나면서 보험사들은 회사의 이미지가 실추될까 봐 ________________ 하고 있대요.

6. **가 :** 와, 정말 맛있다! 이거 도대체 누가 만든 거야?
   둘이 먹다가 하나가 죽어도 모르겠네. 누구 솜씨인지 대단하다!
   나 : 너, ________________ 이/가 너무 심한 거 아니야? 칭찬이란 원래 다른 사람이 해줘야 빛나는 거야.

7. **가 :** 요즘 전기요금, 가스요금이 너무 올라서 부담이 돼요.
   나 : 그래요? 우리 집은 에너지 절약형 아파트여서 생활비가 훨씬 적게 들어요.
   태양광 발전 시설이 갖추어져 있어 전기를 자체 생산할 수 있기 때문에 난방과 샤워용 온수에 쓰이는 거의 100% ________________ 이/가 가능해요.

8. **가 :** 영수야, 개학이 얼마 남지 않았는데 숙제는 언제 하려고 그렇게 놀러만 다니니? 너 그렇게 숙제를__________________ 미루다가는 나중에 크게 후회한다.

나 : 내일부터 할 거예요. 내일부터.

9. **가 :** 포도주의 인기가 식을 줄 모른다지요?

나 : 네, 아마 도수가 높지 않고 향도 좋고 또 건강을 중요하게 생각하는 요즘의 분위기와 잘 맞아서 그런가 봐요.

가 : 포도주 같은 술은 어디까지나 음식에 곁들여 마시는 것이기 때문에 음식이 더 중요해요. 그런데 지금은__________________ 되어서 음식을 포도주에 맞추려는 사람들까지 있어요.

10. **가 :** 드디어 일일 연속극 '한국어학당'이 평균 시청률 1위를 기록했어요.

나 : 그래요? 저도 즐겨보는 드라마인데 소재가 참신하고 이야기가 흥미진진해요.

가 : 외국인 배우들의 열연에 힘입어 방송 사상__________________ 한 시청률 59%를 기록했답니다.

정답 · 색인

Answers
Index

01 정답

01 · 동사 I

1. ❶
2. ❶
3. ❹
4. ❶
5. ❷
6. ❸
7. ❸
8. ❹
9. ❷
10. ❸
11. ❶
12. ❷
13. ❶
14. ❸
15. ❷
16. ❹
17.❸
18. ❹
19. ❹
20. ❶
21. ❷
22. 갉다
23. 개다
24. 가라앉다
25. 기하다
26. 거스르다
27. 거두다
28. 감다
29. 꼬이다
30. 꿰다

02 · 동사 II

1. ❷
2. ❶
3. ❷
4. ❸
5. ❶
6. ❷
7. ❹
8. ❷
9. ❷
10. ❹
11. ❹
12. ❸
13. ❹
14. ❸
15. ❶
16. ❶
17. ❶
18. ❸
19. ❶
20. ❶
21. ❹
22. ❹
23. ❷
24. 날리다
25. 대다
26. 다지다
27. 다듬다
28. 돌리다
29. 배다
30. 달다

03 · 동사 III

1. ❷
2. ❶
3. ❸
4. ❶
5. ❶
6. ❹
7. ❶
8. ❹
9. ❸
10. ❸
11. ❶
12. ❸
13. ❷
14. ❹
15. ❹
16. ❹
17. ❸
18. ❸
19. ❷
20. ❶
21. ❷
22. ❷
23. ❸
24. ❹
25. 엿보다
26. 새기다
27. 시달리다
28. 헤아리다
29. 지다
30. 잠기다

04 · 명사 I

1. ❹
2. ❷
3. ❷
4. ❸
5. ❹
6. ❶
7. ❷
8. ❷
9. ❶
10. ❹
11. ❶
12. ❷
13. ❷
14. ❸
15. ❷
16. ❶
17. ❸
18. ❶
19. ❶
20. ❸
21. ❸
22. ❹
23. ❷
24. ❸
25. ❷
26. ❹
27. ❶
28. ❹
29. ❸
30. 바이러스
31. 구조
32. 매장
33. 난리
34. 마찰
35. ❹
36. ❶

05 · 명사 II

1. ❷
2. ❶
3. ❷
4. ❹
5. ❸
6. ❸
7. ❶
8. ❷
9. ❷
10. ❹
11. ❹
12. ❶
13. ❹
14. ❸
15. ❶
16. ❹

17. ❷
18. ❹
19. ❹
20. ❶
21. ❸
22. ❸
23. ❸
24. ❷
25. ❹
26. ❶
27. 운명
28. 안정
29. 빈곤
30. 보람
31. 사례
32. 수명

06 · 명사Ⅲ

1. ❶
2. ❷
3. ❹
4. ❷
5. ❸
6. ❷
7. ❷
8. ❸
9. ❶
10. ❶
11. ❷
12. ❸
13. ❸
14. ❷
15. ❶
16. ❷
17. ❶
18. ❹
19. ❸
20. ❶
21. ❸
22. ❹
23. ❷
24. ❷
25. ❹
26. ❶
27. ❹
28. ❸
29. ❹
30. ❶
31. ❹
32. 전망
33. 지원
34. 현상
35. 지지
36. 틈
37. ❸
38. ❷
39. ❷

07 · 형용사 Ⅰ

1. ❹
2. ❸
3. ❷
4. ❸
5. ❶
6. ❸
7. ❷
8. ❹
9. ❶
10. ❸
11. ❸
12. ❷
13. ❸
14. ❷
15. ❶
16. ❷
17. ❶
18. ❹
19. ❹
20. ❶
21. ❸
22. ❶
23. ❸
24. ❹
25. ❶
26. ❷
27. ❹
28. ❹
29. ❷
30. 고소하다
31. 기막히다
32. 든든하다
33. 귀하다
34. 굳다
35. 딱딱하다

08 · 형용사Ⅱ

1. ❸
2. ❶
3. ❸
4. ❸
5. ❹
6. ❷
7. ❷
8. ❶
9. ❹
10. ❸
11. ❷
12. ❹
13. ❸
14. ❶
15. ❶
16. ❹
17. ❸
18. ❶
19. ❹
20. ❹
21. ❷
22. ❹
23. ❶
24. ❹
25. ❶
26. ❷
27. ❶
28. ❸
29. ❷
30. ❸
31. ❶
32. ❷
33. ❹
34. 씁쓸하다
35. 어설프다
36. 빡빡하다

09 · 형용사Ⅲ

1. ❸
2. ❷
3. ❹
4. ❹
5. ❶
6. ❹
7. ❷
8. ❹
9. ❸
10. ❷
11. ❸
12. ❶
13. ❹
14. ❶
15. ❸
16. ❶
17. ❸
18. ❹
19. ❶
20. ❷
21. ❹
22. ❶
23. ❸
24. ❹
25. ❷
26. ❶
27. ❷
28. ❸
29. ❶
30. ❸

31. ❷
32. 짜다
33. 캄캄하다
34. ❷
35. ❶

10 · 부사 I

1. ❹
2. ❶
3. ❷
4. ❹
5. ❶
6. ❷
7. ❶
8. ❹
9. ❸
10. ❶
11. ❸
12. ❷
13. ❶
14. ❹
15. ❶
16. ❹
17. ❷
18. ❸
19. ❶
20. ❸
21. ❸
22. ❷
23. ❹
24. ❷
25. ❹
26. ❷
27. ❸
28. ❸
29. ❹
30. ❸

11 · 부사 II

1. ❹
2. ❸
3. ❶
4. ❷
5. ❶
6. ❹
7. ❷
8. ❹
9. ❸
10. ❶
11. ❶
12. ❷
13. ❶
14. ❷
15. ❸
16. ❹
17. ❷
18. ❸
19. ❸
20. ❷
21. ❶
22. ❸
23. ❸
24. ❸
25. ❹
26. ❶
27. ❹
28. ❹
29. ❷
30. ❸

12 · 부사 III

1. ❷
2. ❸
3. ❷
4. ❶
5. ❹
6. ❹
7. ❸
8. ❸
9. ❶
10. ❷
11. ❸
12. ❶
13. ❷
14. ❶
15. ❹
16. ❹
17. ❸
18. ❷
19. ❹
20. ❸
21. ❷
22. ❹
23. ❶
24. ❶
25. ❶
26. ❷
27. ❶
28. ❸
29. ❷
30. ❶

13 의성어 · 의태어

의성어

1. 껄껄
2. 둥둥
3. 찰칵
4. 찰싹찰싹
5. 통탕통탕
6. ❹
7. ❹
8. ❸
9. ❷
10. 꽝

의성의태어

1. 앙앙
2. 짝짝
3. 뚜벅뚜벅
4. ❹
5. ❶
6. 똑똑

의태어

1. 사뿐사뿐
2. 듬성듬성
3. 뒤죽박죽
4. 알록달록
5. 와들와들
6. 갈팡질팡
7. 모락모락
8. 꼬깃꼬깃
9. ❸
10. ❹
11. ❷
12. ❷
13. ❹
14. ❶
15. ❶
16. ❸
17. ❶
18. 띄엄띄엄
19. 들썩들썩
20. 들쭉날쭉

14 접두사 · 접미사

접두사

1. 헛소문이에요
2. 덧나서
3. 한복판
4. 되돌아가서
5. 맨손으로
6. 군살이
7. 풋사랑과
8. 휘날리며
9. 외톨이가
10. 날고기를

접미사

1. 학생답
2. 거짓말투성이야
3. 울렁거려서
4. 자유롭
5. 자랑스러워요
6. 구경꾼이
7. 욕심꾸러기
8. 게으름뱅이가
9. 별난
10. 고집쟁이

15 · 속담

속담 1

1. 개구리 올챙이 적 생각 못 하
2. 매도 먼저 맞는 게 낫다고
3. 개똥(쇠똥)도 약에 쓰려면 없다고
4. 남의 떡이 커
5. 떡 본 김에 제사 지낸다고
6. 과부 사정 홀아비가 안다고
7. 똥 묻은 개가 겨 묻은 개 나무란다고
8. 같은 값이면 다홍치마라고
9. 등잔 밑이 어둡다고
10. 벼는 익을수록 고개는 숙인다는

속담 2

1. 사공이 많으면 배가 산으로 간다
2. 십 년이면 강산도 변하는데
3. 우물을 파도 한 우물을 파라고
4. 열 길 물속은 알아도 한 길 사람 속은 모른다고
5. 쥐구멍에도 볕들 날 있다고
6. 짚신도 짝이 있다는데
7. 웃는 낯에 침 뱉을
8. 오르지 못할 나무는 쳐다보지도 말라고
9. 수박 겉핥기로
10. 선무당이 사람 잡는다고

속담 3

1. 친구 따라 강남 간다
2. 달면 삼키고 쓰면 뱉는
3. 개천에서 용 났다고
4. 비 온 뒤에 땅이 굳어진다
5. 공든 탑이 무너지
6. 가지 많은 나무 바람 잘 날 없다
7. 백지장도 맞들면 낫다
8. 서당 개 삼 년에 풍월을 한다(읊는다)
9. 송충이는 솔잎을 먹어야 산다
10. 소문난 잔치에 먹을 것 없다

속담 4

1. 옥에 티였어요
2. 종로에서 뺨 맞고 한강에서 화풀이 한다
3. 입이 열 개라도 할 말이 없습니다
4. 열 번 찍어 안 넘어가는 나무 없다
5. 새 술은 새 부대에 라는
6. 한 번 엎지른 물은 다시 주워 담지 못 한다
7. 중이 제 머리 못 깎는다
8. 잘 자랄 나무는 떡잎부터 알아본다
9. 첫 술에 배부르
10. 안 되면 조상 탓 잘 되면 제 탓이라고

16 · 관용어

관용어 1

1. 간에 기별도 안 간다. (안 가겠다)
2. 겉 다르고 속 다른
3. 간이 콩알만 해지
4. 개미 새끼 한 마리 얼씬하지 않는 군요.
5. 그 사람이 그 사람이
6. 꿀 먹은 벙어리
7. 가려운 곳을 긁어 줬어
8. 굶기를 밥 먹듯 하
9. 검은 머리가 파뿌리가 되도록 살
10. 다람쥐 쳇바퀴 돌 듯

관용어 2

1. 마음은 굴뚝같
2. 모기 소리만 하
3. 도마 위에 오른
4. 두 다리 쭉 뻗고 잤어.
5. 물 쓰듯 하면
6. 물거품이 됐군요.
7. 바닥이 나서
8. 양다리를 걸치
9. 손때가 묻은
10. 둘이 먹다가 하나가 죽어도 모르

관용어 3

1. 발을 맞춰
2. 등을 돌리
3. 가지를 치
4. 걸음마 단계/ 걸음마 단계여서
5. 값을 치르려고/ 값을 치러야
6. 무릎을 꿇/ 무릎을 꿇어야
7. 고개를 돌리
8. 발목이 잡/ 발목을 잡혔다
9. 기를 죽이/ 기가 죽
10. 거울삼아/ 거울 삼아서

관용어 4

1. 손이 많이 가는, 손이 많이 간다.
2. 얼굴 깎이는
3. 손발이 맞아요, 손발이 맞
4. 빛을 보는, 빛을 볼
5. 뿌리 뽑는, 뿌리 뽑
6. 시치미를 떼면, 시치미를 떼
7. 입을 모아
8. 마침표를 찍
9. 배가 부른, 배가 불러요
10. 찬물을 끼얹었다.

관용어 5

1. 트집을 잡아서
2. 날개 돋친 듯이 팔리
3. 발등에 불이 떨어진
4. 발 벗고 나서서
5. 내 코가 석자야
6. 난다 긴다 하는
7. 뒤 끝이 없어서
8. 꼬리에 꼬리를 물
9. 눈독을 들이
10. 베일에 가려져서

관용어 6

1. 얼굴에 먹칠을 하
2. 죽이 맞아야
3. 코가 납작해졌어
4. 재미를 보
5. 불똥이 튈지
6. 사서 고생하니
7. 눈살을 찌푸렸어요
8. 눈 밖에 나
9. 싼 게 비지떡이라고
10. 열을 올리

17 · 한자성어

한자성어 1

1. 과대망상
2. 견물생심이라고
3. 동분서주
4. 금시초문이야
5. 동고동락
6. 구태의연
7. 감언이설
8. 마이동풍이었잖아요
9. 당연지사
10. 무궁무진

한자성어 2

1. 속수무책이었지만
2. 시기상조
3. 무위도식
4. 무용지물이
5. 반신반의
6. 심사숙고
7. 애지중지, 애지중지
8. 비일비재
9. 산전수전
10. 새옹지마라더니

한자성어 3

1. 양자택일
2. 이구동성으로
3. 일구이언
4. 오십보백보야
5. 어부지리로
6. 일사천리로
7. 의기양양
8. 오리무중
9. 약방감초
10. 왈가왈부

한자성어 4

1. 일편단심은
2. 포복절도
3. 학수고대
4. 죽마고우여서
5. 전전긍긍
6. 자화자찬이
7. 자급자족이
8. 차일피일
9. 주객전도
10. 전무후무

02 색인

표: 표제어(headwords), **유**: 유의어(synonyms), **반**: 반의어(antonyms), **관**: 관련어(related words)

외국인을 위한 **한국어 어휘 연습 (고급)**

편저자 연세대학교 한국어학당 교재편찬위원회
집필진 전나영 · 임지숙 · 전지인 · 강은정
펴낸곳 연세대학교 출판문화원

주소 서울시 서대문구 연세로 50
전화 2123-3380~2
팩스 2123-8673
ysup@yonsei.ac.kr
http://www.yonsei.ac.kr/press
등록 1955년 10월 13일 제9-60호
인쇄 (주)화신문화

2011년 8월 22일 1판 1쇄
2024년 6월 14일 1판 7쇄
ISBN 978-89-7141-961-8 (03710)

값 **25,000원**